Why WileyPLUS for Computer Science?

WileyPLUS for Computer Science is a dy[...] [...] spend more time practicing the problems and explore[...] [...]ed.

"I used the homework problems to pra[...] [...]e problems on my own and then checked WileyPLUS to compare an[...]

● The integrated, online text offers students a low-cost alternative to the printed text, enhanced with direct links to specific portions of the text, plus interactive animations and videos to help students visualize concepts.

● Select WileyPLUS courses include LabRat, the programming assignment tool allows you to choose from hundreds of programming exercises to automate the process of assigning, completing, compiling, testing, submitting, and evaluating programming assignments. When students spend more time practicing, they come to class better prepared.

Try WileyPLUS with LabRat:
www.wileyplus.com/tours

See and try WileyPLUS in action!
Details and Demo: www.wileyplus.com

WileyPLUS combines robust course management tools with the complete online text and all of the interactive teaching & learning resources you and your students need in one easy-to-use system.

"Overall the WileyPLUS package made the material more interesting than if it was just a book with no additional material other than what you need to know."
– Edin Alic, North Dakota State University

Students easily access source code for example problems, as well as self-study materials and all the exercises and readings you assign.

All instructional materials, including PowerPoints, illustrations and visual tools, source code, exercises, solutions and gradebook organized in one easy-to-use system.

"WileyPLUS made it a lot easier to study. I got an A!"
– Student Jeremiah Ellis Mattson, North Dakota State University

C++
for Everyone

C++
for Everyone

Cay Horstmann

SAN JOSE STATE UNIVERSITY

WILEY

John Wiley & Sons, Inc.

EXECUTIVE PUBLISHER:	Don Fowley
ASSOCIATE PUBLISHER:	Dan Sayre
SENIOR EDITORIAL ASSISTANT:	Carolyn Weisman
MEDIA EDITOR:	Lauren Sapira
SENIOR PRODUCTION EDITOR:	Ken Santor
SENIOR DESIGNER:	Madelyn Lesure
TEXT DESIGNER:	Nancy Field
COVER DESIGNER:	Howard Grossman
COVER ILLUSTRATOR:	Susan Cyr
PHOTO EDITOR:	Lisa Gee
PRODUCTION MANAGEMENT:	Cindy Johnson

This book was set in 10.5/12 Stempel Garamond by Publishing Services and printed and bound by R.R. Donnelley – Jefferson City. The cover was printed by R.R. Donnelley.

This book is printed on acid-free paper ∞

ISBN 978-0-470-38329-2

Printed in the United States of America

10 9 8 7 6 5 4 3 2 1

Preface

This book gives an introduction into C++ and computer programming that focuses on the essentials—and on effective learning. The book is suitable for a first course in programming for computer scientists, engineers, and students in other technical or scientific disciplines. No prior programming experience is required, and only a modest amount of high school algebra is needed. Here are the key features of this new book:

- *A visual approach motivates the reader and eases navigation.* This book contains many more photographs, diagrams, and tables than other programming books. It is easy to get the "lay of the land" by browsing the visuals, before focusing on the textual material.

Visual features help the reader with navigation.

- *Guidance and worked examples help students succeed.* Beginning programmers often ask "How do I start? Now what do I do?" Of course, an activity as complex as programming cannot be reduced to cookbook-style instructions. However, step-by-step guidance is immensely helpful for building confidence and providing an outline for the task at hand. The book contains a large number of "How To" guides for common tasks, together with additional worked examples on the web.

- *Practice makes perfect.* Of course, programming students need to be able to implement nontrivial programs, but they first need to have the confidence that they can succeed. This book contains a substantial number of self-check questions (at the end of each section), simple programming assignments, and an electronic test bank.

- *Teach computer science principles, not just C++ or object-orientation.* This book uses the C++ programming language as a vehicle for introducing computer science concepts. A substantial subset of the C++ language is covered, focusing on the modern features of standard C++ that make students productive. The book starts gently by showing how to use objects (in particular, strings and streams). Then it takes a traditional route, stressing functions and procedural decomposition, before turning to the design of classes in the final chapters.
- *Focus on the essentials while being technically accurate.* An encyclopedic coverage is not helpful for a beginning programmer, but neither is the opposite—reducing the material to a list of simplistic bullet points. In this book, the essential essentials of each subject are presented in digestible chunks, with separate notes that go deeper into good practices or language features when the reader is ready for the additional information. You will not find artificial over-simplifications that give an illusion of knowledge.

A Tour of the Book

The core material of the book is:

Chapter 1. Introduction
Chapter 2. Fundamental Data Types
Chapter 3. Decisions
Chapter 4. Loops
Chapter 5. Functions
Chapter 6. Arrays and Vectors

In a course for engineers with a need for systems and embedded programming, you will want to cover Chapter 7 on pointers. Sections 7.1 and 7.4 are sufficient for using pointers with polymorphism in Chapter 10.

File processing is the subject of Chapter 8. Section 8.1 is sufficient for an introduction into reading and writing text files. The remainder of the chapter gives additional material for practical applications.

Chapters 9 and 10 introduce the object-oriented features of C++. Chapter 9 contains an introduction to class design and implementation. Chapter 10 covers inheritance and polymorphism.

✚ Four additional chapters are available on the Web. They can be used individually for a capstone chapter, or they can be combined for teaching a two-semester course. (They can also be incorporated into a custom print version of the text; ask your Wiley sales representative for details.)

Chapter 11. Recursion
Chapter 12. Sorting and Searching
Chapter 13. Lists, Queues, and Stacks
Chapter 14. Sets, Maps, and Priority Queues

Figure 1 shows the dependencies between the chapters.

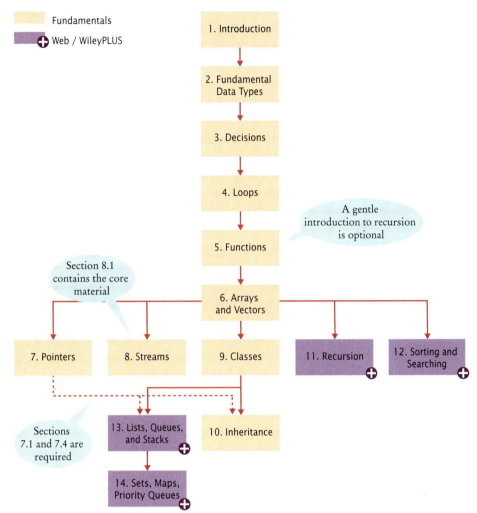

Figure 1
Chapter
Dependencies

Appendices

Appendix A contains a programming style guide. Using a style guide for programming assignments benefits students by directing them toward good habits and reducing gratuitous choice. The style guide is available in electronic form so that instructors can modify it to reflect their preferred style.

Appendices B and C summarize C++ reserved words and operators.

Appendix D lists character escape sequences and ASCII character code values.

Appendix E documents all of the library functions and classes used in this book. An expanded version of this Appendix that includes the functions and classes used in the four optional chapters, 11–14, is available on the Web and in WileyPLUS.

Appendices F, G, and H cover number systems, bit and shift operations, and a comparison of C++ and Java; all three are on the Web and in WileyPLUS.

The Pedagogical Structure

The pedagogical elements in this book work together to focus on and reinforce key concepts and fundamental principles of programming, with additional tips and detail organized to support and deepen these fundamentals. In addition to traditional features, such as chapter objectives and a wealth of exercises, each chapter contains elements geared to today's visual learner.

Throughout each chapter, **margin notes** show where new concepts are introduced and provide an outline of key ideas.

Annotated **syntax boxes** provide a quick, visual overview of new language constructs.

Annotations explain required components and point to more information on common errors or best practices associated with the syntax.

146   CHAPTER 4 ▪ Loops

4.2 The for Loop

> The for loop is used when a value runs from a starting point to an ending point with a constant increment or decrement.

It often happens that you want to execute a sequence of statements a given number of times. You can use a while loop that is controlled by a counter, as in the following example:

```
counter = 1; // Initialize the counter
while (counter <= 10) // Check the counter
{
    cout << counter << endl;
    counter++; // Update the counter
}
```

Because this loop type is so common, there is a special form for it, called the for loop (see Syntax 4.2).

```
for (counter = 1; counter <= 10; counter++)
{
    cout << counter << endl;
}
```

In general, the for loop:

```
for (initialization; condition; update)
{
    statements
}
```

has exactly the same effect as the while loop:

```
initialization;
while (condition)
{
    statements
    update
}
```

You can visualize the for loop as an orderly sequence of steps.

SYNTAX 4.2 **for Statement**

These three expressions should be related. See page 150.

This *initialization* happens once before the loop starts.

The loop is executed while this *condition* is true.

This *update* is executed after each iteration.

```
for (int i = 5; i <= 10; i++)
{
    sum = sum + i;
}
```

The variable i is defined only in this for loop. See page 148.

This loop executes 6 times. See page 151.

Like a variable in a computer program, a parking space has an identifier and a contents.

Analogies to everyday objects are used to explain the nature and behavior of concepts such as variables, data types, loops, and more.

Memorable photos reinforce analogies and help students remember the concepts.

194   CHAPTER 5 ▪ **Functions**

pie(fruit)   pie(fruit)

A recipe for a fruit pie may say to use any kind of fruit. Here, "fruit" is an example of a parameter variable.

Now consider what happens in a subsequent call `cube_volume(10)`. A new parameter variable is created. (Recall that the previous parameter variable was removed when the first call to `cube_volume` returned.) It is initialized with 10, and the process repeats. After the second function call is complete, its variables are again removed.

SELF CHECK

10. What does this program print? Use a diagram like Figure 3 to find the answer.

```
double mystery(int x, int y)
{
    double z = x + y;
    z = z / 2.0;
    return z;
}
int main()
{
    int a = 5;
    int b = 7;
    cout << mystery(a, b) << endl;
}
```

Self-check exercises at the end of each section are designed to make students think through the new material.

find the answer.

Example tables support beginners with multiple, concrete examples. These tables include common errors and present another quick reference to the section's topic.

Table 1 Variable Definitions in C++	
Variable Name	**Comment**
`int cans = 6;`	Defines an integer variable and initializes it with 6.
`int total = cans + bottles;`	The initial value need not be a constant. (Of course, cans and bottles must have been previously defined.)
🚫 `bottles = 1;`	**Error:** The type is missing. This statement is not a definition but an assignment of a new value to an existing variable—see Section 2.3.
🚫 `int bottles = "10";`	**Error:** You cannot initialize a number with a string.
`int bottles;`	Defines an integer variable without initializing it. This can be a cause for errors—see Common Error 2.2 on page 40.
`int cans, bottles;`	Defines two variables in a single statement. In this book, we will define each variable in a separate statement.

gure 3 to find the

ch05/intname.cpp

```
 1  #include <iostream>
 2  #include <string>
 3
 4  using namespace std;
 5
 6  /**
 7      Turns a digit into its English name.
 8      @param digit an integer between 1 and 9
 9      @return the name of digit ("one" ... "nine")
10  */
11  string digit_name(int digit)
12  {
13      if (digit == 1) return "one";
14      if (digit == 2) return "two";
15      if (digit == 3) return "three";
16      if (digit == 4) return "four";
17      if (digit == 5) return "five";
18      if (digit == 6) return "six";
19      if (digit == 7) return "seven";
20      if (digit == 8) return "eight";
21      if (digit == 9) return "nine";
22      return "";
23  }
24
25  /**
26      Turns a number between 10 and 19 into its English name.
27      @param number an integer between 10 and 19
28      @return the name of the given number ("ten" ... "nineteen")
29  */
30  string teen_name(int number)
31  {
32      if (number == 10) return "ten";
```

Program listings are carefully designed for easy reading, going well beyond simple color coding. Functions are set off by a subtle color outline.

Special Features

Seven special features add detail and provide step-by-step guidance. Identified with the icons shown here, they are set off so they don't interrupt the flow of the main material. Some of these are quite short; others extend over a page. Each topic is given the space that is needed for a full and convincing explanation—instead of being forced into a one-paragraph "tip". You can use the tables on pages xxii–xxv to see the features in each chapter and the page numbers where they can be found.

How To Guides give step-by-step guidance for common programming tasks, emphasizing planning and testing. They answer the beginner's question, "Now what do I do?" and integrate key concepts into a problem-solving sequence.

How To 4.1

Write a Loop

This How To walks you through the process of implementing a loop statement. We illustrate the steps with the following example problem:

Read twelve temperature values (one for each month), and display the number of the month with the highest temperature. For example, according to http://worldclimate.com, the average maximum temperatures for Death Valley are (in order by month):

18.2 22.6 26.4 31.1 36.6 42.2
45.7 ...

In the ...
(45.7 ...
displ...

Worked Example 4.1

Credit Card Processing

This Worked Example uses a loop to remove sp...

Worked Examples apply the steps in the How To to a different example, illustrating how they can be used to plan, implement, and test a solution to another programming problem.

Common Error 4.3

Off-by-One Errors

Consider our computation of the number of years that are required to double an inv...

```
int year = 0;
while (balance < TARGET)
{
   year++;
   balance = balance * (1 + RATE / 100);
}
cout << "The investment doubled after "
   << year << " years." << endl;
```

Should year start at 0 or at 1? Should you test for balance < TARGET or for balance <= TARGET? It is easy to be *off by one* in these expressions.

Some people try to solve off-by-one errors by randomly inserting +1 or -1 until the program seems to work—a terrible strategy. It can take a long time to compile and test all the various possibilities. Expending a small amount of mental effort is a real time saver.

Common Errors describe the kinds of errors that students often make, with an explanation of why the errors occur, and what to do about them.

Quality Tip 4.3

Count Iterations

Finding the correct lower and upper bounds for an iteration can be confusing. Should you start at 0 or at 1? Should you use <= b or < b as a termination condition?

Counting the number of iterations is a very useful device for better understanding a loop. Counting is easier for loops with asymmetric bounds. The loop

```
for (i = a; i < b; i++)
```

is executed b - a times. For example, the loop traversing the characters in a string,

```
for (i = 0; i < str.length(); i++)
```

runs str.length() times. That makes perfect sense, since there are str. ... in a string.

The loop with symmetric bounds,

Quality Tips explain good programming practices. These notes carefully motivate the reason behind the advice, and explain why the effort will be repaid later.

Advanced Topic 5.1

Function Declarations

Functions need to be known before they can be used. This can be achieved easily if you first define lower-level helper functions, then the midlevel workhorse functions, and finally main in your program.

Some programmers prefer to list the main function first in their programs. If you share that preference, you need to learn how to declare the other ... gram. A declaration of a function lists the ... ables, but it contains no body:

```
double cube_volume(double side_length)
```

This is an advertisement that promises that the r... to distinguish declarations from definitions: Declaratio... tions are followed by a {...} block. Declarations are also called *prot*...

The declarations of common functions such as pow are contained in header files. If you

Advanced Topics cover optional and challenging material.

PRODUCTIVITY HINT 5.2

Turn Repeated Code Into a Function

When you write nearly identical code multiple times, you should probably introduce a function. Consider these statements:

```
int hours;
do
{
   cout << "Enter a value between 1 and 12: ";
   cin >> hours;
} while (hours <

int minutes;
do
{
   cout << "Enter
   cin >> minutes
} while (minutes
```

Here, we read two v
easy to extract the co

Since n > 0, we repeat the loop. Now digit becomes 2, sum is se

n	sum	digit
1729	0	
172	9	9
17	11	2

Because n is still not zero, we repeat the loop, setting digit to 7, sum to 11 + 7 = 18, and n to 1.

n	sum	digit
1729	0	
172	9	9
17	11	2
1	18	7

19, and n becomes zero. The

> **Productivity Hints** teach students how to use their time and tools more effectively. They encourage students to be more productive with tips and techniques such as hand-tracing.

RANDOM FACT 9.1

Electronic Voting Machines

In the 2000 presidential elections in the United States, votes we... machines. Some machines processed cardboard ballots into which vo... indicate their choices (see Figure 6). When voters were not careful, re... now infamous "chads"—were partially stuck in the punch cards, cau... counted. A manual recount was necessary, but it was not carried out ev... constraints and procedural wrangling. The election was very close, and ... in the minds of many people whether the election outcome would have b... voting machines had accurately counted the intent of the voters.

Subsequently, voting machine manufacturers have argued that electronic voti... would avoid the problems caused by punch cards or optically scanned forms. In a... tronic voting machine, voters indicate their preferences by pressing buttons or touching icons on a computer screen. Typically, each voter is presented with a summary screen for review before casting the ballot. The process is very similar to using an automatic bank teller machine (see Figure 7).

It seems plausible that these machines make it more likely that a vote is counted in the same way that the voter intends. However, there has been significant controversy surrounding some types of electronic voting machines. If a machine si... and prints out the totals after the election has been completed, then h...

> **Random Facts** provide historical and social information on computing, as required to fulfill the "historical and social context" requirements of the ACM/IEEE curriculum guidelines.

> **Progressive figures** trace code segments to help students understand C++ conventions. Color is used consistently to make variables and other code elements easily recognizable.

initialized with the corresponding parameter value.

Consider the function call illustrated in Figure 3:

```
double result1 = cube_volume(2);
```

- The parameter variable side_length of the cube_volume function is created. **1**
- The parameter variable is initialized with the value that was passed in the call. In our case, side_length is set to 2. **2**
- The function computes the expression side_length * side_length * side_length, which has the value 8. That value is stored in the variable volume. **3**
- The function returns. All of its variables are removed. The return value is transferred to the *caller*, that is, the function calling the cube_volume function. **4**

1 Function call

	result1 =
	side_length =

2 Initializing function parameter

	result1 =
	side_length = 2

3 About to return to the caller

	result1 =
	side_length = 2
	volume = 8

4 After function call

| | result1 = 8 |

Figure 3 Parameter Passing

Web Resources

The book is supplemented by a complete suite of online resources and a robust WileyPLUS course.

Student and Instructor Resources

The following resources for students and instructors can be obtained by visiting www.wiley.com/college/horstmann (or the WileyPLUS course for the book). Two companion web sites accompany the book—one for students, and a password-protected site for instructors only.

- Solutions to all exercises (for instructors only)
- A test bank (for instructors only)
- Lecture presentation slides that summarize each chapter and include code listings and figures from the book (for instructors only)
- Source code for all examples in the book
- Additional worked examples and appendices (identified by an icon, ⊕)
- Four additional chapters on recursion, sorting and searching, and data structures
- The programming style guide in electronic form, so you can modify it to suit local preferences

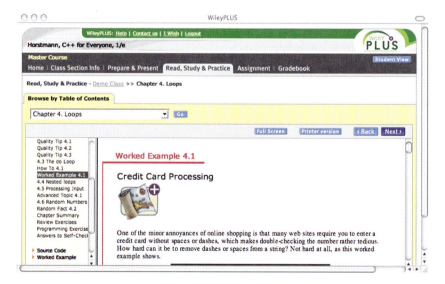

Students can locate the Worked Examples and other content marked with a plus icon, ⊕, in the WileyPLUS course or on the web site for the book at www.wiley.com/college/horstmann.

WileyPLUS

The first two pages of this book describe an innovative online tool for teachers and students: WileyPLUS is an online learning environment that combines all of the resources of a learning management system with an ebook.

With WileyPLUS, instructors can manage reading and homework assignments, create tests, assign quizzes, and store results in an online gradebook. A WileyPLUS adoption also enables students to purchase an eBook at a fraction of the price of the print edition. In addition to the eBook, WileyPLUS integrates all of the instructor and student web resources into an online version of this text. For more information and a demo, please visit the web site listed on pages i-ii, or talk to your Wiley representative.

Acknowledgments

Many thanks to Dan Sayre, Lauren Sapira, Lisa Gee, and Carolyn Weisman at John Wiley & Sons, and to the team at Publishing Services for their hard work and support for this book project. An especially deep acknowledgment and thanks to Cindy Johnson, who, through enormous patience and attention to detail, made this book a reality. We would also like to thank Jonathan Tolstedt, *North Dakota State University*, for working with us to prepare the solutions.

We are very grateful to the many individuals who reviewed the book and made many valuable suggestions for improvement. They include:

Charles D. Allison, *Utah Valley State College*
Fred Annexstein, *University of Cincinnati*
Stefano Basagni, *Northeastern University*
Noah D. Barnette, *Virginia Tech*
Peter Breznay, *University of Wisconsin, Green Bay*
Kuang-Nan Chang, *Eastern Kentucky University*
Joseph DeLibero, *Arizona State University*
Subramaniam Dharmarajan, *Arizona State University*
Stephen Gilbert, *Orange Coast Community College*
Barbara Guillott, *Louisiana State University*
Jon Hanrath, *Illinois Institute of Technology*
Neil Harrison, *Utah Valley University*
Debbie Kaneko, *Old Dominion University*
Mir Behrad Khamesee, *University of Waterloo*
Sung-Sik Kwon, *North Carolina Central University*
W. James MacLean, *University of Toronto*
Ethan V. Munson, *University of Wisconsin, Milwaukee*

Philip Regalbuto, *Trident Technical College*
John P. Russo, *Wentworth Institute of Technology*
Kurt Schmidt, *Drexel University*
William Shay, *University of Wisconsin, Green Bay*
Michele A. Starkey, *Mount Saint Mary College*
William Stockwell, *University of Central Oklahoma*
Jonathan Tolstedt, *North Dakota State University*
Kerstin Voigt, *California State University, San Bernardino*
David P. Voorhees, *Le Moyne College*
Salih Yurttas, *Texas A&M University*

Contents

Contents

Appendices

Alphabetical List of Syntax Boxes

Assignment   **43**
C++ Program   **13**
Class Interface   **372**
Comparisons   **91**
Constructor with Base-Class Initializer   **427**

Defining an Array   **241**
Defining a Vector   **245**
Derived-Class Definition   **425**
Dynamic Memory Allocation   **306**

for Statement   **146**
Function Definition   **189**

if Statement   **83**
Input Statement   **45**

Member Function Definition   **379**

Output Statement   **14**

Pointer Syntax   **290**

Two-Dimensional Array Definition   **266**

Variable Definition   **36**

while Statement   **137**
Working with File Streams   **330**

Introduction

CHAPTER GOALS

- To learn about the architecture of computers
- To learn about machine languages and higher-level programming languages
- To become familiar with your compiler
- To compile and run your first C++ program
- To recognize syntax and logic errors
- To understand the notion of an algorithm
- To understand the activity of programming

This chapter contains a brief introduction to the architecture of computers and an overview of programming languages. You will learn about the activity of programming: how to write and run your first C++ program, how to diagnose and fix programming errors, and how to plan your programming activities.

CHAPTER CONTENTS

1.1 What Is a Computer?

> Computers execute very basic operations in rapid succession.

You have probably used a computer for work or fun. Many people use computers for everyday tasks such as electronic banking or writing a term paper. Computers are good for such tasks. They can handle repetitive chores, such as totaling up numbers or placing words on a page, without getting bored or exhausted.

The flexibility of a computer is quite an amazing phenomenon. The same machine can balance your checkbook, print your term paper, and play a game. In contrast, other machines carry out a much narrower range of tasks; a car drives and a toaster toasts. Computers can carry out a wide range of tasks because they execute different programs, each of which directs the computer to work on a specific task.

> A computer program is a sequence of instructions and decisions.

The computer itself is a machine that stores data (numbers, words, pictures), interacts with devices (the monitor, the sound system, the printer), and executes programs. A *computer program* tells a computer, in minute detail, the sequence of steps that are needed to fulfill a task. The physical computer and peripheral devices are collectively called the *hardware*. The programs the computer executes are called the *software*.

Today's computer programs are so sophisticated that it is hard to believe that they are composed of extremely primitive operations. A typical operation may be one of the following:

- Put a red dot at this screen position.
- Add up these two numbers.
- If this value is negative, continue the program at a certain instruction.

The computer user has the illusion of smooth interaction because a program contains a huge number of such operations, and because the computer can execute them at great speed.

> **Programming is the act of designing and implementing computer programs.**

The act of designing and implementing computer programs is called *programming*. In this book, you will learn how to program a computer—that is, how to direct the computer to execute tasks.

To write a computer game with motion and sound effects or a word processor that supports fancy fonts and pictures is a complex task that requires a team of many highly skilled programmers. Your first programming efforts will be more mundane. The concepts and skills you learn in this book form an important foundation, and you should not be disappointed if your first programs do not rival the sophisticated software that is familiar to you. Actually, you will find that there is an immense thrill even in simple programming tasks. It is an amazing experience to see the computer precisely and quickly carry out a task that would take you hours of drudgery, to make small changes in a program that lead to immediate improvements, and to see the computer become an extension of your mental powers.

SELF CHECK

1. What is required to play music on a computer?
2. Why is a CD player less flexible than a computer?
3. What does a computer user need to know about programming in order to play a video game?

1.2 The Anatomy of a Computer

To understand the programming process, you need to have a rudimentary understanding of the building blocks that make up a computer. We will look at a personal computer. Larger computers have faster, larger, or more powerful components, but they have fundamentally the same design.

At the heart of the computer lies the *central processing unit (CPU)* (see Figure 1). It consists of a single *chip*, or a small number of chips. A computer chip (integrated circuit) is a component with a plastic or metal housing, metal connectors, and inside wiring made principally from silicon. For a CPU chip, the inside wiring is enormously complicated. For example, the Pentium chip (a popular CPU for personal

Figure 1
Central Processing Unit

computers at the time of this writing) is composed of several million structural elements, called *transistors*.

The CPU performs program control and data processing. That is, the CPU locates and executes the program instructions; it carries out arithmetic operations such as addition, subtraction, multiplication, and division; it fetches data from external memory or devices and stores data back. All data must travel through the CPU whenever it is moved from one location to another.

> The central processing unit (CPU) performs program control and data processing.

The computer stores data and programs in *memory*. There are two kinds of memory. *Primary storage* is made from memory chips: *random-access memory* (RAM) and *read-only memory* (ROM). Read-only memory contains certain programs that must always be present—for example, the code needed to start the computer. Random-access memory might have been better called "read-write memory", because the CPU can read data from it and write data back to it. That makes RAM suitable to hold changing data and programs that do not have to be available permanently. RAM memory has two disadvantages. It is comparatively expensive, and it loses all its data when the power is turned off. *Secondary storage*, usually a *hard disk* (see Figure 2), provides less expensive storage that persists without electricity. A hard disk consists of rotating platters, which are coated with a magnetic material, and read/write heads, which can detect and change the magnetic flux on the platters. Programs and data are typically stored on the hard disk and loaded into RAM when the program starts. The program then updates the data in RAM and writes the modified data back to the hard disk.

> Storage devices include random-access memory (RAM) and secondary storage.

To interact with a human user, a computer requires peripheral devices. The computer transmits information (called *output*) to the user through a display screen, speakers, and printers. The user can enter information (called *input*) for the computer by using a keyboard or a pointing device such as a mouse.

Figure 2   A Hard Disk

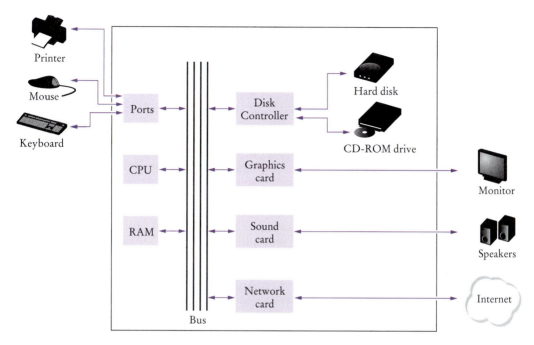

Figure 3 Schematic Design of a Personal Computer

Some computers are self-contained units, whereas others are interconnected through *networks*. Through the network cabling, the computer can read data and programs from central storage locations or send data to other computers. For the user of a networked computer it may not even be obvious which data reside on the computer itself and which are transmitted through the network.

Figure 3 gives a schematic overview of the architecture of a personal computer. Program instructions and data (such as text, numbers, audio, or video) are stored on the hard disk, on a CD-ROM, or elsewhere on the network. When a program is started, it is brought into RAM memory, from where the CPU can read it. The CPU reads the program one instruction at a time. As directed by these instructions, the CPU reads data, modifies it, and writes it back to RAM memory or the hard disk. Some program instructions will cause the CPU to place dots on the display screen or printer or to vibrate the speaker. As these actions happen many times over and at great speed, the human user will perceive images and sound. Some program instructions read user input from the keyboard or mouse. The program analyzes the nature of these inputs and then executes the next appropriate instructions.

SELF CHECK

4. Where is a program stored when it is not currently running?
5. Which part of the computer carries out arithmetic operations, such as addition and multiplication?

RANDOM FACT 1.1

The ENIAC and the Dawn of Computing

The ENIAC (*e*lectronic *n*umerical *i*ntegrator *a*nd *c*omputer) was the first usable electronic computer. It was designed by J. Presper Eckert and John Mauchly at the University of Pennsylvania and was completed in 1946—two years before transistors were invented. The computer was housed in a large room and consisted of many cabinets containing about 18,000 vacuum tubes (see Figure 4). Vacuum tubes burned out at the rate of several tubes per day. An attendant with a shopping cart full of tubes constantly made the rounds and replaced defective ones. The computer was programmed by connecting wires on panels. Each wiring configuration would set up the computer for a particular problem. To have the computer work on a different problem, the wires had to be replugged.

Work on the ENIAC was supported by the U.S. Navy, which was interested in computations of ballistic tables that would give the trajectory of a projectile, depending on the wind resistance, initial velocity, and atmospheric conditions. To compute the trajectories, one must find the numerical solutions of certain differential equations; hence the name "numerical integrator". Before machines like the ENIAC were developed, humans did this kind of work, and until the 1950s the word "computer" referred to these people. The ENIAC was later used for peaceful purposes such as the tabulation of U.S. Census data.

Figure 4   The ENIAC

1.3 Machine Code and Programming Languages

On the most basic level, computer instructions are extremely primitive. The processor executes *machine instructions*. A typical sequence of machine instructions is

1. Move the contents of memory location 40000 into the CPU.
2. If that value is > 100, continue with the instruction that is stored in memory location 11280.

> Computer programs are stored as machine instructions in a code that depends on the processor type.

Actually, machine instructions are encoded as numbers so that they can be stored in memory. On a Pentium processor, this sequence of instruction is encoded as the sequence of numbers

161 40000 45 100 127 11280

On a processor from a different manufacturer, the encoding would be different. When this kind of processor fetches this sequence of numbers, it decodes them and executes the associated sequence of commands.

How can we communicate the command sequence to the computer? The simplest method is to place the actual numbers into the computer memory. This is, in fact, how the very earliest computers worked. However, a long program is composed of thousands of individual commands, and it is a tedious and error-prone affair to look up the numeric codes for all commands and place the codes manually into memory. As already mentioned, computers are really good at automating tedious and error-prone activities. It did not take long for computer programmers to realize that the computers themselves could be harnessed to help in the programming process.

A special computer program, a *compiler*, translates the higher-level description into machine instructions for a particular processor.

For example, in C++, the high-level programming language that we will use in this book, you might give the following instruction:

```
if (int_rate > 100) { cout << "Interest rate error"; }
```

This means, "If the interest rate is over 100, display an error message". It is then the job of the compiler program to look at each C++ instruction and translate it into the machine instructions for the particular processor.

> High-level programming languages are independent of the processor.

High-level languages are independent of the underlying hardware. C++ instructions work equally well on an Intel Pentium and a processor in a cell phone. Of course, the compiler-generated machine instructions are different, but the programmer who uses the compiler need not worry about these differences.

SELF CHECK

6. Is the compiler a part of the computer hardware or software?
7. Does a person who uses a computer for office work ever run a compiler?

1.4 The Evolution of C++

C++ is built upon the C programming language, which was developed to be translated into fast machine code with a minimum of housekeeping overhead. C++ built on C by adding features for "object-oriented programming", a programming style that enables modeling of real-world objects.

The initial version of the C language was designed about 1972. Additional features were added to it over the years. Because different compiler writers added different features, the language actually sprouted various dialects. Some programming instructions were understood by one compiler but rejected by another. Such divergence is a major obstacle to a programmer who wants to move code from one computer to another. An effort got underway to iron out the differences and come up with a standard version of C. The design process ended in 1989 with the completion of the ANSI (American National Standards Institute) standard. In the meantime, Bjarne Stroustrup of AT&T added features of the language Simula (an object-oriented language designed for carrying out simulations) to C. The resulting language was called C++.

From 1985 until today, C++ has grown by the addition of many features. A standardization process culminated in the publication of the international C++ standard in 1998. A minor update to the standard was issued in 2003, and a major revision is expected to come to fruition around 2010.

> C++ is a general-purpose language that is in widespread use for systems and embedded programming.

At this time, C++ is the most commonly used language for developing system software such as databases and operating systems. Just as importantly, C++ is increasingly used for programming "embedded systems", small computers that control devices such as automobile engines or cellular telephones.

SELF CHECK

8. What was added to the C language to create C++?
9. What are the most important uses for C++?

RANDOM FACT 1.2

Standards Organizations

Two organizations, the American National Standards Institute (ANSI) and the International Organization for Standardization (ISO), have jointly developed the definitive standard for the C++ language.

Why have standards? You encounter the benefits of standardization every day. When you buy a light bulb, you can be assured that it fits in the socket without having to measure the socket at home and the bulb in the store. In fact, you may have experienced how painful the lack of standards can be if you have ever purchased a flashlight with nonstandard bulbs. Replacement bulbs for such a flashlight can be difficult and expensive to obtain.

The ANSI and ISO standards organizations are associations of industry professionals who develop standards for everything from car tires and credit card shapes to programming languages. Having a standard for a programming language such as C++ means that you can take a program that you developed on one system with one manufacturer's compiler to a different system and be assured that it will continue to work.

1.5 Becoming Familiar with Your Computer

Set aside some time to become familiar with the computer system and the C++ compiler that you will use for your class work.

As you use this book, you may well be doing your work on an unfamiliar computer system. You should spend some time making yourself familiar with the computer. Because computer systems vary widely, this book can only give an outline of the steps you need to follow. Using a new and unfamiliar computer system can be frustrating. Look for training courses that your campus offers, or just ask a friend to give you a brief tour.

Step 1 Log In

If you use your own home computer, you don't need to worry about logging in. Computers in a lab, however, are usually not open to everyone. Access is usually restricted to those who paid the necessary fees and who can be trusted to use the lab responsibly. You will likely need an account number and a password to gain access to the system.

Step 2 Locate the C++ Compiler

Computer systems differ greatly in this regard. Some systems let you start the compiler by selecting an icon or menu. On other systems you must use the keyboard to type a command to launch the compiler. On many personal computers there is an *integrated environment* in which you can write and test your programs. On other computers you must first launch one program that functions like a word processor, in which you can enter your C++ instructions; then launch another program to translate them to machine code; and then run the resulting machine code.

Step 3 Understand Files and Folders

As a programmer, you will write C++ programs, try them out, and improve them. You will be provided a place on the computer to store them, and you need to find out where that place is. You will store your programs in *files*. A C++ file is a container of C++ instructions. Files have names, and the rules for legal names differ from one system to another. Some systems allow spaces in file names; others don't. Some distinguish between upper- and lowercase letters; others don't. Most C++ compilers require that C++ files end in an *extension* .cpp, .cc, or .C; for example, test.cpp.

Figure 5
A Directory Hierarchy

Files are stored in *folders* or *directories*. These file containers can be nested. A folder can contain files as well as other folders, which themselves can contain more files and folders (see Figure 5). This hierarchy can be quite large, especially on networked computers where some of the files may be on your local disk, others elsewhere on the network. While you need not be concerned with every branch of the hierarchy, you should familiarize yourself with your local environment. Different systems have different ways of showing files and directories. Some use a graphical display and let you move around by clicking the mouse on folder icons. In other systems, you must enter commands to visit or inspect different locations.

Step 4   Write a Simple Program

In the next section, we will introduce a very simple program. You will need to learn how to type it in, run it, and fix mistakes.

Step 5   Save Your Work

> Develop a strategy for keeping backup copies of your work before disaster strikes.

You will spend many hours typing C++ programs in and improving them. The resulting program files have some value, and you should treat them as you would other important property. A conscientious safety strategy is particularly important for computer files. They are more fragile than paper documents or other more tangible objects. It is easy to delete a file by accident, and occasionally files are lost because of a computer malfunction. Unless you keep another copy, you must retype the contents. Because you are unlikely to remember the entire file, you will likely find yourself spending almost as much time as you did to enter and improve it in the first place. This lost time may cause you to miss deadlines. It is therefore crucially important that you learn how to safeguard files and get in the habit of doing so *before* disaster strikes. You can make safety or *backup* copies of files by saving copies on a memory stick or on another computer.

SELF CHECK

10. How are programming projects stored on a computer?
11. What do you do to protect yourself from data loss when you work on programming projects?

PRODUCTIVITY HINT 1.1

Backup Copies

Backing up files on a memory stick is an easy and convenient storage method for many people. Another increasingly popular form of backup is Internet file storage. Here are a few pointers to keep in mind.

- *Back up often.* Backing up a file takes only a few seconds, and you will hate yourself if you have to spend many hours recreating work that you could have saved easily. I recommend that you back up your work once every thirty minutes.
- *Rotate backups.* Use more than one directory for backups, and rotate them. That is, first back up onto the first directory. Then back up onto the second directory. Then use the third, and then go back to the first. That way you always have three recent backups. If your recent changes made matters worse, you can then go back to the older version.
- *Back up source files only.* The compiler translates the files that you write into files consisting of machine code. There is no need to back up the machine code files, since you can recreate them easily by running the compiler again. Focus your backup activity on those files that represent your effort. That way your backup disks won't fill up with files that you don't need.
- *Pay attention to the backup direction.* Backing up involves copying files from one place to another. It is important that you do this right—that is, copy from your work location to the backup location. If you do it the wrong way, you will overwrite a newer file with an older version.
- *Check your backups once in a while.* Double-check that your backups are where you think they are. There is nothing more frustrating than to find out that the backups are not there when you need them.
- *Relax, then restore.* When you lose a file and need to restore it from backup, you are likely to be in an unhappy, nervous state. Take a deep breath and think through the recovery process before you start. It is not uncommon for an agitated computer user to wipe out the last backup when trying to restore a damaged file.

1.6 Compiling a Simple Program

You are now ready to write and run your first C++ program. The traditional choice for the very first program in a new programming language is a program that displays a simple greeting: "Hello, World!" We follow that tradition. Here is the "Hello, World!" program in C++.

ch01/hello.cpp

```
1  #include <iostream>
2
3  using namespace std;
4
5  int main()
6  {
7     cout << "Hello, World!" << endl;
8     return 0;
9  }
```

Program Run

```
Hello, World!
```

We will explain this program in a minute. For now, you should make a new program file and call it `hello.cpp`. Enter the program instructions and compile and run the program, following the procedure that is appropriate for your compiler. (The line numbers are not part of the program. They are included so that your instructor can reference them during lectures.)

When you type in this program, be aware that C++ is *case-sensitive*. You must enter upper- and lowercase letters exactly as they appear in the program listing. Do not type MAIN or Return. On the other hand, C++ has *free-form layout*. The amount of spaces, tabs, and line breaks (collectively called *white space*) used for layout is not important. You can even write the entire program on a single line:

```
int main(){cout<<"Hello, World!"<<endl;return 0;}
```

However, you should always use a layout that makes your programs easy to read.

When you run the program, the message

```
Hello, World!
```

will appear on the screen. On some systems, you may need to switch to a different window to find the message.

Now that you have seen the program working, it is time to understand its makeup. The basic structure of a C++ program is shown in Syntax 1.1.

The first line,

```
#include <iostream>
```

tells the compiler to include a service for "stream input/output". You will learn in Chapter 8 what a stream is. For now, you should simply remember to add this line into all programs that perform input or output.

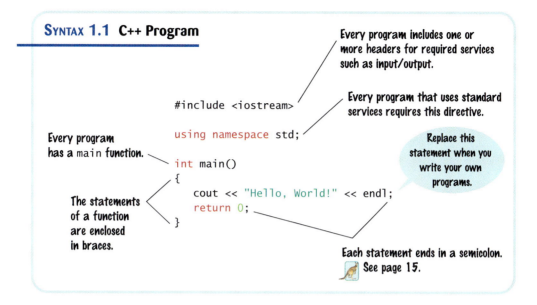

SYNTAX **1.1 C++ Program**

Every program includes one or more headers for required services such as input/output.

```
#include <iostream>
```

Every program that uses standard services requires this directive.

```
using namespace std;
```

Every program has a main function.

Replace this statement when you write your own programs.

```
int main()
{
    cout << "Hello, World!" << endl;
    return 0;
}
```

The statements of a function are enclosed in braces.

Each statement ends in a semicolon. See page 15.

The next line,

```
using namespace std;
```

tells the compiler to use the "standard namespace". Namespaces are a mechanism for avoiding naming conflicts in large programs. You need not be concerned about namespaces. For the programs that you will be writing in this book, you will always use the standard namespace. Simply add the directive using namespace std; at the top of every program that you write, just below the #include directives.

> Every C++ program contains #include directives and a function called main.

The construction

```
int main()
{
    ...
    return 0;
}
```

defines a *function* called main that "returns" the integer 0 (which indicates that the program finished successfully). A function is a collection of programming instructions that carry out a particular task. Every C++ program must have a main function. Most C++ programs contain other functions besides main, but it will take us until Chapter 5 to discuss functions and return values.

For now, it is a good idea to consider all these parts as the plumbing that is necessary to write a simple program. Simply place the code that you want to execute inside the braces of the main function.

> Use cout and the << operator to display values on the screen.

To display values on the screen, you send them to an entity called cout. The << operator denotes the "send to" command. For example, the statement

```
cout << 39 + 3;
```

displays the number 42.

SYNTAX 1.2 Output Statement

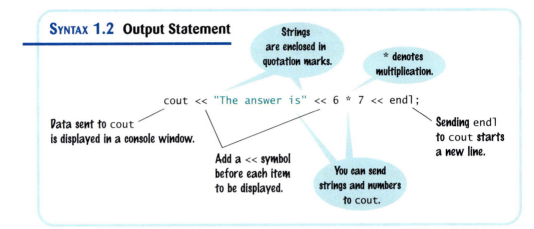

The statement

Enclose text strings in quotation marks.

```
cout << "Hello";
```

displays the *string* Hello. A string is a sequence of characters. You must enclose the contents of a string inside quotation marks so that the compiler knows you literally mean the text "Hello" and not a function with the same name.

Use + to add two numbers and * to multiply two numbers.

You can send more than one item to cout. Use a << before each one of them. For example,

```
cout << "The answer is " << 6 * 7;
```

displays The answer is 42 (in C++, the * denotes multiplication).

Send endl to cout to end a line of displayed output.

The endl symbol denotes an *end of line* marker. When this marker is sent to cout, the cursor is moved to the first column in the next screen row. If you don't use an end of line marker, then the next displayed item will simply follow the current string on the same line. In this program we only printed one item, but in general we will want to print multiple items, and it is a good habit to end all lines of output with an end of line marker.

End each statement with a semicolon.

Finally, note that each statement in C++ ends in a semicolon, just as every English sentence ends in a period.

SELF CHECK

12. How do you modify the hello.cpp program to greet you instead?

13. What is wrong with this program?

```
#include <iostream>
using namespace std;
int main()
{
    cout << Goodbye, World! << endl;
    return 0;
}
```

14. What does the following sequence of statements print?

```
cout << "Hello";
cout << "World";
```

15. What does the following statement print?

```
cout << 2 * 2 << 2;
```

16. What does the following statement print?

```
cout << "Hello" << endl << endl << "World";
```

COMMON ERROR 1.1

Omitting Semicolons

In C++ every statement must end in a semicolon. Forgetting to type a semicolon is a common error. It confuses the compiler because the compiler uses the semicolon to find where one statement ends and the next one starts. The compiler does not use line ends or closing braces to recognize the ends of statements. For example, the compiler considers

```
cout << "Hello, World!" << endl
return 0;
```

a single statement, as if you had written

```
cout << "Hello, World!" << endl return 0;
```

and then it doesn't understand that statement, because it does not expect the word return in the middle of an output command. The remedy is simple. Just scan every statement for a terminating semicolon, just as you would check that every English sentence ends in a period.

ADVANCED TOPIC 1.1

Escape Sequences

How can you display a string containing quotation marks, such as

```
Hello, "World"
```

You can't use

```
cout << "Hello, "World"";
```

As soon as the compiler reads "Hello, ", it thinks the string is finished, and then it gets all confused about World. Compilers have a one-track mind, and if a simple analysis of the input doesn't make sense to them, they just refuse to go on, and they report an error. In contrast, a human would probably realize that the second and third quotation marks were supposed to be part of the string.

Well, how do we then display quotation marks on the screen? The designers of C++ provided an escape hatch. Mark each quotation mark with a backslash character (\), like this:

```
cout << "Hello, \"World\"";
```

The sequence \" denotes a literal quote, not the end of a string. Such a sequence is called an *escape sequence*.

There are a few other escape sequences. If you actually want to show a backslash on the display, you use the escape sequence \\. The statement

```
cout << "Hello\\World";
```

prints

```
Hello\World
```

Finally, the escape sequence \n denotes a *newline* character that starts a new line on the screen. The command

```
cout << "Hello, World!\n";
```

has exactly the same effect as

```
cout << "Hello, World!" << endl;
```

1.7 Errors

Programming languages follow very strict conventions. When you talk to another person, and you scramble or omit a word or two, your conversation partner will usually still understand what you have to say. But when you make an error in a C++ program, the compiler will not try to guess what you meant. (This is actually a good thing. If the compiler were to guess wrongly, the resulting program would do the wrong thing—quite possibly with disastrous effects.) It is important that you learn to understand the compiler's error messages.

Experiment a little with the hello.cpp program. What happens if you make a typing error such as

```
cot << "Hello, World!" << endl;
cout << "Hello, World! << endl;
cout << "Hollo, World!" << endl;
```

> A syntax error is a part of a program that does not conform to the rules of the programming language.

In the first case, the compiler will complain that it has no clue what you mean by cot. The exact wording of the error message is dependent on the compiler, but it might be something like "Undefined symbol cot". This is a *compile-time error* or *syntax error*. Something is wrong according to the language rules, and the compiler finds it.

When the compiler finds one or more errors, it will not translate the program to machine code, and as a consequence there is no program to run. You must fix the error and compile again. It is common to go through several rounds of fixing compile-time errors before compilation succeeds for the first time.

If the compiler finds an error, it will not simply stop and give up. It will try to report as many errors as it can find, so you can fix them all at once. Sometimes, however, one error throws it off track. This is likely to happen with the error in the second line. Since the programmer forgot the closing quote, the compiler will keep looking for the end of the string. In such cases, it is common for the compiler to emit bogus error reports for neighboring lines. You should fix only those error messages that make sense to you and then recompile.

The error in the third line is of a different kind. The program will compile and run, but its output will be wrong. It will print

```
Hollo, World!
```

Logic errors are errors in a program that executes without performing the intended action.

This is a *run-time error* or *logic error*. The program is syntactically correct and does something, but it doesn't do what it is supposed to do. The compiler cannot find the error, and it must be flushed out when the program runs, by testing it and carefully looking at its output.

During program development, errors are unavoidable. Once a program is longer than a few lines, it requires superhuman concentration to enter it correctly without slipping up once. You will find yourself omitting semicolons or quotes more often than you would like, but the compiler will track down these problems for you.

The programmer is responsible for inspecting and testing the program to guard against logic errors.

Logic errors are more troublesome. The compiler will not find them—in fact, the compiler will cheerfully translate any program as long as its syntax is correct—but the resulting program will do something wrong. It is the responsibility of the program author to test the program and find any logic errors. Program testing is an important topic that you will encounter many times in this book.

SELF CHECK

17. Suppose you omit the `()` characters after `main` from the `hello.cpp` program. Will you get a compile-time error or a run-time error?

18. How can you find logic errors in a program?

COMMON ERROR 1.2

Misspelling Words

If you accidentally misspell a word, strange things may happen, and it may not always be completely obvious from the error messages what went wrong. Here is a good example of how simple spelling errors can cause trouble:

```cpp
#include <iostream>

using namespace std;

int Main()
{
    cout << "Hello, World!" << endl;
    return 0;
}
```

This code defines a function called `Main`. The compiler will not consider this to be the same as the `main` function, because `Main` starts with an uppercase letter and the C++ language is *case-sensitive*. Upper- and lowercase letters are considered to be completely different from each other, and to the compiler `Main` is no better match for `main` than `rain`. The compiler will compile your Main function, but when the linker is ready to build the executable file (see Section 1.8), it will complain about the missing main function and refuse to link the program. Of course, the message "missing main function" should give you a clue where to look for the error.

If you get an error message that seems to indicate that the compiler is on the wrong track, it is a good idea to check for spelling and capitalization. In C++, most names use only lowercase letters. If you misspell the name of a symbol (for example out instead of cout), the compiler will complain about an "undefined symbol". This error message is usually a good clue that you made a spelling error.

1.8 The Compilation Process

Some C++ development environments are very convenient to use. You just enter the code in one window, click on a button or menu to compile, and click on another button or menu to run your code. Error messages show up in a second window, and the program runs in a third window. Figure 6 shows the screen layout of a popular C++ compiler with these features. With such an environment you are completely shielded from the details of the compilation process. On other systems you must carry out every step manually.

Even if you use a convenient C++ environment, it is useful to know what goes on behind the scenes, mainly because knowing the process helps you solve problems when something goes wrong.

Figure 6   Screen Layout of an Integrated C++ Environment

You first enter the program statements into a text editor. The editor stores the text and gives it a name such as `hello.cpp`. If the editor window shows a name like `noname.cpp`, you should change the name. You should *save* the file to disk frequently, because otherwise the editor only stores the text in the computer's RAM memory. If something goes wrong with the computer and you need to restart it, the contents of the RAM (including your program text) are lost, but anything stored on a hard disk is permanent even if you need to restart the computer.

> The compiler translates C++ programs into machine code.

When you compile your program, the compiler translates the C++ *source code* (that is, the statements that you wrote) into *machine code*. The resulting file consists of machine instructions and information on how to load the program into memory prior to execution. Machine code is sometimes called *object code*, but we do not use that terminology to avoid confusion with C++ objects. Machine code files usually have the extension `.obj` or `.o`. For example, the machine code for the `hello.cpp` program might be stored in `hello.obj`.

> The linker combines machine code with library code into an executable program.

The machine code file contains only the translation of the code that you wrote. That is not enough to actually run the program. To display a string on a window, quite a bit of low-level activity is necessary. The authors of the `iostream` package (which defines `cout` and its functionality) have implemented all necessary actions and placed the required machine code into a *library*. A library is a collection of code that has been programmed and translated by someone else, ready for you to use in your program. (More complicated programs are built from more than one machine code file and more than one library.) A special program called the *linker* takes your machine code file and the necessary parts from the `iostream` library and builds an *executable file*. (Figure 7 gives an overview of these steps.) The executable file is usually called `hello.exe` or `hello`, depending on your computer system. It contains all machine code necessary to run the program. You can run the program by typing `hello` at a command prompt, or by clicking on the file icon, even after you exit the C++ environment. You can email that file to another user who doesn't

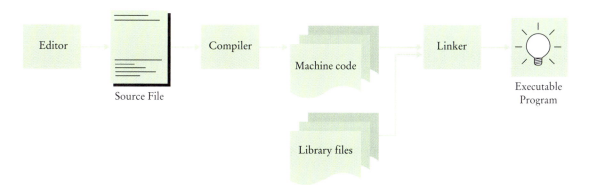

Figure 7 From Source Code to Executable Program

have a C++ compiler or who may not know that there is such a thing as C++, and that person can run the program in the same way.

Your programming activity centers around these files. You start in the editor, writing the source file. You compile the program and look at the error messages. You go back to the editor and fix the syntax errors. When the compiler succeeds, the linker builds the executable file. You run the executable file. If you find an error, you need to find the cause of the error, go back to the editor and fix it. You compile, link, and run again to see whether the error has gone away. If not, you go back to the editor. This is called the *edit-compile-run loop* (see Figure 8).

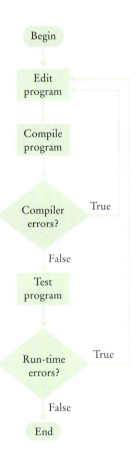

Figure 8
Edit-Compile-Run Loop

SELF CHECK

19. What do you expect to see when you load an executable file into your text editor?

20. Why can't you test a program for run-time errors when it has compiler errors?

1.9 Algorithms

You will soon learn how to program calculations and decision making in C++. But before we look at the mechanics of implementing computations in the next chapter, let's consider the planning process that precedes implementation.

You may have run across advertisements that encourage you to pay for a computerized service that matches you up with a love partner. Think how this might work. You fill out a form and send it in. Others do the same. The data are processed by a computer program. Is it reasonable to assume that the computer can perform the task of finding the best match for you? Suppose your younger brother, not the computer, had all the forms on his desk. What instructions could you give him? You can't say, "Find the best-looking person of the opposite sex who likes inline skating and browsing the Internet". There is no objective standard for good looks, and your brother's opinion (or that of a computer program analyzing the digitized photo) will likely be different from yours. If you can't give written instructions for someone to solve the problem, there is no way the computer can magically solve the problem. The computer can only do what you tell it to do. It just does it faster, without getting bored or exhausted.

Now consider the following investment problem:

> You put $10,000 into a bank account that earns 5 percent interest per year. How many years does it take for the account balance to be double the original?

Could you solve this problem by hand? Sure, you could. You figure out the balance as follows:

year	balance
0	10000
1	10500.00 = 10000.00 x 1.05
2	11025.00 = 10500.00 x 1.05
3	11576.25 = 11025.00 x 1.05
4	12155.06 = 11576.25 x 1.05

You keep going until the balance is at least $20,000. Then the last number in the year column is the answer.

Of course, carrying out this computation is intensely boring to you or your younger brother. But computers are very good at carrying out repetitive calculations quickly and flawlessly. What is important to the computer is a description of the steps for finding the solution. Each step must be clear and unambiguous, requiring no guesswork. Here is such a description:

Start with a year value of 0 and a balance of $10,000.

year	balance
0	10000

Repeat the following steps while the balance is less than $20,000.
   Add 1 to the year value.
   Multiply the balance value by 1.05 (a 5 percent increase).

year	balance
0	10000
1	10500
14	19799.32
⑮	20789.28

Report the final year value as the answer.

> Pseudocode is an informal description of a sequence of steps for solving a problem.

Of course, these steps are not yet in a language that a computer can understand, but you will soon learn how to formulate them in C++. This informal description is called *pseudocode*. What is important is that the method described is

- Unambiguous
- Executable
- Terminating

A method is *unambiguous* when there are precise instructions for what to do at each step and where to go next. There is no room for guesswork or creativity. A method is *executable* when each step can be carried out in practice. Had we asked to use the actual interest rate that will be charged in years to come, and not a fixed rate of 5 percent per year, our method would not have been executable, because there is no way for anyone to know what that interest rate will be. A method is *terminating* if it will eventually come to an end. In our example, it requires a bit of thought to see that the method will not go on forever: With every step, the balance goes up by at least $500, so eventually it must reach $20,000.

An algorithm is a recipe for finding a solution.

An algorithm for solving a problem is a sequence of steps that is unambiguous, executable, and terminating.

A sequence of steps that is unambiguous, executable, and terminating is called an *algorithm*. We have found an algorithm to solve our investment problem, and thus we can find the solution by programming a computer. The existence of an algorithm is an essential prerequisite for programming a task. You need to first discover and describe an algorithm for the task that you want to solve before you start programming (see Figure 9).

Figure 9
The Software Development Process

SELF CHECK

21. Suppose the interest rate was 20 percent. How long would it take for the investment to double?

22. Suppose your cell phone carrier charges you $29.95 for up to 300 minutes of calls, and $0.45 for each additional minute, plus 12.5 percent taxes and fees. Give an algorithm to compute the monthly charge from a given number of minutes.

HOW TO 1.1

Describing an Algorithm with Pseudocode

This is the first of many "How To" sections in this book that give you step-by-step procedures for carrying out important tasks in developing computer programs.

Before you are ready to write a program in C++, you need to develop an algorithm—a method for arriving at a solution for a particular problem. Describe the algorithm in pseudocode: a sequence of precise steps formulated in English.

For example, consider this problem: You have the choice of buying two cars. One is more fuel efficient than the other, but also more expensive. You know the price and fuel efficiency (in miles per gallon, mpg) of both cars. You plan to keep the car for ten years. Assume a price of $4 per gallon of gas and usage of 15,000 miles per year. You will pay cash for the car and not worry about financing costs. Which car is the better deal?

Step 1   Determine the inputs and outputs.

In our sample problem, we have these inputs:

- **purchase price1** and **fuel efficiency1**, the price and fuel efficiency (in mpg) of the first car
- **purchase price2** and **fuel efficiency2**, the price and fuel efficiency of the second car

We simply want to know which car is the better buy. That is the desired output.

Step 2   Break down the problem into smaller tasks.

For each car, we need to know the total cost of driving it. Let's do this computation separately for each car. Once we have the total cost for each car, we can decide which car is the better deal.

The total cost for each car is **purchase price + operating cost**.

We assume a constant usage and gas price for ten years, so the operating cost depends on the cost of driving the car for one year.

The operating cost is **10 x annual fuel cost**.

The annual fuel cost is **price per gallon x annual fuel consumed**.

The annual fuel consumed is **annual miles driven / fuel efficiency**. For example, if you drive the car for 15,000 miles and the fuel efficiency is 15 miles/gallon, the car consumes 1,000 gallons.

Step 3   Describe each subtask in pseudocode.

In your description, arrange the steps so that any intermediate values are computed before they are needed in other computations. For example, list the step

    total cost = purchase price + operating cost

after you have computed **operating cost**.

Here is the algorithm for deciding which car to buy.

    For each car, compute the total cost as follows:
        annual fuel consumed = annual miles driven / fuel efficiency
        annual fuel cost = price per gallon x annual fuel consumed
        operating cost = 10 x annual fuel cost
        total cost = purchase price + operating cost

> If total cost1 < total cost2
>   Choose car1
> Else
>   Choose car2

Step 4 Test your pseudocode by working a problem.

We will use these sample values:

> Car 1: $25,000, 50 miles/gallon
> Car 2: $20,000, 30 miles/gallon

Here is the calculation for the cost of the first car.

> annual fuel consumed = annual miles driven / fuel efficiency = 15000 / 50 = 300
> annual fuel cost = price per gallon x annual fuel consumed = 4 x 300 = 1200
> operating cost = 10 x annual fuel cost = 10 x 1200 = 12000
> total cost = purchase price + operating cost = 25000 + 12000 = 37000

Similarly, the total cost for the second car is $40,000. Therefore, the output of the algorithm is to choose car 1.

WORKED EXAMPLE 1.1

Writing an Algorithm for Tiling a Floor

This Worked Example shows how to develop an algorithm for laying tile in an alternating pattern of colors.

CHAPTER SUMMARY

1. Computers execute very basic operations in rapid succession.

2. A computer program is a sequence of instructions and decisions.

3. Programming is the act of designing and implementing computer programs.

4. The central processing unit (CPU) performs program control and data processing.

5. Storage devices include random-access memory (RAM) and secondary storage.

6. Computer programs are stored as machine instructions in a code that depends on the processor type.

7. High-level programming languages are independent of the processor.

8. C++ is a general-purpose language that is in widespread use for systems and embedded programming.

9. Set aside some time to become familiar with the computer system and the C++ compiler that you will use for your class work.

10. Develop a strategy for keeping backup copies of your work before disaster strikes.

11. Every C++ program contains #include directives and a function called main.

12. Use cout and the << operator to display values on the screen.

13. Enclose text strings in quotation marks.

14. Use + to add two numbers and * to multiply two numbers.

15. Send endl to cout to end a line of displayed output.

16. End each statement with a semicolon.

17. A syntax error is a part of a program that does not conform to the rules of the programming language.

18. Logic errors are errors in a program that executes without performing the intended action.

19. The programmer is responsible for inspecting and testing the program to guard against logic errors.

20. The compiler translates C++ programs into machine code.

21. The linker combines machine code with library code into an executable program.

22. Pseudocode is an informal description of a sequence of steps for solving a problem.

23. An algorithm for solving a problem is a sequence of steps that is unambiguous, executable, and terminating.

REVIEW EXERCISES

Exercise R1.1. Explain the difference between using a computer program and programming a computer.

Exercise R1.2. Which parts of a computer can store program code? Which can store user data?

Exercise R1.3. Which parts of a computer serve to give information to the user? Which parts take user input?

Exercise R1.4. A toaster is a single-function device, but a computer can be programmed to carry out different tasks. Is your cell phone a single-function device, or is it a programmable computer? (Your answer will depend on your cell phone model.)

Exercise R1.5. Explain two benefits of using C++ over machine code.

Exercise R1.6. On your own computer or on your lab computer, find the exact location (folder or directory name) of

a. The sample file hello.cpp (after you saved it in your development environment).

b. The standard header file iostream.

Exercise R1.7. What does this program print?

```
#include <iostream>
using namespace std;
int main()
{
   cout << "6 * 7 = " << 6 * 7 << endl;
   return 0;
}
```

Exercise R1.8. What does this program print?

```
#include <iostream>
using namespace std;
int main()
{
   cout << "Hello" << "World" << endl;
   return 0;
}
```

Pay close attention to spaces.

Exercise R1.9. What does this program print?

```
#include <iostream>
using namespace std;
int main()
{
   cout << "Hello" << endl << "World" << endl;
   return 0;
}
```

Exercise R1.10. Write three versions of the hello.cpp program that have different syntax errors. Write a version that has a logic error.

Exercise R1.11. How do you discover syntax errors? How do you discover logic errors?

Exercise R1.12. Write an algorithm to settle the following question: A bank account starts out with $10,000. Interest is compounded monthly at 6 percent per year (0.5 percent per month). Every month, $500 is withdrawn to meet college expenses. After how many years is the account depleted?

Exercise R1.13. Consider the question in Exercise R1.12. Suppose the numbers ($10,000, 6 percent, $500) were user selectable. Are there values for which the algorithm you developed would not terminate? If so, change the algorithm to make sure it always terminates.

Exercise R1.14. In order to estimate the cost of painting a house, a painter needs to know the surface area of the exterior. Develop an algorithm for computing that value. Your inputs are the width, length, and height of the house, the number of windows and doors, and their dimensions. (Assume the windows and doors have a uniform size.)

Exercise R1.15. You want to decide whether you should drive your car to work or take the train. You know the one-way distance from your home to your place of work, and the fuel efficiency of your car (in miles per gallon). You also know the one-way price of a train ticket. You assume the cost of gas at $4 per gallon, and car maintenance at 5 cents per mile. Write an algorithm to decide which commute is cheaper.

Exercise R1.16. You want to find out which fraction of your car use is for commuting to work, and which is for personal use. You know the one-way distance from your home to your place of work. For a particular period, you recorded the beginning and ending mileage on the odometer and the number of work days. Write an algorithm to settle this question.

Exercise R1.17. In the problem described in How To 1.1 on page 24, you made assumptions about the price of gas and the annual usage. Ideally, you would like to know which car is the better deal without making these assumptions. Why can't a computer program solve that problem?

Exercise R1.18. The value of π can be computed according to the following formula:

$$\frac{\pi}{4} = 1 - \frac{1}{3} + \frac{1}{5} - \frac{1}{7} + \frac{1}{9} - \cdots$$

Write an algorithm to compute π. Because the formula is an infinite series and an algorithm must stop after a finite number of steps, you should stop when you have the result determined to six significant digits.

Exercise R1.19. Suppose you put your younger brother in charge of backing up your work. Write a set of detailed instructions for carrying out his task. Explain how often he should do it, and what files he needs to copy from which folder to which location. Explain how he should verify that the backup was carried out correctly.

PROGRAMMING EXERCISES

Exercise P1.1. Write a program that prints a greeting of your choice, perhaps in another language.

Exercise P1.2. Write a program that prints the message, "Hello, my name is Hal!" Then, on a new line, the program should print the message "What would you like me to do?" Then it's the user's turn to type in an input. You haven't yet learned how to do it—just use the following lines of code:

```
string user_input;
getline(cin, user_input);
```

Finally, the program should ignore the user input and print the message "I am sorry, I cannot do that."

This program uses the `string` data type. To access this feature, you must place the line

```
#include <string>
```

before the `main` function.

Here is a typical program run. The user input is printed in color.

```
Hello, my name is Hal!
What would you like me to do?
Clean up my room
I am sorry, I cannot do that.
```

When running the program, remember to hit the Enter key after typing the last word of the input line.

Exercise P1.3. Write a program that prints out a message "Hello, my name is Hal!" Then, on a new line, the program should print the message "What is your name?" As in Exercise P1.2, just use the following lines of code:

```
string user_name;
getline(cin, user_name);
```

Finally, the program should print the message "Hello, *user name*. I am glad to meet you!" To print the user name, simply use

```
cout << user_name;
```

As in Exercise P1.2, you must place the line

```
#include <string>
```

before the `main` function.

Here is a typical program run. The user input is printed in color.

```
Hello, my name is Hal!
What is your name?
Dave
Hello, Dave. I am glad to meet you!
```

Exercise P1.4. Write a program that prints the sum of the first ten positive integers, $1 + 2 + \cdots + 10$.

Exercise P1.5. Write a program that prints the product of the first ten positive integers, $1 \times 2 \times \cdots \times 10$. (Remember to use * for multiplication in C++.)

Exercise P1.6. Write a program that prints the balance of an account that earns 5 percent interest per year after the first, second, and third year.

Exercise P1.7. Write a program that displays your name inside a box on the terminal screen, like this:

```
 Dave 
```

Do your best to approximate lines with characters such as | - +.

Exercise P1.8. Write a program that prints your name in large letters, such as

```
*    *    **    ****    ****    *    *
*    *   *  *   *    *   *    *  *    *
*****   *    *  ****    ****     *  *
*    *  ******  *    *  *    *     *
*    *  *    *  *    *  *    *     *
```

Exercise P1.9. Write a program that prints a face similar to (but different from) the following:

```
 /////
 +-----+
(| o o |)
 |  ^  |
 | '_' |
 +-----+
```

Exercise P1.10. Write a program that prints a house that looks exactly like the following:

```
   /\
  /  \
 +----+
 | .-.|
 | | ||
 +-+-++
```

Exercise P1.11. Write a program that prints an animal speaking a greeting, similar to (but different from) the following

```
 /\_/\      -----
( ' ' )  / Hello \
(  -  ) <  Junior |
 | | |   \ Coder!/
(_|_)      -----
```

Exercise P1.12. Write a program that prints three items, such as the names of your three best friends or favorite movies, on three separate lines.

Exercise P1.13. Write a program that prints a poem of your choice. If you don't have a favorite poem, search the Internet for "Emily Dickinson" or "e e cummings".

Exercise P1.14. Write a program that prints an imitation of a Piet Mondrian painting. (Search the Internet if you are not familiar with his paintings.) Use character sequences such as @@@ or ::: to indicate different colors, and use - and | to form lines.

Exercise P1.15. Write a program that prints the United States flag, using * and = characters.

ANSWERS TO SELF-CHECK QUESTIONS

1. A program that reads the data on the CD and sends output to the speakers and the screen.
2. A CD player can do one thing—play music CDs. It cannot execute programs.
3. Nothing.
4. In secondary storage, typically a hard disk.
5. The central processing unit.
6. Software.
7. No—a compiler is intended for programmers, to translate high-level programming instructions into machine code.
8. Support for object-oriented programming.
9. System software and embedded systems
10. Programs are stored in files, and files are stored in folders or directories.
11. You back up your files and folders.
12. Replace "World" with your name, for example:

    ```
    cout << "Hello, Harry!" << endl;
    ```
13. There are no quotes around Goodbye, World!.
14. It prints HelloWorld, without a space or comma.
15. 42, without a space.
16. Hello

    World

    with a blank line between the two words.
17. A compile-time error.
18. Run the program and observe its behavior.
19. A sequence of random characters, some funny-looking. Executable files contain machine instructions that are encoded as binary numbers.
20. When a program has compiler errors, no executable file is produced, and there is nothing to run.
21. 4 years:

    0 10,000

    1 12,000

    2 14,400

    3 17,280

    4 20,736

22. Is the number of minutes at most 300?

    a. If so, the answer is $29.95 × 1.125 = $33.70.

    b. If not,

        1. Compute the difference: (number of minutes) – 300.

        2. Multiply that difference by 0.45.

        3. Add $29.95.

        4. Multiply the total by 1.125. That is the answer.

Fundamental Data Types

CHAPTER GOALS

- To understand the properties and limitations of integer and floating-point numbers

- To write arithmetic expressions and assignment statements in C++

- To appreciate the importance of comments and good code layout

- To be able to define and initialize variables and constants

- To learn how to read user input and display program output

- To use the standard C++ `string` type to define and manipulate character strings

- To be able to write simple programs that read numbers and text, process the input, and display the results

In this and the four following chapters, you will learn the basic skills needed to write programs in C++. This chapter teaches you how to manipulate numbers and character strings in C++. The goal of this chapter is to write simple programs using these basic data types.

CHAPTER CONTENTS

2.1 Defining Variables

When your program carries out computations, you will want to store values so that you can use them later. In a C++ program, you use *variables* to store values. In this section, you will learn how to define and use variables.

To illustrate the use of variables, we will develop a program that solves the following problem. Soft drinks are sold in cans and bottles. A store offers a six-pack of 12-ounce cans for the same price as a two-liter bottle. Which should you buy? (12 fluid ounces equal approximately 0.355 liters.)

In our program, we will define variables for the number of cans per pack and for the volume of each can. Then we will compute the volume of a six-pack in liters and print out the answer.

What contains more soda? A six-pack of 12-ounce cans or a two-liter bottle?

2.1.1 Variable Definitions

The following statement defines a variable named cans_per_pack:

```
int cans_per_pack = 6;
```

Like a variable in a computer program, a parking space has an identifier and a contents.

A variable is a storage location with a name.

A variable is a storage location in a computer program. Each variable has a name and holds a value.

A variable is similar to a parking space in a parking garage. The parking space has an identifier (such as "J 053"), and it can hold a vehicle. A variable has a name (such as cans_per_pack), and it can hold a value (such as 6).

When defining a variable, you usually specify an initial value.

When defining a variable, you usually want to *initialize* it. That is, you specify the value that should be stored in the variable. Consider again this variable definition:

```
int cans_per_pack = 6;
```

The variable cans_per_pack is initialized with the value 6.

When defining a variable, you also specify the type of its values.

Like a parking space that is restricted to a certain type of vehicle (such as a compact car, motorcycle, or electric vehicle), a variable in C++ stores data of a specific *type*. C++ supports quite a few data types: numbers, text strings, files, dates, and many others. You must specify the type whenever you define a variable (see Syntax 2.1).

Each parking space is suitable for a particular type of vehicle, just as each variable holds a value of a particular type.

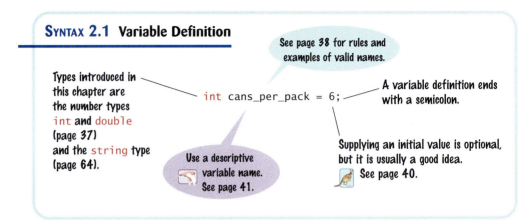

SYNTAX 2.1   Variable Definition

See page 38 for rules and examples of valid names.

Types introduced in this chapter are the number types int and double (page 37) and the string type (page 64).

`int cans_per_pack = 6;`

A variable definition ends with a semicolon.

Use a descriptive variable name. See page 41.

Supplying an initial value is optional, but it is usually a good idea. See page 40.

The `cans_per_pack` variable is an *integer*, a whole number without a fractional part. In C++, this type is called `int`. (See the next section for more information about number types in C++.)

Note that the type comes before the variable name:

```
int cans_per_pack = 6;
```

Table 1 shows variations of variable definitions.

Table 1   Variable Definitions in C++

Variable Name	Comment
`int cans = 6;`	Defines an integer variable and initializes it with 6.
`int total = cans + bottles;`	The initial value need not be a constant. (Of course, cans and bottles must have been previously defined.)
🚫 `bottles = 1;`	**Error:** The type is missing. This statement is not a definition but an assignment of a new value to an existing variable—see Section 2.2.
🚫 `int bottles = "10";`	**Error:** You cannot initialize a number with a string.
`int bottles;`	Defines an integer variable without initializing it. This can be a cause for errors—see Common Error 2.2 on page 40.
`int cans, bottles;`	Defines two integer variables in a single statement. In this book, we will define each variable in a separate statement.

2.1.2 Number Types

Use the `int` type for numbers that cannot have a fractional part.

In C++, there are several different types of numbers. You use the *integer* number type, called `int` in C++, to denote a whole number without a fractional part. For example, there must be an integer number of cans in any pack of cans—you cannot have a fraction of a can.

When a fractional part is required (such as in the number 0.335), we use *floating-point numbers*. The most commonly used type for floating-point numbers in C++ is called `double`. (If you want to know the reason, read Advanced Topic 2.1 on page 41.) Here is the definition of a floating-point variable:

```
double can_volume = 0.335;
```

Use the `double` type for floating-point numbers.

When a value such as 6 or 0.335 occurs in a C++ program, it is called a number *literal*. Table 2 shows how to write integer and floating-point literals in C++.

Table 2 Number Literals in C++

Number	Type	Comment
6	int	An integer has no fractional part.
−6	int	Integers can be negative.
0	int	Zero is an integer.
0.5	double	A number with a fractional part has type double.
1.0	double	An integer with a fractional part .0 has type double.
1E6	double	A number in exponential notation: 1×10^6 or 1000000. Numbers in exponential notation always have type double.
2.96E-2	double	Negative exponent: 2.96×10^{-2} = 2.96 / 100 = 0.0296
🚫 100,000		**Error:** Do not use a comma as a decimal separator.
🚫 3 1/2		**Error:** Do not use fractions; use decimal notation: 3.5

2.1.3 Variable Names

When you define a variable, you should pick a name that explains its purpose. For example, it is better to use a descriptive name, such as can_volume, than a terse name, such as cv.

In C++, there are a few simple rules for variable names:

1. Variable names must start with a letter or the underscore (_) character, and the remaining characters must be letters, numbers, or underscores.

2. You cannot use other symbols such as $ or %. Spaces are not permitted inside names either. You can use an underscore instead, as in can_volume.

3. Variable names are *case-sensitive*, that is, CanVolume and canvolume are different names. For that reason, it is a good idea to use only lowercase letters in variable names.

4. You cannot use *reserved words* such as double or return as names; these words are reserved exclusively for their special C++ meanings. (See Appendix B.)

Table 3 shows examples of legal and illegal variable names in C++.

Table 3   Variable Names in C++

Variable Name	Comment
can_volume1	Variable names consist of letters, numbers, and the underscore character.
x	In mathematics, you use short variable names such as x or y. This is legal in C++, but not very common, because it can make programs harder to understand (see Quality Tip 2.1 on page 41).
⚠ CanVolume	**Caution:** Variable names are case-sensitive. This variable name is different from canvolume.
🚫 6pack	**Error:** Variable names cannot start with a number.
🚫 can volume	**Error:** Variable names cannot contain spaces.
🚫 double	**Error:** You cannot use a reserved word as a variable name.
🚫 ltr/fl.oz	**Error:** You cannot use symbols such as / or .

2.1.4 Comments

As your programs get more complex, you should add *comments*, explanations for human readers of your code. For example, here is a comment that explains the value used in a variable initialization:

```
double can_volume = 0.355; // Liters in a 12-ounce can
```

> Use comments to add explanations for humans who read your code. The compiler ignores comments.

This comment explains the significance of the value 0.355 to a human reader. The compiler does not process comments at all. It ignores everything from a // delimiter to the end of the line.

You use the // syntax for short comments. If you have a longer comment, enclose it between /* and */ delimiters. The compiler ignores these delimiters and everything in between.

Here is a typical example, a long comment at the beginning of a program, to explain the program's purpose:

```
/*
    This program computes the volume (in liters) of a six-pack of
    soda cans.
*/
```

We are now ready to finish our program. The program consists of the two variable definitions that we just discussed, followed by a statement to print their product. Since the result is larger than 2, we know that the six-pack contains more soda than the two-liter bottle.

ch02/volume1.cpp

```
1   #include <iostream>
2
3   using namespace std;
4
5   /*
6       This program computes the volume (in liters) of a six-pack of
7       soda cans.
8   */
9   int main()
10  {
11      int cans_per_pack = 6;
12      double can_volume = 0.355; // Liters in a 12-ounce can
13
14      cout << "A six-pack of 12-ounce cans contains "
15          << cans_per_pack * can_volume << " liters." << endl;
16
17      return 0;
18  }
```

Program Run

```
A six-pack of 12-ounce cans contains 2.13 liters.
```

SELF CHECK

1. Define a variable suitable for holding the number of bottles in a case.
2. What is wrong with the following variable definition?

   ```
   int ounces per liter = 28.35
   ```
3. Define and initialize two variables, `unit_price` and `quantity`, to contain the unit price of a single bottle and the number of bottles purchased. Use reasonable initial values.
4. Use the variables defined in Self Check 3 to display the total purchase price.
5. Some drinks are sold in four-packs instead of six-packs. How would you change the `volume1.cpp` program to compute the total volume?
6. What is wrong with this comment?

   ```
   double can_volume = 0.355; /* Liters in a 12-ounce can //
   ```
7. Suppose the type of the `cans_per_pack` variable in the `volume1.cpp` was changed from `int` to `double`. What would be the effect on the program?

COMMON ERROR 2.1

Using Undefined Variables

You must define a variable before you use it for the first time. For example, the following sequence of statements would not be legal:

```
double can_volume = 12 * liter_per_ounce;
double liter_per_ounce = 0.0296;
```

In your program, the statements are compiled in order. When the compiler reaches the first statement, it does not know that `liter_per_ounce` will be defined in the next line, and it reports an error.

COMMON ERROR 2.2

Using Uninitialized Variables

If you define a variable but leave it uninitialized, then your program can act unpredictably. To understand why, consider what happens when you define a variable. Just enough space is set aside in memory to hold values of the type you specify. For example, with the definition

```
int bottles;
```

a block of memory big enough to hold integers is reserved. There is already *some* value in that memory. After all, you don't get freshly minted transistors—just an area of memory that has previously been used, filled with flotsam left over from prior computations. (In this regard, a variable differs from a parking space. A parking space can be empty, containing no vehicle. But a variable always holds some value.)

If you use the variable without initializing it, then that prior value will be used, yielding unpredictable results. For example, consider the program segment

```
int bottles; // Forgot to initialize
int bottle_volume = bottles * 2; // Result is unpredictable
```

There is no way of knowing what value will be computed. If you are unlucky, a plausible value will happen to appear when you run the program at home, and an entirely different result will occur when the program is graded.

QUALITY TIP 2.1

Choose Descriptive Variable Names

We could have saved ourselves a lot of typing by using shorter variable names, as in

```
double cv = 0.355;
```

Compare this definition with the one that we actually used, though. Which one is easier to read? There is no comparison. Just reading `can_volume` is a lot less trouble than reading `cv` and then *figuring out* it must mean "can volume".

In practical programming, this is particularly important when programs are written by more than one person. It may be obvious to *you* that `cv` stands for can volume and not current velocity, but will it be obvious to the person who needs to update your code years later? For that matter, will you remember yourself what `cv` means when you look at the code three months from now?

ADVANCED TOPIC 2.1

Numeric Types in C++

In addition to the `int` and `double` types, C++ has several other numeric types.

C++ has two floating-point types. The `float` type uses half the storage of the `double` type that we use in this book, but it can only store 6–7 digits. Many years ago, when computers had far less memory than they have today, `float` was the standard type for floating-point computations, and programmers would indulge in the luxury of "double precision" only when they needed the additional digits. Today, the `float` type is rarely used.

By the way, these numbers are called "floating-point" because of their internal representation in the computer. Consider numbers 29600, 2.96, and 0.0296. They can be represented in a very similar way: namely, as a sequence of the significant digits—296—and an indication of the position of the decimal point. When the values are multiplied or divided by 10, only the position of the decimal point changes; it "floats". Computers use base 2, not base 10, but the principle is the same.

In addition to the `int` type, C++ has integer types `short`, `long`, and `long long`. For each integer type, there is an `unsigned` equivalent. For example, the `short` type typically has a range from –32,768 to 32,767, whereas `unsigned short` has a range from 0 to 65,535. These strange-looking limits are the result of the use of binary numbers in computers. A `short` value uses 16 binary digits, which can encode 2^{16} = 65,536 values. Keep in mind that the ranges for integer types are not standardized, and they differ among compilers. The following table contains typical values.

Table 4 Number Types

Type	Typical Range	Typical Size
int	−2,147,483,648 ... 2,147,483,647 (about 2 billion)	4 bytes
unsigned	0 ... 4,294,967,295	4 bytes
short	−32,768 ... 32,767	2 bytes
unsigned short	0 ... 65,535	2 bytes
long long	−9,223,372,036,854,775,808 ... 9,223,372,036,854,775,807	8 bytes
double	The double-precision floating-point type, with a range of about $\pm 10^{308}$ and about 15 significant decimal digits	8 bytes
float	The single-precision floating-point type, with a range of about $\pm 10^{38}$ and about 7 significant decimal digits	4 bytes

ADVANCED TOPIC 2.2

Numeric Ranges and Precisions

Because numbers are represented in the computer with a limited number of digits, they cannot represent arbitrary integer or floating-point numbers.

The int type has a *limited range*: On most platforms, it can represent numbers up to a little more than two billion. For many applications, this is not a problem, but you cannot use an int to represent the world population.

If a computation yields a value that is outside the int range, the result *overflows*. No error is displayed. Instead, the result is truncated, yielding a useless value. For example,

```
int one_billion = 1000000000;
cout << 3 * one_billion << endl;
```

displays −1294967296.

In situations such as this, you can switch to double values. However, read Common Error 2.6 on page 58 for more information about a related issue: roundoff errors.

2.2 Modifying Variables

The contents of a variable can vary over time. In the following three sections, you will see how to change the value of a variable.

2.2.1 The Assignment Statement

> An assignment statement stores a new value in a variable, replacing the previously stored value.

You use the *assignment statement* to place a new value into a variable. Here is an example:

```
cans_per_pack = 8;
```

The left-hand side of an assignment statement consists of a variable. The right-hand side is an expression that has a value. That value is stored in the variable, overwriting its previous contents.

There is an important difference between a variable definition and an assignment statement:

```
int cans_per_pack = 6; // Variable definition
...
cans_per_pack = 8; // Assignment statement
```

The first statement is the *definition* of cans_per_pack. It is an instruction to create a new variable of type int, to give it the name cans_per_pack, and to initialize it with 6. The second statement is an *assignment statement:* an instruction to replace the contents of the *existing* variable cans_per_pack with another value.

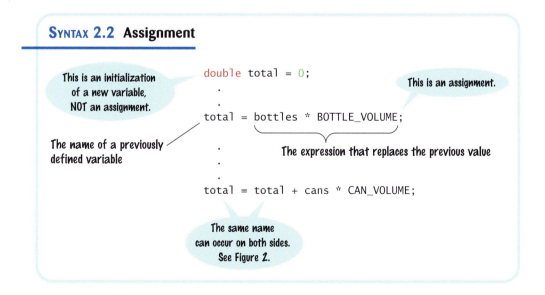

SYNTAX 2.2 Assignment

```
double total = 0;
    .
    .
total = bottles * BOTTLE_VOLUME;
    .
    .
    .
total = total + cans * CAN_VOLUME;
```

This is an initialization of a new variable, NOT an assignment.

The name of a previously defined variable

This is an assignment.

The expression that replaces the previous value

The same name can occur on both sides. See Figure 2.

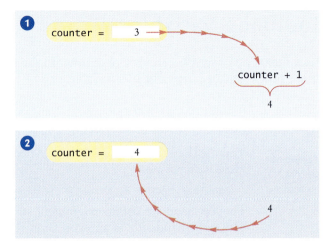

Figure 1   Incrementing a Variable

The assignment operator = does *not* denote mathematical equality.

The = sign doesn't mean that the left-hand side *is equal* to the right-hand side but that the right-hand side value is copied into the left-hand side variable. You should not confuse this *assignment operation* with the = used in algebra to denote *equality*. The assignment operator is an instruction to do something, namely place a value into a variable. The mathematical equality states the fact that two values are equal. For example, in C++, it is perfectly legal to write

```
counter = counter + 1;
```

It means to look up the value stored in the variable counter, add 1 to it, and store the result into counter. (See Figure 1.) The net effect of executing this statement is to increment counter by 1. For example, if counter was 3 before execution of the statement, it is set to 4 afterwards. Of course, in mathematics it would make no sense to write that counter = counter + 1; no value can equal itself plus 1.

2.2.2 Increment and Decrement

The ++ operator adds 1 to a variable; the -- operator subtracts 1.

Changing a variable by adding or subtracting 1 is so common that there is a special shorthand for it, namely

```
counter++;
counter--;
```

The ++ increment operator gave the C++ programming language its name. C++ is the incremental improvement of the C language.

2.2.3 Input

In this section, you will see how to place user input into a variable. Consider for example the `volume1.cpp` program on page 39. Rather than assuming that the price for the two-liter bottle and the six-pack of cans are identical, we can ask the program user for the prices.

When a program asks for user input, it should first print a message that tells the user which input is expected. Such a message is called a *prompt*.

```
cout << "Please enter the number of bottles: "; // Display prompt
```

Do not add an `endl` after the prompt. You want the input to appear after the colon, not on the following line.

> Use the >> operator to read a value and place it in a variable.

Next, the program issues a command to read the input. The `cin` object reads input from the console window. You use the `>>` operator to place an input value into a variable, like this:

```
int bottles;
cin >> bottles;
```

When the program executes the input statement, it waits for the user to provide input. The user also needs to hit the Enter key so that the program accepts the input. After the user supplies the input, the number is placed into the `bottles` variable, and the program continues.

You can read more than one value in a single input statement:

```
cout << "Please enter the number of bottles and cans: ";
cin >> bottles >> cans;
```

The user can supply both inputs on the same line:

```
Please enter the number of bottles and cans: 2 6
```

Alternatively, the user can hit the Enter key after each input:

```
Please enter the number of bottles and cans: 2
6
```

SYNTAX 2.3 Input Statement

Don't use endl here.

Display a prompt in the console window.
```
cout << "Enter the number of bottles: ";
```
Define a variable to hold the input value. —— `int bottles;`
```
cin >> bottles;
```
The program waits for user input, then places the input into the variable.

2.2.4 Constants

> You cannot change the value of a variable that is defined as const.

When a variable is defined with the reserved word const, its value can never change. Constants are commonly written using capital letters to distinguish them visually from regular variables:

```
const double BOTTLE_VOLUME = 2;
```

It is good programming style to use named constants in your program to explain the meanings of numeric values. For example, compare the statements

```
double volume = bottles * 2;
```

and

```
double volume = bottles * BOTTLE_VOLUME;
```

A programmer reading the first statement may not understand the significance of the number 2. The second statement, with a named constant, makes the computation much clearer.

The following program demonstrates the use of assignment statements, input operations, and constants. The program computes the total volume of a number of bottles and cans. First, we ask for the number of bottles and set total_volume to the volume of the bottles. Then we ask for the number of cans and *add* their volume to the total, using the following statement:

```
total_volume = total_volume + cans * CAN_VOLUME;
```

It means, "Compute the volume from the cans (cans * CAN_VOLUME), add it to the value of total_volume, *and place the result again into the variable* total_volume" (see Figure 2).

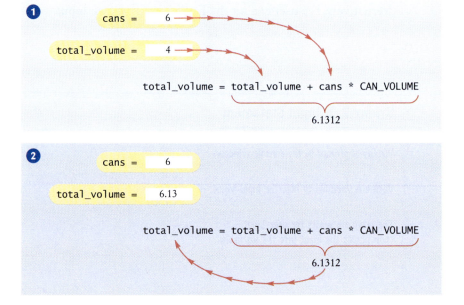

Figure 2
Assignment

ch02/volume2.cpp

```cpp
1   #include <iostream>
2
3   using namespace std;
4
5   int main()
6   {
7      const double BOTTLE_VOLUME = 2;
8      const double LITER_PER_OUNCE = 0.0296;
9      const double CAN_VOLUME = 12 * LITER_PER_OUNCE;
10
11     double total_volume = 0;
12
13     // Read number of bottles
14
15     cout << "Please enter the number of bottles: ";   // Display prompt
16     int bottles;
17     cin >> bottles;
18
19     // Start the computation of the total volume
20
21     total_volume = bottles * BOTTLE_VOLUME;
22
23     // Read number of cans
24
25     cout << "Please enter the number of cans: ";
26     int cans;
27     cin >> cans;
28
29     // Update the total volume
30
31     total_volume = total_volume + cans * CAN_VOLUME;
32
33     cout << "Total volume: " << total_volume << endl;
34
35     return 0;
36  }
```

Program Run

```
Please enter the number of bottles: 2
Please enter the number of cans: 6
Total volume: 6.1312
```

SELF CHECK

8. What is the value of mystery after this sequence of statements?

```cpp
int mystery = 1;
mystery = 1 - 2 * mystery;
mystery++;
```

9. What is wrong with the following sequence of statements?

```
int mystery = 1;
mystery++;
int mystery = 1 - 2 * mystery;
```

10. How would you explain assignment using the parking space analogy?

11. What is wrong with the following statement sequence?

```
cout << "Please enter the unit price: ";
double unit_price;
cin >> unit_price;
int quantity;
cin >> quantity;
```

12. What is problematic about the following statement sequence?

```
cout << "Please enter the unit price: ";
int unit_price;
cin >> unit_price;
```

13. Why can the variables cans and bottles not be declared as const?

Table 5 Modifying a Variable

Statements	Contents of counter	Comments
`counter = 1;`	1	The previous content of the variable has been replaced.
`counter = counter + 1;`	2	Adds 1 to counter. Note that = is not mathematical equality.
`counter++;`	3	++ is a shorthand for adding 1 to a variable.
`counter--;`	2	-- is a shorthand for subtracting 1.
`cin >> counter;`	The input value	Waits for the user to enter a value, and stores the value in the variable.
🚫 `int counter = 4;`		**Error:** This is not an assignment but an attempt to define a second variable named counter.

ADVANCED TOPIC 2.3

Combining Assignment and Arithmetic

In C++, you can combine arithmetic and assignment. For example, the instruction

```
total += cans * CAN_VOLUME;
```

is a shortcut for

```
total = total + cans * CAN_VOLUME;
```

Similarly,

```
total *= 2;
```

is another way of writing

```
total = total * 2;
```

Many programmers find this a convenient shortcut. If you like it, go ahead and use it in your own code. For simplicity, we won't use it in this book, though.

QUALITY TIP 2.2

Do Not Use Magic Numbers

A *magic number* is a numeric constant that appears in your code without explanation. For example,

```
total_volume = bottles * 2;
```

Why 2? Are bottles twice as voluminous as cans? No, the reason is that every bottle contains 2 liters. Use a named constant to make the code self-documenting:

```
const double BOTTLE_VOLUME = 2;
total_volume = bottles * BOTTLE_VOLUME;
```

There is another reason for using named constants. Suppose circumstances change, and the bottle volume is now 1.5 liters. If you used a named constant, you make a single change, and you are done. Otherwise, you have to look at every value of 2 in your program and ponder whether it meant a bottle volume, or something else. In a program that is more than a few pages long, that is incredibly tedious and error-prone.

Even the most reasonable cosmic constant is going to change one day. You think there are seven days per week? Your customers on Mars are going to be pretty unhappy about your silly prejudice. Make a constant

```
const int DAYS_PER_WEEK = 7;
```

2.3 Arithmetic

In the following sections, you will learn how to carry out arithmetic calculations in C++.

2.3.1 Arithmetic Operators

C++ supports the same four basic arithmetic operations as a calculator—addition, subtraction, multiplication, and division—but it uses different symbols for multiplication and division.

You must write a * b to denote multiplication. Unlike in mathematics, you can not write a b, a · b or a × b. Similarly, division is always indicated with a /, never a ÷ or a fraction bar.

For example, $\frac{a+b}{2}$ becomes (a + b) / 2.

Parentheses are used just as in algebra: to indicate in which order the subexpressions should be computed. For example, in the expression (a + b) / 2, the sum a + b is computed first, and then the sum is divided by 2. In contrast, in the expression

    a + b / 2

only b is divided by 2, and then the sum of a and b / 2 is formed. Just as in regular algebraic notation, multiplication and division have a *higher precedence* than addition and subtraction. For example, in the expression a + b / 2, the / is carried out first, even though the + operation occurs further to the left.

2.3.2 Integer Division and Remainder

> If both arguments of / are integers, the remainder is discarded.

Division works as you would expect, as long as at least one of the numbers involved is a floating-point number. That is,

    7.0 / 4.0
    7 / 4.0
    7.0 / 4

all yield 1.75. However, if *both* numbers are integers, then the result of the division is always an integer, with the remainder discarded. That is,

    7 / 4

evaluates to 1 because 7 divided by 4 is 1 with a remainder of 3 (which is discarded). This can be a source of subtle programming errors—see Common Error 2.3 on page 56.

> The % operator computes the remainder of an integer division.

If you are interested in the remainder only, use the % operator:

    7 % 4

is 3, the remainder of the integer division of 7 by 4. The % symbol has no analog in algebra. It was chosen because it looks similar to /, and the remainder operation is related to division. The operator is called *modulus*.

Integer division and the % operator yield the dollar and cent values of a piggybank full of pennies.

(Some people call it *modulo* or *mod.*) It has no relationship with the percent operation that you find on some calculators.

Here is a typical use for the integer / and % operations. Suppose you have an amount of pennies in a piggybank:

```
int pennies = 1729;
```

You want to determine the value in dollars and cents. You obtain the dollars through an integer division by 100.

```
int dollars = pennies / 100;   // Sets dollars to 17
```

The integer division discards the remainder. To obtain the remainder, use the % operator:

```
int cents = pennies % 100;   // Sets cents to 29
```

Table 6 Arithmetic Expressions

Mathematical Expression	C++ Expression	Comments
$\dfrac{x+y}{2}$	(x + y) / 2	The parentheses are required; x + y / 2 computes $x + \frac{y}{2}$.
$\dfrac{xy}{2}$	x * y / 2	Parentheses are not required; operators with the same precedence are evaluated left to right.
$\left(1 + \dfrac{r}{100}\right)^n$	pow(1 + r / 100, n)	Remember to add #include <cmath> to the top of your program.
$\sqrt{a^2 + b^2}$	sqrt(a * a + b * b)	a * a is simpler than pow(a, 2).
$\dfrac{i+j+k}{3}$	(i + j + k) / 3.0	If i, j, and k are integers, using a denominator of 3.0 forces floating-point division.

2.3.3 Powers and Roots

The C++ library defines many mathematical functions such as sqrt (square root) and pow (raising to a power).

In C++, there are no symbols for powers and roots. To compute them, you must call *functions*. To take the square root of a number, you use the sqrt function. For example, $\sqrt{x}$ is written as sqrt(x). To compute x^n, you write pow(x, n).

To use the sqrt and pow functions, you must place the line #include <cmath> at the top of your program file. The header file cmath is a standard C++ header that is available with all C++ systems, as is iostream.

As you can see, the effect of the /, sqrt, and pow operations is to flatten out mathematical terms. In algebra, you use fractions, exponents, and roots to arrange expressions in a compact two-dimensional form. In C++, you have to write all expressions in a linear arrangement. For example, the mathematical expression

$$b \times \left(1 + \frac{r}{100}\right)^n$$

becomes

```
b * pow(1 + r / 100, n)
```

Figure 3 shows how to analyze such an expression.

Table 7 shows additional functions that are declared in the cmath header. Inputs and outputs are floating-point numbers.

Table 7   Other Mathematical Functions

Function	Description
sin(x)	sine of x (x in radians)
cos(x)	cosine of x
tan(x)	tangent of x
log10(x)	(decimal log) $\log_{10}(x)$, $x > 0$
fabs(x)	absolute value $|x|$

2.3.4 Converting Floating-Point Numbers to Integers

When a floating-point value is assigned to an integer variable, the fractional part is discarded:

```
double price = 2.55;
int dollars = price;  // Sets dollars to 2
```

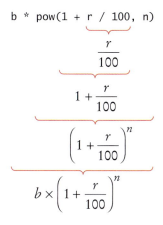

Figure 3 Analyzing an Expression

Discarding the fractional part is not always what you want. Often, you want to round to the *nearest* integer. To round a positive floating-point value to the nearest integer, add 0.5 and then convert to an integer:

```
int dollars = price + 0.5; // Rounds to the nearest integer
```

In our example, adding 0.5 turns all values above 2.5 into values above 3. In particular, 2.55 is turned into 3.05, which is then truncated to 3. (For a negative floating-point value, you subtract 0.5.)

Because truncation is a potential cause for errors, your compiler may issue a warning that assigning a floating-point value to an integer variable is unsafe. See Advanced Topic 2.4 on page 59 on how to avoid this warning.

2.3.5 Formatted Output

When you print the result of a computation, you often want some control over its appearance. For example, when you print an amount in dollars and cents, you usually want it to be rounded to two significant digits. That is, you want the output to look like

```
Price per liter: 1.22
```

instead of

```
Price per liter: 1.21997
```

> You send manipulators to cout to specify how values should be formatted.

The following command instructs cout to use two digits after the decimal point for all floating-point numbers:

```
cout << fixed << setprecision(2);
```

This command does not produce any output; it just manipulates cout so that it will change the output format. The values fixed and setprecision are called *manipulators*. We will discuss manipulators in detail in Chapter 8.

You use manipulators to line up
your output in neat columns.

For now, just remember to include the statement given above whenever you want currency values displayed neatly.

To use manipulators, you must include the `iomanip` header in your program:

```
#include <iomanip>
```

You can combine the manipulators and the values to be displayed into a single statement.

```
cout << fixed << setprecision(2)
    << "Price per liter: "
    << price_per_liter << endl;
```

There is another manipulator that is sometimes handy. When you display several rows of data, you usually want the columns to line up.

You use the `setw` manipulator to set the *width* of the next output field. The width is the total number of characters used for showing the value, including digits, the decimal point, and spaces. Controlling the width is important when you want columns of numbers to line up.

Table 8 Formatting Output

Output Statement	Output	Comment
`cout << 12.345678;`	12.3457	By default, a number is printed with 6 significant digits.

`cout << fixed`
`    << setprecision(2)`
`    << 12.3;`
	12.30	Use the `fixed` and `setprecision` manipulators to control the number of digits after the decimal point.

`cout << ":" << setw(6)` `    << 12;`	: 12	Four spaces are printed before the number, for a total width of 6 characters.
`cout << ":" << setw(2)` `    << 123;`	:123	If the width not sufficient, it is ignored.
`cout << setw(6)` `    << ":" << 12;`	:12.3	The width only refers to the next item. Here, the : is preceded by five spaces.

For example, if you want a number to be printed in a column that is eight characters wide, you use

```
cout << setw(8) << price_per_liter;
```

This command prints the value `price_per_liter` in a field of width 8, for example

```
       1 . 2 2
```

(where each ▪ represents a space).

There is a notable difference between the `setprecision` and `setw` manipulators. Once you set the precision, that value is used for all subsequent floating-point numbers. But the width affects only the *next* value. Subsequent values are formatted without any padding.

Our next example program will prompt for the price of a six-pack and then print out the price per liter. The program puts to work what you just learned about arithmetic and formatting.

ch02/volume3.cpp

```
 1  #include <iostream>
 2  #include <iomanip>
 3
 4  using namespace std;
 5
 6  int main()
 7  {
 8     // Read price per pack
 9
10     cout << "Please enter the price for a six-pack: ";
11     double pack_price;
12     cin >> pack_price;
13
14     // Compute pack volume
15
16     const double LITER_PER_OUNCE = 0.0296;
17     double CAN_VOLUME = 12 * LITER_PER_OUNCE;
18     double PACK_VOLUME = 6 * CAN_VOLUME;
19
20     // Compute and print price per liter
21
22     double price_per_liter = pack_price / PACK_VOLUME;
23
24     cout << fixed << setprecision(2);
25     cout << "Price per liter: " << price_per_liter << endl;
26
27     return 0;
28  }
```

Program Run

```
Please enter the price for a six-pack: 2.60
Price per liter: 1.22
```

SELF CHECK

14. A bank account earns interest of p percent per year. In C++, how do you compute the interest earned in one year? Assume variables p and balance of type double have already been defined.

15. In C++, how do you compute the side length of a square whose area is stored in the variable area?

16. The volume of a sphere is given by $V = \frac{4}{3}\pi r^3$.

    If the radius is given by a variable radius of type double, write a C++ expression for the volume. You may assume that π is defined by a constant PI.

17. What is the value of 1729 / 10 and 1729 % 10?

18. Suppose a punch recipe calls for a given amount of orange soda, measured in ounces.

    ```
    int amount = 32;
    ```

    We can compute the number of 12-ounce cans needed, assuming that the amount does not evenly divide into 12:

    ```
    int cans_needed = amount / 12 + 1;
    ```

    Use the % operator to determine how many ounces will be left over. For example, if 32 ounces are required, we need 3 cans and have 4 ounces left over.

19. What is the output of the following statement sequence?

    ```
    double bottles = 10;
    cout << "The total volume is" << 2 * bottles;
    ```

20. Using the setw manipulator, improve the output statement

    ```
    cout << "Bottles: " << bottles << endl
         << "Cans: " << cans << endl;
    ```

    so that the output looks like this:

    ```
    Bottles:        8
    Cans:          24
    ```

    The numbers to the right should line up. (You may assume that the numbers have at most 8 digits.)

COMMON ERROR 2.3

Unintended Integer Division

It is unfortunate that C++ uses the same symbol, namely /, for both integer and floating-point division. These are really quite different operations. It is a common error to use integer division by accident. Consider this segment that computes the average of three integers.

```
cout << "Please enter your last three test scores: ";
int s1;
int s2;
int s3;
cin >> s1 >> s2 >> s3;
```

```
double average = (s1 + s2 + s3) / 3; // Error
cout << "Your average score is " << average << endl;
```

What could be wrong with that? Of course, the average of s1, s2, and s3 is

$$\frac{s1+s2+s3}{3}$$

Here, however, the / does not mean division in the mathematical sense. It denotes integer division because both s1 + s2 + s3 and 3 are integers. For example, if the scores add up to 14, the average is computed to be 4, the result of the integer division of 14 by 3. That integer 4 is then moved into the floating-point variable average. The remedy is to make the numerator or denominator into a floating-point number:

```
double total = s1 + s2 + s3;
double average = total / 3;
```

or

```
double average = (s1 + s2 + s3) / 3.0;
```

COMMON ERROR 2.4

Unbalanced Parentheses

Consider the expression

```
(-(b * b - 4 * a * c) / (2 * a)
```

What is wrong with it? Count the parentheses. There are three (and two). The parentheses are *unbalanced*. This kind of typing error is very common with complicated expressions. Now consider this expression.

```
-(b * b - (4 * a * c))) / 2 * a)
```

This expression has three (and three), but it still is not correct. In the middle of the expression,

```
-(b * b - (4 * a * c))) / 2 * a)
                    ↑
```

there are only two (but three), which is an error. In the middle of an expression, the count of (must be greater than or equal to the count of), and at the end of the expression the two counts must be the same.

Here is a simple trick to make the counting easier without using pencil and paper. It is difficult for the brain to keep two counts simultaneously. Keep only one count when scanning the expression. Start with 1 at the first opening parenthesis, add 1 whenever you see an opening parenthesis, and subtract one whenever you see a closing parenthesis. Say the numbers aloud as you scan the expression. If the count ever drops below zero, or is not zero at the end, the parentheses are unbalanced. For example, when scanning the previous expression, you would mutter

```
-(b * b - (4 * a * c ) ) ) / 2 * a)
 1         2          1 0 -1
```

and you would find the error.

COMMON ERROR 2.5

Forgetting Header Files

Every program that carries out input or output needs the iostream header. If you use mathematical functions such as sqrt, you need to include cmath. If you forget to include the appropriate header file, the compiler will not know symbols such as cout or sqrt. If the compiler complains about an undefined function or symbol, check your header files.

Sometimes you may not know which header file to include. Suppose you want to compute the absolute value of an integer using the abs function. As it happens, abs is not defined in cmath but in cstdlib. How can you find the correct header file? You need to locate the documentation of the abs function, preferably using the online help of your development environment or a reference site on the Internet such as http://www.cplusplus.com (see Figure 4). The documentation includes a short description of the function and the name of the header file that you must include.

Figure 4   Online Documentation

COMMON ERROR 2.6

Roundoff Errors

Roundoff errors are a fact of life when calculating with floating-point numbers. You probably have encountered that phenomenon yourself with manual calculations. If you calculate 1/3 to two decimal places, you get 0.33. Multiplying again by 3, you obtain 0.99, not 1.00.

In the processor hardware, numbers are represented in the binary number system, not in decimal. You still get roundoff errors when binary digits are lost. They just may crop up at different places than you might expect. Here is an example.

```
#include <iostream>

using namespace std;

int main()
{
   double price = 4.35;
   int cents = 100 * price; // Should be 100 * 4.35 = 435
   cout << cents << endl; // Prints 434!
   return 0;
}
```

Of course, one hundred times 4.35 is 435, but the program prints 434.

Most computers represent numbers in the binary system. In the binary system, there is no exact representation for 4.35, just as there is no exact representation for 1/3 in the decimal system. The representation used by the computer is just a little less than 4.35, so 100 times that value is just a little less than 435. When a floating-point value is converted to an integer, the entire fractional part, which is almost 1, is thrown away, and the integer 434 is stored in cents. The remedy is to add 0.5 in order to round to the nearest integer:

```
int cents = 100 * price + 0.5;
```

ADVANCED TOPIC 2.4

Casts

Occasionally, you need to store a value into a variable of a different type. Whenever there is the risk of *information loss*, the compiler issues a warning. For example, if you store a double value into an int variable, you can lose information in two ways:

- The fractional part is lost.
- The magnitude may be too large.

For example,

```
int n = 1.0E100; // NO
```

is not likely to work, because 10^{100} is larger than the largest representable integer.

Nevertheless, sometimes you do want to convert a floating-point value into an integer value. If you are prepared to lose the fractional part and you know that this particular floating-point number is not larger than the largest possible integer, then you can turn off the warning by using a *cast*. A cast is a conversion from one type (such as double) to another type (such as int) that is not safe in general, but that you know to be safe in a particular circumstance. You express a cast in C++ as follows:

```
int cents = static_cast<int>(100 * price + 0.5);
```

QUALITY TIP 2.3

Spaces in Expressions

It is easier to read

```
x1 = (-b + sqrt(b * b - 4 * a * c)) / (2 * a);
```

than

```
x1=(-b+sqrt(b*b-4*a*c))/(2*a);
```

Simply put spaces around all operators + - * / % =. However, don't put a space after a *unary* minus: a – used to negate a single quantity, such as -b. That way, it can be easily distinguished from a *binary* minus, as in a - b.

It is customary not to put a space after a function name. That is, write sqrt(x) and not sqrt (x).

RANDOM FACT 2.1

The Pentium Floating-Point Bug

In 1994, Intel Corporation released what was then its most powerful processor, the Pentium. Unlike previous generations of its processors, it had a very fast floating-point unit. Intel's goal was to compete aggressively with the makers of higher-end processors for engineering workstations. The Pentium was a huge success immediately.

In the summer of 1994, Dr. Thomas Nicely of Lynchburg College in Virginia ran an extensive set of computations to analyze the sums of reciprocals of certain sequences of prime numbers. The results were not always what his theory predicted, even after he took into account the inevitable roundoff errors. Then Dr. Nicely noted that the same program did produce the correct results when running it on the slower 486 processor that preceded the Pentium in Intel's lineup. This should not have happened. The optimal roundoff behavior of floating-point calculations has been standardized by the Institute for Electrical and Electronic Engineers (IEEE) and Intel claimed to adhere to the IEEE standard in both the 486 and the Pentium processors. Upon further checking, Dr. Nicely discovered that indeed there was a very small set of numbers for which the product of two numbers was computed differently on the two processors. For example,

$$4,195,835 - \left(\left(4,195,835/3,145,727 \right) \times 3,145,727 \right)$$

is mathematically equal to 0, and it did compute as 0 on a 486 processor. On his Pentium processor the result was 256.

As it turned out, Intel had independently discovered the bug in its testing and had started to produce chips that fixed it. The bug was caused by an error in a table that was used to speed up the floating-point multiplication algorithm of the processor. Intel determined that the problem was exceedingly rare. They claimed that under normal use, a typical consumer would only notice the problem once every 27,000 years. Unfortunately for Intel, Dr. Nicely had not been a normal user.

Now Intel had a real problem on its hands. It figured that the cost of replacing all Pentium processors that it had already sold would cost a great deal of money. Intel already had more orders for the chip than it could produce, and it would be particularly galling to have to give out the scarce chips as free replacements instead of selling them. Intel's management decided to punt on the issue and initially offered to replace the processors only for those customers who could prove that their work required absolute precision in mathematical calculations. Naturally, that did not go over well with the hundreds of thousands of customers who had paid retail prices of $700 and more for a Pentium chip and did not want to live with the nagging feeling that perhaps, one day, their income tax program would produce a faulty return.

Ultimately, Intel caved in to public demand and replaced all defective chips, at a cost of about 475 million dollars.

HOW TO 2.1

Carrying out Computations

Many programming problems require that you carry out arithmetic computations. This How To shows you how to turn a problem statement into pseudocode and, ultimately, a C++ program.

Step 1   Understand the problem: What are the inputs? What are the desired outputs?

For example, suppose you are asked to write a program that simulates a vending machine. A customer selects an item for purchase and inserts a bill into the vending machine. The vending machine dispenses the purchased item and gives change. We will assume that all item prices are multiples of 25 cents, and the machine gives all change in dollar coins and quarters. Your task is to compute how many coins of each type to return.

A vending machine takes bills and gives change in coins.

In this problem, there are two inputs:
- The denomination of the bill that the customer inserts
- The price of the purchased item

There are two desired outputs:
- The number of dollar coins that the machine returns
- The number of quarters that the machine returns

Step 2 Work out examples by hand.

This is a very important step. If you can't compute a couple of solutions by hand, it's unlikely that you'll be able to write a program that automates the computation.

Let's assume that a customer purchased an item that cost $2.25 and inserted a $5 bill. The customer is due $2.75, or two dollar coins and three quarters.

That is easy for you to see, but how can a C++ program come to the same conclusion? The key is to work in pennies, not dollars. The amount due the customer is 275 pennies. Dividing by 100 yields 2, the number of dollars. Dividing the remainder (75) by 25 yields 3, the number of quarters.

Step 3 Write pseudocode for computing the answers.

In the previous step, you worked out a specific instance of the problem. You now need to come up with a method that works in general.

Given an arbitrary item price and payment, how can you compute the coins due? First, compute the amount due in pennies:

amount due = 100 x bill value - item price in pennies

To get the dollars, divide by 100 and discard the remainder:

dollar coins = amount due / 100 (without remainder)

The remaining amount due can be computed in two ways. If you are familiar with the modulus operator, you can simply compute

amount due = amount due % 100

Alternatively, subtract the penny value of the dollar coins from the amount due:

amount due = amount due - 100 x dollar coins

To get the quarters due, divide by 25:

quarters = amount due / 25

Step 4 Define the variables and constants that you need, and specify their types.

Here, we have five variables:
- bill_value
- item_price
- amount_due
- dollar_coins
- quarters

Should we introduce constants to explain 100 and 25 as PENNIES_PER_DOLLAR and PENNIES_PER_QUARTER? Doing so will make it easier to convert the program to international markets, so we will take this step.

It is very important that amount_due and PENNIES_PER_DOLLAR are of type int because the computation of dollar_coins uses integer division. Similarly, the other variables are integers.

Step 5 Turn the pseudocode into C++ statements.

If you did a thorough job with the pseudocode, this step should be easy. Of course, you have to know how to express mathematical operations (such as powers or integer division) in C++.

```
amount_due = PENNIES_PER_DOLLAR * bill_value - item_price;
dollar_coins = amount_due / PENNIES_PER_DOLLAR;
amount_due = amount_due % PENNIES_PER_DOLLAR;
quarters = amount_due / PENNIES_PER_QUARTER;
```

Step 6 Provide input and output.

Before starting the computation, we prompt the user for the bill value and item price:

```
cout << "Enter bill value (1 = $1 bill, 5 = $5 bill, etc.): ";
cin >> bill_value;
cout << "Enter item price in pennies: ";
cin >> item_price;
```

When the computation is finished, we display the result. For extra credit, we use the setw manipulator to make sure that the output lines up neatly.

```
cout << "Dollar coins: " << setw(6) << dollar_coins << endl
     << "Quarters:     " << setw(6) << quarters << endl;
```

Step 7 Include the required headers and provide a main function.

We need the iostream header for all input and output. Because we use the setw manipulator, we also require iomanip. This program does not use any special mathematical functions. Therefore, we do not include the cmath header.

In the main function, you need to define constants and variables (Step 4), carry out computations (Step 5), and provide input and output (Step 6). Clearly, you will want to first get the input, then do the computations, and finally show the output. Define the constants at the beginning of the function, and define each variable just before it is needed.

Here is the complete program, ch02/vending.cpp:

```cpp
#include <iostream>
#include <iomanip>

using namespace std;

int main()
{
   const int PENNIES_PER_DOLLAR = 100;
   const int PENNIES_PER_QUARTER = 25;

   cout << "Enter bill value (1 = $1 bill, 5 = $5 bill, etc.): ";
   int bill_value;
   cin >> bill_value;
   cout << "Enter item price in pennies: ";
   int item_price;
   cin >> item_price;

   int amount_due = PENNIES_PER_DOLLAR * bill_value - item_price;
   int dollar_coins = amount_due / PENNIES_PER_DOLLAR;
   amount_due = amount_due % PENNIES_PER_DOLLAR;
   int quarters = amount_due / PENNIES_PER_QUARTER;

   cout << "Dollar coins: " << setw(6) << dollar_coins << endl
      << "Quarters:     " << setw(6) << quarters << endl;
}
```

Program Run

```
Enter bill value (1 = $1 bill, 5 = $5 bill, etc.): 5
Enter item price in pennies: 225
Dollar coins:      2
Quarters:          3
```

WORKED EXAMPLE 2.1

Computing the Cost of Stamps

This Worked Example uses arithmetic functions to simulate a stamp vending machine.

2.4 Strings

> Strings are sequences of characters.

Many programs process text, not numbers. Text consists of *characters*: letters, numbers, punctuation, spaces, and so on. A *string* is a sequence of characters. For example, the string "Harry" is a sequence of five characters.

2.4.1 The string Type

You can define variables that hold strings.

```
string name = "Harry";
```

The string type is a part of the C++ standard. To use it, simply include the header file, string:

```
#include <string>
```

We distinguish between string variables (such as the variable name defined above) and string *literals* (character sequences enclosed in quotes, such as "Harry"). The string stored in a string variable can change. A string literal denotes a particular string, just as a number literal (such as 2) denotes a particular number.

Unlike number variables, string variables are guaranteed to be initialized even if you do not supply an initial value. By default, a string variable is set to an empty string: a string containing no characters. An empty string literal is written as "". The definition

```
string response;
```

has the same effect as

```
string response = "";
```

2.4.2 Concatenation

> Use the + operator to *concatenate* strings; that is, put them together to yield a longer string.

Given two strings, such as "Harry" and "Morgan", you can *concatenate* them to one long string. The result consists of all characters in the first string, followed by all characters in the second string. In C++, you use the + operator to concatenate two strings.

For example,

```
string fname = "Harry";
string lname = "Morgan";
string name = fname + lname;
```

results in the string

```
"HarryMorgan"
```

What if you'd like the first and last name separated by a space? No problem:

```
string name = fname + " " + lname;
```

This statement concatenates three strings: fname, the string literal " ", and lname. The result is

```
"Harry Morgan"
```

You cannot use the + operator to concatenate two string literals. For example, the expression "Harry" + " " is not legal. Simply use "Harry " instead.

2.4.3 String Input

You can read a string from the console:

```
cout << "Please enter your name: ";
string name;
cin >> name;
```

When a string is read with the >> operator, only one word is placed into the string variable. For example, suppose the user types

```
Harry Morgan
```

as the response to the prompt. This input consists of two words. After the call cin >> name, the string "Harry" is placed into the variable name. Use another input statement to read the second word.

2.4.4 String Functions

The length member function yields the number of characters in a string.

The number of characters in a string is called the *length* of the string. For example, the length of "Harry" is 5. You can compute the length of a string with the length function. Unlike the sqrt or pow function, the length function is invoked with the *dot notation*. That is, you write the string whose length you want, then a period, then the name of the function, followed by parentheses:

```
int n = name.length();
```

A member function is invoked using the dot notation.

Many C++ functions require you to use this dot notation, and you must memorize (or look up) which do and which don't. These functions are called *member functions*. We say that the member function length is *invoked on* the variable name.

Once you have a string, you can extract substrings by using the substr member function. The member function call

```
s.substr(start, length)
```

returns a string that is made from the characters in the string s, starting at character start, and containing length characters. Here is an example:

```
string greeting = "Hello, World!";
string sub = greeting.substr(0, 5);
// sub is "Hello"
```

Table 9   String Operations

Statement	Result	Comment
`string str = "C";` `str = str + "++";`	str is set to "C++"	When applied to strings, + denotes concatenation.
🚫 `string str = "C" + "++";`	Error	**Error:** You cannot concatenate two string literals.

`cout << "Enter name: ";`
`cin >> name;`
(User input: Harry Morgan)
	name contains "Harry"	The >> operator places the next word into the string variable.

`cout << "Enter name: ";`
`cin >> name >> last_name;`
(User input: Harry Morgan)
	name contains "Harry", last_name contains "Morgan"	Use multiple >> operators to read more than one word.

`string greeting = "H & S";` `int n = greeting.length();`	n is set to 5	Each space counts as one character.
`string str = "Sally";` `string str2 = str.substr(1, 3);`	str2 is set to "all"	Extracts the substring of length 3 starting at position 1. (The initial position is 0.)
`string str = "Sally";` `string str2 = str.substr(1);`	str2 is set to "ally"	If you omit the length, all characters from the position until the end are included.
`string a = str.substr(0, 1);`	a is set to the initial letter in str	Extracts the substring of length 1 starting at position 0.
`string b = str.substr(` `   str.length() - 1);`	b is set to the last letter in str	The last letter has position str.length() - 1. We need not specify the length.

Use the substr member function to extract a substring of a string.

The substr operation makes a string that consists of five characters taken from the string greeting. Indeed, "Hello" is a string of length 5 that occurs inside greeting. A curious aspect of the substr operation is the starting position. Starting position 0 means "start at the beginning of the string". The first position in a string is labeled 0, the second one 1, and so on. For example, here are the position numbers in the greeting string:

H	e	l	l	o	,		W	o	r	l	d	!
0	1	2	3	4	5	6	7	8	9	10	11	12

The position number of the last character (12) is always one less than the length of the string.

Let's figure out how to extract the substring "World". Count characters starting at 0, not 1. You find that W, the 8th character, has position number 7. The string you want is 5 characters long. Therefore, the appropriate substring command is

```
string w = greeting.substr(7, 5);
```

If you omit the length, you get all characters from the given position to the end of the string. For example,

```
greeting.substr(7)
```

is the string "World!" (including the exclamation mark).

Here is a simple program that puts these concepts to work. The program asks for your name and that of your significant other. It then prints out your initials.

The operation first.substr(0, 1) makes a string consisting of one character, taken from the start of first. The program does the same for the second. Then it concatenates the resulting one-character strings with the string literal "&" to get a string of length 3, the initials string. (See Figure 5.)

first =
R	o	d	o	l	f	o
0	1	2	3	4	5	6

second =
S	a	l	l	y
0	1	2	3	4

initials =
R	&	S
0	1	2

Figure 5 Building the initials String

Initials are formed from the first letter of each name.

ch02/initials.cpp

```
1  #include <iostream>
2  #include <string>
3
4  using namespace std;
5
6  int main()
7  {
8     cout << "Enter your first name: ";
9     string first;
10    cin >> first;
11    cout << "Enter your significant other's first name: ";
12    string second;
13    cin >> second;
14    string initials = first.substr(0, 1)
15       + "&" + second.substr(0, 1);
16    cout << initials << endl;
17
18    return 0;
19 }
```

Program Run

```
Enter your first name: Rodolfo
Enter your significant other's first name: Sally
R&S
```

SELF CHECK

21. What is the length of the string "C++ Program"?

22. Consider this string variable.

```
string str = "C++ Program";
```

Give a call to the substr member function that returns the substring "gram".

23. Use string concatenation to turn the string variable str from Self Check 22 to "C++ Programming".

24. What does the following statement sequence print?

```
string str = "Harry";
cout << str.substr(0, 1) + str.substr(str.length() - 1);
```

25. Give an input statement to read a name of the form "John Q. Public".

RANDOM FACT 2.2

The First Programmer

Before pocket calculators and personal computers existed, navigators and engineers used mechanical adding machines, slide rules, and tables of logarithms and trigonometric functions to speed up computations. Unfortunately, the tables—for which values had to be computed by hand—were notoriously inaccurate. The mathematician Charles Babbage (1791–1871) had the insight that if a machine could be constructed that produced printed tables automatically, both calculation and typesetting errors could be avoided. Babbage set out to develop a machine for this purpose, which he called a *Difference Engine* because it used successive differences to compute polynomials. For example, consider the function $f(x) = x^3$. Write down the values for $f(1)$, $f(2)$, $f(3)$, and so on. Then take the *differences* between successive values:

```
  1
       7
  8
       19
 27
       37
 64
       61
125
       91
216
```

Repeat the process, taking the difference of successive values in the second column, and then repeat once again:

```
  1
       7
  8         12
       19         6
 27         18
       37         6
 64         24
       61         6
125         30
       91
216
```

Now the differences are all the same. You can retrieve the function values by a pattern of additions—you need to know the values at the fringe of the pattern and the constant difference. This method was very attractive, because mechanical addition machines had been known for some time. They consisted of cog wheels, with 10 cogs per wheel, to represent digits, and mechanisms to handle the carry from one digit to the next. Mechanical multiplication machines, on the other hand, were fragile and unreliable. Babbage built a successful prototype of the Difference Engine (the Babbage's Difference Engine figure) and, with his own money and government grants, proceeded to build the table-printing machine. However, because of funding problems and the difficulty of building the machine to the required precision, it was never completed.

While working on the Difference Engine, Babbage conceived of a much grander vision that he called the *Analytical Engine*. The Difference Engine was designed to carry out a limited set of computations—it was no smarter than a pocket calculator is today. But Babbage realized that such a machine could be made *programmable* by storing programs as well

Babbage's Difference Engine

as data. The internal storage of the Analytical Engine was to consist of 1,000 registers of 50 decimal digits each. Programs and constants were to be stored on punched cards—a technique that was, at that time, commonly used on looms for weaving patterned fabrics.

Ada Augusta, Countess of Lovelace (1815–1852), the only child of Lord Byron, was a friend and sponsor of Charles Babbage. Ada Lovelace was one of the first people to realize the potential of such a machine, not just for computing mathematical tables but for processing data that were not numbers. She is considered by many to be the world's first programmer.

CHAPTER SUMMARY

1. A variable is a storage location with a name.

2. When defining a variable, you usually specify an initial value.

3. When defining a variable, you also specify the type of its values.

4. Use the int type for numbers that cannot have a fractional part.

5. Use the double type for floating-point numbers.

6. Use comments to add explanations for humans who read your code. The compiler ignores comments.

7. An assignment statement stores a new value in a variable, replacing the previously stored value.

8. The assignment operator = does not denote mathematical equality.

9. The ++ operator adds 1 to a variable; the -- operator subtracts 1.

10. Use the >> operator to read a value and place it in a variable.

11. You cannot change the value of a variable that is defined as const.

12. If both arguments of / are integers, the remainder is discarded.

13. The % operator computes the remainder of an integer division.

14. The C++ library defines many mathematical functions such as sqrt (square root) and pow (raising to a power).

15. You send manipulators to cout to specify how values should be formatted.

16. Strings are sequences of characters.

17. Use the + operator to *concatenate* strings; that is, put them together to yield a longer string.

18. The length member function yields the number of characters in a string.

19. A member function is invoked using the dot notation.

20. Use the substr member function to extract a substring of a string.

REVIEW EXERCISES

Exercise R2.1. Write the following mathematical expressions in C++.

$$s = s_0 + v_0 t + \frac{1}{2} g t^2$$

$$G = 4\pi^2 \frac{a^3}{p^2(m_1 + m_2)}$$

$$FV = PV \cdot \left(1 + \frac{INT}{100}\right)^{YRS}$$

$$c = \sqrt{a^2 + b^2 - 2ab \cos \gamma}$$

Exercise R2.2. Write the following C++ expressions in mathematical notation.

a. `dm = m * (sqrt(1 + v / c) / sqrt(1 - v / c) - 1);`

b. `volume = PI * r * r * h;`

c. `volume = 4 * PI * pow(r, 3) / 3;`

d. `z = sqrt(x * x + y * y);`

Exercise R2.3. What are the values of the following expressions? In each line, assume that

```
double x = 2.5;
double y = -1.5;
int m = 18;
int n = 4;
string s = "Hello";
string t = "World";
```

a. `x + n * y - (x + n) * y`

b. `m / n + m % n`

c. `5 * x - n / 5`

d. `1 - (1 - (1 - (1 - (1 - n))))`

e. `sqrt(sqrt(n))`

f. `s.length() + t.length()`

g. `s.substr(1, 2)`

h. `s.substr(s.length() / 2, 1)`

i. `s + t`

j. `t + s`

Exercise R2.4. Find at least five *syntax* errors in the following program.

```
#include iostream

int main();
{
   cout << "Please enter two numbers:"
   cin << x, y;
   cout << "The sum of << x << "and" << y
      << "is: " x + y << endl;
   return;
}
```

Exercise R2.5. Find at least four *logic* errors in the following program.

```
#include <iostream>

using namespace std;

int main()
{
   int total;
   int x1;
   cout << "Please enter a number:";
   cin >> x1;
   total = total + x1;
   cout << "Please enter another number:";
   int x2;
   cin >> x2;
   total = total + x1;
   double average = total / 2;
   cout << "The average of the two numbers is "
      << average << "endl";
   return 0;
}
```

Exercise R2.6. Explain the differences between 2, 2.0, "2", and "2.0".

Exercise R2.7. Explain what each of the following program segments computes:

a. x = 2;
   y = x + x;
b. s = "2";
   t = s + s;

Exercise R2.8. Write pseudocode for a program that reads a word and then prints the first character, the last character, and the characters in the middle. For example, if the input is Harry, the program prints H y arr.

Exercise R2.9. Write pseudocode for a program that reads a name (such as Harold James Morgan) and then prints a monogram consisting of the initial letters of the first, middle, and last name (such as HJM).

Exercise R2.10. Write pseudocode for a program that computes the first and last digit of a number. For example, if the input is 23456, the program should print out 2 and 6. *Hint:* %, log10.

Exercise R2.11. Modify the pseudocode for the program in How To 2.1 on page 61 so that the program gives change in quarters, dimes, and nickels. You can assume that the price is a multiple of 5 cents.

Exercise R2.12. The following pseudocode describes how to obtain the name of a day, given the day number (0 = Sunday, 1 = Monday, and so on.)

> Define a string called names containing "SunMonTueWedThuFriSat".
> Compute the starting position as 3 x the day number.
> Extract the substring of names at the starting position with length 3.

Check this pseudocode, using the day number 4. Draw a diagram of the string that is being computed, similar to Figure 5.

Exercise R2.13. The following pseudocode describes how to swap two letters in a word.

> We are given a string str and two positions i and j. (i comes before j)
> Set first to the substring from the start of the string to the last position before i.
> Set middle to the substring from positions i + 1 to j - 1.
> Set last to the substring from position j + 1 to the end of the string.
> Concatenate the following five strings: first, the string containing just the character at position j,
>   middle, the string containing just the character at position i, and last.

Check this pseudocode, using the string "Gateway" and positions 2 and 4. Draw a diagram of the string that is being computed, similar to Figure 5.

Exercise R2.14. Run the following program, and explain the output you get.

```cpp
#include <iostream>

using namespace std;

int main()
{
   int total;
   cout << "Please enter a number: ";
   double x1;
   cin >> x1;
   total = total + x1;
   cout << "total: " << total << endl;
   cout << "Please enter a number: ";
   double x2;
   cin >> x2;
   total = total + x2;
   cout << "total: " << total << endl;
   total = total / 2;
   cout << "total: " << total << endl;
   cout << "The average is " << total << endl;
   return 0;
}
```

Note the *trace messages* that are inserted to show the current contents of the total variable. How do you fix the program? (The program has two separate errors.)

Exercise R2.15. Write a program that prints the values

```
3 * 1000 * 1000 * 1000
3.0 * 1000 * 1000 * 1000
```

Explain the results.

Exercise R2.16. This chapter contains a number of recommendations regarding variables and constants that make programs easier to read and maintain. Briefly summarize these recommendations.

PROGRAMMING EXERCISES

Exercise P2.1. Write a program that reads a number and displays the square, cube, and fourth power. Use the pow function only for the fourth power.

Exercise P2.2. Write a program that prompts the user for two integers and then prints

- The sum
- The difference
- The product
- The average
- The distance (absolute value of the difference)
- The maximum (the larger of the two)
- The minimum (the smaller of the two)

Hint: The max and min functions are defined in the algorithm header.

Exercise P2.3. Write a program that prompts the user for a measurement in meters and then converts it to miles, feet, and inches.

Exercise P2.4. Write a program that prompts the user for a radius and then prints

- The area and circumference of a circle with that radius
- The volume and surface area of a sphere with that radius

Exercise P2.5. Write a program that asks the user for the lengths of the sides of a rectangle. Then print

- The area and perimeter of the rectangle
- The length of the diagonal (use the Pythagorean theorem)

Exercise P2.6. Improve the program discussed in the How To on page 61 to allow input of quarters in addition to bills.

Exercise P2.7. Write a program that helps a person decide whether to buy a hybrid car. Your program's inputs should be:

- The cost of a new car
- The estimated miles driven per year
- The estimated gas price
- The estimated resale value after 5 years

Compute the total cost of owning the car for 5 years. (For simplicity, we will not take the cost of financing into account.) Obtain realistic prices for a new and used hybrid and a comparable car from the Web. Run your program twice, using today's gas price and 15,000 miles per year. Include pseudocode and the program runs with your assignment.

Exercise P2.8. The following pseudocode describes how a bookstore computes the price of an order from the total price and the number of the books that were ordered.

```
Read the total book price and the number of books.
Compute the tax (7.5% of the total book price).
Compute the shipping charge ($2 per book).
The price of the order is the sum of the total book price, the tax, and the shipping charge.
Print the price of the order.
```

Translate this pseudocode into a C++ program.

Exercise P2.9. The following pseudocode describes how to turn a string containing a ten-digit phone number (such as "4155551212") into a more readable string with parentheses and dashes, like this: "(415) 555-1212".

```
Take the substring consisting of the first three characters and surround it with "(" and ")". This is the
    area code.
Concatenate the area code, the substring consisting of the next three characters, a hyphen, and the
    substring consisting of the last four characters. This is the formatted number.
```

Translate this pseudocode into a C++ program that reads a telephone number into a string variable, computes the formatted number, and prints it.

Exercise P2.10. The following pseudocode describes how to extract the dollars and cents from a price given as a floating-point value. For example, a price 2.95 yields values 2 and 95 for the dollars and cents.

```
Assign the price to an integer variable dollars.
Multiply the difference price - dollars by 100 and add 0.5.
Assign the result to an integer variable cents.
```

Translate this pseudocode into a C++ program. Read a price and print the dollars and cents. Test your program with inputs 2.95 and 4.35.

Exercise P2.11. *Giving change.* Implement a program that directs a cashier how to give change. The program has two inputs: the amount due and the amount received from the customer. Display the dollars, quarters, dimes, nickels, and pennies that the customer should receive in return.

Exercise P2.12. Write a program that asks the user to input

- The number of gallons of gas in the tank
- The fuel efficiency in miles per gallon
- The price of gas per gallon

Then print the cost per 100 miles and how far the car can go with the gas in the tank.

Exercise P2.13. *File names and extensions.* Write a program that prompts the user for the drive letter (C), the path (\Windows\System), the file name (Readme), and the extension (txt). Then print the complete file name C:\Windows\System\Readme.txt. (If you use UNIX or a Macintosh, skip the drive name and use / instead of \ to separate directories.)

Exercise P2.14. Write a program that reads a number greater than or equal to 1,000 from the user and prints it *with a comma separating the thousands*. Here is a sample dialog; the user input is in color:

```
Please enter an integer >= 1000: 23456
23,456
```

Exercise P2.15. Write a program that reads a number between 1,000 and 999,999 from the user, where the user enters a comma in the input. Then print the number without a comma. Here is a sample dialog; the user input is in color:

```
Please enter an integer between 1,000 and 999,999: 23,456
23456
```

Hint: Read the input as a string. Measure the length of the string. Suppose it contains n characters. Then extract substrings consisting of the first $n - 4$ characters and the last three characters.

Exercise P2.16. *Printing a grid.* Write a program that prints the following grid to play tic-tac-toe.

```
+--+--+--+
|  |  |  |
+--+--+--+
|  |  |  |
+--+--+--+
|  |  |  |
+--+--+--+
```

Of course, you could simply write seven statements of the form

```
cout << "+--+--+--+";
```

You should do it the smart way, though. Define string variables to hold two kinds of patterns: a comb-shaped pattern and the bottom line. Print the comb three times and the bottom line once.

Exercise P2.17. Write a program that reads in an integer and breaks it into a sequence of individual digits. For example, the input 16384 is displayed as

```
1 6 3 8 4
```

You may assume that the input has no more than five digits and is not negative.

Exercise P2.18. Write a program that reads two times in military format (0900, 1730) and prints the number of hours and minutes between the two times. Here is a sample run. User input is in color.

```
Please enter the first time: 0900
Please enter the second time: 1730
8 hours 30 minutes
```

Extra credit if you can deal with the case where the first time is later than the second:

```
Please enter the first time: 1730
Please enter the second time: 0900
15 hours 30 minutes
```

Exercise P2.19. *Writing large letters.* A large letter H can be produced like this:

```
*    *
*    *
*****
*    *
*    *
```

It can be defined as a string constant like this:

```
const string LETTER_H =
   "*    *\n*    *\n*****\n*    *\n*    *\n";
```

(The \n character is explained in Advanced Topic 1.1.) Do the same for the letters E, L, and O. Then write the message

```
H
E
L
L
O
```

in large letters.

Exercise P2.20. Write a program that transforms numbers 1, 2, 3, …, 12 into the corresponding month names January, February, March, …, December. *Hint:* Make a very long string "January February March ...", in which you add spaces such that each month name has *the same length*. Then use substr to extract the month you want.

ANSWERS TO SELF-CHECK QUESTIONS

1. One possible answer is

   ```
   int bottles_per_case = 8;
   ```

   You may choose a different variable name or a different initialization value, but your variable should have type int.
2. There are three errors:
   - You cannot have spaces in variable names.
   - The variable type should be double because it holds a fractional value.
   - There is a semicolon missing at the end of the statement.

3.
```
double unit_price = 1.95;
int quantity = 2;
```

4. `cout << "Total price: " << unit_price * quantity << endl;`

5. Change the definition of `cans_per_pack` to

`int cans_per_pack = 4;`

6. You need to use a `*/` delimiter to close a comment that begins with a `/*`:

`double can_volume = 0.355; /* Liters in a 12-ounce can */`

7. The program would compile, and it would display the same result. However, a person reading the program might find it confusing that fractional cans are being considered.

8. The variable `mystery` is initialized to 1. The assignment statement changes `mystery` to –1. The increment statement changes it to 0.

9. The last statement is a variable definition, but `mystery` has already been defined. Remedy: Drop the `int` in the last statement.

10. Assignment would occur when one car is replaced by another in the parking space.

11. There is no prompt that alerts the program user to enter the quantity.

12. The `unit_price` variable is defined as an `int`. If the user were to enter a price such as `1.95`, only the 1 would be placed into the variable.

13. Their values are modified by the input statements.

14. `double interest = balance * p / 100;`

15. `double side_length = sqrt(area);`

16. `4 * PI * pow(radius, 3) / 3`
or `(4.0 / 3) * PI * pow(radius, 3),`
but not `(4 / 3) * PI * pow(radius, 3)`

17. 172 and 9

18. `int leftover = 12 - amount % 12;`

19. The output is

`The total volume is20`

Note that there is no space between the `is` and `20`.

20.
```
cout << "Bottles: " << setw(8) << bottles << endl
     << "Cans:    " << setw(8) << cans << endl;
```

Note that the `setw` manipulator appears twice. Also note the added spaces in the string `"Cans:    "`.

21. The length is 11. The space counts as a character.

22. `str.substr(7, 4)`

23. `str = str + "ming";`

24. `Hy`

25. `cin >> first_name >> middle_initial >> last_name;`

Decisions

CHAPTER GOALS

- To be able to implement decisions using if statements
- To learn how to compare integers, floating-point numbers, and strings
- To understand the Boolean data type
- To develop strategies for validating user input

The programs you have seen to this point are able to do fast computations but they are very inflexible. Except for variations in the input, they work the same way with every program run.

One of the essential features of nontrivial computer programs is their ability to make decisions and to carry out different actions, depending on the nature of the inputs. In this chapter, you will learn how to program simple and complex decisions. You will apply what you learn to the task of checking that user-supplied input can safely be used in your program.

CHAPTER CONTENTS

3.1 The if Statement

> The if statement allows a program to carry out different actions depending on the nature of the data to be processed.

The if statement is used to implement a decision. When a condition is fulfilled, one set of statements is executed. Otherwise, another set of statements is executed (see Syntax 3.1).

An if statement is like a fork in the road. Depending upon a decision, different parts of the program are executed.

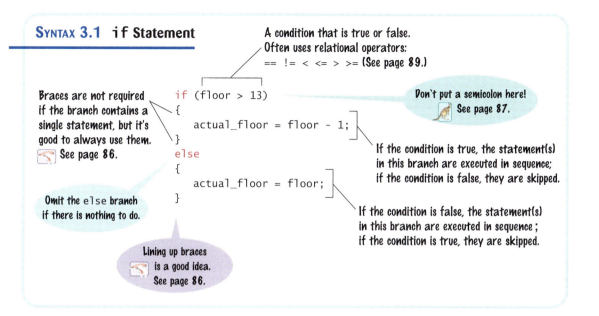

SYNTAX 3.1 if Statement

A condition that is true or false. Often uses relational operators:
== != < <= > >= (See page 89.)

Braces are not required if the branch contains a single statement, but it's good to always use them. See page 86.

```
if (floor > 13)
{
    actual_floor = floor - 1;
}
else
{
    actual_floor = floor;
}
```

Don't put a semicolon here! See page 87.

If the condition is true, the statement(s) in this branch are executed in sequence; if the condition is false, they are skipped.

Omit the else branch if there is nothing to do.

If the condition is false, the statement(s) in this branch are executed in sequence; if the condition is true, they are skipped.

Lining up braces is a good idea. See page 86.

Here is an example using the if statement. In many countries, the number 13 is considered unlucky. Rather than offending superstitious tenants, building owners sometimes skip the thirteenth floor; floor 12 is immediately followed by floor 14. Of course, floor 13 is not usually left empty or, as some conspiracy theorists believe, filled with secret offices and research labs. It is simply called floor 14. The computer that controls the building elevators needs to compensate for this foible and adjust all floor numbers above 13.

Let's simulate this process in C++. We will ask the user to type in the desired floor number and then compute the actual floor. When the input is above 13, then we need to decrement the input to obtain the actual floor. For example, if the user provides an input of 20, the program determines the actual floor as 19. Otherwise, we simply use the supplied floor number.

This elevator panel "skips" the thirteenth floor. The floor is not actually missing—the computer that controls the elevator adjusts the floor numbers above 13.

```
int actual_floor;

if (floor > 13)
{
    actual_floor = floor - 1;
```

```
   }
   else
   {
      actual_floor = floor;
   }
```

The flowchart in Figure 1 shows the branching behavior.

In our example, each branch of the `if` statement contains a single statement. You can include as many statements in each branch as you like. Sometimes, it happens that there is nothing to do in the `else` branch of the statement. In that case, you can omit it entirely, such as in this example:

```
int actual_floor = floor;

if (floor > 13)
{
   actual_floor--;
} // No else needed
```

The following program puts the `if` statement to work. This program asks for the desired floor and then prints out the actual floor.

ch03/elevator1.cpp

```
 1  #include <iostream>
 2
 3  using namespace std;
 4
 5  int main()
 6  {
 7     int floor;
 8     cout << "Floor: ";
 9     cin >> floor;
10     int actual_floor;
11     if (floor > 13)
12     {
13        actual_floor = floor - 1;
14     }
15     else
16     {
17        actual_floor = floor;
18     }
19
20     cout << "The elevator will travel to the actual floor "
21        << actual_floor << endl;
22
23     return 0;
24  }
```

Program Run

```
Floor: 20
The elevator will travel to the actual floor 19
```

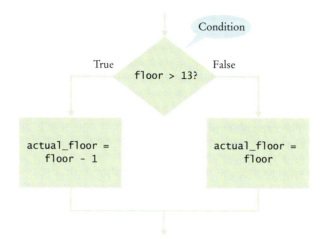

Figure 1 Flowchart for if Statement

SELF CHECK

1. In some Asian countries, the number 14 is considered unlucky. Some building owners play it safe and skip *both* the thirteenth and the fourteenth floor. How would you modify the sample program to handle such a building?

2. Consider the following if statement to compute a discounted price:

```
if (original_price > 100)
{
    discounted_price = original_price - 20;
}
else
{
    discounted_price = original_price - 10;
}
```

What is the discounted price if the original price is 95? 100? 105?

3. Compare this if statement with the one in Self Check 2:

```
if (original_price < 100)
{
    discounted_price = original_price - 10;
}
else
{
    discounted_price = original_price - 20;
}
```

Do the two statements always compute the same value? If not, when do the values differ?

4. Consider the following statements to compute a discounted price:

```
discounted_price = original_price;
if (original_price > 100)
{
   discounted_price = original_price - 10;
}
```

What is the discounted price if the original price is 95? 100? 105?

5. The variables `fuel_amount` and `fuel_capacity` hold the actual amount of fuel and the size of the fuel tank of a vehicle. If less than 10 percent is remaining in the tank, a status light should show a red color; otherwise it shows a green color. Simulate this process by printing out either "red" or "green".

QUALITY TIP 3.1

Brace Layout

The compiler doesn't care where you place braces. In this book, we follow the simple rule of making { and } line up.

```
if (floor > 13)
{
   floor--;
}
```

This style makes it easy to spot matching braces. Some programmers put the opening brace on the same line as the `if`:

```
if (floor > 13) {
   floor--;
}
```

This style makes it harder to match the braces, but it saves a line of code, allowing you to view more code on the screen without scrolling. There are passionate advocates of both styles.

It is important that you pick a layout style and stick with it consistently within a given programming project. Which style you choose may depend on your personal preference or a coding style guide that you need to follow.

QUALITY TIP 3.2

Always Use Braces

When the body of an `if` statement consists of a single statement, you need not use braces. For example, the following is legal:

```
if (floor > 13)
   floor--;
```

However, it is a good idea to always include the braces:

```
if (floor > 13)
{
    floor--;
}
```

The braces makes your code easier to read, and you are less likely to make errors such as the one described in Common Error 3.1.

COMMON ERROR 3.1

A Semicolon After the if Condition

The following code fragment has an unfortunate error:

```
if (floor > 13) ; // ERROR
{
    floor--;
}
```

There should be no semicolon after the if condition. The compiler interprets this statement as follows: If floor is greater than 13, execute the statement that is denoted by a single semicolon, that is, the do-nothing statement. The statement enclosed in braces is no longer a part of the if statement. It is always executed. In other words even if the value of floor is not above 13, it is decremented.

PRODUCTIVITY HINT 3.1

Tabs

Block-structured code has the property that nested statements are indented by one or more levels:

```
int main()
{
|   int floor;
|   ...
|   if (floor > 13)
|   {
|   |   floor--;
|   } |
|   ...
|   return 0;
} | |
0  1  2
Indentation level
```

How do you move the cursor from the leftmost column to the appropriate indentation level? A perfectly reasonable strategy is to hit the space bar a sufficient number of times. However, many programmers use the Tab key instead. A tab moves the cursor to the next indentation level.

As nice as tabs are for data entry, they have one disadvantage: They can lead to problems when you send your file to another person or a printer. There is no universal agreement on the width of indentations, and some software will ignore tabs altogether. It is therefore best to save your files with spaces instead of tabs. Most development environments have settings to automatically convert all tabs to spaces. Look at the documentation of your development environment to find out how to activate this useful setting.

You use the Tab key to move the cursor to the next indentation level.

ADVANCED TOPIC 3.1

The Selection Operator

C++ has a *selection operator* of the form

   condition ? *value₁* : *value₂*

The value of that expression is either $value_1$ if the test passes or $value_2$ if it fails. For example, we can compute the actual floor number as

```
actual_floor = floor > 13 ? floor - 1 : floor;
```

which is equivalent to

```
if (floor > 13) { actual_floor =  floor - 1; }
else { actual_floor = floor; }
```

You can use the selection operator anywhere that a value is expected, for example:

```
cout << "Actual floor: " << (floor > 13 ? floor - 1 : floor);
```

We don't use the selection operator in this book, but it is a convenient construct that you will find in many C++ programs.

QUALITY TIP 3.3

Avoid Duplication in Branches

Look to see whether you *duplicate code* in each branch. If so, move it out of the if statement. Here is an example of such duplication:

```
if (floor > 13)
{
```

```
    actual_floor = floor - 1;
    cout << "Actual floor: " << actual_floor << endl;
}
else
{
    actual_floor = floor;
    cout << "Actual floor: " << actual_floor << endl;
}
```

The output statement is exactly the same in both branches. This is not an error—the program will run correctly. However, you can simplify the program by moving the duplicated statement, like this:

```
if (floor > 13)
{
    actual_floor = floor - 1;
}
else
{
    actual_floor = floor;
}
cout << "Actual floor: " << actual_floor << endl;
```

Removing duplication is particularly important when programs are maintained for a long time. When there are two sets of statements with the same effect, it can easily happen that a programmer modifies one set but not the other.

3.2 Relational Operators

Relational operators
(< <= > >= == !=)
are used to compare
numbers and strings.

Every if statement contains a condition. In many cases, the condition involves comparing two values. For example, in the previous examples we tested floor > 13. The comparison > is called a *relational operator*. C++ has six relational operators (see Table 1).

Table 1   Relational Operators

C++	Math Notation	Description
>	>	Greater than
>=	$\geq$	Greater than or equal
<	<	Less than
<=	$\leq$	Less than or equal
==	=	Equal
!=	$\neq$	Not equal

As you can see, only two C++ relational operators (> and <) look as you would expect from the mathematical notation. Computer keyboards do not have keys for ≥, ≤, or ≠, but the >=, <=, and != operators are easy to remember because they look similar. The == operator is initially confusing to most newcomers to C++. In C++, = already has a meaning, namely assignment. The == operator denotes equality testing:

```
floor = 13; // Assign 13 to floor
if (floor == 13)  // Test whether floor equals 13
```

You must remember to use == inside tests and to use = outside tests. (See Common Error 3.2 on page 92 for more information.)

You can compare strings as well:

```
if (input == "Quit") ...
```

Use != to check whether two strings are different. In C++, letter case matters. For example, "Quit" and "quit" are not the same string.

Table 2 summarizes how to use relational operators in C++.

In C++, you use a relational operator to check whether one value is greater than another.

Table 2 Relational Operator Examples

Expression	Value	Comment
3 <= 4	true	3 is less than 4; <= tests for "less than or equal".
🚫 3 =< 4	Error	The "less than or equal" operator is <=, not =<, with the "less than" symbol first.
3 > 4	false	> is the opposite of <=.
4 < 4	false	The left-hand side must be strictly smaller than the right-hand side.
4 <= 4	true	Both sides are equal; <= tests for "less than or equal".
3 == 5 - 2	true	== tests for equality.
3 != 5 - 1	true	!= tests for inequality. It is true that 3 is not 5 – 1.
🚫 3 = 6 / 2	Error	Use == to test for equality.
1.0 / 3.0 == 0.333333333	false	Although the values are very close to one another, they are not exactly equal. See Common Error 3.3 on page 93.
🚫 "10" > 5	Error	You cannot compare a string to a number.

SYNTAX 3.2 Comparisons

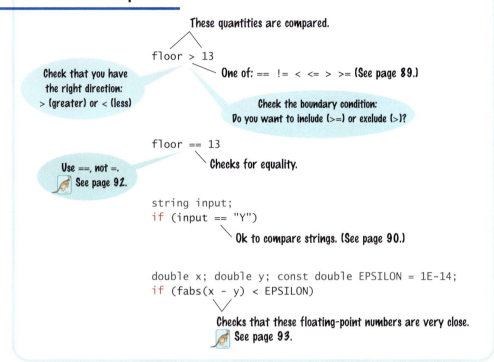

These quantities are compared.

floor > 13

Check that you have the right direction:
> (greater) or < (less)

One of: == != < <= > >= (See page 89.)

Check the boundary condition:
Do you want to include (>=) or exclude (>)?

floor == 13

Checks for equality.

Use ==, not =.
See page 92.

```
string input;
if (input == "Y")
```

Ok to compare strings. (See page 90.)

```
double x; double y; const double EPSILON = 1E-14;
if (fabs(x - y) < EPSILON)
```

Checks that these floating-point numbers are very close.
See page 93.

SELF CHECK

6. Which of the following conditions are true, provided a is 3 and b is 4?
  a. a + 1 <= b
  b. a + 1 >= b
  c. a + 1 != b

7. Give the opposite of the condition
  ```
  floor > 13
  ```

8. What is the error in this statement?
  ```
  if (score_a = score_b)
  {
      cout << "Tie" << endl;
  }
  ```

9. Supply a condition in this if statement to test whether the user entered a Y:
  ```
  string input;
  cout << "Enter Y to quit." << endl;
  cin >> input;
  if (...)
  {
  ```

```
        cout << "Goodbye." << endl;
        return 0;
    }
```

10. How do you test that a string `str` is not the empty string?

COMMON ERROR 3.2

Confusing = and ==

The rule for the correct usage of = and == is very simple: In tests, always use == and never use =. If it is so simple, why can't the compiler be helpful and flag any errors?

Actually, the C++ language allows the use of = inside tests. To understand this, we have to go back in time. The creators of C, the predecessor to C++, were very frugal. They did not want to have special values `true` and `false`. Instead, they allowed any numeric value inside a condition, with the convention that 0 denotes false and any non-0 value denotes true. Furthermore, in C and C++ assignments have values. For example, the value of the assignment expression `floor = 13` is 13.

These two features—namely that numbers can be used as truth values and that assignments are expressions with values—conspire to make a horrible pitfall. The test

```
    if (floor = 13) // ERROR
```

is legal C++, but it does not test whether `floor` and 13 are equal. Instead, the code sets `floor` to 13, and since that value is not zero, the condition of the `if` statement is always fulfilled.

Fortunately, most compilers issue a warning when they encounter such a statement. You should take such warnings seriously. (See Quality Tip 3.4 on page 92 for more advice about compiler warnings.)

Some shell-shocked programmers are so nervous about using = that they use == even when they want to make an assignment:

```
    floor == floor - 1; // ERROR
```

This statement tests whether `floor` equals `floor - 1`. It doesn't do anything with the outcome of the test, but that is not an error. Some compilers will warn that "the code has no effect", but others will quietly accept the code.

QUALITY TIP 3.4

Compile with Zero Warnings

There are two kinds of messages that the compiler gives you: *errors* and *warnings*. Error messages are fatal; the compiler will not translate a program with one or more errors. Warning messages are advisory; the compiler will translate the program, but there is a good chance that the program will not do what you expect it to do.

It is a good idea to learn how to activate warnings with your compiler, and to write code that emits no warnings at all. For example, consider the test

```
    if (floor = 13)
```

One C++ compiler emits a curious warning message: "Suggest parentheses around assignment used as truth value". Sadly, the message is misleading because it was not written for students. Nevertheless, such a warning gives you another chance to look at the offending statement and fix it, in this case, by replacing the = with an ==.

In order to make warnings more visible, many compilers require you to take some special action. This might involve clicking a checkbox in an integrated environment or supplying a special option on the command line. Ask your instructor or lab assistant how to turn on warnings for your compiler.

COMMON ERROR 3.3

Exact Comparison of Floating-Point Numbers

Floating-point numbers have only a limited precision, and calculations can introduce round-off errors. You must take these inevitable roundoffs into account when comparing floating-point numbers. For example, the following code multiplies the square root of 2 by itself. Ideally, we expect to get the answer 2:

```
double r = sqrt(2.0);
if (r * r == 2)
{
   cout << "sqrt(2) squared is 2" << endl;
}
else
{
   cout << "sqrt(2) squared is not 2 but "
      << setprecision(18) << r * r << endl;
}
```

This program displays

```
sqrt(2) squared is not 2 but 2.00000000000000044
```

It does not make sense in most circumstances to compare floating-point numbers exactly. Instead, we should test whether they are *close enough*. That is, the magnitude of their difference should be less than some threshold. Mathematically, we would write that x and y are close enough if

$$|x - y| < \varepsilon$$

for a very small number, ε. ε is the Greek letter epsilon, a letter used to denote a very small quantity. It is common to set ε to 10^{-14} when comparing double numbers:

```
const double EPSILON = 1E-14;
double r = sqrt(2.0);
if (fabs(r * r - 2) < EPSILON)
{
   cout << "sqrt(2) squared is approximately 2";
}
```

Include the <cmath> header to use the fabs function.

Lexicographic Ordering of Strings

If you compare strings using < <= > >=, they are compared in "lexicographic" order. This ordering is very similar to the way in which words are sorted in a dictionary.

For example, consider this code fragment.

```
string name = "Tom";
if (name < "Dick") ...
```

> Lexicographic order is used to compare strings.

The condition is not fulfilled, because in the dictionary Dick comes before Tom. There are a few differences between the ordering in a dictionary and in C++. In C++:

- All uppercase letters come before the lowercase letters. For example, "z" comes before "a".
- The space character comes before all printable characters.
- Numbers come before letters.
- For the ordering of punctuation marks, see Appendix D.

To see which of two terms comes first in the dictionary, consider the first letter in which they differ.

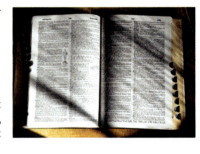

When comparing two strings, you compare the first letters of each word, then the second letters, and so on, until either one of the strings ends or you find the first letter pair that doesn't match.

If one of the strings ends, the longer string is considered the "larger" one. For example, compare "car" with "cart". The first three letters match, and we reach the end of the first string. Therefore "car" comes before "cart" in lexicographic ordering.

When you reach a mismatch, the string containing the "larger" character is considered "larger". For example, let's compare "cat" with "cart". The first two letters match. Since t comes after r, the string "cat" comes after "cart" in the lexicographic ordering. (See Figure 2.)

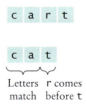

Figure 2   Lexicographic Ordering

HOW TO 3.1

Implementing an if Statement

This How To walks you through the process of implementing an if statement. We will illustrate the steps with the following example problem:

The university bookstore has a Kilobyte Day sale every October 24, giving an 8 percent discount on all computer accessory purchases if the price is less than $128, and a 16 percent discount if the price is at least $128. Write a program that asks the cashier for the original price and then prints the discounted price.

Sales discounts are often higher for expensive products. Use the if statement to implement such a decision.

Step 1   Decide upon the branching condition.

In our sample problem, the obvious choice for the condition is:

```
original price < 128?
```

That is just fine, and we will use that condition in our solution.

But you could equally well come up with a correct solution if you choose the opposite condition: Is the original price at least $128? You might choose this condition if you put yourself into the position of a shopper who wants to know when the bigger discount applies.

Step 2   Give pseudocode for the work that needs to be done when the condition is fulfilled.

In this step, you list the action or actions that are taken in the "positive" branch. The details depend on your problem. You may want to print a message, compute values, or even exit the program.

In our example, we need to apply an 8 percent discount:

```
discounted price = 0.92 x original price
```

Step 3   Give pseudocode for the work (if any) that needs to be done when the condition is *not* fulfilled.

What do you want to do in the case that the condition of Step 1 is not fulfilled? Sometimes, you want to do nothing at all. In that case, use an if statement without an else branch.

In our example, the condition tested whether the price was less than $128. If that condition is *not* fulfilled, the price is at least $128, so the higher discount of 16 percent applies to the sale:

```
discounted price = 0.84 x original price
```

Step 4   Double-check relational operators.

First, be sure that the test goes in the right *direction*. It is a common error to confuse > and <. Next, consider whether you should use the < operator or its close cousin, the <= operator.

What should happen if the original price is exactly $128? Reading the problem carefully, we find that the lower discount applies if the original price is *less than* $128, and the higher discount applies when it is *at least* $128. A price of $128 should therefore *not* fulfill our condition, and we must use <, not <=.

Step 5   Remove duplication.

Check which actions are common to both branches, and move them outside. (See Quality Tip 3.3 on page 88.)

In our example, we have two statements of the form

```
discounted price = ___ x original price
```

They only differ in the discount rate. It is best to just set the rate in the branches, and to do the computation afterwards:

```
If original price < 128
{
    discount rate = 0.92
}
Else
{
    discount rate = 0.84
}
discounted price = discount rate x original price
```

Step 6   Test both branches.

Formulate two test cases, one that fulfills the condition of the if statement, and one that does not. Ask yourself what should happen in each case. Then follow the pseudocode and act each of them out.

In our example, let us consider two scenarios for the original price: $100 and $200. We expect that the first price is discounted by $8, the second by $32.

When the original price is 100, then the condition 100 < 128 is true, and we get

```
discount rate = 0.92
discounted price = 0.92 x 100 = 92
```

When the original price is 200, then the condition 200 < 128 is false, and

```
discount rate = 0.84
discounted price = 0.84 x 200 = 168
```

In both cases, we get the expected answer.

Step 7   Assemble the if statement in C++.

Type the skeleton

```
if ()
{
}
else
{
}
```

and fill it in, as shown in Syntax 3.1 on page 83. Omit the else branch if it is not needed.

In our example, the completed statement is

```
if (original_price < 128)
{
    discount_rate = 0.92;
```

```
   }
   else
   {
      discount_rate = 0.84;
   }
   discounted_price = discount_rate * original_price;
```

WORKED EXAMPLE 3.1

Extracting the Middle

This Worked Example shows how to extract the middle character from a string, or the two middle characters if the length of the string is even.

RANDOM FACT 3.1

The Denver Airport Luggage Handling System

Making decisions is an essential part of any computer program. Nowhere is this more obvious than in a computer system that helps sort luggage at an airport. After scanning the luggage identification codes, the system sorts the items and routes them to different conveyor belts. Human operators then place the items onto trucks. When the city of Denver built a huge airport to replace an outdated and congested facility, the luggage system contractor went a step further. The new system was designed to replace the human operators with robotic carts. Unfortunately, the system plainly did not work. It was plagued by mechanical problems, such as luggage falling onto the tracks and jamming carts. Just as frustrating were the software glitches. Carts would uselessly accumulate at some locations when they were needed elsewhere.

The Denver airport originally had a fully automatic system for moving luggage, replacing human operators with robotic carts. Unfortunately, the system never worked and was dismantled before the airport was opened.

The airport had been scheduled for opening in 1993, but without a functioning luggage system, the opening was delayed for over a year while the contractor tried to fix the problems. The contractor never succeeded, and ultimately a manual system was installed. The delay cost the city and airlines close to a billion dollars, and the contractor, once the leading luggage systems vendor in the United States, went bankrupt.

Clearly, it is very risky to build a large system based on a technology that has never been tried in a smaller scale. As robots and the software that controls them get better over time, they will take on a larger share of luggage handling in the future. But it is likely that this will happen in an incremental fashion.

3.3 Multiple Alternatives

> Multiple if statements can be combined to evaluate complex decisions.

In Section 3.1, you saw how to program a two-way branch with an if statement. In many situations, there are more than two cases. In this section, you will see how to implement a decision with multiple alternatives.

For example, consider a program that displays the effect of an earthquake, as measured by the Richter scale (see Table 3). The Richter scale is a measurement of the strength of an earthquake. Every step in the scale, for example from 6.0 to 7.0, signifies a tenfold increase in the strength of the quake.

The 1989 Loma Prieta earthquake that damaged the Bay Bridge in San Francisco and destroyed many buildings measured 7.1 on the Richter scale.

Table 3 Richter Scale

Value	Effect
8	Most structures fall
7	Many buildings destroyed
6	Many buildings considerably damaged, some collapse
4.5	Damage to poorly constructed buildings

In this case, there are five branches: one each for the four descriptions of damage, and one for no destruction. Figure 3 shows the flowchart for this multiple-branch statement.

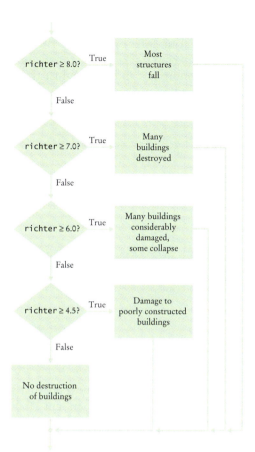

Figure 3
Multiple Alternatives

You use multiple `if` statements to implement multiple alternatives, like this:

```
if (richter >= 8.0)
{
   cout << "Most structures fall";
}
else if (richter >= 7.0)
{
   cout << "Many buildings destroyed";
}
else if (richter >= 6.0)
{
   cout << "Many buildings considerably damaged, some collapse";
}
else if (richter >= 4.5)
{
   cout << "Damage to poorly constructed buildings";
}
else
{
   cout << "No destruction of buildings";
}
```

As soon as one of the four tests succeeds, the effect is displayed, and no further tests are attempted. If none of the four cases applies, the final else clause applies, and a default message is printed. (See ch03/richter.cpp for the full program.)

Here you must sort the conditions and test against the largest cutoff first. Suppose we reverse the order of tests:

```
if (richter >= 4.5) // Tests in wrong order
{
   cout << "Damage to poorly constructed buildings";
}
else if (richter >= 6.0)
{
   cout << "Many buildings considerably damaged, some collapse";
}
else if (richter >= 7.0)
{
   cout << "Many buildings destroyed";
}
else if (richter >= 8.0)
{
   cout << "Most structures fall";
}
```

> When using multiple if statements, pay attention to the order of the conditions.

This does not work. Suppose the value of richter is 7.1. That value is at least 4.5, matching the first case. The other tests will never be attempted.

In this example, it is also important that we use an if/else/else sequence, not just multiple independent if statements. Consider this sequence of independent tests.

```
if (richter >= 8.0) // Didn't use else
{
   cout << "Most structures fall";
}
if (richter >= 7.0)
{
   cout << "Many buildings destroyed";
}
if (richter >= 6.0)
{
   cout << "Many buildings considerably damaged, some collapse";
}
if (richter >= 4.5)
{
   cout << "Damage to poorly constructed buildings";
}
```

Now the alternatives are no longer exclusive. If richter is 7.1, then the last *three* tests all match, and three messages are printed.

SELF CHECK

11. In a game program, the scores of players A and B are stored in variables score_a and score_b. Assuming that the player with the larger score wins, write an if/else/else sequence that prints out "A won", "B won", or "Game tied".

12. Write a conditional statement with three branches that sets s to 1 if x is positive, to –1 if x is negative, and to 0 if x is zero.

13. How could you achieve the task of Self Check 12 with only two branches?

14. Beginners sometimes write statements such as the following:

```
if (price > 100)
{
   discounted_price = price - 20;
}
else if (price <= 100)
{
   discounted_price = price - 10;
}
```

Explain how this code can be improved.

15. Suppose the user enters -1 into the richter.cpp program. What is printed?

16. Suppose we want to have the richter.cpp program check whether the user entered a negative number. What branch would you add to the if statement, and where?

ADVANCED TOPIC 3.3

The switch Statement

A sequence of if/else/else that compares a *single integer value* against several *constant* alternatives can be implemented as a switch statement. For example,

```
int digit;
...
switch (digit)
{
   case 1: digit_name = "one"; break;
   case 2: digit_name = "two"; break;
   case 3: digit_name = "three"; break;
   case 4: digit_name = "four"; break;
   case 5: digit_name = "five"; break;
   case 6: digit_name = "six"; break;
   case 7: digit_name = "seven"; break;
   case 8: digit_name = "eight"; break;
   case 9: digit_name = "nine"; break;
   default: digit_name = ""; break;
}
```

This is a shortcut for

```
int digit;
if (digit == 1) { digit_name = "one"; }
```

```
else if (digit == 2) { digit_name = "two"; }
else if (digit == 3) { digit_name = "three"; }
else if (digit == 4) { digit_name = "four"; }
else if (digit == 5) { digit_name = "five"; }
else if (digit == 6) { digit_name = "six"; }
else if (digit == 7) { digit_name = "seven"; }
else if (digit == 8) { digit_name = "eight"; }
else if (digit == 9) { digit_name = "nine"; }
else { digit_name = ""; }
```

Well, it isn't much of a shortcut, but it has one advantage—it is obvious that all branches test the *same* value, namely digit.

The switch statement can be applied only in narrow circumstances. The test cases must be constants, and they must be integers. You cannot use

```
switch (digit_name)
{
    case "one": value = 1; break; // Error
    ...
}
```

Every branch of the switch must be terminated by a break instruction. If the break is missing, execution *falls through* to the next branch, and so on, until finally a break or the end of the switch is reached. In practice, this fall-through behavior is rarely useful, but it is a common cause of errors. If you accidentally forget the break statement, your program compiles but executes unwanted code. Many programmers consider the switch statement somewhat dangerous and prefer the if statement.

We leave it to you to use the switch statement for your own code or not. At any rate, you need to have a reading knowledge of switch in case you find it in other programmers' code.

3.4 Nested Branches

It is often necessary to include an if statement inside another. Such an arrangement is called a *nested* set of statements. Here is a typical example.

In the United States different tax rates are used depending on the taxpayer's marital status. There are different tax schedules for single and for married taxpayers. Married taxpayers add their income together and pay taxes on the total. Table 4 gives the tax rate computations, using a simplification of the schedules in effect for the 2008 tax year. A different tax rate applies to each "bracket". In this schedule, the

Computing income taxes requires multiple levels of decisions.

Table 4	Federal Tax Rate Schedule			
If your status is Single and if the taxable income is over	**but not over**	**the tax is**	**of the amount over**
$0	$32,000	10%	$0
$32,000		$3,200 + 25%	$32,000
If your status is Married and if the taxable income is over	**but not over**	**the tax is**	**of the amount over**
$0	$64,000	10%	$0
$64,000		$6,400 + 25%	$64,000

income at the first bracket is taxed at 10 percent, and the income at the second bracket is taxed at 25 percent. The income limits for each bracket depend on the marital status.

Now compute the taxes due, given a filing status and an income figure. The key point is that there are two *levels* of decision making. First, you must branch on the marital status. Then, for each filing status, you must have another branch on income level.

The two-level decision process is reflected in two levels of if statements in the program at the end of this section. (See Figure 4 for a flowchart.) In theory, nesting can go deeper than two levels. A three-level decision process (first by state, then by filing status, then by income level) requires three nesting levels.

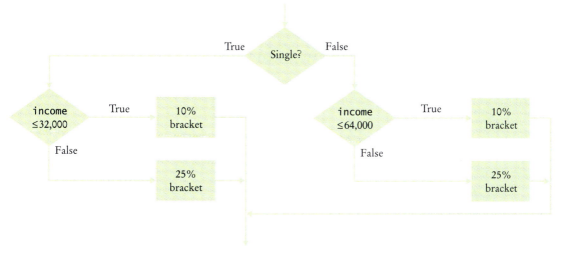

Figure 4 Income Tax Computation

ch03/tax.cpp

```cpp
 1  #include <iostream>
 2  #include <string>
 3
 4  using namespace std;
 5
 6  int main()
 7  {
 8     const double RATE1 = 0.10;
 9     const double RATE2 = 0.25;
10     const double RATE1_SINGLE_LIMIT = 32000;
11     const double RATE1_MARRIED_LIMIT = 64000;
12
13     double tax1 = 0;
14     double tax2 = 0;
15
16     double income;
17     cout << "Please enter your income: ";
18     cin >> income;
19
20     cout << "Please enter s for single, m for married: ";
21     string marital_status;
22     cin >> marital_status;
23
24     if (marital_status == "s")
25     {
26        if (income <= RATE1_SINGLE_LIMIT)
27        {
28           tax1 = RATE1 * income;
29        }
30        else
31        {
32           tax1 = RATE1 * RATE1_SINGLE_LIMIT;
33           tax2 = RATE2 * (income - RATE1_SINGLE_LIMIT);
34        }
35     }
36     else
37     {
38        if (income <= RATE1_MARRIED_LIMIT)
39        {
40           tax1 = RATE1 * income;
41        }
42        else
43        {
44           tax1 = RATE1 * RATE1_MARRIED_LIMIT;
45           tax2 = RATE2 * (income - RATE1_MARRIED_LIMIT);
46        }
47     }
48
49     double total_tax = tax1 + tax2;
50
51     cout << "The tax is $" << total_tax << endl;
52     return 0;
53  }
```

Program Run

```
Please enter your income: 80000
Please enter s for single, m for married: m
The tax is $10400
```

SELF CHECK

17. What is the amount of tax that a single taxpayer pays on an income of $32,000?

18. Would that amount change if the first nested if statement changed from

```
if (income <= RATE1_SINGLE_LIMIT)
```

to

```
if (income < RATE1_SINGLE_LIMIT)
```

19. Suppose Harry and Sally each make $40,000 per year. Would they save taxes if they married?

20. How would you modify the tax.cpp program in order to check that the user entered a correct value for the marital status (i.e., s or m)?

21. Some people object to higher tax rates for higher incomes, claiming that you might end up with less money after taxes when you get a raise for working hard. What is the flaw in this argument?

PRODUCTIVITY HINT 3.2

Hand-Tracing

A very useful technique for understanding whether a program works correctly is called *hand-tracing*. You simulate the program's activity on a sheet of paper. You can use this method with pseudocode or C++ code.

Get an index card, a cocktail napkin, or whatever sheet of paper is within reach. Make a column for each variable. Have the program code ready. Use a marker, such as a paper clip, to mark the current statement. In your mind, execute statements one at a time. Every time the value of a variable changes, cross out the old value and write the new value below the old one.

For example, let's trace the tax program with the data from the program run on page 104. In lines 13 and 14, tax1 and tax2 are initialized to 0.

```
 6  int main()
 7  {
 8      const double RATE1 = 0.10;
 9      const double RATE2 = 0.25;
10      const double RATE1_SINGLE_LIMIT = 32000;
11      const double RATE1_MARRIED_LIMIT = 64000;
12
13      double tax1 = 0;
14      double tax2 = 0;
15
```

tax1	tax2	income	marital status
0	0		

In lines 18 and 22, `income` and `marital_status` are initialized by input statements

```
16    double income;
17    cout << "Please enter your income: ";
18    cin >> income;
19
20    cout << "Please enter s for single, m for married: ";
21    string marital_status;
22    cin >> marital_status;
23
```

tax1	tax2	income	marital status
0	0	80000	m

Because `marital_status` is not `"s"`, we move to the `else` branch of the outer `if` statement (line 36)

```
24    if (marital_status == "s")
25    {
26       if (income <= RATE1_SINGLE_LIMIT)
27       {
28          tax1 = RATE1 * income;
29       }
30       else
31       {
32          tax1 = RATE1 * RATE1_SINGLE_LIMIT;
33          tax2 = RATE2 * (income - RATE1_SINGLE_LIMIT);
34       }
35    }
36    else
37    {
```

Since `income` is not <= 64000, we move to the `else` branch of the inner `if` statement (line 42)

```
38       if (income <= RATE1_MARRIED_LIMIT)
39       {
40          tax1 = RATE1 * income;
41       }
42       else
43       {
44          tax1 = RATE1 * RATE1_MARRIED_LIMIT;
45          tax2 = RATE2 * (income - RATE1_MARRIED_LIMIT);
46       }
```

The values of `tax1` and `tax2` are updated.

```
43       {
44          tax1 = RATE1 * RATE1_MARRIED_LIMIT;
45          tax2 = RATE2 * (income - RATE1_MARRIED_LIMIT);
46       }
47    }
```

tax1	tax2	income	marital status
~~0~~	~~0~~	80000	m
6400	4000		

Their sum `total_tax` is computed and printed. Then the program ends.

```
48
49    double total_tax = tax1 + tax2;
50
51    cout << "The tax is $" << total_tax << endl;
52    return 0;
53 }
```

tax1	tax2	income	marital status	total tax
~~0~~	~~0~~	80000	m	
6400	4000			10400

Because the program trace shows the expected output ($10,400), it successfully demonstrated that this test case works correctly.

QUALITY TIP 3.5

Prepare Test Cases Ahead of Time

Consider how to test the tax computation program. Of course, you cannot try out all possible inputs of filing status and income level. Even if you could, there would be no point in trying them all. If the program correctly computes one or two tax amounts in a given bracket, then we have a good reason to believe that all amounts will be correct.

You want to aim for complete coverage of all decision points. Here is a plan for obtaining a comprehensive set of test cases:

- There are two possibilities for the filing status and two tax brackets for each status, yielding four test cases.
- Test a handful of *boundary* conditions, such as an income that is at the boundary between two brackets, and a zero income.
- If you are responsible for error checking (which is discussed in Section 3.7), also test an invalid input, such as a negative income.

Make a list of the test cases and the expected outputs:

Test Case		Expected Output	Comment
30,000	s	3,000	10% bracket
72,000	s	13,200	3,200 + 25% of 40,000
50,000	m	5,000	10% bracket
10,400	m	16,400	6,400 + 25% of 40,000
32,000	m	3,200	boundary case
0		0	boundary case

It is always a good idea to design test cases *before* starting to code. Working through the test cases gives you a better understanding of the algorithm that you are about to implement.

PRODUCTIVITY HINT 3.3

Make a Schedule and Make Time for Unexpected Problems

Commercial software is notorious for being delivered later than promised. For example, Microsoft originally promised that its Windows Vista operating system would be available late in 2003, then in 2005, then in March 2006; it finally was released in January 2007. Some of the early promises might not have been realistic. It was in Microsoft's interest to let prospective customers expect the imminent availability of the product. Had customers known the actual delivery date, they might have switched to a different product in the meantime. Undeniably, though, Microsoft had not anticipated the full complexity of the tasks it had set itself to solve.

Microsoft can delay the delivery of its product, but it is likely that you cannot. As a student or a programmer, you are expected to manage your time wisely and to finish your assignments on time. You can probably do simple programming exercises the night before the due date, but an assignment that looks twice as hard may well take four times as long, because more things can go wrong. You should therefore make a schedule whenever you start a programming project.

First, estimate realistically how much time it will take you to:

- Design the program logic.
- Develop test cases.
- Type the program in and fix syntax errors.
- Test and debug the program.

For example, for the income tax program I might estimate an hour for the design; 30 minutes for developing test cases; an hour for data entry and fixing syntax errors; and an hour for testing and debugging. That is a total of 3.5 hours. If I work two hours a day on this project, it will take me almost two days.

Make a schedule for your programming work and build in time for problems.

Then think of things that can go wrong. Your computer might break down. You might be stumped by a problem with the computer system. (That is a particularly important concern for beginners. It is *very* common to lose a day over a trivial problem just because it takes time to track down a person who knows the magic command to overcome it.) As a rule of thumb, *double* the time of your estimate. That is, you should start four days, not two days, before the due date. If nothing went wrong, great; you have the program done two days early. When the inevitable problem occurs, you have a cushion of time that protects you from embarrassment and failure.

COMMON ERROR 3.4

The Dangling else Problem

When an if statement is nested inside another if statement, the following error may occur.

```
double shipping_charge = 5.00; // $5 inside continental U.S.
if (country == "USA")
   if (state == "HI")
      shipping_charge = 10.00; // Hawaii is more expensive
else // Pitfall!
   shipping_charge = 20.00; // As are foreign shipments
```

The indentation level seems to suggest that the else is grouped with the test country == "USA". Unfortunately, that is not the case. The compiler ignores all indentation and matches the else with the preceding if. That is, the code is actually

```
double shipping_charge = 5.00; // $5 inside continental U.S.
if (country == "USA")
   if (state == "HI")
      shipping_charge = 10.00; // Hawaii is more expensive
   else // Pitfall!
      shipping_charge = 20.00; // As are foreign shipments
```

That isn't what you want. You want to group the else with the first if.

The ambiguous `else` is called a *dangling* `else`. You can avoid this pitfall if you *always use braces,* as recommended in Quality Tip 3.2 on page 86:

```
double shipping_charge = 5.00; // $5 inside continental U.S.
if (country == "USA")
{
   if (state == "HI")
   {
      shipping_charge = 10.00; // Hawaii is more expensive
   }
}
else
{
   shipping_charge = 20.00; // As are foreign shipments
}
```

3.5 Boolean Variables and Operators

Sometimes, you need to evaluate a logical condition in one part of a program and use it elsewhere. To store a condition that can be true or false, you use a *Boolean variable*. Boolean variables are named after the mathematician George Boole.

> The Boolean type `bool` has two values, `false` and `true`.

In C++, the `bool` data type represents the Boolean type. Variables of type `bool` can hold exactly two values, denoted false and true. These values are not strings or integers; they are special values, just for Boolean variables. Here is a definition of a Boolean variable:

```
bool failed = true;
```

You can use the value later in your program to make a decision:

```
if (failed) // Only executed if failed has been set to true
{
   ...
}
```

Boolean variables are named after the mathematician George Boole (1815–1864), a pioneer in the study of logic.

> C++ has two Boolean operators that combine conditions: && (and) and || (or).

When you make complex decisions, you often need to combine Boolean values. An operator that combines Boolean conditions is called a *Boolean operator*. In C++, the && operator (called *and*) yields true only when both conditions are true. The || operator (called *or*) yields the result true if at least one of the conditions is true.

A	B	A && B
true	true	true
true	false	false
false	Any	false

A	B	A || B
true	Any	true
false	true	true
false	false	false

A	!A
true	false
false	true

Figure 5   Boolean Truth Tables

Suppose you write a program that processes temperature values, and you want to test whether a given temperature corresponds to liquid water. (At sea level, water freezes at 0 degrees Celsius and boils at 100 degrees.) Water is liquid if the temperature is greater than zero *and* less than 100:

```
if (temp > 0 && temp < 100) { cout << "Liquid"; }
```

The condition of the test has two parts, joined by the && operator. Each part is a Boolean value that can be true or false. The combined expression is true if both individual expressions are true. If either one of the expressions is false, then the result is also false (see Figure 5).

Conversely, let's test whether water is not liquid at a given temperature. That is the case when the temperature is at most 0 *or* at least 100. Use the || (or) operator to combine the expressions:

```
if (temp <= 0 || temp >= 100) { cout << "Not liquid"; }
```

Figure 6 shows flowcharts for these examples.

At this geyser in Iceland, you can see ice, liquid water, and steam.

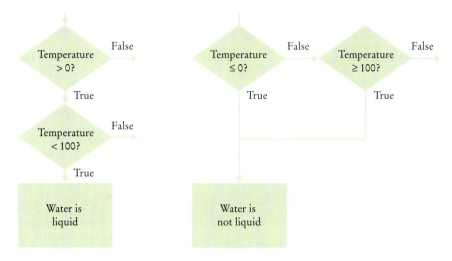

Figure 6 Flowcharts for *and* and *or* Combinations

To invert a condition, use the ! (not) operator.

Sometimes you need to *invert* a condition with the *not* logical operator. The ! operator takes a single condition and evaluates to true if that condition is false and to false if the condition is true. In this example, output occurs if the value of the Boolean variable frozen is false:

```
if (!frozen) { cout << "Not frozen"; }
```

Table 5 illustrates additional examples of evaluating Boolean operators.

Table 5 Boolean Operators

Expression	Value	Comment
0 < 200 && 200 < 100	false	Only the first condition is true.
0 < 200 || 200 < 100	true	The first condition is true.
0 < 200 || 100 < 200	true	The || is not a test for "either-or". If both conditions are true, the result is true.
🚫 0 < 200 < 100	true	**Error:** The expression 0 < 200 is true, which is converted to 1. The expression 1 < 100 is true. You never want to write such an expression; see Common Error 3.5 on page 112.

Table 5 Boolean Operators (continued)

Expression	Value	Comment
🚫 -10 && 10 > 0	true	**Error:** –10 is not zero. It is converted to true. You never want to write such an expression; see Common Error 3.5.
0 < x && x < 100 || x == -1	(0 < x && x < 100) || x == -1	The && operator binds more strongly than the || operator.
!(0 < 200)	false	0 < 200 is true, therefore its negation is false.
frozen == true	frozen	There is no need to compare a Boolean variable with true.
frozen == false	!frozen	It is clearer to use ! than to compare with false.

SELF CHECK

22. Suppose x and y are two integers. How do you test whether both of them are zero?
23. How do you test whether at least one of them is zero?
24. How do you test whether *exactly one of them* is zero?
25. What is the value of !!frozen?
26. What is the advantage of using the type bool rather than strings "false"/"true" or integers 0/1?

COMMON ERROR 3.5

Combining Multiple Relational Operators

Consider the expression

```
if (0 <= temp <= 100) // Error
```

This looks just like the mathematical test $0 \le temp \le 100$. Unfortunately, it is not.

Let us dissect the expression 0 <= temp <= 100. The first half, 0 <= temp, is a test with outcome true or false, depending on the value of temp. The outcome of that test (true or false) is then compared against 100. This seems to make no sense. Can one compare truth values and floating-point numbers? Is true larger than 100 or not? Unfortunately, to stay compatible with the C language, C++ converts false to 0 and true to 1. Therefore, the expression will always evaluate to true.

You must be careful not to mix logical and arithmetic expressions in your programs. Instead, use *and* to combine two separate tests:

```
if (0 <= temp && temp <= 100) ...
```

Another common error, along the same lines, is to write

```
if (x && y > 0) ... // Error
```

instead of

```
if (x > 0 && y > 0) ...
```

Unfortunately, the compiler will not issue an error message. Instead, it converts x to `true` or `false`. Zero is converted to `false`, and any nonzero value is converted to `true`. If x is not zero, then it tests whether y is greater than 0, and finally it computes the *and* of these two truth values. Naturally, that computation makes no sense.

COMMON ERROR 3.6

Confusing && and || Conditions

It is a surprisingly common error to confuse *and* and *or* conditions. A value lies between 0 and 100 if it is at least 0 *and* at most 100. It lies outside that range if it is less than 0 *or* greater than 100. There is no golden rule; you just have to think carefully.

Often the *and* or *or* is clearly stated, and then it isn't too hard to implement it. But sometimes the wording isn't as explicit. It is quite common that the individual conditions are nicely set apart in a bulleted list, but with little indication of how they should be combined. Consider these instructions for filing a tax return. You can claim single filing status if any one of the following is true:

• You were never married.
• You were legally separated or divorced on the last day of the tax year.
• You were widowed, and did not remarry.

Since the test passes if *any one* of the conditions is true, you must combine the conditions with *or*. Elsewhere, the same instructions state that you may use the more advantageous status of married filing jointly if all five of the following conditions are true:

• Your spouse died less than two years ago and you did not remarry.
• You have a child whom you can claim as dependent.
• That child lived in your home for all of the tax year.
• You paid over half the cost of keeping up your home for this child.
• You filed a joint return with your spouse the year he or she died.

Because *all* of the conditions must be true for the test to pass, you must combine them with an *and*.

ADVANCED TOPIC 3.4

Lazy Evaluation of Boolean Operators

> The && and || operators are computed *lazily*: As soon as the truth value is determined, no further conditions are evaluated.

The && and || operators are computed using *lazy evaluation*. In other words, logical expressions are evaluated from left to right, and evaluation stops as soon as the truth value is determined. When an && is evaluated and the first condition is false, the second condition is not evaluated, because it does not matter what the outcome of the second test is.

For example, consider the expression

```
quantity > 0 && price / quantity < 10
```

Suppose the value of quantity is zero. Then the test quantity > 0 fails, and the second test is not attempted. That is just as well, because it is illegal to divide by zero.

Similarly, when the first condition of an || expression is true, then the remainder is not evaluated since the result must be true.

ADVANCED TOPIC 3.5

De Morgan's Law

Humans generally have a hard time comprehending logical conditions with *not* operators applied to *and/or* expressions. De Morgan's Law, named after the logician Augustus De Morgan (1806–1871), can be used to simplify these Boolean expressions.

Suppose we want to charge a higher shipping rate if we don't ship within the continental United States.

```
if (!(country == "USA"
      && state != "AK"
      && state != "HI"))
   shipping_charge = 20.00;
```

This test is a little bit complicated, and you have to think carefully through the logic. When it is *not* true that the country is USA *and* the state is not Alaska *and* the state is not Hawaii, then charge $20.00. Huh? It is not true that some people won't be confused by this code.

The computer doesn't care, but it takes human programmers to write and maintain the code. Therefore, it is useful to know how to simplify such a condition.

> De Morgan's law tells you how to negate && and || conditions.

De Morgan's Law has two forms: one for the negation of an *and* expression and one for the negation of an *or* expression:

!(A && B)	is the same as	!A || !B
!(A || B)	is the same as	!A && !B

Pay particular attention to the fact that the *and* and *or* operators are *reversed* by moving the *not* inward. For example, the negation of "the state is Alaska *or* it is Hawaii",

```
!(state == "AK" || state == "HI")
```

is "the state is not Alaska *and* it is not Hawaii":

```
!(state == "AK") && !(state == "HI")
```

That is, of course, the same as

```
state != "AK" && state != "HI"
```

Now apply the law to our shipping charge computation:

```
!(country == "USA"
    && state != "AK"
    && state != "HI")
```

is equivalent to

```
!(country == "USA")
    || !(state != "AK")
    || !(state != "HI")
```

That yields the simpler test

```
country != "USA"
    || state == "AK"
    || state == "HI"
```

To simplify conditions with negations of *and* or *or* expressions, it is usually a good idea to apply De Morgan's Law to move the negations to the innermost level.

RANDOM FACT 3.2

Artificial Intelligence

When one uses a sophisticated computer program such as a tax preparation package, one is bound to attribute some intelligence to the computer. The computer asks sensible questions and makes computations that we find a mental challenge. After all, if doing one's taxes were easy, we wouldn't need a computer to do it for us.

As programmers, however, we know that all this apparent intelligence is an illusion. Human programmers have carefully "coached" the software in all possible scenarios, and it simply replays the actions and decisions that were programmed into it.

Would it be possible to write computer programs that are genuinely intelligent in some sense? From the earliest days of computing, there was a sense that the human brain might be nothing but an immense computer, and that it might well be feasible to program computers to imitate some processes of human thought. Serious research into *artificial intelligence* began in the mid-1950s, and the first twenty years brought some impressive successes. Programs that play chess—surely an activity that appears to require remarkable intellectual powers—have become so good that they now routinely beat all but the best human players. As far back as 1975, an *expert-system* program called Mycin gained fame for being better in diagnosing meningitis in patients than the average physician.

However, there were serious setbacks as well. From 1982 to 1992, the Japanese government embarked on a massive research project, funded at over 40 billion Japanese yen. It was known as the *Fifth-Generation Project*. Its goal was to develop new hardware and software to greatly improve the performance of expert system software. At its outset, the project created fear in other countries that the Japanese computer industry was about to become the undisputed leader in the field. However, the end results were disappointing and did little to bring artificial intelligence applications to market.

From the very outset, one of the stated goals of the AI community was to produce software that could translate text from one language to another, for example from English to

Russian. That undertaking proved to be enormously complicated. Human language appears to be much more subtle and interwoven with the human experience than had originally been thought. Even the grammar-checking tools that come with word-processing programs today are more of a gimmick than a useful tool, and analyzing grammar is just the first step in translating sentences.

The CYC (from en*cyc*lopedia) project, started by Douglas Lenat in 1984, tries to codify the implicit assumptions that underlie human speech and writing. The team members started out analyzing news articles and asked themselves what unmentioned facts are necessary to actually understand the sentences. For example, consider the sentence "Last fall she enrolled in Michigan State". The reader automatically realizes that "fall" is not related to falling down in this context, but refers to the season. While there is a state of Michigan, here Michigan State denotes the university. A priori, a computer program has none of this knowledge. The goal of the CYC project is to extract and store the requisite facts—that is, (1) people enroll in universities; (2) Michigan is a state; (3) many states have universities named X State University, often abbreviated as X State; (4) most people enroll in a university in the fall. By 1995, the project had codified about 100,000 common-sense concepts and about a million facts of knowledge relating them. Even this massive amount of data has not proven sufficient for useful applications.

Figure 7   The Winner of the 2007 DARPA Urban Challenge

In recent years, artificial intelligence technology has seen substantial advances. One of the most astounding examples is the outcome of a series of "grand challenges" for autonomous vehicles posed by the Defense Advanced Research Projects Agency (DARPA). Competitors were invited to submit a computer-controlled vehicle that had to complete an obstacle course without a human driver or remote control. The first event, in 2004, was a disappointment, with none of the entrants finishing the route. In 2005, five vehicles completed a grueling 212 km course in the Mojave desert. Stanford's Stanley came in first, with an average speed of 30 km/h. In 2007, DARPA moved the competition to an "urban" environment, an abandoned air force base. Vehicles had to be able to interact with each other, following California traffic laws. As Stanford's Sebastian Thrun explained: "In the last Grand Challenge, it didn't really matter whether an obstacle was a rock or a bush, because either way you'd just drive around it. The current challenge is to move from just sensing the environment to understanding the environment."

3.6 Application: Input Validation

Like a quality control worker, you want to make sure that user input is correct before processing it.

An important application for the `if` statement is *input validation*. Whenever your program accepts user input, you need to make sure that the user-supplied values are valid before you use them in your computations.

Consider our elevator program. Assume that the elevator panel has buttons labeled 1 through 20 (but not 13). The following are illegal inputs:

- The number 13
- Zero or a negative number
- A number larger than 20
- A value that is not a sequence of digits, such as `five`

In each of these cases, we will want to give an error message and exit the program.

It is simple to guard against an input of 13:

```
if (floor == 13)
{
   cout << "Error: There is no thirteenth floor." << endl;
   return 1;
}
```

The statement

```
return 1;
```

immediately exits the `main` function and therefore terminates the program. It is a convention to return with the value 0 if the program completed normally, and with a non-zero value when an error was encountered.

Here is how you ensure that the user doesn't enter a number outside the valid range:

```
if (floor <= 0 || floor > 20)
{
   cout << "Error: The floor must be between 1 and 20." << endl;
   return 1;
}
```

However, dealing with an input that is not a valid integer is a more serious problem. When the statement

```
cin >> floor;
```

is executed, and the user types in an input that is not an integer (such as `five`), then the integer variable `floor` is not set. Instead, the input stream `cin` is set to a failed state. You call the `fail` member function to test for that failed state.

```
if (cin.fail())
{
```

```
        cout << "Error: Not an integer." << endl;
        return 1;
    }
```

Use the `fail` function to test whether stream input has failed.

The order of the `if` statements is important. You must *first* test for `cin.fail()`. After all, if the input failed, no value has been assigned to `floor`, and it makes no sense to compare it against other values.

Input failure is quite serious in C++. Once input has failed, all subsequent attempts at input will fail as well. You will learn in Chapter 8 how to write programs that are more tolerant of bad input. For now, our goal is simply to detect bad input and to exit the program when it occurs.

Here is the complete elevator program with input validation.

ch03/elevator2.cpp

```
1  #include <iostream>
2
3  using namespace std;
4
5  int main()
6  {
7     int floor;
8     cout << "Floor: ";
9     cin >> floor;
10
11    // The following statements check various input errors
12    if (cin.fail())
13    {
14       cout << "Error: Not an integer." << endl;
15       return 1;
16    }
17    if (floor == 13)
18    {
19       cout << "Error: There is no thirteenth floor." << endl;
20       return 1;
21    }
22    if (floor <= 0 || floor > 20)
23    {
24       cout << "Error: The floor must be between 1 and 20." << endl;
25       return 1;
26    }
27
28    // Now we know that the input is valid
29    int actual_floor;
30    if (floor > 13)
31    {
32       actual_floor = floor - 1;
33    }
34    else
35    {
36       actual_floor = floor;
37    }
38
```

```
39      cout << "The elevator will travel to the actual floor "
40         << actual_floor << endl;
41
42      return 0;
43   }
```

Program Run

```
Floor: 13
Error: There is no thirteenth floor.
```

SELF CHECK

27. Consider the `elevator2.cpp` program. What output do you get when the input is

   a. 100

   b. −1

   c. 20

   d. thirteen

28. Your task is to rewrite the `elevator2.cpp` program so that there is a single `if` statement with a complex condition:

```
if (...)
{
   cout << "Error: Bad input" << endl;
   return 1;
}
```

What is the condition?

29. In the Sherlock Holmes story "The Adventure of the Sussex Vampire", the inimitable detective uttered these words: "Matilda Briggs was not the name of a young woman, Watson, ... It was a ship which is associated with the giant rat of Sumatra, a story for which the world is not yet prepared." Over a hundred years later, researchers found giant rats in Western New Guinea, another part of Indonesia.

When processing inputs, you want to reject values that are too large. But how large is too large? These giant rats, found in Western New Guinea, are about five times the size of a city rat.

Suppose you are charged with writing a program that processes rat weights. It contains the statements

```
double weight;
cout << "Enter weight in kg: ";
cin >> weight;
```

What input checks should you supply?

30. Consider the following test program:

```cpp
int main()
{
   int m = 1;
   cout << "Enter an integer: ";
   cin >> m;
   int n = 2;
   cout << "Enter another integer: ";
   cin >> n;
   cout << m << " " << n << endl;
   return 0;
}
```

Run this program and enter three at the first prompt. What happens? Why?

CHAPTER SUMMARY

1. The if statement allows a program to carry out different actions depending on the nature of the data to be processed.

2. Relational operators (< <= > >= == !=) are used to compare numbers and strings.

3. Lexicographic order is used to compare strings.

4. Multiple if statements can be combined to evaluate complex decisions.

5. When using multiple if statements, pay attention to the order of the conditions.

6. The Boolean type bool has two values, false and true.

7. C++ has two Boolean operators that combine conditions: && (and) and || (or).

8. To invert a condition, use the ! (not) operator.

9. The && and || operators are computed lazily: As soon as the truth value is determined, no further conditions are evaluated.

10. De Morgan's law tells you how to negate && and || conditions.

11. Use the `fail` function to test whether stream input has failed.

REVIEW EXERCISES

Exercise R3.1. Find the errors in the following `if` statements.

   a. `if x > 0 then cout << x;`

   b. `if (1 + x > pow(x, sqrt(2)) { y = y + x; }`

   c. `if (x = 1) { y++; }`

   d. `cin >> x; if (cin.fail()) { y = y + x; }`

Exercise R3.2. What do these code fragments print?

   a. `int n = 1; int m = -1;`
      `if (n < -m) { cout << n; } else { cout << m; }`

   b. `int n = 1; int m = -1;`
      `if (-n >= m) { cout << n; } else { cout << m; }`

   c. `double x = 0; double y = 1;`
      `if (fabs(x - y) < 1) { cout << x; } else { cout << y; }`

   d. `double x = sqrt(2); double y = 2;`
      `if (x * x == y) { cout << x; } else { cout << y; }`

Exercise R3.3. Suppose x and y are variables of type `double`. Write a code fragment that sets y to x if x is positive and to 0 otherwise.

Exercise R3.4. Suppose x and y are variables of type `double`. Write a code fragment that sets y to the absolute value of x without calling the `fabs` function. Use an `if` statement.

Exercise R3.5. Explain why it is more difficult to compare floating-point numbers than integers. Write C++ code to test whether an integer n equals 10 and whether a floating-point number x equals 10.

Exercise R3.6. Common Error 3.2 on page 92 explains that a C++ compiler will not report an error when you use an assignment operator instead of a test for equality, but it may issue a warning. Write a test program containing a statement

   `if (floor = 13)`

What does your compiler do when you compile the program?

Exercise R3.7. Each square on a chess board can be described by a letter and number, such as g5 in this example:

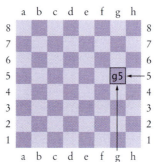

The following pseudocode describes an algorithm that determines whether a square with a given letter and number is dark (black) or light (white).

```
If the letter is an a, c, e, or g
{
    If the number is odd
    {
        color = "black"
    }
    Else
    {
        color = "white"
    }
}
Else
{
    If the number is even
    {
        color = "black"
    }
    Else
    {
        color = "white"
    }
}
```

Using the procedure in Productivity Hint 3.2 on page 105, trace this pseudocode with input g5.

Exercise R3.8. Give a set of four test cases for the algorithm of Exercise R3.7 that covers all branches.

Exercise R3.9. In a scheduling program, we want to check whether two appointments overlap. For simplicity, appointments start at a full hour, and we use military time (with hours 0–24). The following pseudocode describes an algorithm that determines whether the appointment with start time **start1** and end time **end1** overlaps with the appointment with start time **start2** and end time **end2**.

```
If start1 > start2
{
    s = start1
}
Else
{
    s = start2
}
If end1 < end2
{
    e = end1
}
Else
{
    e = end2
}
If s < e
{
    The appointments overlap.
}
Else
{
    The appointments don't overlap.
}
```

Trace this algorithm with an appointment from 10–12 and one from 11–13, then with an appointment from 10–11 and one from 12–13.

Exercise R3.10. Write pseudocode for a program that prompts the user for a month and day and prints out whether it is one of the following four holidays:

- New Year's Day (January 1)
- Independence Day (July 4)
- Veterans Day (November 11)
- Christmas Day (December 25)

Exercise R3.11. Write pseudocode for a program that assigns letter grades for a quiz, according to the following table:

```
Score    Grade
90-100   A
80-89    B
70-79    C
60-69    D
< 60     F
```

Exercise R3.12. Explain how the lexicographic ordering of strings in C++ differs from the ordering of words in a dictionary or telephone book. *Hint:* Consider strings such as IBM, wiley.com, Century 21, and While-U-Wait.

Exercise R3.13. Of the following pairs of strings, which comes first in lexicographic order?

a. `"Tom"`, `"Dick"`

b. `"Tom"`, `"Tomato"`

c. `"church"`, `"Churchill"`

d. `"car manufacturer"`, `"carburetor"`

e. `"Harry"`, `"hairy"`

f. `"C++"`, `" Car"`

g. `"Tom"`, `"Tom"`

h. `"Car"`, `"Carl"`

i. `"car"`, `"bar"`

Exercise R3.14. Explain the difference between an `if/else/else` sequence and nested `if` statements. Give an example for each.

Exercise R3.15. Give an example for an `if/else/else` sequence where the order of the tests does not matter. Give an example where the order of the tests matters.

Exercise R3.16. Give a set of test cases for the tax program in Exercise P3.18. Manually compute the expected results.

Exercise R3.17. Make up another C++ code example that shows the dangling `else` problem, using the following statement. A student with a GPA of at least 1.5, but less than 2, is on probation. With less than 1.5, the student is failing.

Exercise R3.18. Complete the following truth table by finding the truth values of the Boolean expressions for all combinations of the Boolean inputs p, q, and r.

p	q	r	(p && q) || !r	!(p && (q || !r))
false	false	false		
false	false	true		
false	true	false		
		. . .		
	5 more combinations			
		. . .		

Exercise R3.19. True or false? *A* && *B* is the same as *B* && *A* for any Boolean conditions *A* and *B*.

Exercise R3.20. The "advanced search" features of many search engines allow you to use Boolean operators for complex queries, such as "(cats OR dogs) AND NOT pets". Contrast these search operators with the Boolean operators in C++.

Exercise R3.21. Suppose the value of b is `false` and the value of x is 0. What is the value of the following expressions?

   a. `b && x == 0`

   b. `b || x == 0`

   c. `!b && x == 0`

   d. `!b || x == 0`

   e. `b && x != 0`

   f. `b || x != 0`

   g. `!b && x != 0`

   h. `!b || x != 0`

Exercise R3.22. Simplify the following expressions. Here, b is a variable of type `bool`.

   a. `b == true`

   b. `b == false`

   c. `b != true`

   d. `b != false`

Exercise R3.23. Simplify the following statements. Here, b is a variable of type `bool` and n is a variable of type `int`.

   a. `if (n == 0) { b = true; } else { b = false; }`
      (*Hint:* What is the value of n == 0?)

   b. `if (n == 0) { b = false; } else { b = true; }`

   c. `b = false; if (n > 1) { if (n < 2) { b = true; } }`

   d. `if (n < 1) { b = true; } else { b = n > 2; }`

Exercise R3.24. What is wrong with the following program?

```
cout << "Enter the number of quarters: ";
cin >> quarters;
total = total + quarters * 0.25;
cout << "Total: " << total << endl;
if (cin.fail()) cout << "Input error.";
```

Exercise R3.25. Reading numbers is surprisingly difficult because a C++ input stream looks at the input one character at a time. First, white space is skipped. Then the stream consumes those input characters that can be a part of a number. Once the stream has recognized a number, it stops reading if it finds a character that cannot be a part of a number. However, if the first non-white space character is not a digit or a sign, or if the first character is a sign and the second one is not a digit, then the stream fails.

Consider a program reading an integer:

```
cout << "Enter the number of quarters: ";
int quarters;
cin >> quarters;
```

For each of the following user inputs, circle how many characters have been read and whether the stream is in the failed state or not.

   a. 15.9

   b. 15 9

   c. +159

   d. -15A9

   e. Fifteen

   f. -Fifteen

   g. + 15

   h. 1.5E3

   i. +1+5

PROGRAMMING EXERCISES

Exercise P3.1. Write a program that reads a temperature value and the letter C for Celsius or F for Fahrenheit. Print whether water is liquid, solid, or gaseous at the given temperature at sea level.

Exercise P3.2. The boiling point of water drops by about one degree centigrade for every 300 meters (or 1,000 feet) of altitude. Improve the program of Exercise P3.1 to allow the user to supply the altitude in meters or feet.

Exercise P3.3. Write a program that translates a letter grade into a number grade. Letter grades are A, B, C, D, and F, possibly followed by + or –. Their numeric values are 4, 3, 2, 1, and 0. There is no F+ or F–. A + increases the numeric value by 0.3, a – decreases it by 0.3. However, an A+ has value 4.0.

```
Enter a letter grade: B-
The numeric value is 2.7.
```

Exercise P3.4. Write a program that translates a number between 0 and 4 into the closest letter grade. For example, the number 2.8 (which might have been the average of several grades) would be converted to B–. Break ties in favor of the better grade; for example 2.85 should be a B.

Exercise P3.5. Write a program that takes user input describing a playing card in the following shorthand notation:

```
A              Ace
2 ... 10       Card values
J              Jack
```

Q	Queen
K	King
D	Diamonds
H	Hearts
S	Spades
C	Clubs

Your program should print the full description of the card. For example,

```
Enter the card notation: QS
Queen of Spades
```

Exercise P3.6. Write a program that prompts the user for a wavelength value and prints a description of the corresponding part of the electromagnetic spectrum, as given in Table 6.

Table 6 Electromagnetic Spectrum		
Type	**Wavelength (m)**	**Frequency (Hz)**
Radio Waves	$> 10^{-1}$	$< 3 \times 10^9$
Microwaves	10^{-3} to 10^{-1}	3×10^9 to 3×10^{11}
Infrared	7×10^{-7} to 10^{-3}	3×10^{11} to 4×10^{14}
Visible light	4×10^{-7} to 7×10^{-7}	4×10^{14} to 7.5×10^{14}
Ultraviolet	10^{-8} to 4×10^{-7}	7.5×10^{14} to 3×10^{16}
X-rays	10^{-11} to 10^{-8}	3×10^{16} to 3×10^{19}
Gamma rays	$< 10^{-11}$	$> 3 \times 10^{19}$

Exercise P3.7. Repeat Exercise P3.6, modifying the program so that it prompts for the frequency instead.

Exercise P3.8. Repeat Exercise P3.6, modifying the program so that it first asks the user whether the input will be a wavelength or a frequency.

Exercise P3.9. Write a program that reads in three floating-point numbers and prints the largest of the three inputs. For example:

```
Please enter three numbers: 4 9 2.5
The largest number is 9.
```

Exercise P3.10. Write a program that reads in three strings and sorts them lexicographically.

```
Enter three strings: Charlie Able Baker
Able
Baker
Charlie
```

Exercise P3.11. When two points in time are compared, each given as hours (in military time, ranging from 0 and 23) and minutes, the following pseudocode determines which comes first.

```
If hour1 < hour2
{
    time1 comes first.
}
Else if hour1 and hour2 are the same
{
    If minute1 < minute2
    {
        time1 comes first.
    }
    Else if minute1 and minute2 are the same
    {
        time1 and time2 are the same.
    }
    Else
    {
        time2 comes first.
    }
}
Else
{
    time2 comes first.
}
```

Write a program that prompts the user for two points in time and prints the time that comes first, then the other time.

Exercise P3.12. The following algorithm yields the season (Spring, Summer, Fall, or Winter) for a given month and day.

```
If month is 1, 2, or 3 { season = "Winter" }
Else if month is 4, 5, or 6 { season = "Spring" }
Else if month is 7, 8, or 9 { season = "Summer" }
Else if month is 10, 11, or 12 { season = "Fall" }
If month is divisible by 3 and day >= 21
{
    If season is "Winter" { season = "Spring" }
    Else if season is "Spring" { season = "Summer" }
    Else if season is "Summer" { season = "Fall" }
    Else { season = "Winter" }
}
```

Write a program that prompts the user for a month and day and then prints the season, as determined by this algorithm.

Exercise P3.13. Write a program that reads in two floating-point numbers and tests whether they are the same up to two decimal places. Here are two sample runs.

```
Enter two floating-point numbers: 2.0 1.99998
They are the same up to two decimal places.
Enter two floating-point numbers: 2.0 1.98999
They are different.
```

Exercise P3.14. Write a program to simulate a bank transaction. There are two bank accounts: checking and savings. First, ask for the initial balances of the bank accounts; reject negative balances. Then ask for the transactions; options are deposit, withdrawal, and transfer. Then ask for the account; options are checking and savings. Then ask for the amount; reject transactions that overdraw an account. At the end, print the balances of both accounts.

Exercise P3.15. Write a program that reads in the name and salary of an employee. Here the salary will denote an *hourly* wage, such as $9.25. Then ask how many hours the employee worked in the past week. Be sure to accept fractional hours. Compute the pay. Any overtime work (over 40 hours per week) is paid at 150 percent of the regular wage. Print a paycheck for the employee.

Exercise P3.16. Write a program that prompts for the day and month of the user's birthday and then prints a horoscope. Make up fortunes for programmers, like this:

```
Please enter your birthday (month and day): 6 16
Gemini are experts at figuring out the behavior of complicated programs.
You feel where bugs are coming from and then stay one step ahead. Tonight,
your style wins approval from a tough critic.
```

Each fortune should contain the name of the astrological sign. (You will find the names and date ranges of the signs at a distressingly large number of sites on the Internet.)

Exercise P3.17. The original U.S. income tax of 1913 was quite simple. The tax was

- 1 percent on the first $50,000.
- 2 percent on the amount over $50,000 up to $75,000.
- 3 percent on the amount over $75,000 up to $100,000.
- 4 percent on the amount over $100,000 up to $250,000.
- 5 percent on the amount over $250,000 up to $500,000.
- 6 percent on the amount over $500,000.

There was no separate schedule for single or married taxpayers. Write a program that computes the income tax according to this schedule.

Exercise P3.18. Write a program that computes taxes for the following schedule.

If your status is Single and if the taxable income is over	but not over	the tax is	of the amount over
$0	$8,000	10%	$0
$8,000	$32,000	$800 + 15%	$8,000
$32,000		$4,400 + 25%	$32,000
If your status is Married and if the taxable income is over	**but not over**	**the tax is**	**of the amount over**
$0	$16,000	10%	$0
$16,000	$64,000	$1,600 + 15%	$16,000
$64,000		$8,800 + 25%	$64,000

Exercise P3.19. The `tax.cpp` program uses a simplified version of the 2008 U.S. income tax schedule. Look up the tax brackets and rates for the current year, for both single and married filers, and implement a program that computes the actual income tax.

Exercise P3.20. *Unit conversion.* Write a unit conversion program that asks the users from which unit they want to convert (fl. oz, gal, oz, lb, in, ft, mi) and to which unit they want to convert (ml, l, g, kg, mm, cm, m, km). Reject incompatible conversions (such as gal → km). Ask for the value to be converted, then display the result:

```
Convert from? gal
Convert to? ml
Value? 2.5
2.5 gal = 9462.5 ml
```

Exercise P3.21. Write a program that prompts the user to provide a single character from the alphabet. Print Vowel or Consonant, depending on the user input. If the user input is not a letter (between a and z or A and Z), or is a string of length > 1, print an error message.

Exercise P3.22. *Roman numbers.* Write a program that converts a positive integer into the Roman number system. The Roman number system has digits

I	1
V	5
X	10
L	50
C	100

D   500

M   1,000

Numbers are formed according to the following rules. (1) Only numbers up to 3,999 are represented. (2) As in the decimal system, the thousands, hundreds, tens, and ones are expressed separately. (3) The numbers 1 to 9 are expressed as

I   1

II   2

III   3

IV   4

V   5

VI   6

VII   7

VIII   8

IX   9

As you can see, a I preceding a V or X is subtracted from the value, and you can never have more than three I's in a row. (4) Tens and hundreds are done the same way, except that the letters X, L, C and C, D, M are used instead of I, V, X, respectively.

Your program should take an input, such as 1978, and convert it to Roman numerals, MCMLXXVIII.

Exercise P3.23. Write a program that asks the user to enter a month (1 for January, 2 for February, and so on) and then prints the number of days in the month. For February, print "28 or 29 days".

```
Enter a month: 5
30 days
```

Exercise P3.24. A year with 366 days is called a leap year. A year is a leap year if it is divisible by four (for example, 1980), except that it is not a leap year if it is divisible by 100 (for example, 1900); however, it is a leap year if it is divisible by 400 (for example, 2000). There were no exceptions before the introduction of the Gregorian calendar on October 15, 1582 (1500 was a leap year). Write a program that asks the user for a year and computes whether that year is a leap year.

ANSWERS TO SELF-CHECK QUESTIONS

1. Change the if statement to

```
if (floor > 14)
{
    actual_floor = floor - 2;
}
```

2. 85. 90. 85.

3. The only difference is if `original_price` is 100. The statement in Self Check 2 sets `discounted_price` to 90; this one sets it to 80.

4. 95. 100. 95

5.
```
if (fuel_amount < 0.10 * fuel_capacity)
{
    cout << "red" << endl;
}
else
{
    cout << "green" << endl;
}
```

6. (a) and (b) are both true, (c) is false.

7. `floor <= 13`

8. The values should be compared with `==`, not `=`.

9. `input == "Y"`

10. `str != "" or str.length() > 0`

11.
```
if (score_a > score_b) { cout << "A won"; }
else if (score_a < score_b) { cout << "B won"; }
else { cout << "Game tied"; }
```

12.
```
if (x > 0) { s = 1; }
else if (x < 0) { s = -1; }
else { s = 0; }
```

13. You could first set s to one of the three values:
```
s = 0;
if (x > 0) { s = 1; }
else if (x < 0) { s = -1; }
```

14. The `if (price <= 100)` can be omitted, making it clear that the `else` branch is the sole alternative.

15. No destruction of buildings

16. Add a branch
```
else if (richter < 0) { cout << "Error: Negative input" << endl; }
```
before the final `else`.

17. 3200

18. No. Then the computation is $0.10 \times 32000 + 0.25 \ (32000 - 32000)$.

19. No. Their individual tax is $5,200 each, and if they married, they would pay $10,400. Actually, taxpayers in higher tax brackets (which our program does not model) may pay higher taxes when they marry, a phenomenon known as the *marriage penalty*.

20. Change `else` in line 36 to `else if (marital_status == "m")`, and add another branch after line 47:
```
else { cout << "Error: marital status should be s or m." << endl; }
```

21. The higher tax rate is only applied on the income in the higher bracket. Suppose you are single and make $31,900. Should you try to get a $200 raise? Absolutely: you get to keep 90 percent of the first $100 and 75 percent of the next $100.

22. `x == 0 && y == 0`

23. `x == 0 || y == 0`

24. `(x == 0 && y != 0) || (y == 0 && x != 0)`

25. The same as the value of `frozen`.

26. You are guaranteed that there are no other values. With strings or integers, you would need to check that no values such as `"maybe"` or −1 enter your calculations.

27. (a) `Error: The floor must be between 1 and 20.` (b) `Error: The floor must be between 1 and 20.` (c) 19 (d) `Error: Not an integer.`

28. `cin.fail() || floor == 13 || floor <= 0 || floor > 20`

29. Check for `cin.fail()`, to make sure a researcher didn't supply an input such as `oh my`. Check for `weight <= 0`, since any rat must surely have a positive weight. We don't know how giant a rat could be, but the New Guinea rats weighed no more than 2 kg. A regular house rat (*rattus rattus*) weighs up to 0.2 kg, so we'll say that any weight > 10 kg was surely an input error, perhaps confusing grams and kilograms. Thus, the checks are

```
if (cin.fail())
{
   cout << "Error: Not an integer" << endl;
   return 1;
}

if (weight < 0)
{
   cout << "Error: Weight cannot be negative." << endl;
   return 1;
}

if (weight > 10)
{
   cout << "Error: Weight > 10 kg." << endl;
   return 1;
}
```

30. The first input fails. The value of `m` is unchanged. Because a previous input failed, the next input doesn't even try to get additional keystrokes. It also fails, and `n` is unchanged. The program prints 1 2.

Loops

CHAPTER GOALS

- To learn about while, for, and do loops
- To avoid infinite loops and off-by-one errors
- To understand nested loops
- To implement programs that read and process data sets
- To use a computer for simulations

This chapter presents the various iteration constructs that are available in C++. These constructs execute one or more statements repeatedly until a goal is reached. You will see how the techniques that you learn in this chapter can be applied to the processing of input data and the programming of simulations.

CHAPTER CONTENTS

4.1 The while Loop

In this section, you will learn how to repeatedly execute statements until a goal has been reached.

Recall the investment problem from Chapter 1. You put $10,000 into a bank account that earns 5 percent interest per year. How many years does it take for the account balance to be double the original investment?

In Chapter 1 we developed the following algorithm for this problem:

Because the interest earned also earns interest, a bank balance grows exponentially.

Start with a year value of 0 and a balance of $10,000.

year	balance
0	$10,000

Repeat the following steps while the balance is less than $20,000.
   Add 1 to the year value.
   Multiply the balance value by 1.05 (a 5 percent increase).
Report the final year value as the answer.

You now know how to define and update the variables in C++. What you don't yet know is how to carry out "Repeat steps while the balance is less than $20,000".

In a particle accelerator, subatomic particles traverse a loop-shaped tunnel multiple times, gaining the speed required for physical experiments. Similarly, in computer science, statements in a loop are executed while a condition is true.

In C++, the while statement implements such a repetition (see Syntax 4.1). The code

```
while (condition)
{
    statements
}
```

keeps executing the statements while the condition is true. In our case, we want to increment the year counter and add interest while the balance is less than the target balance of $20,000:

```
while (balance < TARGET)
{
    year++;
    balance = balance * (1 + RATE / 100);
}
```

> Loops execute a block of code repeatedly while a condition remains true.

A while statement is an example of a *loop*. If you draw a flowchart, the flow of execution loops again to the point where the condition is tested (see Figure 1).

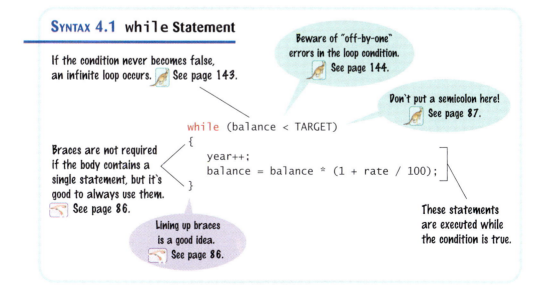

SYNTAX 4.1 while Statement

Beware of "off-by-one" errors in the loop condition. See page 144.

If the condition never becomes false, an infinite loop occurs. See page 143.

Don't put a semicolon here! See page 87.

```
while (balance < TARGET)
{
    year++;
    balance = balance * (1 + rate / 100);
}
```

Braces are not required if the body contains a single statement, but it's good to always use them. See page 86.

Lining up braces is a good idea. See page 86.

These statements are executed while the condition is true.

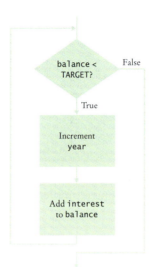

Figure 1
Flowchart of a while Loop

Here is the program that solves the investment problem. Figure 2 illustrates the program's execution.

ch04/doublinv.cpp

```
1   #include <iostream>
2
3   using namespace std;
4
5   int main()
6   {
7      const double RATE = 5;
8      const double INITIAL_BALANCE = 10000;
9      const double TARGET = 2 * INITIAL_BALANCE;
10
11     double balance = INITIAL_BALANCE;
12     int year = 0;
13
14     while (balance < TARGET)
15     {
16        year++;
17        balance = balance * (1 + RATE / 100);
18     }
19
20     cout << "The investment doubled after "
21        << year << " years." << endl;
22
23     return 0;
24  }
```

Program Run

```
The investment doubled after 15 years.
```

① Check the loop condition   The condition is true

```
while (balance < TARGET)
{
```
balance = 10000

```
    year++;
    balance = balance * (1 + rate / 100);
```
year = 0
```
}
```

② Execute the statements in the loop

```
while (balance < TARGET)
{
```
balance = 10500

```
    year++;
    balance = balance * (1 + rate / 100);
```
year = 1
```
}
```

③ Check the loop condition again   The condition is still true

```
while (balance < TARGET)
{
```
balance = 10500

```
    year++;
    balance = balance * (1 + rate / 100);
```
year = 1
```
}
```

⋮

④ After 15 iterations   The condition is no longer true

```
while (balance < TARGET)
{
```
balance = 20789.28

```
    year++;
    balance = balance * (1 + rate / 100);
```
year = 15
```
}
```

⑤ Execute the statement following the loop

```
while (balance < TARGET)
{
```
balance = 20789.28

```
    year++;
    balance = balance * (1 + rate / 100);
```
year = 15
```
}
cout << year << endl;
```

Figure 2   Execution of the doublinv Loop

SELF CHECK

1. How many years does it take for the investment to triple? Modify the program and run it.
2. If the interest rate is 10 percent per year, how many years does it take for the investment to double? Modify the program and run it.

3. Modify the program so that the balance after each year is printed. How did you do that?

4. Suppose we change the program so that the condition of the `while` loop is

```
while (balance <= TARGET)
```

What is the effect on the program? Why?

5. What does the following loop print?

```
int n = 1;
while (n < 100)
{
   n = 2 * n;
   cout << n << " ";
}
```

Table 1   while Loop Examples

Loop	Output	Explanation

`i = 5;`
`while (i > 0)`
`{`
`   cout << i << " ";`
`   i--;`
`}`
	5 4 3 2 1	When i is 0, the loop condition is false, and the loop ends.

`i = 5;`
`while (i > 0)`
`{`
`   cout << i << " ";`
`   i++;`
`}`
	5 6 7 8 9 10 11 ...	The i++ statement is an error causing an "infinite loop" (see Common Error 4.1 on page 143).

`i = 5;`
`while (i > 5)`
`{`
`   cout << i << " ";`
`   i--;`
`}`
	(No output)	The statement i > 5 is false, and the loop is never executed.

`i = 5;`
`while (i < 0)`
`{`
`   cout << i << " ";`
`   i--;`
`}`
	(No output)	The programmer probably thought, "Stop when i is less than 0". However, the loop condition controls when the loop is executed, not when it ends (see Common Error 4.2 on page 144).

`i = 5;`
`while (i > 0) ;`
`{`
`   cout << i << " ";`
`   i--;`
`}`
	(No output, program does not terminate)	Note the semicolon before the {. This loop has an empty body. It runs forever, checking whether i > 0 and doing nothing in the body.

PRODUCTIVITY HINT 4.1

Hand-Tracing Loops

In Productivity Hint 3.2, you learned about the method of hand tracing. This method is particularly effective for understanding how a loop works.

Consider this example. What value is displayed?

```cpp
int n = 1729;
int sum = 0;
while (n > 0)
{
   int digit = n % 10;
   sum = sum + digit;
   n = n / 10;
}
cout << sum << endl;
```

There are three variables: n, sum, and digit.

n	sum	digit

The first two variables are initialized with 1729 and 0 before the loop is entered.

n	sum	digit
1729	0	

Now enter the loop. The variable digit is set to 9 (the remainder of dividing 1729 by 10). The variable sum is set to 0 + 9 = 9. Finally, n becomes 172. (Recall that the remainder in the division 1729 / 10 is discarded because both arguments are integers.). Cross out the old values and write the new ones under the old ones.

n	sum	digit
~~1729~~	~~0~~	
172	9	9

Since n > 0, we repeat the loop. Now digit becomes 2, sum is set to 9 + 2 = 11, and n is set to 17.

n	sum	digit
1~~729~~	0̸	
17~~2~~	9̸	9̸
17	11	2

Because n is still not zero, we repeat the loop, setting digit to 7, sum to 11 + 7 = 18, and n to 1.

n	sum	digit
1~~729~~	0̸	
17~~2~~	9̸	9̸
1~~7~~	1̸1̸	2̸
1	18	7

We enter the loop for one last time. Now digit is set to 1, sum to 19, and n becomes zero. The condition n > 0 is now false, and we continue with the output statement after the loop. The value that is output is 19.

n	sum	digit
1~~729~~	0̸	
17~~2~~	9̸	9̸
1~~7~~	1̸1̸	2̸
~~1~~	1̸8̸	7̸
0	19	1

Of course, you can get the same answer by just running the code. The hope is that by hand-tracing, you gain an *insight*. Consider again what happens in each iteration:

• We extract the last digit of n.
• We add that digit to sum.
• We strip the digit off n.

In other words, the loop forms the sum of the digits in n. You now know what the loop does for any value of n, not just the one in the example.

   Why would anyone want to form the sum of the digits? Operations of this kind are useful for checking the validity of credit card numbers and other forms of ID numbers—see Exercise P4.2.

COMMON ERROR 4.1

Infinite Loops

A very annoying loop error is an *infinite loop:* a loop that runs forever and can be stopped only by killing the program or restarting the computer. If there are output statements in the program, then reams and reams of output flash by on the screen. Otherwise, the program just sits there and *hangs*, seeming to do nothing. On some systems, you can kill a hanging program by hitting Ctrl + C. On others, you can close the window in which the program runs.

A common reason for infinite loops is forgetting to update the variable that controls the loop:

```
year = 1;
while (year <= 20)
{
    balance = balance * (1 + RATE / 100);
}
```

Here the programmer forgot to add a year++ command in the loop. As a result, the year always stays at 1, and the loop never comes to an end.

Another common reason for an infinite loop is accidentally incrementing a counter that should be decremented (or vice versa). Consider this example:

```
year = 20;
while (year > 0)
{
    balance = balance * (1 + RATE / 100);
    year++;
}
```

The year variable really should have been decremented, not incremented. This is a common error because incrementing counters is so much more common than decrementing that your fingers may type the ++ on autopilot. As a consequence, year is always larger than 0, and the loop never ends. (Actually, year may eventually exceed the largest representable positive integer and *wrap around* to a negative number. Then the loop ends—of course, with a completely wrong result.)

In this famous engraving by M.C. Escher, the hooded figures traverse an infinite loop, a loop that never ends.

COMMON ERROR 4.2

Don't Think "Are We There Yet?"

When doing something repetitive, most of us want to know when we are done. For example, you may think, "I want to get at least $20,000," and set the loop condition to

```
balance >= TARGET
```

But the while loop thinks the opposite: How long am I allowed to keep going? The correct loop condition is

```
while (balance < TARGET)
```

In other words: "Keep at it while the balance is less than the target".

When writing a loop condition, don't ask, "Are we there yet?" The condition determines how long the loop will keep going.

COMMON ERROR 4.3

Off-by-One Errors

Consider our computation of the number of years that are required to double an investment:

```
int year = 0;
while (balance < TARGET)
{
   year++;
   balance = balance * (1 + RATE / 100);
}
cout << "The investment doubled after "
   << year << " years." << endl;
```

Should year start at 0 or at 1? Should you test for balance < TARGET or for balance <= TARGET? It is easy to be *off by one* in these expressions.

Some people try to solve off-by-one errors by randomly inserting +1 or -1 until the program seems to work—a terrible strategy. It can take a long time to compile and test all the various possibilities. Expending a small amount of mental effort is a real time saver.

> An off-by-one error is a common error when programming loops. Think through simple test cases to avoid this type of error.

Fortunately, off-by-one errors are easy to avoid, simply by thinking through a couple of test cases and using the information from the test cases to come up with a rationale for your decisions.

Should year start at 0 or at 1? Look at a scenario with simple values: an initial balance of $100 and an interest rate of 50 percent. After year 1, the balance is $150, and after year 2 it is $225, or over $200. So the investment doubled after 2 years. The loop executed two times, incrementing year each time. Hence year must start at 0, not at 1.

year	balance
0	$100
1	$150
2	$225

In other words, the balance variable denotes the balance after the end of the year. At the outset, the balance variable contains the balance after year 0 and not after year 1.

Next, should you use a < or <= comparison in the test? This is harder to figure out, because it is rare for the balance to be exactly twice the initial balance. There is one case when this happens, namely when the interest is 100 percent. The loop executes once. Now year is 1, and balance is exactly equal to 2 * INITIAL_BALANCE. Has the investment doubled after one year? It has. Therefore, the loop should not execute again. If the test condition is balance < TARGET, the loop stops, as it should. If the test condition had been balance <= TARGET, the loop would have executed once more.

In other words, you keep adding interest while the balance *has not yet doubled*.

RANDOM FACT 4.1

The First Bug

According to legend, the first bug was found in the Mark II, a huge electromechanical computer at Harvard University. It really was caused by a bug—a moth was trapped in a relay switch.

Actually, from the note that the operator left in the log book next to the moth (see Figure 3), it appears as if the term "bug" had already been in active use at the time.

The pioneering computer scientist Maurice Wilkes wrote: "Somehow, at the Moore School and afterwards, one had always assumed there would be no particular difficulty in getting programs right. I can remember the exact instant in time at which it dawned on me that a great part of my future life would be spent finding mistakes in my own programs."

Figure 3   The First Bug

4.2 The for Loop

> The for loop is used when a value runs from a starting point to an ending point with a constant increment or decrement.

It often happens that you want to execute a sequence of statements a given number of times. You can use a while loop that is controlled by a counter, as in the following example:

```
counter = 1; // Initialize the counter
while (counter <= 10) // Check the counter
{
    cout << counter << endl;
    counter++; // Update the counter
}
```

Because this loop type is so common, there is a special form for it, called the for loop (see Syntax 4.2).

```
for (counter = 1; counter <= 10; counter++)
{
    cout << counter << endl;
}
```

In general, the for loop:

```
for (initialization; condition; update)
{
    statements
}
```

has exactly the same effect as the while loop:

```
initialization;
while (condition)
{
    statements
    update
}
```

You can visualize the for loop as an orderly sequence of steps.

SYNTAX 4.2 for Statement

These three expressions should be related.
See page 150.

This *initialization* happens once before the loop starts.

The loop is executed while this *condition* is true.

This *update* is executed after each iteration.

```
for (int i = 5; i <= 10; i++)
{
    sum = sum + i;
}
```

The variable i is defined only in this for loop.
See page 148.

This loop executes 6 times.
See page 151.

When a loop is controlled by a counter, the for loop looks neater than a while loop because it groups the initialization, condition, and update expressions together. However, it is important to realize that these expressions are not executed together (see Figure 4).

- The initialization is executed once, before the loop is entered. **❶**
- The condition is checked before each iteration. **❷** **❺**
- The update is executed after each iteration. **❹**

A for loop can count down instead of up:

```
for (counter = 10; counter >= 0; counter--) ...
```

The increment or decrement need not be in steps of 1:

```
for (counter = 0; counter <= 10; counter = counter + 2) ...
```

See Table 2 on page 150 for additional variations.

❶ Initialize counter

```
counter =     1
```

```
for (counter = 1; counter <= 10; counter++)
{
    cout << counter << endl;
}
```

❷ Check condition

```
counter =     1
```

```
for (counter = 1; counter <= 10; counter++)
{
    cout << counter << endl;
}
```

❸ Execute loop body

```
counter =     1
```

```
for (counter = 1; counter <= 10; counter++)
{
    cout << counter << endl;
}
```

❹ Update counter

```
counter =     2
```

```
for (counter = 1; counter <= 10; counter++)
{
    cout << counter << endl;
}
```

❺ Check condition again

```
counter =     2
```

```
for (counter = 1; counter <= 10; counter++)
{
    cout << counter << endl;
}
```

Figure 4 Execution of a for Loop

So far, we assumed that the counter variable had already been defined before the for loop. Alternatively, you can define a variable in the loop initialization. Such a variable is defined only in the loop:

```
for (int counter = 1; counter <= 10; counter++)
{
   . . .
} // counter no longer defined here
```

Here is a typical use of the for loop. We want to print the balance of our savings account over a period of years, as shown in this table:

Year	Balance
1	10500.00
2	11025.00
3	11576.25
4	12155.06
5	12762.82

Figure 5
Flowchart of a for Loop

The for loop pattern applies because the variable year starts at 1 and then moves in constant increments until it reaches the target:

```
for (int year = 1; year <= nyears; year++)
{
    Update balance.
    Print year and balance.
}
```

Here is the complete program. Figure 5 shows the corresponding flowchart.

ch04/invtable.cpp

```cpp
 1  #include <iostream>
 2  #include <iomanip>
 3
 4  using namespace std;
 5
 6  int main()
 7  {
 8      const double RATE = 5;
 9      const double INITIAL_BALANCE = 10000;
10      double balance = INITIAL_BALANCE;
11      int nyears;
12      cout << "Enter number of years: ";
13      cin >> nyears;
14
15      cout << fixed << setprecision(2);
16      for (int year = 1; year <= nyears; year++)
17      {
18          balance = balance * (1 + RATE / 100);
19          cout << setw(4) << year << setw(10) << balance << endl;
20      }
21
22      return 0;
23  }
```

Program Run

```
Enter number of years: 10
  1  10500.00
  2  11025.00
  3  11576.25
  4  12155.06
  5  12762.82
  6  13400.96
  7  14071.00
  8  14774.55
  9  15513.28
 10  16288.95
```

SELF CHECK

6. Write the for loop of the `invtable.cpp` program as a `while` loop.

7. How many numbers does this loop print?

```
for (int n = 10; n >= 0; n--)
{
    cout << n << endl;
}
```

8. Write a for loop that prints all even numbers between 10 and 20 (inclusive).

9. Write a for loop that computes the sum of the integers from 1 to n.

10. How would you modify the for loop of the `invtable.cpp` program to print all balances until the investment has doubled?

Table 2 for Loop Examples

Loop	Values of i	Comment
`for (i = 0; i <= 5; i++)`	0 1 2 3 4 5	Note that the loop is executed 6 times. (See Quality Tip 4.3 on page 151.)
`for (i = 5; i >= 0; i--)`	5 4 3 2 1 0	Use `i--` for decreasing values.
`for (i = 0; i < 9; i = i + 2)`	0 2 4 6 8	Use `i = i + 2` for a step size of 2.
`for (i = 0; i != 9; i = i + 2)`	0 2 4 6 8 10 12 14 ... (infinite loop)	You can use `<` or `<=` instead of `!=` to avoid this problem.
`for (i = 1; i <= 20; i = i * 2)`	1 2 4 8 16	You can specify any rule for modifying i, such as doubling it in every step.
`for (i = 0; i < str.length(); i++)`	0 1 2 ... until the last valid index of the string str	In the loop body, use the expression `str.substr(i, 1)` to get a string containing the `i`th character.

QUALITY TIP 4.1

Use for Loops for Their Intended Purpose Only

A for loop is an *idiom* for a loop of a particular form. A value runs from the start to the end, with a constant increment or decrement.

The compiler won't check whether the initialization, condition, and update expressions are related. For example, the following loop is legal:

```
// Confusing—unrelated expressions
for (cout << "Inputs: "; cin >> x; sum = sum + x)
{
```

```
        count++;
    }
```

However, programmers reading such a for loop will be confused because it does not match their expectations. Use a while loop for iterations that do not follow the for idiom.

QUALITY TIP 4.2

Choose Loop Bounds That Match Your Task

Suppose you want to print line numbers that go from 1 to 10. Of course, you will want to use a loop

```
    for (int i = 1; i <= 10; i++)
```

The values for i are bounded by the relation $1 \leq i \leq 10$. Because there are $\leq$ on both bounds, the bounds are called *symmetric*.

When traversing the characters in a string, it is more natural to use the bounds

```
    for (int i = 0; i < str.length(); i++)
```

In this loop, i traverses all valid positions in the string. You can access the ith character as str.substr(i, 1). The values for i are bounded by $0 \leq i < str.length()$, with a $\leq$ to the left and a $<$ to the right. That is appropriate, because str.length() is not a valid position. Such bounds are called *asymmetric*.

In this case, it is not a good idea to use symmetric bounds:

```
    for (int i = 0; i <= str.length() - 1; i++) // Use < instead
```

The asymmetric form is easier to understand.

QUALITY TIP 4.3

Count Iterations

Finding the correct lower and upper bounds for an iteration can be confusing. Should you start at 0 or at 1? Should you use <= b or < b as a termination condition?

Counting the number of iterations is a very useful device for better understanding a loop. Counting is easier for loops with asymmetric bounds. The loop

```
    for (int i = a; i < b; i++)
```

is executed b - a times. For example, the loop traversing the characters in a string,

```
    for (int i = 0; i < str.length(); i++)
```

runs str.length() times. That makes perfect sense, since there are str.length() characters in a string.

The loop with symmetric bounds,

```
    for (int i = a; i <= b; i++)
```

is executed b - a + 1 times. That "+1" is the source of many programming errors.

For example,

```
for (int i = 0; i <= 10; i++)
```

runs 11 times. Maybe that is what you want; if not, start at 1 or use < 10.

One way to visualize this "+1" error is by looking at a fence. Each section has one fence post to the left, and there is a final post on the right of the last section. Forgetting to count the last value is often called a "fence post error".

How many posts do you need for a fence with four sections? It is easy to be "off by one" with problems such as this one.

4.3 The do Loop

The do loop is appropriate when the loop body must be executed at least once.

Sometimes you want to execute the body of a loop at least once and perform the loop test after the body is executed. The do loop serves that purpose:

```
do
{
    statements
}
while (condition);
```

The body of the do loop is executed first, then the condition is tested.

A typical example for such a loop is input validation. Suppose you ask a user to enter a value < 100. If the user didn't pay attention and entered a larger value, you ask again, until the value is correct. Of course, you cannot test the value until the user has entered it. This is a perfect fit for the do loop (see Figure 6):

```
int value;
do
{
    cout << "Enter a value < 100: ";
    cin >> value;
}
while (value >= 100);
```

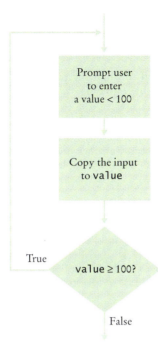

Figure 6   Flowchart of a do Loop

SELF CHECK

11. Suppose that we want to check for inputs that are at least 0 and at most 100. Modify the do loop for this check.

12. Rewrite the input check using a while loop. What is the disadvantage of your solution?

13. Suppose C++ didn't have a do loop. Could you rewrite any do loop as a while loop?

14. Write a do loop that reads integers and computes their sum. Stop when reading the value 0.

15. Write a do loop that reads positive integers and computes their sum. Stop when reading the same value twice in a row. For example, if the input is 1 2 3 4 4, then the sum is 14 and the loop stops.

HOW TO 4.1

Writing a Loop

This How To walks you through the process of implementing a loop statement. We will illustrate the steps with the following example problem:

Read twelve temperature values (one for each month), and display the number of the month with the highest temperature. For example, according to http://worldclimate.com, the average maximum temperatures for Death Valley are (in order by month):

18.2 22.6 26.4 31.1 36.6 42.2
45.7 44.5 40.2 33.1 24.2 17.6

In this case, the month with the highest temperature (45.7 degrees Celsius) is July, and the program should display 7.

Step 1   Decide what work must be done *inside* the loop.

Every loop needs to do some kind of repetitive work, such as

- Reading another item.
- Updating a value (such as a bank balance or total).
- Incrementing a counter.

If you can't figure out what needs to go inside the loop, start by writing down the steps that you would take if you solved the problem by hand. For example, with the temperature reading problem, you might write

Read first value.
Read second value.
If second value is higher than the first, set highest temperature to that value, highest month to 2.
Read next value.
If value is higher than the first and second, set highest temperature to that value, highest month to 3.
Read next value.
If value is higher than the highest temperature seen so far, set highest temperature to that value,
    highest month to 4.
. . .

Now look at these steps and reduce them to a set of *uniform* actions that can be placed into the loop body. The first action is easy:

Read next value.

The next action is trickier. In our description, we used tests "higher than the first", "higher than the first and second", "higher than the highest temperature seen so far". We need to settle on one test that works for all iterations. The last formulation is the most general.

Similarly, we must find a general way of setting the highest month. We need a variable that stores the current month, running from 1 to 12. Then we can formulate the second loop action:

If value is higher than the highest temperature, set highest temperature to that value,
    highest month to current month.

Altogether our loop is

```
Loop
{
    Read next value.
    If value is higher than the highest temperature, set highest temperature to that value,
        highest month to current month.
    Increment current month.
}
```

Step 2 Specify the loop condition.

What goal do you want to reach in your loop? Typical examples are

- Has the counter reached the final value?
- Have you read the last input value?
- Has a value reached a given threshold?

In our example, we simply want the current month to reach 12.

Step 3 Find out how often the loop is repeated, and choose the loop type.

- If you know in advance how many times a loop is repeated, use a `for` loop.
- If the loop must be executed at least once, use a `do` loop.
- Otherwise, use a `while` loop.

In our example, we read 12 temperature values. Therefore, we choose a `for` loop.

Step 4 Set up variables for entering the loop for the first time.

List all variables that are used and updated in the loop, and determine how to initialize them. Commonly, counters are initialized with 0 or 1, totals with 0.

In our example, the variables are

```
current month
highest value
highest month
```

We need to be careful how we set up the highest temperature value. We can't simply set it to 0. After all, our program needs to work with temperature values from Antarctica, all of which may be negative.

A good option is to set the highest temperature value to the first input value. Of course, then we need to remember to only read in another 11 values, with the current month starting at 2.

We also need to initialize the highest month with 1. After all, in an Australian city, we may never find a month that is warmer than January.

Step 5 Process the result after the loop has finished.

In many cases, the desired result is simply a variable that was updated in the loop body. For example, in our temperature program, the result is the highest month. Sometimes, the loop computes values that contribute to the final result. For example, suppose you are asked to average the temperatures. Then the loop should compute the sum, not the average. After the loop has completed, you are ready compute the average: divide the sum by the number of inputs.

Here is our complete loop.

```
Read first value; store as highest value.
highest month = 1
for (current month = 2; current month <= 12; current month++)
{
    Read next value.
    If value is higher than the highest value, set highest value to that value,
        highest month to current month.
}
```

Step 6   Trace the loop with typical examples.

Hand trace your loop code, as described in Productivity Hint 4.1 on page 141. Choose example values that are not too complex—executing the loop 3–5 times is enough to check for the most common errors. Pay special attention when entering the loop for the first and last time.

Sometimes, you want to make a slight modification to make tracing feasible. For example, when hand tracing the investment doubling problem, use an interest rate of 20 percent rather than 5 percent. When hand tracing the temperature loop, use 4 data values, not 12.

Let's say the data are 22.6 36.6 44.5 24.2. Here is the walkthrough:

current month	current value	highest month	highest value
		~~1~~	~~22.6~~
~~2~~	~~36.6~~	~~2~~	~~36.6~~
~~3~~	~~44.5~~	3	44.5
4	24.2		

The trace demonstrates that **highest month** and **highest value** are properly set.

Step 7   Implement the loop in C++.

Here's the loop for our example. Exercise P4.1 asks you to complete the program.

```cpp
double highest_value;
cin >> highest_value;
int highest_month = 1;
for (int current_month = 2; current_month <= 12; current_month++)
{
    double next_value;
    cin >> next_value;
    if (next_value > highest_value)
    {
        highest_value = next_value;
        highest_month = current_month;
    }
}
cout << highest_month << endl;
```

WORKED EXAMPLE 4.1

Credit Card Processing

This Worked Example uses a loop to remove spaces from a credit card number.

4.4 Nested Loops

> Nested loops are commonly used for processing tabular structures.

In Section 3.4, you saw how to nest two `if` statements. Similarly, complex iterations sometimes require a nested loop: a loop inside another loop statement. When processing tables, nested loops occur naturally. An outer loop iterates over all rows of the table. An inner loop deals with the columns in the current row.

In this section you will see how to print a table. For simplicity, we will simply print powers x^n, as in the table at right.

Here is the pseudocode for printing the table.

```
Print table header.
For x from 1 to 10
{
    Print table row.
    Print endl.

}
```

x^1	x^2	x^3	x^4
1	1	1	1
2	4	8	16
3	9	27	81
...	...	...	...
10	100	1000	10000

How do you print a table row? You need to print a value for each exponent. This requires a second loop.

```
For n from 1 to 4
{
    Print xⁿ.
}
```

This loop must be placed inside the preceding loop. We say that the inner loop is *nested* inside the outer loop.

There are 10 rows in the outer loop. For each x, the program prints four columns in the inner loop. Thus, a total of $10 \times 4 = 40$ values are printed.

The hour and minute displays in a digital clock are an example of nested loops. The hours loop 12 times, and for each hour, the minutes loop 60 times.

Here is the complete program. Note that we also use loops to print the table header. However, those loops are not nested.

ch04/powtable.cpp

```
 1  #include <iostream>
 2  #include <iomanip>
 3  #include <cmath>
 4
 5  using namespace std;
 6
 7  int main()
 8  {
 9     const int NMAX = 4;
10     const double XMAX = 10;
11
12     // Print table header
13
14     for (int n = 1; n <= NMAX; n++)
15     {
16        cout << setw(10) << n;
17     }
18     cout << endl;
19     for (int n = 1; n <= NMAX; n++)
20     {
21        cout << setw(10) << "x ";
22     }
23     cout << endl << endl;
24
25     // Print table body
26
27     for (double x = 1; x <= XMAX; x++)
28     {
29        // Print table row
30
31        for (int n = 1; n <= NMAX; n++)
32        {
33           cout << setw(10) << pow(x, n);
34        }
35        cout << endl;
36     }
37
38     return 0;
39  }
```

Program Run

```
         1         2         3         4
         x         x         x         x

         1         1         1         1
         2         4         8        16
         3         9        27        81
         4        16        64       256
         5        25       125       625
```

6	36	216	1296
7	49	343	2401
8	64	512	4096
9	81	729	6561
10	100	1000	10000

SELF CHECK

16. Why is there a statement cout << endl in the outer loop but not in the inner loop?

17. How would you change the program so that all powers from x^0 to x^5 are displayed?

18. If you make the change in Self Check 17, how many values are displayed?

19. What do the following nested loops display?
```
for (int i = 0; i < 3; i++)
{
   for (int j = 0; j < 4; j++)
   {
      cout << i + j;
   }
   cout << endl;
}
```

20. Write nested loops that make the following pattern of brackets:
```
[][][][]
[][][][]
[][][][]
```

Table 3 Nested Loop Examples

Nested Loops	Output	Explanation

```for (i = 1; i <= 3; i++)```
```{```
   ```for (j = 1; j <= 4; j++) { cout << "*"; }```
   ```cout << endl;```
```}```
	****
	****
	****
		Prints 3 rows of 4 asterisks each.

```for (i = 1; i <= 4; i++)```
```{```
   ```for (j = 1; j <= 3; j++) { cout << "*"; }```
   ```cout << endl;```
```}```
	***
	***
	***
	***
		Prints 4 rows of 3 asterisks each.

```for (i = 1; i <= 4; i++)```
```{```
   ```for (j = 1; j <= i; j++) { cout << "*"; }```
   ```cout << endl;```
```}```
	*
	**
	***
	****
		Prints 4 rows of lengths 1, 2, 3, and 4.

Table 3 Nested Loop Examples, continued		
Nested Loops	**Output**	**Explanation**
| ```
for (i = 1; i <= 3; i++)
{
   for (j = 1; j <= 5; j++)
   {
      if (j % 2 == 0) { cout << "*"; }
      else { cout << "-"; }
   }
   cout << endl;
}
``` | -\*-\*-<br>-\*-\*-<br>-\*-\*- | Prints asterisks in even columns, dashes in odd columns. |
| ```
for (i = 1; i <= 3; i++)
{
   for (j = 1; j <= 5; j++)
   {
      if ((i + j) % 2 == 0) { cout << "*"; }
      else { cout << " "; }
   }
   cout << endl;
}
``` | \* \* \*<br> \* \*<br>\* \* \* | Prints a checkerboard pattern. |

4.5 Processing Input

In this section, you will learn how to read and process a sequence of input values.

A sentinel value denotes the end of a data set, but it is not part of the data.

Whenever you read a sequence of inputs, you need to have some method of indicating the end of the sequence. Sometimes you are lucky and no input value can be zero. Then you can prompt the user to keep entering numbers, or 0 to finish the sequence. If zero is allowed but negative numbers are not, you can use –1 to indicate termination. Such a value, which is not an actual input, but serves as a signal for termination, is called a *sentinel*.

In the military, a sentinel guards a border. In computer science, a sentinel value denotes the border between a data set and unrelated input.

Let's put this technique to work in a program that computes the average of a set of salary values. In our sample program, we will use –1 as a sentinel. An employee would surely not work for a negative salary, but there may be volunteers who work for free.

Inside the loop, we read an input. If the input is not –1, we process it. In order to compute the average, we need the total sum of all salaries, and the number of inputs.

```cpp
cin >> salary;
if (salary != -1)
{
   sum = sum + salary;
   count++;
}
```

We stay in the loop while the sentinel value is not detected.

```cpp
while (salary != -1)
{
   ...
}
```

There is just one problem: When the loop is entered for the first time, no data value has been read. We must make sure to initialize salary with some value other than the sentinel:

```cpp
double salary = 0; // Any value other than -1 will do
```

After the loop has finished, we compute and print the average. Here is the complete program.

ch04/sentinel.cpp

```cpp
1  #include <iostream>
2
3  using namespace std;
4
5  int main()
6  {
7     double sum = 0;
8     int count = 0;
9     double salary = 0;
10    cout << "Enter salaries, -1 to finish: ";
11    while (salary != -1)
12    {
13       cin >> salary;
14       if (salary != -1)
15       {
16          sum = sum + salary;
17          count++;
18       }
19    }
20    if (count > 0)
21    {
```

```
22          double average = sum / count;
23          cout << "Average salary: " << average << endl;
24       }
25       else
26       {
27          cout << "No data" << endl;
28       }
29       return 0;
30    }
```

Program Run

```
Enter salaries, -1 to finish: 10 10 40 -1
Average salary: 20
```

Sentinels only work if there is some restriction on the input. In many cases, though, there isn't. Suppose you want to compute the average of a data set that may contain 0 or negative values. Then you cannot use 0 or –1 to indicate the end of the input.

In such a situation, you can read input data until input fails. As you have seen in Section 3.6, the condition

```
cin.fail()
```

is true if the preceding input has failed. For example, suppose that the input was read with these statements:

```
double value;
cin >> value;
```

If the user enters a value that is not a number (such as Q), then the input fails.

We now encounter an additional complexity. You only know that input failed after you have entered the loop and attempted to read it. To remember the failure, use a Boolean variable:

> You can use a Boolean variable to control a loop. Set the variable to true before entering the loop, then set it to false to leave the loop.

```
cout << "Enter values, Q to quit: ";
bool more = true;
while (more)
{
   cin >> value;
   if (cin.fail())
   {
      more = false;
   }
   else
   {
      Process value.
   }
}
```

Some programmers dislike the introduction of a Boolean variable to control a loop. Advanced Topic 4.1 on page 163 shows an alternative mechanism for leaving a loop. However, when reading from a stream, there is an easier way. The expression

```
cin >> value
```

can be used in a condition. It evaluates to `true` if the stream has *not* failed after reading `value`. Therefore, you can read and process a set of inputs with the following loop:

```
cout << "Enter values, Q to quit: ";
while (cin >> value)
{
    Process value.
}
```

This loop is suitable for processing a single sequence of inputs. You will learn more about reading inputs in Chapter 8.

SELF CHECK

21. What does the `sentinel.cpp` program print when the user immediately types –1 when prompted for a value?

22. Why does the `sentinel.cpp` program have *two* checks of the form
    ```
    salary != -1
    ```

23. What would happen if the definition of the `salary` variable in `sentinel.cpp` was changed to
    ```
    double salary = -1;
    ```

24. We prompt the user "Enter values, Q to quit." What happens when the user enters a different letter?

25. What is wrong with the following loop for reading a sequence of values?
    ```
    cout << "Enter values, Q to quit: ";
    while (!cin.fail())
    {
        double value;
        cin >> value;
        sum = sum + value;
        count++;
    }
    ```

ADVANCED TOPIC 4.1

The Loop-and-a-Half Problem and the break Statement

Some programmers dislike loops that are controlled by a Boolean variable, such as:

```
bool more = true;
while (more)
{
    cin >> value;
    if (cin.fail())
    {
        more = false;
```

```
        }
        else
        {
            Process value.
        }
    }
```

The actual test for loop termination is in the middle of the loop, not at the top. This is called a *loop and a half* because one must go halfway into the loop before knowing whether one needs to terminate.

As an alternative, you can use the break reserved word.

```
while (true)
{
    cin >> value;
    if (cin.fail()) { break; }
    Process value.
}
```

The break statement breaks out of the enclosing loop, independent of the loop condition.

In the loop-and-a-half case, break statements can be beneficial. But it is difficult to lay down clear rules as to when they are safe and when they should be avoided. We do not use the break statement in this book.

4.6 Random Numbers and Simulations

In a simulation program, you use the computer to simulate an activity. You can introduce randomness by calling the random number generator.

A *simulation program* uses the computer to simulate an activity in the real world (or an imaginary one). Simulations are commonly used for predicting climate change, analyzing traffic, picking stocks, and many other applications in science and business. In the following sections, you will learn how to implement simulations that model phenomena with a degree of randomness.

4.6.1 Generating Random Numbers

Many events in the real world are difficult to predict with absolute precision, yet we can sometimes know the average behavior quite well. For example, a store may know from experience that a customer arrives every five minutes. Of course, that is an average—customers don't arrive in five minute intervals. To accurately model customer traffic, you want to take that random fluctuation into account. Now, how can you run such a simulation in the computer?

The C++ library has a *random number generator*, which produces numbers that appear to be completely random. Calling rand() yields a random integer between 0 and RAND_MAX (which is an implementation-dependent constant, typically, but not always, the largest valid `int` value). Call `rand()` again, and you get a different number. The `rand` function is defined in the `cstdlib` header.

The following program calls the `rand` function ten times.

ch04/random.cpp

```cpp
1   #include <iostream>
2   #include <cstdlib>
3
4   using namespace std;
5
6   int main()
7   {
8      for (int i = 1; i <= 10; i++)
9      {
10        int r = rand();
11        cout << r << endl;
12     }
13     return 0;
14  }
```

Program Run

```
1804289383
846930886
1681692777
1714636915
1957747793
424238335
719885386
1649760492
596516649
118964142
```

Actually, the numbers are not completely random. They are drawn from sequences of numbers that don't repeat for a long time. These sequences are actually computed from fairly simple formulas; they just behave like random numbers. For that reason, they are often called *pseudorandom* numbers.

Try running the program again. You will get the *exact same output*! This confirms that the random numbers are generated by formulas. However, when running simulations, you don't always want to get the same results. To overcome this problem, specify a *seed* for the random number sequence. Every time you use a new seed, the random number generator starts generating a new sequence. The seed is set with the `srand` function. A simple value to use as a seed is the current time:

```cpp
srand(time(0));
```

Simply make this call once in your program, before generating any random numbers. Then the random numbers will be different in every program run.

4.6.2 Simulating Die Tosses

In actual applications, you need to transform the output from the random number generator into different ranges. For example, to simulate the throw of a die, you need random numbers between 1 and 6.

Here is the general recipe for computing random integers between two bounds a and b. As you know from Quality Tip 4.3 on page 151, there are b - a + 1 values between a and b, including the bounds themselves. First compute rand() % (b - a + 1) to obtain a random value between 0 and b - a, then add a, yielding a random value between a and b:

```
int r = rand() % (b - a + 1) + a;
```

Here is a program that simulates the throw of a pair of dice:

ch04/dice.cpp

```cpp
1  #include <iostream>
2  #include <string>
3  #include <cstdlib>
4  #include <ctime>
5
6  using namespace std;
7
8  int main()
9  {
10     srand(time(0));
11
12     for (int i = 1; i <= 10; i++)
13     {
14        int d1 = rand() % 6 + 1;
15        int d2 = rand() % 6 + 1;
16        cout << d1 << " " << d2 << endl;
17     }
18     cout << endl;
19     return 0;
20  }
```

Program Run

```
5 1
2 1
1 2
5 1
1 2
6 4
4 4
6 1
6 3
5 2
```

4.6.3 The Monte Carlo Method

The Monte Carlo method is an ingenious method for finding approximate solutions to problems that cannot be precisely solved. (The method is named after the famous casino in Monte Carlo.) Here is a typical example. It is difficult to compute the number π, but you can approximate it quite well with the following simulation.

Simulate shooting a dart into a square surrounding a circle of radius 1. That is easy: generate random x and y coordinates between –1 and 1.

If the generated point lies inside the circle, we count it as a *hit*. That is the case when $x^2 + y^2 \leq 1$. Because our shots are entirely random, we expect that the ratio of *hits / tries* is approximately equal to the ratio of the areas of the circle and the square, that is, $\pi / 4$. Therefore, our estimate for π is $4 \times$ *hits / tries*. This method yields an estimate for π, using nothing but simple arithmetic.

To run the Monte Carlo simulation, you have to work a little harder with random number generation. When you throw a die, it has to come up with one of six faces. When throwing a dart, however, there are many possible outcomes. You must generate a random *floating-point number*.

First, generate the following value:

```
double r = rand() * 1.0 / RAND_MAX; // Between 0 and 1
```

The value r is a random floating-point value between 0 and 1. (You have to multiply by 1.0 to ensure that one of the operands of the / operator is a floating-point number. The division rand() / RAND_MAX would be an integer division—see Common Error 2.3.)

To generate a random value between –1 and 1, you compute:

```
double x = -1 + 2 * r; // Between -1 and 1
```

As r ranges from 0 to 1, x ranges from $-1 + 2 \times 0 = -1$ to $-1 + 2 \times 1 = 1$.

Here is the program that carries out the simulation.

ch04/montecarlo.cpp

```
 1  #include <iostream>
 2  #include <cstdlib>
 3  #include <cmath>
 4  #include <ctime>
 5
 6  using namespace std;
 7
 8  int main()
 9  {
10     const int TRIES = 10000;
11
12     srand(time(0));
13
14     int hits = 0;
15     for (int i = 1; i <= TRIES; i++)
16     {
17        double r = rand() * 1.0 / RAND_MAX; // Between 0 and 1
18        double x = -1 + 2 * r; // Between -1 and 1
19        r = rand() * 1.0 / RAND_MAX;
20        double y = -1 + 2 * r;
21        if (x * x + y * y <= 1) { hits++; }
22     }
23     double pi_estimate = 4.0 * hits / TRIES;
24     cout << "Estimate for pi: " << pi_estimate << endl;
25     return 0;
26  }
```

Program Run

```
Estimate for pi: 3.1504
```

SELF CHECK

26. How do you simulate a coin toss with the rand function?

27. How do you simulate the picking of a random playing card?

28. Why does the dice.cpp file include the <ctime> header?

29. In many games, you throw a pair of dice to get a value between 2 and 12. What is wrong with this simulated throw of a pair of dice?

    ```
    int sum = rand() % 11 + 2;
    ```

30. How do you generate a random floating-point number between 0 and 100?

RANDOM FACT 4.2

Software Piracy

As you read this, you have written a few computer programs, and you have experienced firsthand how much effort it takes to write even the humblest of programs. Writing a real software product, such as a financial application or a computer game, takes a lot of time and money. Few people, and fewer companies, are going to spend that kind of time and money if they don't have a reasonable chance to make more money from their effort. (Actually, some companies give away their software in the hope that users will upgrade to more elaborate paid versions. Other companies give away the software that enables users to read and use files but sell the software needed to create those files. Finally, there are individuals who donate their time, out of enthusiasm, and produce programs that you can copy freely.)

When selling software, a company must rely on the honesty of its customers. It is an easy matter for an unscrupulous person to make copies of computer programs without paying for them. In most countries that is illegal. Most governments provide legal protection, such as copyright laws and patents, to encourage the development of new products. Countries that tolerate widespread piracy have found that they have an ample cheap supply of foreign software, but no local manufacturers willing to design good software for their own citizens, such as word processors in the local script or financial programs adapted to the local tax laws.

When a mass market for software first appeared, vendors were enraged by the money they lost through piracy. They tried to fight back by various schemes to ensure that only the legitimate owner could use the software. Some manufacturers used *key disks:* disks with special patterns of holes burned in by a laser, which couldn't be copied. Others used *dongles:* devices that are attached to a printer port. Legitimate users hated these measures. They paid for the software, but they had to suffer through the inconvenience of inserting a key disk every time they started the software or having multiple dongles stick out from their computer. In the United States, market pressures forced most vendors to give up on these copy protection schemes, but they are still commonplace in other parts of the world.

Because it is so easy and inexpensive to pirate software, and the chance of being found out is minimal, you have to make a moral choice for yourself. If a package that you would really like to have is too expensive for your budget, do you steal it, or do you stay honest and get by with a more affordable product?

Of course, piracy is not limited to software. The same issues arise for other digital products as well. You may have had the opportunity to obtain copies of songs or movies without payment. Or you may have been frustrated by a copy protection device on your music player that made it difficult for you to listen to songs that you paid for. Admittedly, it can be difficult to have a lot of sympathy for a musical ensemble whose publisher charges a lot of money for what seems to have been very little effort on their part, at least when compared to the effort that goes into designing and implementing a software package. Nevertheless, it seems only fair that artists and authors receive some compensation for their efforts. How to pay artists, authors, and programmers fairly, without burdening honest customers, is an unsolved problem at the time of this writing, and many computer scientists are engaged in research in this area.

CHAPTER SUMMARY

1. Loops execute a block of code repeatedly while a condition remains true.

2. An off-by-one error is a common error when programming loops. Think through simple test cases to avoid this type of error.

3. The for loop is used when a value runs from a starting point to an ending point with a constant increment or decrement.

4. The do loop is appropriate when the loop body must be executed at least once.

5. Nested loops are commonly used for processing tabular structures.

6. A sentinel value denotes the end of a data set, but it is not part of the data.

7. You can use a Boolean variable to control a loop. Set the variable to true before entering the loop, then set it to false to leave the loop.

8. In a simulation program, you use the computer to simulate an activity. You can introduce randomness by calling the random number generator.

REVIEW EXERCISES

Exercise R4.1. Write a loop that computes
   a. The sum of all even numbers between 2 and 100 (inclusive).
   b. The sum of all squares between 1 and 100 (inclusive).

   c. The sum of all odd numbers between a and b (inclusive).
   d. The sum of all odd digits of n. (For example, if n is 32677, the sum would be $3 + 7 + 7 = 17$.)

Exercise R4.2. Provide trace tables for these loops.

```
a. int i = 0; int j = 10; int n = 0;
   while (i < j) { i++; j--; n++; }
b. int i = 0; int j = 0; int n = 0;
   while (i < 10) { i++; n = n + i + j; j++; }
c. int i = 10; int j = 0; int n = 0;
   while (i > 0) { i--; j++; n = n + i - j; }
d. int i = 0; int j = 10; int n = 0;
   while (i != j) { i = i + 2; j = j - 2; n++; }
```

Exercise R4.3. What do these loops print?

```
a. for (int i = 1; i < 10; i++) { cout << i << " "; }
b. for (int i = 1; i < 10; i += 2) { cout << i << " "; }
c. for (int i = 10; i > 1; i--) { cout << i << " "; }
d. for (int i = 0; i < 10; i++) { cout << i << " "; }
e. for (int i = 1; i < 10; i = i * 2) { cout << i << " "; }
f. for (int i = 1; i < 10; i++) { if (i % 2 == 0) { cout << i << " "; } }
```

Exercise R4.4. What is an infinite loop? On your computer, how can you terminate a program that executes an infinite loop?

Exercise R4.5. What is an "off-by-one" error? Give an example from your own programming experience.

Exercise R4.6. What is a sentinel value? Give a simple rule when it is appropriate to use a numeric sentinel value.

Exercise R4.7. Which loop statements does C++ support? Give simple rules when to use each loop type.

Exercise R4.8. Is the following code legal?

```
for (int i = 0; i < 10; i++)
{
   for (int i = 0; i < 10; i++)
   {
      cout << i << " ";
   }
   cout << endl;
}
```

What does it print? Is it good coding style? If not, how would you improve it?

Exercise R4.9. How often do the following loops execute? Assume that i is not changed in the loop body.

  a. `for (int i = 1; i <= 10; i++) ...`
  b. `for (int i = 0; i < 10; i++) ...`
  c. `for (int i = 10; i > 0; i--) ...`
  d. `for (int i = -10; i <= 10; i++) ...`
  e. `for (int i = 10; i >= 0; i++) ...`
  f. `for (int i = -10; i <= 10; i = i + 2) ...`
  g. `for (int i = -10; i <= 10; i = i + 3) ...`

Exercise R4.10. Write pseudocode for a program that prints a calendar such as the following:

```
Su  M  T  W Th  F Sa
             1  2  3  4
 5  6  7  8  9 10 11
12 13 14 15 16 17 18
19 20 21 22 23 24 25
26 27 28 29 30 31
```

Exercise R4.11. Write pseudocode for a program that prints a Celsius/Fahrenheit conversion table such as the following:

```
Celsius | Fahrenheit
--------+-----------
      0 |         32
     10 |         50
     20 |         68
    ...           ...
    100 |        212
```

Exercise R4.12. Write pseudocode for a program that reads a sequence of student records and prints the total score for each student. Each record has the student's first and last name, followed by a sequence of test scores and a sentinel of –1. The sequence is terminated by the word END. Here is a sample sequence:

```
Harry Morgan 94 71 86 95 -1
Sally Lin 99 98 100 95 90 -1
END
```

Provide a trace table for this sample input.

Exercise R4.13. Rewrite the following for loop into a while loop.

```
int s = 0;
for (int i = 1; i <= 10; i++)
{
   s = s + i;
}
```

Exercise R4.14. Rewrite the following do/while loop into a while loop.

```
int n;
cin >> n;
double x = 0;
double s;
do
{
   s = 1.0 / (1 + n * n);
   n++;
   x = x + s;
}
while (s > 0.01);
```

Exercise R4.15. Provide trace tables of the following loops.

```
a. int s = 1;
   int n = 1;
   while (s < 10) { s = s + n; }
   n++;
```

```
b. int s = 1;
   for (int n = 1; n < 5; n++) { s = s + n; }
```

```
c. int s = 1;
   int n = 1;
   do
   {
      s = s + n;
      n++;
   }
   while (s < 10 * n);
```

Exercise R4.16. What do the following loops print? Work out the answer by tracing the code, not by using the computer.

```
a. int s = 1;
   for (int n = 1; n <= 5; n++)
   {
      s = s + n;
      cout << s << " ";
   }
```

```
b. int s = 1;
   for (int n = 1; s <= 10; cout << s << " ")
   {
      n = n + 2;
      s = s + n;
   }
```

```
c. int s = 1;
   int n;
   for (n = 1; n <= 5; n++)
   {
      s = s + n;
      n++;
   }
   cout << s << " " << n;
```

Exercise R4.17. What do the following program segments print? Find the answers by tracing the code, not by using the computer.

a.
```
int n = 1;
for (int i = 2; i < 5; i++) { n = n + i; }
cout << n;
```

b.
```
int i;
double n = 1 / 2;
for (i = 2; i <= 5; i++) { n = n + 1.0 / i; }
cout << i;
```

c.
```
double x = 1;
double y = 1;
int i = 0;
do
{
   y = y / 2;
   x = x + y;
   i++;
}
while (x < 1.8);
cout << i;
```

d.
```
double x = 1;
double y = 1;
int i = 0;
while (y >= 1.5)
{
   x = x / 2;
   y = x + y;
   i++;
}
cout << i;
```

Exercise R4.18. Give an example of a for loop where symmetric bounds are more natural. Give an example of a for loop where asymmetric bounds are more natural.

Exercise R4.19. What are nested loops? Give an example where a nested loop is typically used.

Exercise R4.20. The nested loops

```
for (int i = 1; i <= height; i++)
{
   for (int j = 1; j <= width; j++) { cout << "*"; }
   cout << endl;
}
```

display a rectangle of a given width and height, such as

```
****
****
****
```

Write a *single* for loop that displays the same rectangle.

Exercise R4.21. Suppose you design an educational game to teach children how to read a clock. How do you generate random values for the hours and minutes?

Exercise R4.22. In a travel simulation, Harry will visit one of his friends that are located in three states. He has ten friends in California, three in Nevada, and two in Utah. How do you produce a random number between 1 and 3, denoting the destination state, with a probability that is proportional to the number of friends in each state?

PROGRAMMING EXERCISES

Exercise P4.1. Complete the program in How To 4.1 on page 154. Your program should read twelve temperature values and print the month with the highest temperature.

Exercise P4.2. *Credit Card Number Check.* The last digit of a credit card number is the *check digit*, which protects against transcription errors such as an error in a single digit or switching two digits. The following method is used to verify actual credit card numbers but, for simplicity, we will describe it for numbers with 8 digits instead of 16:

- Starting from the rightmost digit, form the sum of every other digit. For example, if the credit card number is 4358 9795, then you form the sum 5 + 7 + 8 + 3 = 23.
- Double each of the digits that were not included in the preceding step. Add all digits of the resulting numbers. For example, with the number given above, doubling the digits, starting with the next-to-last one, yields 18 18 10 8. Adding all digits in these values yields 1 + 8 + 1 + 8 + 1 + 0 + 8 = 27.
- Add the sums of the two preceding steps. If the last digit of the result is 0, the number is valid. In our case, 23 + 27 = 50, so the number is valid.

Write a program that implements this algorithm. The user should supply an 8-digit number, and you should print out whether the number is valid or not. If it is not valid, you should print out the value of the check digit that would make the number valid.

Exercise P4.3. *Currency conversion.* Write a program that first asks the user to type today's exchange rate between U.S. dollars and Japanese yen, then reads U.S. dollar values and converts each to yen. Use 0 as a sentinel.

Exercise P4.4. Write a program that first asks the user to type in today's exchange rate between U.S. dollars and Japanese yen, then reads U.S. dollar values and converts each to Japanese yen. Use 0 as the sentinel value to denote the end of dollar inputs. Then the program reads a sequence of yen amounts and converts them to dollars. The second sequence is terminated by another zero value.

Exercise P4.5. Write a program that reads a set of floating-point values. Ask the user to enter the values, then print

- the average of the values.
- the smallest of the values.
- the largest of the values.
- the range, that is the difference between the smallest and largest.

Of course, you may only prompt for the values once.

Exercise P4.6. Translate the following pseudocode for finding the minimum value from a set of inputs into a C++ program.

```
Set a Boolean variable "first" to true.
While another value has been read successfully
{
    If first is true
    {
        Set the minimum to the value.
        Set first to false.
    }
    Else if the value is less than the minimum
    {
        Set the minimum to the value.
    }
}
Print the minimum.
```

Exercise P4.7. Translate the following pseudocode for randomly permuting the characters in a string into a C++ program.

```
Read a word.
Repeat word.length() times
{
    Pick a random position i in the word.
    Pick a random position j > i in the word.
    Swap the letters at positions j and i.
}
Print the word.
```

To swap the letters, construct substrings as follows:

first   i   middle   j   last

Then replace the string with

```
first + word.substr(j, 1) + middle + word.substr(i, 1) + last
```

Exercise P4.8. Write a program that reads a word and prints each character of the word on a separate line. For example, if the user provides the input "Harry", the program prints

```
H
a
r
r
y
```

Exercise P4.9. Write a program that reads a word and prints the word in reverse. For example, if the user provides the input "Harry", the program prints

```
yrraH
```

Exercise P4.10. Write a program that reads a word and prints the number of vowels in the word. For this exercise, assume that a e i o u y are vowels. For example, if the user provides the input "Harry", the program prints 2 vowels.

Exercise P4.11. Write a program that reads a word and prints the number of syllables in the word. For this exercise, assume that syllables are determined as follows: Each sequence of vowels a e i o u y, except for the last e in a word, is a vowel. However, if that algorithm yields a count of 0, change it to 1. For example,

Word	Syllables
Harry	2
hairy	2
hare	1
the	1

Exercise P4.12. Write a program that reads a word and prints all substrings, sorted by length. For example, if the user provides the input "rum", the program prints

```
r
u
m
ru
um
rum
```

Exercise P4.13. Write a program that prints all powers of 2 from 2^0 up to 2^{20}.

Exercise P4.14. Write a program that reads a number and prints all of its *binary digits:* Print the remainder number % 2, then replace the number with number / 2. Keep going until the number is 0. For example, if the user provides the input 13, the output should be

```
1
0
1
1
```

Exercise P4.15. *Mean and standard deviation.* Write a program that reads a set of floating-point data values. Choose an appropriate mechanism for prompting for the end of the data set. When all values have been read, print out the count of the values, the average, and the standard deviation. The average of a data set $\{x_1, \ldots, x_n\}$ is $\bar{x} = \sum x_i / n$, where $\sum x_i = x_1 + \ldots + x_n$ is the sum of the input values. The standard deviation is

$$s = \sqrt{\frac{\sum (x_i - \bar{x})^2}{n - 1}}$$

However, this formula is not suitable for the task. By the time the program has computed $\bar{x}$, the individual x_i are long gone. Until you know how to save these values, use the numerically less stable formula

$$s = \sqrt{\frac{\sum x_i^2 - \frac{1}{n}\left(\sum x_i\right)^2}{n - 1}}$$

You can compute this quantity by keeping track of the count, the sum, and the sum of squares as you process the input values.

Exercise P4.16. The *Fibonacci numbers* are defined by the sequence

$$f_1 = 1$$
$$f_2 = 1$$
$$f_n = f_{n-1} + f_{n-2}$$

Reformulate that as

```
fold1 = 1;
fold2 = 1;
fnew = fold1 + fold2;
```

After that, discard `fold2`, which is no longer needed, and set `fold2` to `fold1` and `fold1` to `fnew`. Repeat `fnew` an appropriate number of times.

Implement a program that computes the Fibonacci numbers in that way.

Exercise P4.17. *Factoring of integers.* Write a program that asks the user for an integer and then prints out all its factors. For example, when the user enters 150, the program should print

```
2
3
5
5
```

Exercise P4.18. *Prime numbers.* Write a program that prompts the user for an integer and then prints out all prime numbers up to that integer. For example, when the user enters 20, the program should print

```
2
3
```

```
5
7
11
13
17
19
```

Recall that a number is a prime number if it is not divisible by any number except 1 and itself.

Exercise P4.19. Write a program that prints a multiplication table, like this:

```
 1   2   3   4   5   6   7   8   9  10
 2   4   6   8  10  12  14  16  18  20
 3   6   9  12  15  18  21  24  27  30
...
10  20  30  40  50  60  70  80  90 100
```

Exercise P4.20. Write a program that reads an integer and displays, using asterisks, a filled and hollow square, placed next to each other. For example if the side length is 5, the program should display

```
***** *****
***** *   *
***** *   *
***** *   *
***** *****
```

Exercise P4.21. Write a program that reads an integer and displays, using asterisks, a filled diamond of the given side length. For example, if the side length is 4, the program should display

```
   *
  ***
 *****
*******
 *****
  ***
   *
```

Exercise P4.22. *Projectile flight.* Suppose a cannonball is propelled straight into the air with a starting velocity v_0. Any calculus book will state that the position of the ball after t seconds is $s(t) = -\frac{1}{2}gt^2 + v_0t$, where $g = 9.81$ m/sec^2 is the gravitational force of the earth. No calculus book ever mentions why someone would want to carry out such an obviously dangerous experiment, so we will do it in the safety of the computer.

In fact, we will confirm the theorem from calculus by a simulation. In our simulation, we will consider how the ball moves in very short time intervals Δt. In a short time interval the velocity v is nearly constant, and we can compute the distance the ball moves as $\Delta s = v\Delta t$. In our program, we will simply set

```
const double DELTA_T = 0.01;
```

and update the position by

```
s = s + v * DELTA_T;
```

The velocity changes constantly—in fact, it is reduced by the gravitational force of the earth. In a short time interval, $\Delta v = -g\Delta t$, we must keep the velocity updated as

```
v = v - g * DELTA_T;
```

In the next iteration the new velocity is used to update the distance.

Now run the simulation until the cannonball falls back to the earth. Get the initial velocity as an input (100 m/sec is a good value). Update the position and velocity 100 times per second, but print out the position only every full second. Also print out the values from the exact formula $s(t) = -\frac{1}{2}gt^2 + v_0t$ for comparison.

What is the benefit of this kind of simulation when an exact formula is available? Well, the formula from the calculus book is *not* exact. Actually, the gravitational force diminishes the farther the cannonball is away from the surface of the earth. This complicates the algebra sufficiently that it is not possible to give an exact formula for the actual motion, but the computer simulation can simply be extended to apply a variable gravitational force. For cannonballs, the calculus-book formula is actually good enough, but computers are necessary to compute accurate trajectories for higher-flying objects such as ballistic missiles.

Exercise P4.23. *The game of Nim.* This is a well-known game with a number of variants. The following variant has an interesting winning strategy. Two players alternately take marbles from a pile. In each move, a player chooses how many marbles to take. The player must take at least one but at most half of the marbles. Then the other player takes a turn. The player who takes the last marble loses.

You will write a program in which the computer plays against a human opponent. Generate a random integer between 10 and 100 to denote the initial size of the pile. Generate a random integer between 0 and 1 to decide whether the computer or the human takes the first turn. Generate a random integer between 0 and 1 to decide whether the computer plays *smart* or *stupid*. In stupid mode the computer simply takes a random legal value (between 1 and $n/2$) from the pile whenever it has a turn. In smart mode the computer takes off enough marbles to make the size of the pile a power of two minus 1—that is, 3, 7, 15, 31, or 63. That is always a legal move, except when the size of the pile is currently one less than a power of two. In that case, the computer makes a random legal move.

You will note that the computer cannot be beaten in smart mode when it has the first move, unless the pile size happens to be 15, 31, or 63. Of course, a human player who has the first turn and knows the winning strategy can win against the computer.

Exercise P4.24. *The Drunkard's Walk.* A drunkard in a grid of streets randomly picks one of four directions and stumbles to the next intersection, then again randomly picks one of four directions, and so on. You might think that on average the drunkard doesn't move very far because the choices cancel each other out, but that is actually not the case.

Represent locations as integer pairs (x, y). Implement the drunkard's walk over 100 intersections and print the beginning and ending location.

Exercise P4.25. *The Monty Hall Paradox.* Marilyn vos Savant described the following problem (loosely based on a game show hosted by Monty Hall) in a popular magazine: "Suppose you're on a game show, and you're given the choice of three doors: Behind one door is a car; behind the others, goats. You pick a door, say No. 1, and the host, who knows what's behind the doors, opens another door, say No. 3, which has a goat. He then says to you, "Do you want to pick door No. 2?" Is it to your advantage to switch your choice?"

Ms. vos Savant proved that it is to your advantage, but many of her readers, including some mathematics professors, disagreed, arguing that the probability would not change because another door was opened.

Your task is to simulate this game show. In each iteration, randomly pick a door number between 1 and 3 for placing the car. Randomly have the player pick a door. Randomly have the game show host pick one of the two doors having a goat. Now increment a counter for strategy 1 if the player wins by switching to the third door, and increment a counter for strategy 2 if the player wins by sticking with the original choice. Run 1,000 iterations and print both counters.

Exercise P4.26. *The Buffon Needle Experiment.* The following experiment was devised by Comte Georges-Louis Leclerc de Buffon (1707–1788), a French naturalist. A needle of length 1 inch is dropped onto paper that is ruled with lines 2 inches apart. If the needle drops onto a line, we count it as a *hit*. (See Figure 7.) Buffon conjectured that the quotient *tries/hits* approximates π.

For the Buffon needle experiment, you must generate two random numbers: one to describe the starting position and one to describe the angle of the needle with the *x*-axis. Then you need to test whether the needle touches a grid line.

Generate the *lower* point of the needle. Its *x*-coordinate is irrelevant, and you may assume its *y*-coordinate y_{low} to be any random number between 0 and 2. The angle α between the needle and the *x*-axis can be any value between 0 degrees and 180 degrees (π radians). The upper end of the needle has *y*-coordinate

$$y_{high} = y_{low} + \sin\alpha$$

The needle is a hit if y_{high} is at least 2, as shown in Figure 8.

Figure 7 The Buffon Needle Experiment

Figure 8
A Hit in the Buffon Needle Experiment

Stop after 10,000 tries and print the quotient *tries/hits*. (This program is not suitable for computing the value of π. You need π in the computation of the angle.)

ANSWERS TO SELF-CHECK QUESTIONS

1. 23 years.
2. 7 years.
3. Add a statement
   ```
   cout << balance << endl;
   ```
   as the last statement in the `while` loop.
4. The program prints the same output. This is because the balance after 14 years is slightly below $20,000, and after 15 years, it is slightly above $20,000.
5. `2 4 8 16 32 64 128`
   Note that the value 128 is printed even though it is larger than 100.
6. ```
   int year = 1;
   while (year <= nyears)
   {
      balance = balance * (1 + RATE / 100);
      cout << setw(4) << year << setw(10) << balance << endl;
      year++;
   }
   ```
7. 11 numbers: 10 9 8 7 6 5 4 3 2 1 0
8. ```
   for (int i = 10; i <= 20; i = i + 2)
   {
      cout << n << endl;
   }
   ```
9. ```
   int sum = 0;
   for (int i = 1; i <= n; i++)
   {
   ```
   ```

```
    sum = sum + i;
}
```

10. `for (int year = 1; balance <= 2 * INITIAL_BALANCE; year++)`

However, it is best not to use a for loop in this case because the loop condition does not relate to the year variable. A `while` loop would be a better choice.

11.
```
do
{
    cout << "Enter a value between 0 and 100: ";
    cin >> value;
}
while (value < 0 || value > 100);
```

12.
```
int value = 100;
while (value >= 100)
{
    cout << "Enter a value < 100: ";
    cin >> value;
}
```

Here, the variable value had to be initialized with an artificial value to ensure that the loop is entered at least once.

13. Yes. The do loop

do { *body* } while (*condition*);

is equivalent to this while loop:

```
boolean first = true;
while (first || condition) { body; first = false; }
```

14.
```
int x;
int sum = 0;
do
{
    cin >> x;
    sum = sum + x;
}
while (x != 0);
```

15.
```
int x = 0;
int previous;
do
{
    previous = x;
    cin >> x;
    sum = sum + x;
}
while (previous != x);
```

16. All values in the inner loop should be displayed on the same line.

17. Change lines 14, 19, and 31 to for (int n = 0; n <= NMAX; n++). Change NMAX to 5.

18. 60: The outer loop is executed 10 times, and the inner loop 6 times.

19.
```
0123
1234
2345
```

20.
```
for (int i = 1; i <= 3; i++)
{
   for (int j = 1; j <= 4; j++)
   {
      cout << "[]";
   }
   cout << endl;
}
```

21. No data

22. The first check ends the loop after the sentinel has been read. The second check ensures that the sentinel is not processed as an input value.

23. The while loop would never be entered. The user would never be prompted for input. Since count stays 0, the program would then print "No data".

24. The stream also fails. A more accurate prompt would have been: "Enter values, a key other than a digit to quit." But that might be more confusing to the program user who would need now ponder which key to choose.

25. You don't know whether the input fails until after you try reading input.

26. Compute rand() % 2, and use 0 for heads, 1 for tails, or the other way around.

27. Compute rand() % 4 and associate the numbers 0 ... 3 with the four suits. Then compute rand() % 13 and associate the numbers 0 ... 12 with Jack, Ace, 2 ... 10, Queen, and King

28. It is required for calling the time function.

29. The call will produce a value between 2 and 12, but all values have the same probability. When throwing a pair of dice, the number 7 is six times as likely as the number 2. The correct formula is

```
int sum = rand() % 6 + rand() % 6 + 2;
```

30. rand() * 100.0 / RAND_MAX

Functions

CHAPTER GOALS

- To be able to implement functions
- To become familiar with the concept of parameter passing
- To appreciate the importance of function comments
- To develop strategies for decomposing complex tasks into simpler ones
- To be able to determine the scope of a variable
- To recognize when to use value and reference parameters

Functions are a fundamental building block of C++ programs. A function packages a computation into a form that can be easily understood and reused. In this chapter, you will learn how to design and implement your own functions, and how to break up complex tasks into sets of cooperating functions.

CHAPTER CONTENTS

5.1 Functions as Black Boxes

> A function is a named sequence of instructions.

A *function* is a sequence of instructions with a name. You have already encountered several functions. For example, the function named pow, which was introduced in Chapter 2, contains instructions to compute a power x^y. Moreover, every C++ program has a function called main.

You *call* a function in order to execute its instructions. For example, consider the following program:

```
int main()
{
    double z = pow(2, 3);
    ...
}
```

By using the expression pow(2, 3), main *calls* the pow function, asking it to compute 2^3. The main function is temporarily suspended. The instructions of the pow function execute and compute the result. The pow function *returns* its result back to main, and the main function resumes execution (see Figure 1).

When another function calls the pow function, it provides "inputs", such as the values 2 and 3 in the call pow(2, 3). In order to avoid confusion with inputs that are provided by a human user, these values are called *parameter values*. The "output" that the pow function computes is called the *return value*.

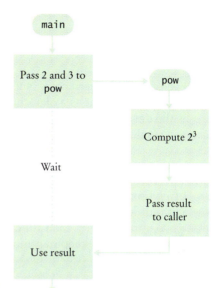

Figure 1
Execution Flow During a Function Call

Functions can have multiple parameter values, but they have only one return value.

> Parameter values are supplied when a function is called. The return value is the result that the function computes.

Note that the return value of a function is returned to the calling function, not displayed on the screen. For example, suppose your program contains a statement

```
double z = pow(2, 3);
```

When the pow function returns its result, the return value is stored in the variable z. If you want the value to be displayed, you need to add a statement such as cout << z.

At this point, you may wonder how the pow function performs its job. For example, how does pow(2, 3) compute that 2^3 is 8? By multiplying $2 \times 2 \times 2$? With logarithms? Fortunately, as a user of the function, you *don't need to know* how the function is implemented. You just need to know the *specification* of the function: If you provide parameter values x and y, the function returns x^y. Engineers use the term *black box* for a device with a given specification but unknown implementation. You can think of pow as a black box, as shown in Figure 2.

Figure 2
The pow Function as a Black Box

Even though a thermostat is usually white, you can think of it as a black box. The input is the desired temperature, and the output is a signal to the heater or air conditioner.

When you design your own functions, you will want to make them appear as black boxes to other programmers. Those programmers want to use your functions without knowing what goes on inside. Even if you are the only person working on a program, making each function into a black box pays off: there are fewer details that you need to keep in mind.

SELF CHECK

1. Consider the function call pow(3, 2). What are the parameter and return values?
2. What is the return value of the function call pow(pow(2, 2), 2)?
3. The ceil function in the C++ standard library takes a single parameter value x and returns the smallest integer $\geq x$. What is the return value of ceil(2.3)?
4. It is possible to determine the answer to Self Check 3 without knowing how the ceil function is implemented. Use an engineering term to describe this aspect of the ceil function.

5.2 Implementing Functions

In this section, you will learn how to implement a function from a given specification. We will use a very simple example: a function to compute the volume of a cube with a given side length.

The cube_volume function uses a given side length to compute the volume of a cube.

> When defining a function, you provide a name for the function, a name and type for each parameter, and a type for the result.

When writing this function, you need to

- Pick a name for the function (cube_volume).
- Give a type and a name for each parameter variable (double side_length).
- Specify the type of the return value (double).

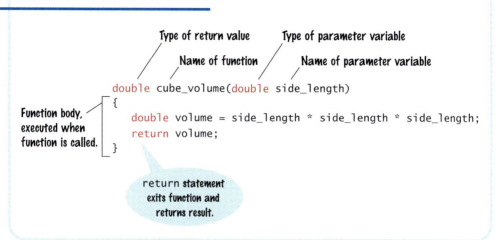

SYNTAX 5.1 Function Definition

Put all this information together to form the first line of the function's definition:

```
double cube_volume(double side_length)
```

Next, specify the *body* of the function: the statements that are executed when the function is called.

The volume of a cube of side length s is $s \times s \times s$. However, for greater clarity, our parameter variable has been called `side_length`, not s, so we need to compute `side_length * side_length * side_length`.

We will store this value in a variable called `volume`:

```
double volume = side_length * side_length * side_length;
```

In order to return the result of the function, use the `return` statement:

```
return volume;
```

The body of a function is enclosed in braces. Here is the complete function:

```
double cube_volume(double side_length)
{
    double volume = side_length * side_length * side_length;
    return volume;
}
```

Let's put this function to use. We'll supply a `main` function that calls the `cube_volume` function twice.

```
int main()
{
    double result1 = cube_volume(2);
    double result2 = cube_volume(10);
    cout << "A cube with side length 2 has volume " << result1 << endl;
    cout << "A cube with side length 10 has volume " << result2 << endl;
```

```
        return 0;
    }
```

When the function is called with different parameter values, the function returns different results. Consider the call cube_volume(2). The parameter value 2 corresponds to the side_length parameter variable. Therefore, in this call, side_length is 2. The function computes side_length * side_length * side_length, or 2 * 2 * 2. When the function is called with a different parameter value, say 10, then the function computes 10 * 10 * 10.

Now we combine both functions into a test program. Because main calls cube_volume, the cube_volume function must be known before the main function is defined. This is easily achieved by placing cube_volume first and main last in the source file. (See Advanced Topic 5.1 on page 197 for an alternative.) Here is the complete program. Note the comment that describes the behavior of the function. (Productivity Hint 5.1 on page 191 describes the format of the comment.)

ch05/cube.cpp

```
 1  #include <iostream>
 2
 3  using namespace std;
 4
 5  /**
 6      Computes the volume of a cube.
 7      @param side_length the side length of the cube
 8      @return the volume
 9  */
10  double cube_volume(double side_length)
11  {
12      double volume = side_length * side_length * side_length;
13      return volume;
14  }
15
16  int main()
17  {
18      double result1 = cube_volume(2);
19      double result2 = cube_volume(10);
20      cout << "A cube with side length 2 has volume " << result1 << endl;
21      cout << "A cube with side length 10 has volume " << result2 << endl;
22
23      return 0;
24  }
```

Program Run

```
A cube with side length 2 has volume 8
A cube with side length 10 has volume 1000
```

SELF CHECK

5. What is the value of `cube_volume(3)`?

6. What is the value of `cube_volume(cube_volume(2))`?

7. Provide an alternate implementation of the body of the `cube_volume` function by calling the `pow` function.

8. Define a function `square_area` that computes the area of a square of a given side length.

9. Consider this function:

```
int mystery(int x, int y)
{
    double result = (x + y) / (y - x);
    return result;
}
```

What is the result of the call `mystery(2, 3)`?

PRODUCTIVITY HINT 5.1

Function Comments

Whenever you write a function, you should *comment* its behavior. Comments are for human readers, not compilers, and there is no universal standard for the layout of a function comment. In this book, we will use the following layout:

```
/**
    Computes the volume of a cube.
    @param side_length the side length of the cube
    @return the volume
*/
double cube_volume(double side_length)
{
    double volume = side_length * side_length * side_length;
    return volume;
}
```

This particular documentation style is borrowed from the Java programming language. It is widely supported by C++ tools as well, for example by the Doxygen tool (http://www.stack.nl/~dimitri/doxygen/).

> Function comments explain the purpose of the function, the meaning of the parameters and return value, as well as any special requirements.

The first line of the comment describes the purpose of the function. Each `@param` clause describes a parameter variable and the `@return` clause describes the return value.

Note that the function comment does not document the implementation (*how* the function does what it does) but rather the design (*what* the function does, its inputs, and its results). The comment allows other programmers to use the function as a "black box".

Turn Repeated Code Into a Function

When you write nearly identical code multiple times, you should probably introduce a function. Consider these statements:

```
int hours;
do
{
   cout << "Enter a value between 1 and 12: ";
   cin >> hours;
}
while (hours < 1 || hours > 12);

int minutes;
do
{
   cout << "Enter a value between 0 and 59: ";
   cin >> minutes;
}
while (minutes < 0 || minutes > 59);
```

Here, we read two variables, making sure that each of them is within a certain range. It is easy to extract the common behavior into a function:

```
/**
   Prompts a user to enter a value in a given range until the user
   provides a valid input.
   @param low the low end of the range
   @param high the high end of the range
   @return the value provided by the user
*/
int read_value_between(int low, int high)
{
   int input;
   do
   {
      cout << "Enter a value between " << low << " and " << high << ": ";
      cin >> input;
   }
   while (input < low || input > high);
   return input;
}
```

Then use this function twice:

```
int hours = read_value_between(1, 12);
int minutes = read_value_between(0, 59);
```

Note how the code has become much easier to understand.

5.3 Parameter Passing

In this section, we examine the mechanism of parameter passing more closely. When a function is called, a variable is created for each parameter. This variable is called a *parameter variable*. (Another commonly used term is *formal parameter*.) In the function call, a value is supplied for each parameter, called the *parameter value*. (Other commonly used terms for this value are *actual parameter* and *argument*.) Each parameter variable is initialized with the corresponding parameter value.

Consider the function call illustrated in Figure 3:

```
double result1 = cube_volume(2);
```

- The parameter variable `side_length` of the `cube_volume` function is created. **1**
- The parameter variable is initialized with the value that was passed in the call. In our case, `side_length` is set to 2. **2**
- The function computes the expression `side_length * side_length * side_length`, which has the value 8. That value is stored in the variable `volume`. **3**
- The function returns. All of its variables are removed. The return value is transferred to the *caller*, that is, the function calling the `cube_volume` function. **4**

Figure 3   Parameter Passing

pie(fruit)   pie(fruit)

A recipe for a fruit pie may say to use any kind of fruit. Here, "fruit" is an example of a parameter variable.

Now consider what happens in a subsequent call cube_volume(10). A new parameter variable is created. (Recall that the previous parameter variable was removed when the first call to cube_volume returned.) It is initialized with 10, and the process repeats. After the second function call is complete, its variables are again removed.

SELF CHECK

10. What does this program print? Use a diagram like Figure 3 to find the answer.

```cpp
double mystery(int x, int y)
{
    double z = x + y;
    z = z / 2.0;
    return z;
}
int main()
{
    int a = 5;
    int b = 7;
    cout << mystery(a, b) << endl;
}
```

11. What does this program print? Use a diagram like Figure 3 to find the answer.

```cpp
int mystery(int x)
{
    int y = x * x;
    return y;
}
int main()
{
    int a = 4;
    cout << mystery(a + 1) << endl;
}
```

12. What does the following program print? Use a diagram like Figure 3 to find the answer.

```cpp
int mystery(int n)
{
```

```
      n++;
      n++;
      return n;
   }
   int main()
   {
      int a = 5;
      cout << mystery(a) << endl;
   }
```

QUALITY TIP 5.1

Do Not Modify Parameter Variables

In C++, a parameter variable is just like any other variable. You can modify the values of the parameter variables in the body of a function. For example,

```
   int total_cents(int dollars, int cents)
   {
      cents = dollars * 100 + cents; // Modifies parameter variable
      return cents;
   }
```

However, many programmers find this practice confusing. It mixes the concept of a parameter (input to the function) with that of a variable (storage for a value). To avoid the confusion, simply introduce a separate variable:

```
   int total_cents(int dollars, int cents)
   {
      int result = dollars * 100 + cents;
      return result;
   }
```

5.4 Return Values

The return statement terminates a function call and yields the function result.

You use the `return` statement to specify the result of a function. When the `return` statement is processed, the function exits *immediately*. This behavior is convenient for handling exceptional cases at the beginning:

```
   double cube_volume(double side_length)
   {
      if (side_length < 0) return 0;
      double volume = side_length * side_length * side_length;
      return volume;
   }
```

If the function is called with a negative value for `side_length`, then the function returns 0 and the remainder of the function is not executed. (See Figure 4.)

Figure 4   A return Statement Exits a Function Immediately

In the preceding example, each `return` statement returned a constant or a variable. Actually, the `return` statement can return the value of any expression. Instead of saving the return value in a variable and returning the variable, it is often possible to eliminate the variable and return a more complex expression:

```
double cube_volume(double side_length)
{
   return side_length * side_length * side_length;
}
```

It is important that every branch of a function return a value. Consider the following incorrect function:

```
double cube_volume(double side_length)
{
   if (side_length >= 0)
   {
      return side_length * side_length * side_length;
   } // Error
}
```

Suppose you call `cube_volume` with a negative value for the side length. Of course, you aren't supposed to call that, but it might happen as the result of a coding error. Because the `if` condition is not true, the `return` statement is not executed. However, the function must return *something*. Depending on circumstances, the compiler might flag this as an error, or the function might return a random value. Protect against this problem by returning some safe value:

```
double cube_volume(double side_length)
{
   if (side_length >= 0)
   {
      return side_length * side_length * side_length;
   }
   return 0;
}
```

The last statement of every function ought to be a `return` statement. This ensures that *some* value gets returned when the function reaches the end.

COMMON ERROR 5.1

Missing Return Value

A function always needs to return something. If the code of the function contains several branches, make sure that each one of them returns a value:

```
int sign(double x)
{
   if (x < 0) return -1;
   if (x > 0) return 1;
   // Error: missing return value if x equals 0
}
```

This function computes the sign of a number: –1 for negative numbers and +1 for positive numbers. If the parameter value is zero, however, no value is returned. Most compilers will issue a warning in this situation, but if you ignore the warning and the function is ever called with a parameter value of 0, a random quantity will be returned.

ADVANCED TOPIC 5.1

Function Declarations

Functions need to be known before they can be used. This can be achieved easily if you first define lower-level helper functions, then the midlevel workhorse functions, and finally `main` in your program.

Some programmers prefer to list the `main` function first in their programs. If you share that preference, you need to learn how to declare the other functions at the top of the program. A declaration of a function lists the return type, function name, and parameter variables, but it contains no body:

```
double cube_volume(double side_length);
```

This is an advertisement that promises that the function is implemented elsewhere. It is easy to distinguish declarations from definitions: Declarations end in a semicolon, whereas definitions are followed by a {...} block. Declarations are also called *prototypes*.

The declarations of common functions such as `pow` are contained in header files. If you have a look inside `cmath`, you will find the declaration of `pow` and the other math functions.

Here is an alternate organization of the `cube.cpp` file:

```
#include <iostream>

using namespace std;

// Declaration of cube_volume
double cube_volume(double side_length);

int main()
{
```

```
    double result1 = cube_volume(2); // Use of cube_volume
    double result2 = cube_volume(10);
    cout << "A cube with side length 2 has volume " << result1 << endl;
    cout << "A cube with side length 10 has volume " << result2 << endl;
    return 0;
}

// Definition of cube_volume
double cube_volume(double side_length)
{
    return side_length * side_length * side_length;
}
```

If you prefer this approach, go ahead and use it in your programs. You just need to be aware of one drawback. Whenever you change the name of a function or one of the parameter types, you need to fix it in both places: in the declaration and in the definition.

How To 5.1

Implementing a Function

> Turn computations that can be reused into functions.

A function is a computation that can be used multiple times with different parameter values, either in the same program or in different programs. Whenever a computation is needed more than once, turn it into a function.

To illustrate this process, suppose that you are helping archaeologists who research Egyptian pyramids. You have taken on the task of writing a function that determines the volume of a pyramid, given its height and base length.

Step 1 Describe what the function should do.

Provide a simple English description, such as "Compute the volume of a pyramid whose base is a square."

Step 2 Determine the function's "inputs".

Make a list of *all* the parameters that can vary. It is common for beginners to implement functions that are overly specific. For example, you may know that the great pyramid of Giza, the largest of the Egyptian pyramids, has a height of 146 meters and a base length of 230 meters. You should *not* use these numbers in your calculation, even if the original problem only asked about the great pyramid. It is just as easy—and far more useful—to write a function that computes the volume of *any* pyramid.

In our case, the parameters are the pyramid's height and base length. At this point, we have enough information to document the function:

```
/**
    Computes the volume of a pyramid whose base is a square.
    @param height  the height of the pyramid
    @param base_length  the length of one side of the pyramid's base
    @return  the volume of the pyramid
*/
```

Step 3 Determine the types of the parameters and the return value.

The height and base length can both be floating-point numbers. Therefore, we will choose the type `double` for both parameter variables. The computed volume is also a floating-point number, yielding a return type of `double`. Therefore, the function will be defined as

```
double pyramid_volume(double height, double base_length)
```

Step 4 Write pseudocode for obtaining the desired result.

In most cases, a function needs to carry out several steps to find the desired answer. You may need to use mathematical formulas, branches, or loops. Express your function in pseudocode.

An Internet search yields the fact that the volume of a pyramid is computed as

volume = 1/3 x height x base area

Since the base is a square, we have

base area = base length x base length

Using these two equations, we can compute the volume from the parameter values.

Step 5 Implement the function body.

In our example, the function body is quite simple. Note the use of the `return` statement to return the result.

```
{
   double base_area = base_length * base_length;
   return height * base_area / 3;
}
```

Step 6 Test your function.

After implementing a function, you should test it in isolation. Such a test is called a *unit test*. Work out test cases by hand, and make sure that the function produces the correct results. For example, for a pyramid with height 9 and base length 10, we expect the area to be $1/3 \times 9 \times 100 = 300$. If the height is 0, we expect an area of 0.

```
int main()
{
   cout << "Volume: " << pyramid_volume(9, 10) << endl;
   cout << "Expected: 300"
   cout << "Volume: " << pyramid_volume(0, 10) << endl;
   cout << "Expected: 0"
   return 0;
}
```

The output confirms that the function worked as expected:

```
Volume: 300
Expected: 300
Volume: 0
Expected: 0
```

Matching and Replacing Parts of a String

This Worked Example creates a function to find the first occurrence of one string in a given string and replace it with a second string.

5.5 Functions Without Return Values

> Use a return type of void to indicate that a function does not return a value.

Sometimes, you need to carry out a sequence of instructions that does not yield a value. If that instruction sequence occurs multiple times, you will want to package it into a function. In C++, you use the return type void to indicate the absence of a return value.

Here is a typical example. Your task is to print a string in a box, like this:

```
-------
!Hello!
-------
```

However, different strings can be substituted for Hello. A function for this task can be defined as follows:

```
void box_string(string str)
```

Now you develop the body of the function in the usual way, by formulating a general method for solving the task.

- Print a line that contains the - character n + 2 times, where n is the length of the string.
- Print a line containing the string, surrounded with a ! to the left and right.
- Print another line containing the - character n + 2 times.

Here is the function implementation:

```
/**
   Prints a string in a box.
   @param str  the string to print
*/
void box_string(string str)
{
   int n = str.length();
   for (int i = 0; i < n + 2; i++) { cout << "-"; }
   cout << endl;
   cout << "!" << str << "!" << endl;
   for (int i = 0; i < n + 2; i++) { cout << "-"; }
   cout << endl;
}
```

Note that this function doesn't compute any value. It performs some actions and then returns to the caller. (See the sample program ch05/box.cpp.)

Because there is no return value, you cannot use box_string in an expression. You can call

```
box_string("Hello");
```

but not

```
result = box_string("Hello"); // Error: box_string doesn't return a result.
```

If you want to return from a void function before reaching the end, you use a return statement without a value. For example,

```
void box_string(string str)
{
   int n = str.length();
   if (n == 0)
   {
      return; //  Return immediately
   }
   ...
}
```

SELF CHECK

13. How do you generate the following printout, using the box_string function?

```
-------
!Hello!
-------
-------
!World!
-------
```

14. What is wrong with the following statement?

```
cout << box_string("Hello");
```

15. Implement a function shout that prints a line consisting of a string followed by three exclamation marks. For example, shout("Hello") should print Hello!!!. The function should not return a value.

16. How would you modify the box_string function to leave a space around the string that is being boxed, like this:

```
---------
! Hello !
---------
```

17. The box_string function contains the code for printing a line of - characters twice. Place that code into a separate function print_line, and use that function to simplify box_string. What is the code of both functions?

5.6 Stepwise Refinement

> Use the process of stepwise refinement to decompose complex tasks into simpler ones.

One of the most powerful strategies for problem solving is the process of *stepwise refinement*. To solve a difficult task, break it down into simpler tasks. Then keep breaking down the simpler tasks into even simpler ones, until you are left with tasks that you know how to solve.

Now apply this process to a problem of everyday life. You get up in the morning and simply must **get coffee**. How do you get coffee? You see whether you can get someone else, such as your mother or mate, to bring

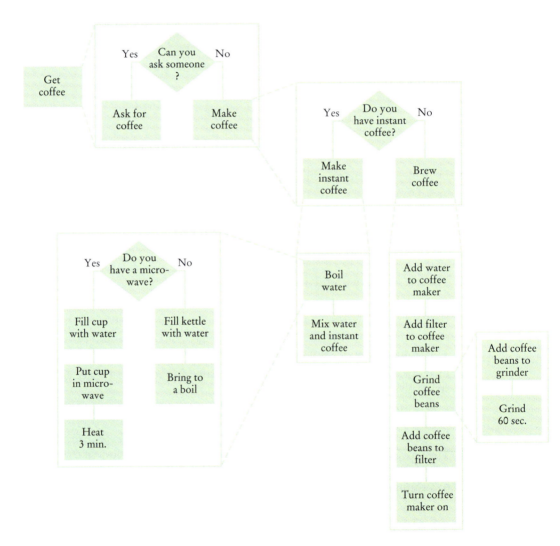

Figure 5   Flowchart of Coffee-Making Solution

you some. If that fails, you must **make coffee**. How do you make coffee? If there is instant coffee available, you can **make instant coffee**. How do you make instant coffee? Simply **boil water** and mix the boiling water with the instant coffee. How do you boil water? If there is a microwave, then you fill a cup with water, place it in the microwave and heat it for three minutes. Otherwise, you fill a kettle with water and heat it on the stove until the water comes to a boil. On the other hand, if you don't have instant coffee, you must **brew coffee**. How do you brew coffee? You add water to the coffee maker, put in a filter, **grind coffee**, put the coffee in the filter, and turn the coffee maker on. How do you grind coffee? You add coffee beans to the coffee grinder and push the button for 60 seconds.

Figure 5 shows a flowchart view of the coffee-making solution. Refinements are shown as expanding boxes. In C++, you implement a refinement as a function. For example, a function `brew_coffee` would call `grind_coffee`, and it would be called from a function `make_coffee`.

Let us apply the process of stepwise refinement to a programming problem. When printing a check, it is customary to write the check amount both as a number ("$274.15") and as a text string ("two hundred seventy four dollars and 15 cents"). Doing so reduces the recipient's temptation to add a few digits in front of the amount (see Figure 6). For a human, this isn't particularly difficult, but how can a computer do this? There is no built-in function that turns 274 into "two hundred seventy four". We need to program this function. Here is the description of the function we want to write:

```
/**
    Turns a number into its English name.
    @param number  a positive integer < 1,000
    @return  the name of number (e.g., "two hundred seventy four")
*/
string int_name(int number)
```

Figure 6   Check Showing the Amount as Both a Number and a String

Before starting to program, we need to have a plan. Consider a simple case. If the number is between 1 and 9, we need to compute "one" ... "nine". In fact, we need the same computation *again* for the hundreds (two hundred). Any time you need something more than once, it is a good idea to turn that into a function. Rather than writing the entire function, write only the comment:

```
/**
    Turns a digit into its English name.
    @param digit  an integer between 1 and 9
    @return  the name of digit ("one" ... "nine")
*/
string digit_name(int digit)
```

This sounds simple enough to implement, using an if statement with nine branches, so we will worry about the implementation later.

Numbers between 10 and 19 are special cases. Let's have a separate function teen_name that converts them into strings "eleven", "twelve", "thirteen", and so on:

```
/**
    Turns a number between 10 and 19 into its English name.
    @param number  an integer between 10 and 19
    @return  the name of the number ("ten" ... "nineteen")
*/
string teen_name(int number)
```

Next, suppose that the number is between 20 and 99. Then we show the tens as "twenty", "thirty", ..., "ninety". For simplicity and consistency, put that computation into a separate function:

```
/**
    Gives the name of the tens part of a number between 20 and 99.
    @param number  an integer between 20 and 99
    @return  the name of the tens part of the number ("twenty" ... "ninety")
*/
string tens_name(int number)
```

Now suppose the number is at least 20 and at most 99. If the number is evenly divisible by 10, we use tens_name, and we are done. Otherwise, we print the tens with tens_name and the ones with digit_name. If the number is between 100 and 999, then we show a digit, the word "hundred", and the remainder as described previously.

Here is the pseudocode of the algorithm.

```
part = number (The part that still needs to be converted)
name = "" (The name of the number)
If part >= 100
{
    name = name of hundreds in part + " hundred"
    Remove hundreds from part.
}

If part >= 20
{
    Append tens_name(part) to name.
    Remove tens from part.
```

```
}
Else if part >= 10
{
    Append teen_name(part) to name.
    part = 0
}

If (part > 0)
{
    Append digit_name(part) to name.
}
```

This pseudocode has a number of important improvements over the verbal description. It shows how to arrange the tests, starting with the comparisons against the larger numbers, and it shows how the smaller number is subsequently processed in further if statements.

On the other hand, this pseudocode is vague about the actual conversion of the pieces, just referring to "name of hundreds" and the like. Furthermore, we were vague about spaces. As it stands, the code would produce strings with no spaces, twohundredseventyfour, for example. Compared to the complexity of the main problem, one would hope that spaces are a minor issue. It is best not to muddy the pseudocode with minor details.

Now turn the pseudocode into real code. The last three cases are easy, because helper functions are already developed for them:

```
if (part >= 20)
{
    name = name + " " + tens_name(part);
    part = part % 10;
}
else if (part >= 10)
{
    name = name + " " + teen_name(part);
    part = 0;
}

if (part > 0)
{
    name = name + " " + digit_name(part);
}
```

Finally, let us tackle the case of numbers between 100 and 999. Because part < 1000, part / 100 is a single digit, and we obtain its name by calling digit_name. Then we add the "hundred" suffix:

```
if (part >= 100)
{
    name = digit_name(part / 100) + " hundred";
    part = part % 100;
}
```

Now you have seen all the important building blocks for the int_name function. Here is the complete program.

ch05/intname.cpp

```
 1  #include <iostream>
 2  #include <string>
 3
 4  using namespace std;
 5
 6  /**
 7     Turns a digit into its English name.
 8     @param digit an integer between 1 and 9
 9     @return the name of digit ("one" ... "nine")
10  */
11  string digit_name(int digit)
12  {
13     if (digit == 1) return "one";
14     if (digit == 2) return "two";
15     if (digit == 3) return "three";
16     if (digit == 4) return "four";
17     if (digit == 5) return "five";
18     if (digit == 6) return "six";
19     if (digit == 7) return "seven";
20     if (digit == 8) return "eight";
21     if (digit == 9) return "nine";
22     return "";
23  }
24
25  /**
26     Turns a number between 10 and 19 into its English name.
27     @param number an integer between 10 and 19
28     @return the name of the given number ("ten" ... "nineteen")
29  */
30  string teen_name(int number)
31  {
32     if (number == 10) return "ten";
33     if (number == 11) return "eleven";
34     if (number == 12) return "twelve";
35     if (number == 13) return "thirteen";
36     if (number == 14) return "fourteen";
37     if (number == 15) return "fifteen";
38     if (number == 16) return "sixteen";
39     if (number == 17) return "seventeen";
40     if (number == 18) return "eighteen";
41     if (number == 19) return "nineteen";
42     return "";
43  }
44
45  /**
46     Gives the name of the tens part of a number between 20 and 99.
47     @param number an integer between 20 and 99
48     @return the name of the tens part of the number ("twenty" ... "ninety")
49  */
50  string tens_name(int number)
51  {
```

```
52      if (number >= 90) return "ninety";
53      if (number >= 80) return "eighty";
54      if (number >= 70) return "seventy";
55      if (number >= 60) return "sixty";
56      if (number >= 50) return "fifty";
57      if (number >= 40) return "forty";
58      if (number >= 30) return "thirty";
59      if (number >= 20) return "twenty";
60      return "";
61   }
62
63   /**
64      Turns a number into its English name.
65      @param number  a positive integer < 1,000
66      @return  the name of the number (e.g. "two hundred seventy four")
67   */
68   string int_name(int number)
69   {
70      int part = number; // The part that still needs to be converted
71      string name; // The return value
72
73      if (part >= 100)
74      {
75         name = digit_name(part / 100) + " hundred";
76         part = part % 100;
77      }
78
79      if (part >= 20)
80      {
81         name = name + " " + tens_name(part);
82         part = part % 10;
83      }
84      else if (part >= 10)
85      {
86         name = name + " " + teen_name(part);
87         part = 0;
88      }
89
90      if (part > 0)
91      {
92         name = name + " " + digit_name(part);
93      }
94
95      return name;
96   }
97
98   int main()
99   {
100     cout << "Please enter a positive integer: ";
101     int input;
102     cin >> input;
103     cout << int_name(input) << endl;
104     return 0;
105  }
```

Program Run

```
Please enter a positive integer: 729
seven hundred twenty nine
```

SELF CHECK

18. Explain how you can improve the int_name function so that it can handle parameter values up to 9999.

19. Why does line 87 set part = 0?

20. What happens when you call int_name(0)? How can you change the int_name function to handle this case correctly?

21. Trace the function call int_name(72), as described in Productivity Hint 5.3.

22. Use the process of stepwise refinement to break down the task of printing the following table into simpler tasks.

```
+-----+-----------+
|   i | i * i * i |
+-----+-----------+
|   1 |         1 |
|   2 |         8 |
   . . .
|  20 |      8000 |
+-----+-----------+
```

QUALITY TIP 5.2

Keep Functions Short

There is a certain cost for writing a function. You need to design, code, and test the function. The function needs to be documented. You need to spend some effort to make the function reusable rather than tied to a specific context. To avoid this cost, it is always tempting just to stuff more and more code in one place rather than going through the trouble of breaking up the code into separate functions. It is quite common to see inexperienced programmers produce functions that are several hundred lines long.

As a rule of thumb, a function that is so long that its code will not fit on a single screen in your development environment should probably be broken up.

PRODUCTIVITY HINT 5.3

Tracing Functions

When you design a complex set of functions, it is a good idea to carry out a manual walk-through before entrusting your program to the computer.

Take an index card, or some other piece of paper, and write down the function call that you want to study. Write the name of the function and the names and values of the parameter variables, like this:

int_name(number = 416)	
part	name

Then write the names of the function variables. Write them in a table, since you will update them as you walk through the code.

int_name(number = 416)	
part	name
416	""

We enter the test part >= 100. part / 100 is 4 and part % 100 is 16. digit_name(4) is easily seen to be "four". (Had digit_name been complicated, you would have started another sheet of paper to figure out that function call. It is quite common to accumulate several sheets in this way.)

Now name has changed to name + " " + digit_name(part / 100) + " hundred", that is "four hundred", and part has changed to part % 100, or 16.

int_name(number = 416)	
part	name
~~416~~	~~""~~
16	"four hundred"

Now you enter the branch part >= 10. teens_name(16) is sixteen, so the variables now have the values

int_name(number = 416)	
part	name
~~416~~	~~""~~
~~16~~	~~"four hundred"~~
0	"four hundred sixteen"

Now it becomes clear why you need to set part to 0. Otherwise, you would enter the next branch and the result would be "four hundred sixteen six". Tracing the code is an effective way to understand the subtle aspects of a function.

PRODUCTIVITY HINT 5.4

Stubs

When writing a larger program, it is not always feasible to implement and test all functions at once. You often need to test a function that calls another, but the other function hasn't yet been implemented. Then you can temporarily replace the missing function with a *stub*. A stub is a function that returns a simple value that is sufficient for testing another function. Here are examples of stub functions.

```
/**
    Turns a digit into its English name.
    @param digit  an integer between 1 and 9
    @return the name of digit ("one" ... "nine")
*/
string digit_name(int digit)
{
    return "mumble";
}

/**
    Gives the name of the tens part of a number between 20 and 99.
    @param number  an integer between 20 and 99
    @return the tens name of the number ("twenty" ... "ninety")
*/
string tens_name(int number)
{
    return "mumblety";
}
```

If you combine these stubs with the int_name function and test it with a parameter value of 274, you will get a result of "mumble hundred mumblety mumble", which indicates that the basic logic of the int_name function is working correctly.

WORKED EXAMPLE 5.2

Calculating a Course Grade

This Worked Example uses stepwise refinement to solve the problem of converting a set of letter grades into an average grade for a course.

5.7 Variable Scope and Global Variables

It is possible to define the same variable name more than once in a program. When the variable name is used, you need to know to which definition it belongs. In this section, we discuss the rules for dealing with multiple definitions of the same name.

In the same way that there can be a street named "Main Street" in different cities, a C++ program can have multiple variables with the same name.

The scope of a variable is the part of the program in which it is visible.

A variable that is defined within a function is visible from the point at which it is defined until the end of the block in which it was defined. This area is called the *scope* of the variable.

Consider the volume variables in the following example:

```cpp
double cube_volume(double side_length)
{
   double volume = side_length * side_length * side_length;
   return volume;
}

int main()
{
   double volume = cube_volume(2);
   cout << volume << endl;

   return 0;
}
```

Each volume variable is defined in a separate function, and their scopes do not overlap.

It is not legal to define two variables with the same name in the same scope. For example, the following is not legal:

```
int main()
{
    double volume = cube_volume(2);
    double volume = cube_volume(10);
        // ERROR: cannot define another volume variable in this scope
    ...
}
```

However, you can define another variable with the same name in a *nested block*. Here, we define two variables called amount.

```
double withdraw(double balance, double amount)
{
    if (...)
    {
        double amount = 10; // Another variable named amount
        ...
    }
    ...
}
```

The scope of the parameter variable amount is the entire function, *except* the nested block. Inside the nested block, amount refers to the variable that was defined in that block. You should avoid this potentially confusing situation in the functions that you write, simply by renaming one of the variables.

A local variable is defined inside a function. A global variable is defined outside a function.

Variables that are defined inside functions are called *local variables*. C++ also supports *global variables:* variables that are defined outside functions. A global variable is visible to all functions that are defined after it. For example, the <iostream> header defines global variables cin and cout.

Here is an example of a global variable:

```
int balance = 10000; // A global variable

void withdraw(double amount)
{
    if (balance >= amount)
    {
        balance = balance - amount;
    }
}

int main()
{
    withdraw(1000);
    cout << balance << endl;
    return 0;
}
```

The scope of the variable balance extends over both the withdraw and the main functions.

Generally, global variables are not a good idea. When multiple functions update global variables, the result can be difficult to predict. Particularly in larger programs that are developed by multiple programmers, it is very important that the effect of each function be clear and easy to understand. You should avoid global variables in your programs.

SELF CHECK

Consider this program:

```
1   int x;
2   int mystery(int x)
3   {
4      int s = 0;
5      for (int i = 0; i < x; x++)
6      {
7         int x = i + 1;
8         s = s + x;
9      }
10     return x;
11  }
12  int main()
13  {
14     x = 4;
15     int s = mystery(x);
16     cout << s << endl;
17  }
```

23. Which line defines a global variable?

24. Which lines define local variables named x?

25. Which lines are in the scope of the definition of x in line 2?

26. Which variable is changed by the assignment in line 14?

27. This program defines two variables with the same name whose scopes don't overlap. What are they?

QUALITY TIP 5.3

Avoid Global Variables

There are a few cases where global variables are required (such as cin and cout), but they are quite rare. Programs with global variables are difficult to maintain and extend because you can no longer view each function as a "black box" that simply receives parameter values and returns a result. When functions modify global variables, it becomes more difficult to understand the effect of function calls. As programs get larger, this difficulty mounts quickly. Instead of using global variables, use function parameters to transfer information from one part of a program to another.

5.8 Reference Parameters

If you want to write a function that changes the value of a parameter, you must use a *reference parameter* in order to allow the change. We first explain why a different parameter type is necessary, then we show you the syntax for reference parameters.

Consider a function that simulates withdrawing a given amount of money from a bank account, provided that sufficient funds are available. If the amount of money is insufficient, a $10 penalty is deducted instead. The function would be used as follows:

```
double harrys_account = 1000;
withdraw(harrys_account, 100); // Now harrys_account is 900
withdraw(harrys_account, 1000); // Insufficient funds. Now harrys_account is 890
```

Here is a first attempt:

```
void withdraw(double balance, double amount) // Does not work
{
   const double PENALTY = 10;
   if (balance >= amount)
   {
      balance = balance - amount;
   }
   else
   {
      balance = balance - PENALTY;
   }
}
```

But this doesn't work.

Let's walk through the function call `withdraw(harrys_account, 100)`—see Figure 7. As the function starts, the parameter variable `balance` is created ❶ and set to the same value as `harrys_account`, and `amount` is set to 100 ❷. Then `balance` is modified ❸. Of course, that modification has no effect on `harrys_account`, because `balance` is a separate variable. When the function returns, `balance` is forgotten, and no money was withdrawn from `harrys_account` ❹.

A parameter such as `balance` is called a *value parameter*, because it is initialized with a value supplied by the caller. All parameters in the functions that we have written so far have been value parameters. In this situation, though, we don't just want `balance` to have the same value as `harrys_account`. We want `balance` to refer to the actual variable `harrys_account` (or `joes_account` or whatever variable is supplied in the call). The contents of *that* variable should be updated.

> A reference parameter refers to a variable that is supplied in a function call.

You use a reference parameter when you want to update a variable that was supplied in the function call. When we make `balance` into a reference parameter, then `balance` is not a new variable but a reference to an existing variable. Any change in `balance` is actually a change in the variable to which `balance` refers in that particular call.

Figure 8 shows the difference between value and reference parameters.

To indicate a reference parameter, you place an & after the type name.

```
void withdraw(double& balance, double amount)
```

1 Function call | harrys_account = 1000

balance =

amount =

2 Initializing function parameters | harrys_account = 1000

balance = 1000

amount = 100

3 About to return to the caller | harrys_account = 1000

balance = 900

amount = 100

4 After function call | harrys_account = 1000

Figure 7   Value Parameters

The type double& is read "a reference to a double" or, more briefly, "double ref".

The withdraw function has two parameters: one of type "double ref" and the other a value parameter of type double. The body of the function is unchanged. What has changed is the meaning of the assignments to the balance variable.

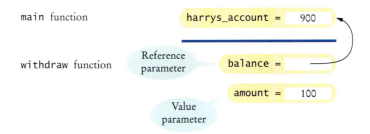

main function   harrys_account = 900

withdraw function   Reference parameter   balance =

amount = 100

Value parameter

Figure 8   Reference and Value Parameters

A reference parameter for a bank balance is like an ATM card—it allows you to change the balance. In contrast, a value parameter can only tell you the balance.

The assignment

```
balance = balance - amount;
```

now changes the variable that was passed to the function. For example, the call

```
withdraw(harrys_account, 500);
```

modifies the variable harrys_account, and the call

```
withdraw(sallys_account, 150);
```

modifies the variable sallys_account.

A reference parameter must always be called with a *variable*. It would be an error to supply a number:

```
withdraw(1000, 500); // Error: reference parameter must be a variable
```

The reason is clear—the function modifies the reference parameter, but it is impossible to change the value of a number. For the same reason, you cannot supply an expression:

```
withdraw(harrys_account + 150, 500);
    // Error: reference parameter must be a variable
```

ch05/account.cpp

```
 1  #include <iostream>
 2
 3  using namespace std;
 4
 5  /**
 6      Withdraws the amount from the given balance, or withdraws
 7      a penalty if the balance is insufficient.
 8      @param balance  the balance from which to make the withdrawal
 9      @param amount  the amount to withdraw
10  */
11  void withdraw(double& balance, double amount)
12  {
```

```
13      const double PENALTY = 10;
14      if (balance >= amount)
15      {
16          balance = balance - amount;
17      }
18      else
19      {
20          balance = balance - PENALTY;
21      }
22   }
23
24   int main()
25   {
26      double harrys_account = 1000;
27      double sallys_account = 500;
28      withdraw(harrys_account, 100);
29          // Now harrys_account is 900
30      withdraw(harrys_account, 1000); // Insufficient funds
31          // Now harrys_account is 890
32      withdraw(sallys_account, 150);
33      cout << "Harry's account: " << harrys_account << endl;
34      cout << "Sally's account: " << sallys_account << endl;
35
36      return 0;
37   }
```

Program Run

```
Harry's account: 890
Sally's account: 350
```

SELF CHECK

28. Would the withdraw function work correctly if the amount parameter was defined as double& instead of double?

29. The following function is intended to transfer the given amount of money from one account to another. Supply the function parameters.

```
void transfer(...)
{
    if (balance1 >= amount)
    {
        balance1 = balance1 - amount;
        balance2 = balance2 + amount;
    }
}
```

30. Change the withdraw function so that it returns a bool value indicating whether the withdrawal was successful. Do not charge a penalty if the balance was insufficient.

31. Write a function minmax so that the call minmax(x, y, a, b) sets a to the smaller of x and y and b to the larger of x and y.

32. What does this program print?

```
void mystery(int& a, int& b)
{
   a = a - b;
   b = b + a;
   a = b - a;
}
int main()
{
   int x = 4;
   int y = 3;
   mystery(x, y);
   cout << x << " " << y << endl;
}
```

QUALITY TIP 5.4

Prefer Return Values to Reference Parameters

Some programmers use reference parameters as a mechanism for setting the result of a function. For example,

```
void cube_volume(double side_length, double& volume)
{
   volume = side_length * side_length * side_length;
}
```

However, this function is less convenient than our previous cube_volume function. It cannot be used in expressions such as cout << cube_volume(2).

Use a reference parameter only when a function needs to update a variable.

ADVANCED TOPIC 5.2

Constant References

It is not very efficient to have a value parameter that is a large object (such as a string value). Copying the object into parameter value is less efficient than using a reference parameter. With a reference parameter, only the location of the variable, not its value, needs to be communicated to the function.

You can instruct the compiler to give you the efficiency of call by reference and the meaning of call by value, by using a *constant reference* as shown below. The function

```
void shout(const string& str)
{
   cout << str << "!!!" << endl;
}
```

works exactly the same as the function

```
void shout(string str)
{
```

```
        cout << str << "!!!" << endl;
    }
```

There is just one difference: Calls to the first function execute a bit faster.

5.9 Recursive Functions (Optional)

A recursive function is a function that calls itself. This is not as unusual as it sounds at first. Suppose you face the arduous task of cleaning up an entire house. You may well say to yourself, "I'll pick a room and clean it, and then I'll clean the other rooms." In other words, the cleanup task calls itself, but with a simpler input. Eventually, all the rooms will be cleaned.

Cleaning up a house can be solved recursively: Clean one room, then clean up the rest.

In C++, a recursive function uses the same principle. Here is a typical example. We want to print triangle patterns like this:

```
[]
[][]
[][][]
[][][][]
```

Specifically, our task is to provide a function

```
void print_triangle(int side_length)
```

The triangle given above is printed by calling `print_triangle(4)`. To see how recursion helps, consider how a triangle with side length 4 can be obtained from a triangle with side length 3.

```
[]
[][]
[][][]
[][][][]
```

Print the triangle with side length 3.
Print a line with four [].

More generally, here are the C++ instructions for an arbitrary side length:

```
print_triangle(side_length - 1);
for (int i = 0; i < side_length; i++)
{
   cout << "[]";
}
cout << endl;
```

There is just one problem with this idea. When the side length is 1, we don't want to call print_triangle(0), print_triangle(-1), and so on. The solution is simply to treat this as a special case, and not to print anything when side_length is less than 1.

```
void print_triangle(int side_length)
{
   if (side_length < 1) return;
   print_triangle(side_length - 1);
   for (int i = 0; i < side_length; i++)
   {
      cout << "[]";
   }
   cout << endl;
}
```

A recursive computation solves a problem by using the solution of the same problem with simpler inputs.

Look at the print_triangle function one more time and notice how utterly reasonable it is. If the side length is 0, nothing needs to be printed. The next part is just as reasonable. Print the smaller triangle *and don't think about why that works*. Then print a row of []. Clearly, the result is a triangle of the desired size.

There are two key requirements to make sure that the recursion is successful:

- Every recursive call must simplify the task in some way.
- There must be special cases to handle the simplest tasks directly.

For a recursion to terminate, there must be special cases for the simplest inputs.

The print_triangle function calls itself again with smaller and smaller side lengths. Eventually the side length must reach 0, and the function stops calling itself.

Here is what happens when we print a triangle with side length 4.

- The call print_triangle(4) calls print_triangle(3).
  - The call print_triangle(3) calls print_triangle(2).
    - The call print_triangle(2) calls print_triangle(1).
      - The call print_triangle(1) calls print_triangle(0).
        - The call print_triangle(0) returns, doing nothing.
      - The call print_triangle(1) prints [].
    - The call print_triangle(2) prints [][].
  - The call print_triangle(3) prints [][][].
- The call print_triangle(4) prints [][][][].

This set of Russian dolls looks similar to the call pattern of a recursive function.

The call pattern of a recursive function looks complicated, and the key to the successful design of a recursive function is *not to think about it*.

Recursion is not really necessary to print triangle shapes. You can use nested loops, like this:

```
for (int i = 0; i < side_length; i++)
{
   for (int j = 0; j < i; j++)
   {
      cout << "[]";
   }
   cout << endl;
}
```

However, this pair of loops is a bit tricky. Many people find the recursive solution simpler to understand.

SELF CHECK

33. Consider this slight modification of the print_triangle function:

```
void print_triangle(int side_length)
{
   if (side_length < 1) return;
   for (int i = 0; i < side_length; i++)
   {
      cout << "[]";
   }
   cout << endl;
   print_triangle(side_length - 1);
}
```

What is the result of print_triangle(4)?

34. Consider this recursive function:

```
int mystery(int n)
{
   if (n <= 0) { return 0; }
   return n + mystery(n - 1);
}
```

What is mystery(4)?

35. Consider this recursive function:

```
int mystery(int n)
{
   if (n <= 0) { return 0; }
   return mystery(n / 2) + 1;
}
```

What is mystery(20)?

36. Write a recursive function for printing n box shapes [] in a row.

37. The int_name function in Section 5.6 accepted parameter values < 1,000. Using a recursive call, extend its range to 999,999. For example an input of 12,345 should return "twelve thousand three hundred forty five".

How To 5.2

Thinking Recursively

To solve a problem recursively requires a different mindset than to solve it by programming loops. In fact, it helps if you are, or pretend to be, a bit lazy and let others do most of the work for you. If you need to solve a complex problem, pretend that "someone else" will do most of the heavy lifting and solve the problem for all simpler inputs. Then you only need to figure out how you can turn the solutions with simpler inputs into a solution for the whole problem.

To illustrate the recursive thinking process, consider the problem of Productivity Hint 4.1, to compute the sum of the digits of a number. We want to design a function digit_sum that computes the sum of the digits of an integer n. For example, digit_sum(1729) = 1 + 7 + 2 + 9 = 19.

Step 1 Break the input into parts that can themselves be inputs to the problem.

> The key step to finding a recursive solution is reducing the input to a simpler input for the same problem.

In your mind, fix a particular input or set of inputs for the task that you want to solve, and think how you can simplify the inputs. Look for simplifications that can be solved by the same task, and whose solutions are related to the original task.

In the digit sum problem, consider how we can simplify an input such as n = 1729. Would it help to subtract 1? After all, digit_sum(1729) = digit_sum(1728) + 1. But consider n = 1000. There seems to be no obvious relationship between digit_sum(1000) and digit_sum(999).

A much more promising idea is to remove the last digit, that is, compute n / 10 = 172. The digit sum of 172 is directly related to the digit sum of 1729.

Step 2 Combine solutions with simpler inputs into a solution of the original problem.

In your mind, consider the solutions for the simpler inputs that you have discovered in Step 1. Don't worry *how* those solutions are obtained. Simply have faith that the solutions are readily available. Just say to yourself: These are simpler inputs, so someone else will solve the problem for me.

> When designing a recursive solution, do not worry about multiple nested calls. Simply focus on reducing a problem to a slightly simpler one.

In the case of the digit sum task, ask yourself how you can obtain digit_sum(1729) if you know digit_sum(172). You simply add the last digit (9), and you are done. How do you get the last digit? As the remainder n % 10. The value digit_sum(n) can therefore be obtained as

```
digit_sum(n / 10) + n % 10
```

Don't worry how digit_sum(n / 10) is computed. The input is smaller, and therefore it just works.

Step 3   Find solutions to the simplest inputs.

A recursive computation keeps simplifying its inputs. To make sure that the recursion comes to a stop, you must deal with the simplest inputs separately. Come up with special solutions for them. That is usually very easy.

Look at the simplest inputs for the digit_sum test:

- A number with a single digit
- 0

A number with a single digit is its own digit sum, so you can stop the recursion when n < 10, and return n in that case. Or, if you prefer, you can be even lazier. If n has a single digit, then digit_sum(n / 10) + n % 10 equals digit_sum(0) + n. You can simply terminate the recursion when n is zero.

Step 4   Implement the solution by combining the simple cases and the reduction step.

Now you are ready to implement the solution. Make separate cases for the simple inputs that you considered in Step 3. If the input isn't one of the simplest cases, then implement the logic you discovered in Step 2.

Here is the complete digit_sum function:

```
int digit_sum(int n)
{
    // Special case for terminating the recursion
    if (n == 0) return 0;
    // General case
    return digit_sum(n / 10) + n % 10;
}
```

Random Fact 5.1

The Explosive Growth of Personal Computers

In 1971, Marcian E. "Ted" Hoff, an engineer at Intel Corporation, was working on a chip for a manufacturer of electronic calculators. He realized that it would be a better idea to develop a *general-purpose* chip that could be *programmed* to interface with the keys and display of a calculator, rather than to do yet another custom design. Thus, the *microprocessor* was born. At the time, its primary application was as a controller for calculators, washing machines, and the like. It took years for the computer industry to notice that a genuine central processing unit was now available as a single chip.

Hobbyists were the first to catch on. In 1974 the first computer *kit,* the Altair 8800, was available from MITS Electronics for about $350. The kit consisted of the microprocessor, a circuit board, a very small amount of memory, toggle switches, and a row of display lights. Purchasers had to solder and assemble it, then program it in machine language through the toggle switches. It was not a big hit.

The first big hit was the Apple II. It was a real computer with a keyboard, a monitor, and a floppy disk drive. When it was first released, users had a $3,000 machine that could play Space Invaders, run a primitive bookkeeping program, or let users program it in BASIC. The original Apple II did not even support lowercase letters, making it worthless for word processing. The breakthrough came in 1979 with a new spreadsheet program, VisiCalc. In a spreadsheet, you enter financial data and their relationships into a grid of rows and columns (see Figure 9). Then you modify some of the data and watch in real time how the others

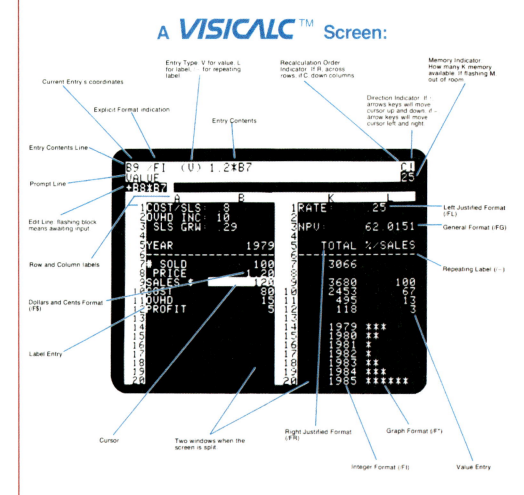

Figure 9   The VisiCalc Spreadsheet Running on an Apple II

change. For example, you can see how changing the mix of widgets in a manufacturing plant might affect estimated costs and profits. Middle managers in companies, who understood computers and were fed up with having to wait for hours or days to get their data runs back from the computing center, snapped up VisiCalc and the computer that was needed to run it. For them, the computer was a spreadsheet machine.

The next big hit was the IBM Personal Computer, ever after known as the PC. It was the first widely available personal computer that used Intel's 16-bit processor, the 8086, whose successors are still being used in personal computers today. The success of the PC was based not on any engineering breakthroughs but on the fact that it was easy to *clone*. IBM published specifications for plug-in cards, and it went one step further. It published the exact source code of the so-called BIOS (Basic Input/Output System), which controls the keyboard, monitor, ports, and disk drives and must be installed in ROM form in every PC. This allowed third-party vendors of plug-in cards to ensure that the BIOS code, and third-party extensions of it, interacted correctly with the equipment. Of course, the code itself was the property of IBM and could not be copied legally. Perhaps IBM did not foresee that functionally equivalent versions of the BIOS nevertheless could be recreated by others. Compaq, one of the first clone vendors, had fifteen engineers, who certified that they had never seen the original IBM code, write a new version that conformed precisely to the IBM specifications. Other companies did the same, and soon a variety of vendors were selling computers that ran the same software as IBM's PC but distinguished themselves by a lower price, increased portability, or better performance. In time, IBM lost its dominant position in the PC market. It is now one of many companies producing IBM PC-compatible computers.

IBM never produced an *operating system* for its PCs—that is, the software that organizes the interaction between the user and the computer, starts application programs, and manages disk storage and other resources. Instead, IBM offered customers the option of three separate operating systems. Most customers couldn't care less about the operating system. They chose the system that was able to launch most of the few applications that existed at the time. It happened to be DOS (Disk Operating System) by Microsoft. Microsoft cheerfully licensed the same operating system to other hardware vendors and encouraged software companies to write DOS applications. A huge number of useful application programs for PC-compatible machines was the result.

PC applications were certainly useful, but they were not easy to learn. Every vendor developed a different *user interface:* the collection of keystrokes, menu options, and settings that a user needed to master to use a software package effectively. Data exchange between applications was difficult, because each program used a different data format. The Apple Macintosh changed all that in 1984. The designers of the Macintosh had the vision to supply an intuitive user interface with the computer and to force software developers to adhere to it. It took Microsoft and PC-compatible manufacturers years to catch up.

Most personal computers are used for accessing information from online sources, entertainment, word processing, and home finance (banking, budgeting, taxes). Some analysts predict that the personal computer will merge with the television set and cable network into an entertainment and information appliance.

CHAPTER SUMMARY

1. A function is a named sequence of instructions.

2. Parameter values are supplied when a function is called. The return value is the result that the function computes.

3. When defining a function, you provide a name for the function, a name and type for each parameter, and a type for the result.

4. Function comments explain the purpose of the function, the meaning of the parameters and return value, as well as any special requirements.

5. Parameter variables hold the parameter values supplied in the function call.

6. The return statement terminates a function call and yields the function result.

7. Turn computations that can be reused into functions.

8. Use a return type of void to indicate that a function does not return a value.

9. Use the process of stepwise refinement to decompose complex tasks into simpler ones.

10. The scope of a variable is the part of the program in which it is visible.

11. A local variable is defined inside a function. A global variable is defined outside a function.

12. A reference parameter refers to a variable that is supplied in a function call.

13. A recursive computation solves a problem by using the solution of the same problem with simpler inputs.

14. For a recursion to terminate, there must be special cases for the simplest inputs.

15. The key step to finding a recursive solution is reducing the input to a simpler input for the same problem.

16. When designing a recursive solution, do not worry about multiple nested calls. Simply focus on reducing a problem to a slightly simpler one.

REVIEW EXERCISES

Exercise R5.1. In which sequence are the lines of the program cube.cpp on page 190 executed, starting with the first line of main?

Exercise R5.2. Give examples of the following, either from the C++ library or from the functions discussed in this chapter:

a. A function with two double parameters and a double return value
b. A function with a double parameter and a double return value
c. A function with two int parameters and an int return value
d. A function with an int parameter and a string return value
e. A function with a string parameter and no return value
f. A function with a double& and a double parameter and no return value
g. A function with no parameter and an int return value

Exercise R5.3. True or false?

a. A function has exactly one return statement.
b. A function has at least one return statement.
c. A function has at most one return value.
d. A function with return value void never has a return statement.
e. When executing a return statement, the function exits immediately.
f. A function with return value void must print a result.
g. A function without parameters always returns the same value.

Exercise R5.4. Consider these functions:

```
double f(double x) { return g(x) + sqrt(h(x)); }
double g(double x) { return 4 * h(x); }
double h(double x) { return x * x + k(x) - 1; }
double k(double x) { return 2 * (x + 1); }
```

Without actually compiling and running a program, determine the results of the following function calls.

a. double x1 = f(2);
b. double x2 = g(h(2));
c. double x3 = k(g(2) + h(2));
d. double x4 = f(0) + f(1) + f(2);
e. double x5 = f(-1) + g(-1) + h(-1) + k(-1);

Exercise R5.5. What is the difference between a parameter value and a return value? What is the difference between a parameter value and a parameter variable? What is the difference between a parameter value and a value parameter?

Exercise R5.6. Write pseudocode for a function that translates a telephone number with letters in it (such as 1-800-FLOWERS) into the actual phone number. Use the standard letters on a phone pad.

Exercise R5.7. For each of the variables in the following program, indicate the scope. Then determine what the program prints, without actually running the program.

```cpp
int a = 0;
int b = 0;
int f(int c)
{
   int n = 0;
   a = c;
   if (n < c)
   {
      n = a + b;
   }
   return n;
}

int g(int c)
{
   int n = 0;
   int a = c;
   if (n < f(c))
   {
      n = a + b;
   }
   return n;
}

int main()
{
   int i = 1;
   int b = g(i);
   cout << a + b + i << endl;
   return 0;
}
```

Exercise R5.8. We have seen three kinds of variables in C++: global variables, parameter variables, and local variables. Classify the variables of Exercise R5.7 according to these categories.

Exercise R5.9. Use the process of stepwise refinement to describe the process of making scrambled eggs. Discuss what you do if you do not find eggs in the refrigerator.

Exercise R5.10. How many parameters does the following function have? How many return values does it have? *Hint:* The C++ notions of "parameter value" and "return value" are not the same as the intuitive notions of "input" and "output".

```
void average(double& avg)
{
    cout << "Please enter two numbers: ";
    double x;
    double y;
    cin >> x >> y;
    avg = (x + y) / 2;
}
```

Exercise R5.11. Perform a walkthrough of the int_name function with the following parameter values:

a. 5

b. 12

c. 21

d. 301

e. 324

f. 0

g. -2

Exercise R5.12. Consider the following function:

```
int f(int n)
{
    if (n <= 1) { return 1; }
    if (n % 2 == 0) // n is even
    {
        return f(n / 2);
    }
    else { return f(3 * n + 1); }
}
```

Perform traces of the computations f(1), f(2), f(3), f(4), f(5), f(6), f(7), f(8), f(9), and f(10).

Exercise R5.13. Consider the following function that is intended to swap the values of two integers:

```
void false_swap1(int& a, int& b)
{
    a = b;
    b = a;
}

int main()
{
    int x = 3;
    int y = 4;
    false_swap1(x, y);
    cout << x << " " << y << endl;
    return 0;
```

```
   }
```

Why doesn't the function swap the contents of x and y? How can you rewrite the function to work correctly?

Exercise R5.14. Consider the following function that is intended to swap the values of two integers:

```
void false_swap2(int a, int b)
{
   int temp = a;
   a = b;
   b = temp;
}

int main()
{
   int x = 3;
   int y = 4;
   false_swap2(x, y);
   cout << x << " " << y << endl;
   return 0;
}
```

Why doesn't the function swap the contents of x and y? How can you rewrite the function to work correctly?

Exercise R5.15. The following function swaps two integers, without requiring a temporary variable.

```
void tricky_swap(int& a, int& b)
{
   a = a - b;
   b = a + b;
   a = b - a;
}
```

However, it fails in one important case, namely when calling tricky_swap(x, x). Explain what should happen and what actually happens.

Exercise R5.16. Give pseudocode for a recursive function for printing all substrings of a given string. For example, the substrings of the string "rum" are "rum" itself, "ru", "um", "r", "u", "m", and the empty string. You may assume that all letters of the string are different.

Exercise R5.17. Give pseudocode for a recursive function that sorts all letters in a string. For example, the string "goodbye" would be sorted into "bdegooy".

PROGRAMMING EXERCISES

Exercise P5.1. Write a function that computes the balance of a bank account with a given initial balance and interest rate, after a given number of years. Assume interest is compounded yearly.

Exercise P5.2. Write a function

```
string repeat(string str, int n)
```

that returns the string str repeated n times. For example, repeat("ho", 3) returns
"hohoho".

Exercise P5.3. Write a function

```
int count_vowels(string str)
```

that returns a count of all vowels in the string str. Vowels are the letters a, e, i, o,
and u, and their uppercase variants.

Exercise P5.4. Write a function

```
int count_words(string str)
```

that returns a count of all words in the string str. Words are separated by spaces.
For example, count_words("Mary had a little lamb") should return 5.

Exercise P5.5. It is a well-known phenomenon that most people are easily able to
read a text whose words have two characters flipped, provided the first and last letter of each word are not changed. For example:

I dn'ot gvie a dman for a man taht can olny sepll a wrod one way. (Mrak Taiwn)

Write a function string scramble(string word) that constructs a scrambled version
of a given word, randomly flipping two characters other than the first and last one.
Then write a program that reads words from cin and prints the scrambled words.

Exercise P5.6. Write functions

```
double sphere_volume(double r)
double sphere_surface(double r)
double cylinder_volume(double r, double h)
double cylinder_surface(double r, double h)
double cone_volume(double r, double h)
double cone_surface(double r, double h)
```

that compute the volume and surface area of a sphere with radius r, a cylinder with
a circular base with radius r and height h, and a cone with a circular base with radius
r and height h. Then write a program that prompts the user for the values of r and h,
calls the six functions, and prints the results.

Exercise P5.7. Write a function

```
double read_double(string prompt)
```

that displays the prompt string, followed by a space, reads a floating-point number
in, and returns it. Here is a typical usage:

```
salary = read_double("Please enter your salary:");
perc_raise = read_double("What percentage raise would you like?");
```

Exercise P5.8. Write a function void sort2(int& a, int& b) that swaps the values of a and b if a is greater than b and otherwise leaves a and b unchanged. For example,

```
int u = 2;
int v = 3;
int w = 4;
int x = 1;
sort2(u, v); // u is still 2, v is still 3
sort2(w, x); // w is now 1, x is now 4
```

Exercise P5.9. Write a function sort3(int& a, int& b, int& c) that swaps its three parameters to arrange them in sorted order. For example,

```
int v = 3;
int w = 4;
int x = 1;
sort3(v, w, x); // v is now 1, w is now 3, x is now 4
```

Hint: Use sort2 of Exercise P5.8.

Exercise P5.10. Enhance the int_name function so that it works correctly for values < 1,000,000,000.

Exercise P5.11. Enhance the int_name function so that it works correctly for negative values and zero. *Caution:* Make sure the improved function doesn't print 20 as "twenty zero".

Exercise P5.12. For some values (for example, 20), the int_name function returns a string with a leading space (" twenty"). Repair that blemish and ensure that spaces are inserted only when necessary. *Hint:* There are two ways of accomplishing this. Either ensure that leading spaces are never inserted, or remove leading spaces from the result before returning it.

Exercise P5.13. Write a program that prints a paycheck. Ask the program user for the name of the employee, the hourly rate, and the number of hours worked. If the number of hours exceeds 40, the employee is paid "time and a half", that is, 150 percent of the hourly rate on the hours exceeding 40. Your check should look similar to that in Figure 6. Use fictitious names for the payer and the bank. Be sure to use stepwise refinement and break your solution into several functions. Use the int_name function to print the dollar amount of the check.

Exercise P5.14. *Leap years.* Write a function

```
bool leap_year(int year)
```

that tests whether a year is a leap year: that is, a year with 366 days. Leap years are necessary to keep the calendar synchronized with the sun because the earth revolves around the sun once every 365.25 days. Actually, that figure is not entirely precise, and for all dates after 1582 the *Gregorian correction* applies. Usually years that are divisible by 4 are leap years, for example 1996. However, years that are divisible by 100 (for example, 1900) are not leap years, but years that are divisible by 400 are leap years (for example, 2000).

Exercise P5.15. Write a program that converts a Roman number such as MCMLXX-VIII to its decimal number representation. *Hint:* First write a function that yields the numeric value of each of the letters. Then use the following algorithm:

```
total = 0
While the roman number string is not empty
{
    If the first character has a larger value than the second, or the string has length 1
    {
        Add value(first character) to total.
        Remove the character.
    }
    Else
    {
        Add value(second character) – value(first character) to total.
        Remove both characters.
    }
}
```

Exercise P5.16. In Exercise P3.22 you were asked to write a program to convert a number to its representation in Roman numerals. At the time, you did not know how to factor out common code, and as a consequence the resulting program was rather long. Rewrite that program by implementing and using the following function:

```
string roman_digit(int n, string one, string five, string ten)
```

That function translates one digit, using the strings specified for the one, five, and ten values. You would call the function as follows:

```
roman_ones = roman_digit(n % 10, "I", "V", "X");
n = n / 10;
roman_tens = roman_digit(n % 10, "X", "L", "C");
...
```

Exercise P5.17. *Postal bar codes.* For faster sorting of letters, the United States Postal Service encourages companies that send large volumes of mail to use a bar code denoting the zip code (see Figure 10).

The encoding scheme for a five-digit zip code is shown in Figure 11. There are full-height frame bars on each side. The five encoded digits are followed by a check

Figure 10 A Postal Bar Code

Figure 11 Encoding for Five-Digit Bar Codes

digit, which is computed as follows: Add up all digits, and choose the check digit to make the sum a multiple of 10. For example, the zip code 95014 has a sum of 19, so the check digit is 1 to make the sum equal to 20.

Each digit of the zip code, and the check digit, is encoded according to the following table where 0 denotes a half bar and 1 a full bar.

	7	4	2	1	0
1	0	0	0	1	1
2	0	0	1	0	1
3	0	0	1	1	0
4	0	1	0	0	1
5	0	1	0	1	0
6	0	1	1	0	0
7	1	0	0	0	1
8	1	0	0	1	0
9	1	0	1	0	0
0	1	1	0	0	0

The digit can be easily computed from the bar code using the column weights 7, 4, 2, 1, 0. For example, 01100 is $0 \times 7 + 1 \times 4 + 1 \times 2 + 0 \times 1 \times 0 \times 0 = 6$. The only exception is 0, which would yield 11 according to the weight formula.

Write a program that asks the user for a zip code and prints the bar code. Use : for half bars, | for full bars. For example, 95014 becomes

```
||:|:::|:|:||::::::||:|::|:::|||
```

Exercise P5.18. Write a program that reads in a bar code (with : denoting half bars and | denoting full bars) and prints out the zip code it represents. Print an error message if the bar code is not correct.

Exercise P5.19. Write a program that prints instructions to get coffee, asking the user for input whenever a decision needs to be made. Decompose each task into a function, for example:

```
void brew_coffee()
{
   cout << "Add water to the coffee maker." << endl;
   cout << "Put a filter in the coffee maker." << endl;
   grind_coffee();
   cout << "Put the coffee in the filter." << endl;
   ...
}
```

Exercise P5.20. Write a recursive function

```
string reverse(string str)
```

that computes the reverse of a string. For example, `reverse("flow")` should return "wolf". *Hint:* Reverse the substring starting at the second character, then add the first character at the end. For example, to reverse "flow", first reverse "low" to "wol", then add the "f" at the end.

Exercise P5.21. Write a recursive function

```
bool is_palindrome(string str)
```

that returns `true` if `str` is a palindrome, that is, a word that is the same when reversed. Examples of palindrome are "deed", "rotor", or "aibohphobia". *Hint:* A word is a palindrome if the first and last letters match and the remainder is also a palindrome.

Exercise P5.22. Use recursion to implement a function `bool find(string str, string match)` that tests whether `match` is contained in `str`:

```
bool b = find("Mississippi", "sip"); // Sets b to true
```

Hint: If `str` starts with `match`, then you are done. If not, consider the string that you obtain by removing the first character.

Exercise P5.23. Use recursion to determine the number of digits in a number n. *Hint:* If n is < 10, it has one digit. Otherwise, it has one more digit than n / 10.

Exercise P5.24. Use recursion to compute a^n, where n is a positive integer. *Hint:* If n is 1, then $a^n = a$. If n is even, then $a^n = (a^{n/2})^2$. Otherwise, $a^n = a \times a^{n-1}$.

ANSWERS TO SELF-CHECK QUESTIONS

1. The parameter values are 3 and 2. The return value is 9.
2. The inner call to pow returns $2^2 = 4$. Therefore, the outer call returns $4^2 = 16$.
3. 3
4. Users of the function can treat it as a *black box*.
5. 27
6. $8 \times 8 \times 8 = 512$
7. ```
double volume = pow(side_length, 3);
return volume;
```
8. ```
double square_area(double side_length)
{
   double area = side_length * side_length;
   return area;
}
```
9. `(2 + 3) / (3 - 2) = 5`

10. When the function is called, x is set to 5, y is set to 7, and z becomes 12. Then z is changed to 6, and that value is returned and printed.

11. When the function is called, x is set to 5. Then y is set to 25, and that value is returned and printed.

12. When the function is called, n is set to 5. Then n is incremented twice, setting it to 7. That value is returned and printed.

13.
```
box_string("Hello");
box_string("World");
```

14. The box_string function does not return a value. Therefore, you cannot use it in a << expression.

15.
```
void shout(string str)
{
   cout << str << "!!!" << endl;
}
```

16.
```
void box_string(string str)
{
   int n = str.length();
   for (int i = 0; i < n + 4; i++) { cout << "-"; }
   cout << endl;
   cout << "! " << str << " !" << endl;
   for (int i = 0; i < n + 4; i++) { cout << "-"; }
   cout << endl;
}
```

17.
```
void print_line(int count)
{
   for (int i = 0; i < count; i++) { cout << "-"; }
   cout << endl;
}
void box_string(string str)
{
   int n = str.length();
   print_line(n + 2);
   cout << "!" << str << "!" << endl;
   print_line(n + 2);
}
```

18. Change line 75 to
```
name = name + digit_name(part / 100) + " hundred";
```
In line 72, add the statement
```
if (part >= 1000)
{
   name = digit_name(part / 1000) + "thousand ";
   part = part % 1000;
}
```
In line 65, change 1000 to 10000 in the comment.

19. In the case of "teens", we already have the last digit as part of the name.

20. Nothing is printed. One way of dealing with this case is to add the following statement before line 70.

```
if (number == 0) { return "zero"; }
```

21. Here is the approximate trace:

int_name(number = 72)	
part	name
~~72~~	~~"seventy"~~
2	" seventy two"

Note that the string starts with a blank space. Exercise P5.12 asks you to eliminate it.

22. Here is one possible solution. Break up the task **print table** into **print header** and **print body**. The **print header** task calls **print separator**, prints the header cells, and calls **print separator** again. The **print body** task repeatedly calls **print row** and then calls **print separator**.

23. 1

24. 2, 7

25. Lines 3, 4, 5, 6, 10, 11, but not 7 through 9

26. The global variable defined in line 1.

27. The variables s defined in lines 4 and 15.

28. Yes, but since the function does not modify the amount parameter variable, there is no need to do so.

29. `void transfer(double& balance1, double& balance2, double amount)`

30.
```
bool withdraw(double& balance, double amount)
{
    if (balance >= amount)
    {
        balance = balance - amount;
        return true;
    }
    else
    {
        return false;
    }
}
```

31.
```
void minmax(double x, double y, double& a, double& b)
{
    if (x < y) { a = x; b = y; }
    else { a = y; b = x; }
}
```

32. The program sets x to 1, then y to 4, then x to 3. It prints 3 4.

33. [][][][]
    [][][]
    [][]
    []

34. 4 + 3 + 2 + 1 + 0 = 10

35. mystery(10) + 1 = mystery(5) + 2 = mystery(2) + 3 = mystery(1) + 4 = mystery(0) + 5 = 5

36. The idea is to print one [], then print n - 1 of them.

```
void print_boxes(int n)
{
   if (n == 0) { return; }
   cout << "[]";
   print_boxes(n - 1);
}
```

37. Simply add the following to the beginning of the function:

```
if (part >= 1000)
{
   return int_name(part / 1000) + " thousand " + int_name(part % 1000);
}
```

Arrays and Vectors

- To become familiar with using arrays and vectors to collect values

- To learn about common algorithms for processing arrays and vectors

- To write functions that receive and return arrays and vectors

- To learn how to use two-dimensional arrays

In many programs, you need to collect large numbers of values. In standard C++, the vector construct allows you to conveniently manage collections that automatically grow to any desired size. A lower-level construct, the array, is less convenient but sometimes required for efficiency or compatibility with older software. In this chapter, you will learn about arrays, vectors, and common algorithms for processing them.

CHAPTER CONTENTS

6.1 Using Arrays and Vectors

Use an array or vector to collect a sequence of values of the same type.

In the following sections, we introduce the array and vector constructs. Arrays and vectors allow you to store a sequence of values of the same type. You will learn how to define and use arrays and vectors, and how to decide which of the two is the best choice for a particular problem.

6.1.1 Arrays

Suppose you write a program that reads a sequence of values and prints out the sequence, marking the largest value, like this:

```
32
54
67.5
29
35
80
115 <= largest value
44.5
100
65
```

You do not know which value to mark as the largest one until you have seen them all. After all, the last value might be the largest one. Therefore, the program must first store all values before it can print them.

Figure 1
An Array of Size 10

Could you simply store each value in a separate variable? If you know that there are ten inputs, then you can store the data in ten variables data1, data2, data3, ..., data10. However, such a sequence of variables is not very practical to use. You would have to write quite a bit of code ten times, once for each of the variables. In C++, an arrray is a much better choice for storing a sequence of values.

Here we define an array that can hold ten values:

```
double data[10];
```

This is the definition of a variable data whose type is "array of double". That is, data stores a sequence of floating-point numbers. The [10] indicates the *size* of the array. (See Figure 1.) The array size must be a constant that is known at compile-time.

When you define an array, you can specify the initial values. For example,

```
double data[] = { 32, 54, 67.5, 29, 35, 80, 115, 44.5, 100, 65 };
```

When you supply initial values, you don't need to specify the array size. The compiler determines the size by counting the values.

> Individual elements in an array data are accessed by an integer index i, using the notation data[i].

In general, array variables are defined as in Syntax 6.1. To access a value in the data array, you must specify which "slot" you want to use. That is done with the [] operator:

```
data[4] = 35;
```

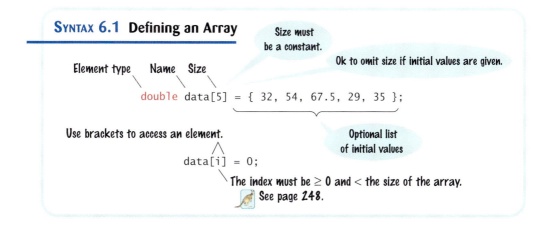

SYNTAX 6.1 **Defining an Array**

Size must be a constant.

Ok to omit size if initial values are given.

Element type   Name   Size

```
double data[5] = { 32, 54, 67.5, 29, 35 };
```

Use brackets to access an element.

Optional list of initial values

```
data[i] = 0;
```

The index must be ≥ 0 and < the size of the array. See page **248**.

Like a post office box that is identified by a box number, an array element is identified by an index.

Now the number 4 slot of data is filled with 35. (See Figure 2). This "slot number" is called an *index*. Each slot in an array is called an *element*.

> An array element can be used like any variable.

Because data is an array of `double` values, each element `data[i]` can be used like any variable of type `double`. For example, you can display the contents of the element with index 4 with the following command:

```
cout << data[4] << endl;
```

Before continuing, we must take care of an important detail of C++ arrays. If you look carefully at Figure 2, you will find that the *fifth* element was filled with data when we changed `data[4]`. In C++, the elements of arrays are numbered *starting at 0*. That is, the legal elements for the data array are

`data[0]`, the first element

`data[1]`, the second element

`data[2]`, the third element

`data[3]`, the fourth element

`data[4]`, the fifth element

...

`data[9]`, the tenth element

You will see in Chapter 7 why this numbering scheme was chosen in C++.

```
data =                    [0]
                          [1]
                          [2]
                          [3]
                   35     [4]
                          [5]
                          [6]
                          [7]
                          [8]
                          [9]
```

Figure 2   Filling an Array Element

An array index must be at least zero and less than the size of the array.

You have to be careful about index values. Trying to access a element that does not exist in the array is a serious error. For example, if data has ten elements, you are not allowed to access data[20]. Attempting to access an element whose index is not within the valid index range is called a *bounds error*. The compiler does not catch this type of error. Even the running program generates *no* error message. If you make a bounds error, you silently read or overwrite another memory location. As a consequence, your program may have random errors, and it can even crash.

The most common bounds error is the following:

A bounds error, which occurs if you supply an invalid array index, can corrupt data or cause your program to terminate.

```
double data[10];
cout << data[10];
```

There is no data[10] in an array with ten elements—the legal index values range from 0 to 9.

To visit all elements of an array, use a variable for the index. Suppose data has ten elements and the integer variable i takes values 0, 1, 2, and so on, up to 9. Then the expression data[i] yields each element in turn. For example, this loop displays all elements.

```
for (int i = 0; i < 10; i++)
{
    cout << data[i] << endl;
}
```

Note that the loop condition is that the index is *less than* 10 because there is no element corresponding to data[10].

Table 1 Defining Arrays

`int numbers[10];`	An array of ten integers.
`const int SIZE = 10;` `int numbers[SIZE];`	It is a good idea to use a named constant for the size.
🚫 `int size = 10;` `int numbers[size];`	**Error:** The size must be a constant.
`int squares[5] = { 0, 1, 4, 9, 16 };`	An array of five integers, with initial values.
`int squares[] = { 0, 1, 4, 9, 16 };`	You can omit the array size if you supply initial values. The size is set to the number of initial values.
`int squares[5] = { 0, 1, 4 };`	If you supply fewer initial values than the size, the remaining values are set to 0. This array contains 0, 1, 4, 0, 0.
`string names[3];`	An array of three strings.

6.1.2 Vectors

A vector stores a sequence of values whose size can change.

When you write a program that collects values from user input, you don't always know how many values you will have. Unfortunately, the size of the array has to be known *when the program is compiled*. The vector construct has been designed to solve this problem. A vector collects a sequence of values, just like an array does, but its size can change.

When you define a vector, you can specify the initial size. For example, here is a definition of a vector whose initial size is 10.

```
vector<double> data(10);
```

Use the push_back member function to add more elements to a vector. Use pop_back to reduce the size.

You access the vector elements as data[i], just like you do with arrays. If you need additional elements, you use the push_back function to add an element to the end of the vector, thereby increasing its size by 1. The push_back function is a member function that you must call with the dot notation, like this:

```
data.push_back(37.5);
```

After this call, the vector data has size 11, and data[10] contains the value 37.5 (see Figure 3).

When you define a vector, you need not specify an initial size. By default, a vector is empty.

```
vector<double> data; // Now data is empty
```

Note that the element type is enclosed in angle brackets.

You can then use the push_back function to fill it. For example,

```
data.push_back(32);   // Now data has size 1 and element 32
data.push_back(54);   // Now data has size 2 and elements 32, 54
data.push_back(67.5); // Now data has size 3 and elements 32, 54, 67.5
```

Figure 3 Adding an Element with push_back

SYNTAX 6.2 **Defining a Vector**

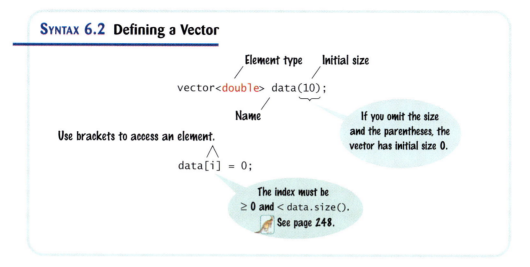

In particular, you will want to use the push_back function when filling a vector with input values.

```
double input;
while (cin >> input)
{
    data.push_back(input);
}
```

Another member function, pop_back, removes the last element of a vector, shrinking its size by one.

```
data.pop_back();
```

Table 2 Defining Vectors

`vector<int> numbers(10);`	A vector of ten integers.
`vector<string> names(3);`	A vector of three strings.
`vector<double> values;`	A vector of size 0.
🚫 `vector<double> values();`	**Error:** Does not define a vector.

`vector<int> numbers;`
`for (int i = 1; i <= 10; i++)`
`{`
`    numbers.push_back(i);`
`}`
	A vector of ten integers, filled with 1, 2, 3, ..., 10.

`vector<int> numbers(10);`
`for (int i = 0; i < numbers.size(); i++)`
`{`
`    numbers[i] = i + 1;`
`}`
	Another way of defining a vector of ten integers and filling it with 1, 2, 3, ..., 10.

Use the size function to obtain the current size of a vector.

The `size` member function returns the current size of a vector. In a loop that visits all vector elements, use the `size` member function like this:

```
for (int i = 0; i < data.size(); i++)
{
   cout << data[i] << endl;
}
```

In order to use vectors in your program, you need to include the `<vector>` header.

6.1.3 Partially-Filled Arrays

Unlike a vector, an array cannot change size at run time. There is no analog to the `push_back` or `pop_back` member functions. This is a problem when you don't know in advance how many elements you need. In that situation, you must come up with a good guess on the maximum number of elements that you need to store. We call this quantity the *capacity*. For example, we may decide that we sometimes want to store more than ten values, but never more than 100:

```
const int CAPACITY = 100;
double data[CAPACITY];
```

With a partially-filled array, keep a companion variable for the current size.

In a typical program run, only a part of the array will be occupied by actual elements. We call such an array a *partially-filled array*. You must keep a *companion variable* that counts how many elements are actually used. In Figure 4 we call the companion variable `size`.

The following loop collects data and fills up the data array.

```
int size = 0;
double input;
while (cin >> input)
{
   if (size < CAPACITY)
   {
      data[size] = x;
      size++;
   }
}
```

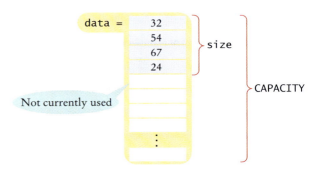

Figure 4
A Partially-Filled Array

At the end of this loop, size contains the actual number of elements in the array. Note that you have to stop accepting inputs if the size of the array reaches the capacity.

To process the gathered array elements, you again use the companion variable, not the capacity. This loop prints the partially filled array:

```
for (int i = 0; i < size; i++)
{
   cout << data[i] << endl;
}
```

SELF CHECK

1. Define an array of integers containing the first five prime numbers.
2. Assume the array primes has been initialized as described in Self Check 1. What is its contents after executing the following loop?

   ```
   for (int i = 0; i < 2; i++)
   {
      primes[4 - i] = primes[i];
   }
   ```

3. Assume the array primes has been initialized as described in Self Check 1. What is its contents after executing the following loop?

   ```
   for (int i = 0; i < 5; i++)
   {
      primes[i]++;
   }
   ```

4. Given the definition

   ```
   const int SIZE = 10;
   double data[SIZE];
   ```

   write statements to put a zero into the elements of the array data with the lowest and the highest valid index.

5. Given the array defined in Self Check 4, write a loop to print the elements of the array data in reverse order, starting with the last element.
6. Define an array called words that can hold ten values of type string.
7. Define an array containing two strings, "Yes", and "No".
8. Define a vector of integers that contains the first five prime numbers (2, 3, 5, 7, and 11).
9. What is the contents of the vector names after the following statements?

   ```
   vector<string> names;
   names.push_back("Ann");
   names.push_back("Bob");
   names.pop_back();
   names.push_back("Cal");
   ```

10. Suppose you want to store the names of the weekdays. Should you use a vector or an array of seven strings?

COMMON ERROR 6.1

Bounds Errors

Perhaps the most common error with using arrays and vectors is accessing a nonexistent element.

```
vector<double> data(10);
data[10] = 5.4;
    // Error—data has 10 elements with subscripts 0 to 9
```

If your program accesses an array or vector through an out-of-bounds subscript, there is no error message. Instead, the program will quietly (or not so quietly) corrupt some memory. Except for very short programs, in which the problem may go unnoticed, that corruption will make the program act unpredictably, and it can even cause the program to terminate. These are serious errors that can be difficult to detect.

PRODUCTIVITY HINT 6.1

Prefer Vectors over Arrays

For most programming tasks, vectors are easier to use than arrays. Vectors can grow and shrink. Even if a vector always stays the same size, it is convenient that a vector remembers its size. For a beginner, the sole advantage of an array is the initialization syntax. Advanced programmers sometimes prefer arrays because they are a bit more efficient. Moreover, you need to know how to use arrays if you work with older programs.

COMMON ERROR 6.2

Arrays Cannot Be Assigned

Suppose you have two arrays

```
int squares[5] = { 0, 1, 4, 9, 16 };
int lucky_numbers[5];
```

The following assignment is an error:

```
lucky_numbers = squares; // Error
```

You must use a loop to copy all elements:

```
for (int i = 0; i < 5; i++) { lucky_numbers[i] = squares[i]; }
```

Vectors do not suffer from this limitation. Consider this example:

```
vector<int> squares;
for (int i = 0; i < 5; i++) { squares.push_back(i * i); }
vector<int> lucky_numbers; // Initially empty
lucky_numbers = squares; // Now lucky_numbers contains the same elements as squares
```

RANDOM FACT 6.1

An Early Internet Worm

In November 1988, Robert Morris, a college student at Cornell University launched a so-called virus program that infected about 6,000 computers connected to the Internet across the United States. Tens of thousands of computer users were unable to read their e-mail or otherwise use their computers. All major universities and many high-tech companies were affected. (The Internet was much smaller then than it is now.)

The particular kind of virus used in this attack is called a worm. The virus program crawled from one computer on the Internet to the next. The worm would attempt to connect to finger, a program in the UNIX operating system for finding information on a user who has an account on a particular computer on the network. Like many programs in UNIX, finger was written in the C language. C does not have vectors, only arrays, and when you construct an array in C, you have to make up your mind how many elements you need. To store the user name to be looked up (say, walters@cs.sjsu.edu), the finger program allocated an array of 512 characters, under the assumption that nobody would ever provide such a long input. Unfortunately, C does not check that an array index is less than the length of the array. If you write into an array, using an index that is too large, you simply overwrite memory locations that belong to some other objects. In some versions of the finger program, the programmer had been lazy and had not checked whether the array holding the input characters was large enough to hold the input. So the worm program purposefully filled the 512-character array with 536 bytes. The excess 24 bytes would overwrite a return address, which the attacker knew was stored just after the line buffer. When that function was finished, it didn't return to its caller but to code supplied by the worm (see Figure 5). That code ran under the same super-user privileges as finger, allowing the worm to gain entry into the remote system. Had the programmer who wrote finger been more conscientious, this particular attack would not be possible. In C++, as in C, all programmers must be very careful not to overrun array boundaries.

One may well speculate what would possess the virus author to spend many weeks to plan the antisocial act of breaking into thousands of computers and disabling them. It appears that the break-in was fully intended by the author, but the disabling of the computers was a bug, caused by continuous reinfection. Morris was sentenced to 3 years probation, 400 hours of community service, and a $10,000 fine.

In recent years, computer attacks have intensified and the motives have become more sinister. Instead of disabling computers, viruses often steal financial data or use the attacked computers for sending spam e-mail. Sadly, many of these attacks continue to be possible because of poorly written programs that are susceptible to buffer overrun errors.

Figure 5
A "Buffer
Overrun" Attack

6.2 Common Array and Vector Algorithms

In the following sections, we discuss some of the most common algorithms for working with arrays and vectors. For simplicity, we will use vectors in our examples. If you use arrays, remember to replace the size member function with the array's size (or the companion variable used to represent it).

6.2.1 Filling

This loop fills a vector with zeroes:

```
for (int i = 0; i < data.size(); i++)
{
   data[i] = 0;
}
```

Here, we fill a vector with squares (0, 1, 4, 9, 16, ...). Note that the element with index 0 contains 0^2, the element with index 1 contains 1^2, and so on.

```
for (int i = 0; i < data.size(); i++)
{
   data[i] = i * i;
}
```

6.2.2 Sum and Average Value

To compute the sum of all elements in a vector, simply keep a running total.

```
double total = 0;
for (int i = 0; i < data.size(); i++)
{
   total = total + data[i];
}
```

To obtain the average, divide by the number of elements:

```
double average = total / data.size();
```

Be sure to check that the size is not zero.

6.2.3 Maximum and Minimum

To compute the largest value in a vector, keep a variable that stores the largest element that you have encountered, and update it when you find a larger one.

```
double largest = data[0];
for (int i = 1; i < data.size(); i++)
{
   if (data[i] > largest)
   {
      largest = data[i];
```

```
      }
   }
```

Note that the loop starts at 1 because we initialize largest with data[0]. Similarly, the following loop computes the smallest value:

```
double smallest = data[0];
for (int i = 1; i < data.size(); i++)
{
   if (data[i] < smallest)
   {
      smallest = data[i];
   }
}
```

The only difference is that we reverse the comparison.

These algorithms require that the vector (or array) contain at least one element.

To find the height of the tallest bus rider, remember the largest value so far, and update it whenever you see a taller one.

6.2.4 Element Separators

When you display the elements of a vector, you usually want to separate them, often with commas or vertical lines, like this:

```
1 | 4 | 9 | 16 | 25
```

Note that there is one fewer separator than there are numbers. Print the separator before each element *except the initial one* (with index 0):

```
for (int i = 0; i < data.size(); i++)
{
   if (i > 0)
   {
      cout << " | ";
   }
   cout << data[i];
}
```

6.2.5 Counting Matches

A common task is to count how many elements of a vector fulfill a particular criterion. Keep a counter and increment it for each matching element. For example, this loop counts how many elements are greater than 100.

```
int count = 0;
for (int i = 0; i < data.size(); i++)
{
   if (data[i] > 100)
   {
      count++;
   }
}
```

6.2.6 Collecting Matches

Sometimes, it is not enough to know how many elements of a vector fulfill a criterion, but you actually want to know what those elements are. This, too, is easily achieved: use a second vector to collect the matches. Here we collect all elements that are greater than 100.

```
vector<double> matches;
for (int i = 0; i < data.size(); i++)
{
   if (data[i] > 100)
   {
      matches.push_back(data[i]);
   }
}
```

Note how similar this loop is to the counting loop. The only difference is that we collect the matches instead of incrementing a counter.

6.2.7 Finding the Position of an Element

You often need to locate the position of an element so that you can replace or remove it. Visit all elements until you have found a match or you have come to the end of the vector. Here we locate the position of the first element that is larger than 100.

```
int pos = 0;
bool found = false;
while (pos < data.size() && !found)
{
   if (data[pos] > 100)
   {
      found = true;
   }
   else
   {
      pos++;
```

```
    }
}
```

6.2.8 Removing an Element

Suppose you want to remove the element with index pos from the vector data. If the elements in the vector are not in any particular order, that task is easy to accomplish. Simply overwrite the element to be removed with the *last* element of the vector, then shrink the size of the vector. (See Figure 6.)

```
int last_pos = data.size() - 1;
data[pos] = data[last_pos];
data.pop_back();
```

The situation is more complex if the order of the elements matters. Then you must move all elements following the element to be removed down (to a lower index), and then shrink the size of the vector. (See Figure 7.)

```
for (int i = pos; i < data.size() - 1; i++)
{
    data[i] = data[i + 1];
}
data.pop_back();
```

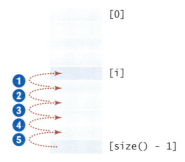

Figure 6
Removing an Element in
an Unordered Vector

Figure 7
Removing an Element in
an Ordered Vector

6.2.9 Inserting an Element

If the order of the elements does not matter, you can simply insert new elements at the end, using the push_back member function.

It is more work to insert an element at a particular position in the middle of a vector. First, add a new element at the end of the vector. Next, move all elements above the insertion location up (to a higher index). Finally, insert the new element.

Note the order of the movement: When you remove an element, you first move the next element down to a lower index, then the one after that, until you finally get

Figure 8

Inserting an Element in an Ordered Vector

to the end of the vector. When you insert an element, you start at the end of the vector, move that element up to a higher index, then move the one before that, and so on until you finally get to the insertion location (see Figure 8).

```cpp
int last_pos = data.size() - 1;
data.push_back(data[last_pos]);
for (int i = last_pos; i > pos; i--)
{
   data[i] = data[i - 1];
}
data[pos] = new_element;
```

The following program solves the task that we set ourselves at the beginning of this chapter, to mark the largest value in an input sequence.

ch06/largest.cpp

```cpp
1   #include <iostream>
2   #include <vector>
3
4   using namespace std;
5
6   int main()
7   {
8      vector<double> data;
9
10     cout << "Please enter values, Q to quit:" << endl;
11     double input;
12     while (cin >> input)
13     {
14        data.push_back(input);
15     }
16
17     double largest = data[0];
18     for (int i = 1; i < data.size(); i++)
19     {
20        if (data[i] > largest)
21        {
22           largest = data[i];
23        }
24     }
25
```

```
26     for (int i = 0; i < data.size(); i++)
27     {
28         cout << data[i];
29         if (data[i] == largest)
30         {
31             cout << " <== largest value";
32         }
33         cout << endl;
34     }
35
36     return 0;
37  }
```

Program Run

```
Please enter values, Q to quit:
35 80 115 44.5 Q
35
80
115 <== largest value
44.5
```

SELF CHECK

11. What is the output of the largest.cpp program when the inputs are

20 10 20 Q

12. Write a loop that counts how many elements in a vector are equal to zero.

13. How can you combine the tasks of Sections 6.2.5 and 6.2.6, that is, count *and* collect matches?

14. Consider the algorithm to find the largest element in a vector. Why don't we initialize largest and i with zero, like this?

```
double largest = 0;
for (int i = 0; i < data.size(); i++)
{
    if (data[i] > largest)
    {
        largest = data[i];
    }
}
```

15. When printing separators, we skipped the separator before the initial element. Rewrite the loop so that the separator is printed *after* each element, except for the last element.

16. What is wrong with these statements for printing a vector with separators?

```
cout << data[0];
for (int i = 1; i < data.size(); i++)
{
    cout << ", " << data[i];
}
```

17. When finding the position of a match, we used a `while` loop, not a `for` loop. What is wrong with using this loop instead?

```
for (pos = 0; pos < data.size() && !found; pos++)
{
   if (data[pos] > 100)
   {
      found = true;
   }
}
```

18. When inserting an element into a vector, we moved the elements with larger index values, starting at the end of the vector. Why is it wrong to start at the insertion location, like this:

```
for (int i = pos; i < data.size() - 1; i++)
{
   data[i + 1] = data[i];
}
```

ADVANCED TOPIC 6.1

Sorting with the C++ Library

You often want to sort the elements of a vector or array. Advanced Topic 6.2 shows you a sorting algorithm that is relatively simple but not very efficient. Efficient sorting algorithms are significantly more complex. Fortunately, the C++ library provides an efficient `sort` function. To sort a vector `data`, make this call:

```
sort(data.begin(), data.end());
```

To sort an array `a` with `size` elements, call

```
sort(a, a + size);
```

To fully understand the curious syntax of these calls, you will need to know advanced C++ that is beyond the scope of this book. But don't hesitate to call the sort function whenever you need to sort an array or vector.

To use the sort function, include the `<algorithm>` header in your program.

ADVANCED TOPIC 6.2

A Sorting Algorithm

A *sorting algorithm* rearranges the elements of a sequence so that they are stored in sorted order. Here is a simple sorting algorithm, called *selection sort*. Consider sorting the following vector data:

[0]	[1]	[2]	[3]	[4]
11	9	17	5	12

An obvious first step is to find the smallest element. In this case the smallest element is 5, stored in `data[3]`. You should move the 5 to the beginning of the vector. Of course, there is already an element stored in data[0], namely 11. Therefore you cannot simply move data[3] into data[0] without moving the 11 somewhere else. You don't yet know where the 11 should end up, but you know for certain that it should not be in data[0]. Simply get it out of the way by *swapping it* with data[3].

Now the first element is in the correct place. In the foregoing figure, the darker color indicates the portion of the vector that is already sorted.

Next take the minimum of the remaining entries data[1]...data[4]. That minimum value, 9, is already in the correct place. You don't need to do anything in this case, simply extend the sorted area by one to the right:

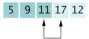

Repeat the process. The minimum value of the unsorted region is 11, which needs to be swapped with the first value of the unsorted region, 17.

Now the unsorted region is only two elements long; keep to the same successful strategy. The minimum element is 12. Swap it with the first value, 17.

That leaves you with an unprocessed region of length 1, but of course a region of length 1 is always sorted. You are done.

Here is the C++ code:

```cpp
for (int unsorted = 0; unsorted < data.size() - 1; unsorted++)
{
   // Find the position of the minimum
   int min_pos = unsorted;
   for (int i = unsorted + 1; i < data.size(); i++)
   {
      if (data[i] < data[min_pos]) { min_pos = i; }
   }
   // Swap the minimum into the sorted area
   if (min_pos != unsorted)
   {
      swap(data[min_pos], data[unsorted]);
   }
}
```

This algorithm is simple to understand, but unfortunately it is not very efficient. Computer scientists have studied sorting algorithms extensively and discovered significantly better algorithms. The sort function of the C++ library provides one such algorithm—see Advanced Topic 6.1.

6.3 Vectors and Arrays in Functions

In this section, we will explore how to write functions that process vectors and arrays, highlighting the key differences in working with each.

> Vectors can occur as function parameters and return values.

You can use vectors as function parameters in exactly the same way as any other values. For example, the following function computes the sum of a vector of floating-point numbers:

```
double sum(vector<double> data)
{
    double total = 0;
    for (int i = 0; i < data.size(); i++)
    {
        total = total + data[i];
    }
    return total;
}
```

This function visits the vector elements, but it does not modify them. If your function modifies the elements, use a reference parameter. The following function multiplies all values of a vector with a given factor.

```
void multiply(vector<double>& data, double factor) // Note the &
{
    for (int i = 0; i < data.size(); i++)
    {
        data[i] = data[i] * factor;
    }
}
```

A function can return a vector. Again, vectors are no different from any other values in this regard. Simply build up the result in the function and return it. In this example, the squares function returns a vector of squares from 0^2 up to $(n-1)^2$:

```
vector<int> squares(int n)
{
    vector<int> result;
    for (int i = 0; i < n; i++)
    {
        result.push_back(i * i);
    }
    return result;
}
```

As you can see, it is easy to use vectors with functions—there are no special rules to keep in mind. You have to be much more careful when using arrays with functions.

When you pass an array to a function, you also need to pass the size of the array. The function has no other way of querying the size of the array—there is no size() member function. Here is the sum function again, this time with an array parameter:

```
double sum(double data[], int size)
{
    double total = 0;
    for (int i = 0; i < size; i++)
    {
```

```
            total = total + data[i];
        }
        return total;
    }
```

Note the special syntax for array parameters. When writing an array parameter, you place an empty [] behind the parameter name. Do not specify the size of the array inside the brackets.

Array parameters are always passed by reference.

Unlike all other parameters, array parameters are *always passed by reference*. (You will see the reason in Chapter 7.) Functions can modify array parameters, and those modifications affect the array that was passed into the function. For example, the following multiply function updates all elements in the array.

```cpp
void multiply(double data[], int size, double factor) // No &
{
    for (int i = 0; i < size; i++)
    {
        data[i] = data[i] * factor;
    }
}
```

A function's return type cannot be an array.

Although arrays can be function parameters, they cannot be function return types. If a function computes multiple values, the caller of the function must provide an array parameter to hold the result.

```cpp
void squares(int n, int result[])
{
    for (int i = 0; i < n; i++)
    {
        result[i] = i * i;
    }
}
```

The following example program reads values from standard input, doubles them, and prints the result. The program uses three functions:

- The read_inputs function returns a vector.
- The multiply function has a vector as a reference parameter.
- The print function has a vector as a value parameter.

ch06/vecfuns.cpp

```cpp
1   #include <iostream>
2   #include <vector>
3
4   using namespace std;
5
6   /**
7       Reads a sequence of floating-point numbers.
8       @return a vector containing the numbers
9   */
10  vector<double> read_inputs()
11  {
```

```
12      vector<double> result;
13      cout << "Please enter values, Q to quit:" << endl;
14      bool more = true;
15      while (more)
16      {
17         double input;
18         cin >> input;
19         if (cin.fail())
20         {
21            more = false;
22         }
23         else
24         {
25            result.push_back(input);
26         }
27      }
28      return result;
29   }
30
31   /**
32      Multiplies all elements of a vector by a factor.
33      @param data a vector
34      @param factor the value with which element is multiplied
35   */
36   void multiply(vector<double>& data, double factor)
37   {
38      for (int i = 0; i < data.size(); i++)
39      {
40         data[i] = data[i] * factor;
41      }
42   }
43
44   /**
45      Prints the elements of a vector, separated by commas.
46      @param data a vector
47   */
48   void print(vector<double> data)
49   {
50      for (int i = 0; i < data.size(); i++)
51      {
52         if (i > 0) { cout << ", "; }
53         cout << data[i];
54      }
55      cout << endl;
56   }
57
58   int main()
59   {
60      vector<double> values = read_inputs();
61      multiply(values, 2);
62      print(values);
63
64      return 0;
65   }
```

Program Run

```
Please enter values, Q to quit:
12 25 20 Q
24, 50, 40
```

SELF CHECK

19. Consider this partially completed function that appends the elements of one vector to another.

    ```
    void append(vector<double>__ target, vector<double>__ source)
    {
       for (int i = 0; i < source.size(); i++)
       {
          target.push_back(source[i]);
       }
    }
    ```

    Specify whether the parameters should be value or reference parameters.

20. What happens if you declare a vector parameter as a reference parameter even though the function never modifies it? For example,

    ```
    double total(vector<double>& data)
    ```

21. What happens if you call the array version of the sum function and you lie about the size? For example, calling

    ```
    double result = sum(data, 1000);
    ```

    even though data has size 100.

22. How do you call the vector version of the squares function to compute the first five squares and store the result in a vector numbers?

23. How do you call the array version of the squares function to compute the first five squares and store the result in an array numbers?

ADVANCED TOPIC 6.3

Constant Vector References and Array Parameters

Passing a vector into a function by value is unfortunately somewhat inefficient, because the function must make a copy of all elements. As explained in Advanced Topic 5.2, the cost of a copy can be avoided by using a constant reference. Simply write

```
double sum(const vector<double>& data)
```

instead of

```
double sum(vector<double> data)
```

This is a useful optimization that greatly increases performance.

Similarly, when a function doesn't modify an array parameter, it is considered good style to add the const reserved word, like this:

```
double sum(const double data[], int size)
```

In this case, the reason is not efficiency. Arrays are always passed by reference. However, the const reserved word helps the reader of the code, making it clear that the function keeps the array elements unchanged.

HOW TO 6.1

Working with Vectors and Arrays

When you process a sequence of values, you usually need to use vectors or arrays. (In some very simple situations, you can process data as you read them in, without storing them.) This How To walks you through the necessary steps.

Consider this example problem: You are given the quiz scores of a student. You are to compute the final quiz score, which is the sum of all scores after dropping the lowest one. For example, if the scores are

    8 7 8.5 9.5 7 5 10

then the final score is 50.

Step 1 Decompose your task into steps.

You will usually want to break down your task into multiple steps, such as

- Reading the data into a vector or array.
- Processing the data in one or more steps.
- Displaying the results.

When deciding how to process the data, you should be familiar with the array algorithms in Section 6.2. Most processing tasks can be solved by using one or more of these algorithms.

In our sample problem, we will want to read the data. Then we will remove the minimum and compute the total. For example, if the input is 8 7 8.5 9.5 7 5 10, we will remove the minimum of 5, yielding 8 7 8.5 9.5 7 10. The sum of those values is the final score of 50.

Thus, we have identified three steps:

    Read inputs.
    Remove the minimum.
    Calculate the sum.

(It is possible to solve this problem using a different sequence of steps—see Exercise P6.3.)

Step 2 Choose between vectors and arrays.

Generally, vectors are more convenient than arrays. You would choose arrays if one of the following applies:

- You know in advance how many elements you will collect, and the size will not change.
- You interact with pre-existing code that uses arrays.

None of these cases applies here, so we will store the scores in a vector.

Step 3 Determine which algorithm(s) you need for each step.

Sometimes, a step corresponds to exactly one of the basic array algorithms. That is the case with calculating the sum. At other times, you need to combine several algorithms. To remove the minimum value, you can find the minimum value (Section 6.2.3), find its position

(Section 6.2.7), and remove the element at that position (Section 6.2.8). (There is a more effi-cient way of removing the minimum from a vector—see Exercise P6.4.)

Step 4 Determine functions, parameters, and return values.

Even though it may be possible to put all steps into the main function, this is rarely a good idea. The simplest and best approach is to make each step into a separate function. In our example, we will implement three functions:
- read_inputs
- remove_min
- sum

If a function modifies a vector, then you need to pass it by reference. Removing the smallest value modifies a vector, but computing the sum does not:

```
void remove_min(vector<double>& data)
double sum(vector<double> data)
```

If you follow Advanced Topic 6.3 on page 261, you can use the more efficient

```
double sum(const vector<double>& data)
```

When reading data, you have two choices. You can return a vector with the data that you read:

```
vector<double> read_inputs()
```

Or you can pass a vector that should be filled:

```
void read_inputs(vector<double>& data)
```

The first approach is generally considered in better taste and easier to understand, but the second is a bit more efficient. We will opt for good taste.

If you had used an array instead of a vector, then the first two functions would have been

```
void remove_min(double data[], int size)
double sum(const double data[], int size) // See Advanced Topic 6.3 for the
                                          // optional const
```

Returning an array from a function is not an option, so the read_inputs function would need to supply a parameter for holding the values that the user supplied. The function also needs to know the capacity of that array, and it needs to set the actual number of values read:

```
void read_inputs(double data[], int capacity, int& size)
```

You can see once again that arrays are not a comfortable choice for storing a data set whose size is unknown.

Step 5 Document and implement each function, using helper functions when needed.

We won't show the code for the read_inputs and sum functions because you have seen them already, but we will consider the function remove_min. A safe strategy is to implement it with three helper functions, minimum, find_first, and remove:

```
/**
    Removes the minimum from a vector.
    @param data a vector of size >= 1
*/
void remove_min(vector<double>& data)
{
    double min = minimum(data);
    int pos = find_first(data, min);
    remove(data, pos);
}
```

The helper functions use the algorithms from Section 6.2.

```
/**
    Gets the minimum value from a vector.
    @param data a vector of size >= 1
    @return the smallest element of data
*/
double minimum(vector<double> data)
{
    double smallest = data[0];
    for (int i = 1; i < data.size(); i++)
    {
        if (data[i] < smallest)
        {
            smallest = data[i];
        }
    }
    return smallest;
}

/**
    Returns the index of the first element that matches a given element.
    @param data a vector
    @param element the element to match
    @return the smallest i such that data[i] == element,
    or -1 if there is no such element
*/
int find_first(vector<double> data, double element)
{
    int pos = 0;
    while (pos < data.size())
    {
        if (data[pos] == element)
        {
            return pos;
        }
        else
        {
            pos++;
        }
    }
    return -1;
}

/**
    Removes an element from a vector. The order of the elements is not
    preserved.
    @param data a vector
    @param pos the index of the element to be removed (must be valid)
*/
void remove(vector<double>& data, int pos)
{
    int last_pos = data.size() - 1;
    data[pos] = data[last_pos];
    data.pop_back();
}
```

Most functions that operate on vectors and arrays are a bit intricate, and you have to be careful that you handle both normal and exceptional situations. What happens with an empty array? An array that contains a single element? When no match is found? When there are multiple matches? Consider these boundary conditions and make sure that your functions work correctly.

In the `remove_min` function, we require that the vector contain at least one element. Therefore, the `minimum` function will find the smallest element. Since that element is a part of the vector, the `find_pos` method will yield a valid position.

What if there are multiple matches? That means that a student had more than one test with a low score. The `remove_min` function removes only one of the occurrences of that low score, and that is the desired behavior.

Step 6 Assemble and test the complete program.

Now we are ready to combine the individual functions into a complete program. Before doing this, consider some test cases and their expected output:

Test Case	Expected Output	Comment
8 7 8.5 9.5 7 5 10	50	See Step 1.
8 7 7 9	24	Only one instance of the low score should be removed.
8	0	After removing the low score, no score remains.
(no inputs)	**Error**	That is not a legal input.

This `main` function completes the solution (see `ch06/scores.cpp`).

```
int main()
{
   vector<double> scores = read_inputs();
   if (scores.size() == 0)
   {
      cout << "At least one score is required." << endl;
   }
   else
   {
      remove_min(scores);
      double total = sum(scores);
      cout << "Final score: " << total << endl;
   }
   return 0;
}
```

WORKED EXAMPLE 6.1

Rolling the Dice

This Worked Example shows how to analyze a set of die tosses to see whether the die is "fair".

6.4 Two-Dimensional Arrays

It often happens that you want to store collections of values that have a two-dimensional layout. Such data sets commonly occur in financial and scientific applications. An arrangement consisting of rows and columns of values is called a *two-dimensional array*, or a *matrix*.

Let's explore how to store the example data shown in Figure 9: the medal counts of the figure skating competitions at the 2006 Winter Olympics.

	Gold	Silver	Bronze
Canada	0	0	1
China	0	1	1
Japan	1	0	0
Russia	3	0	1
Switzerland	0	1	0
Ukraine	0	0	1
United States	0	2	0

Figure 9   Figure Skating Medal Counts

SYNTAX 6.3 Two-Dimensional Array Definition

```
        Element type    Rows      Columns
                    \      \      /
                    int data[4][4] = {
                       /           { 16, 3, 2, 13 },
                    Name           { 5, 10, 11, 8 },
                                   { 9, 6, 7, 12 },
                                   { 4, 15, 14, 1 },
                                };
```

Optional list of initial values

6.4.1 Defining Two-Dimensional Arrays

Use a two-dimensional array to store tabular data.

C++ uses an array with two subscripts to store a two-dimensional array. For example, here is the definition of an array with 7 rows and 3 columns and suitable for storing our medal count data:

```
const int COUNTRIES = 7;
const int MEDALS = 3;
int counts[COUNTRIES][MEDALS];
```

You can initialize the array by grouping each row, as follows:

```
int counts[COUNTRIES][MEDALS] =
    {
        { 0, 0, 1 },
        { 0, 1, 1 },
        { 1, 0, 0 },
        { 3, 0, 1 },
        { 0, 1, 0 },
        { 0, 0, 1 },
        { 0, 2, 0 }
    };
```

Just as with one-dimensional arrays, you cannot change the size of a two-dimensional array once it has been defined.

6.4.2 Accessing Elements

Individual elements in a two-dimensional array are accessed by using two subscripts, m[i][j].

To access a particular element in the two-dimensional array, you need to specify two subscripts in separate brackets to select the row and column, respectively (see Syntax 6.3 and Figure 10):

```
int value = counts[3][1];
```

To access all values in a two-dimensional array, you use two nested loops.

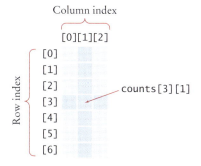

Figure 10   Accessing an Element in a Two-Dimensional Array

For example, the following loop prints all elements of counts.

```
for (int i = 0; i < COUNTRIES; i++)
{
   // Process the ith row
   for (int j = 0; j < MEDALS; j++)
   {
      // Process the jth column in the ith row
      cout << setw(8) << counts[i][j];
   }
   cout << endl; // Start a new line at the end of the row
}
```

6.4.3 Computing Row and Column Totals

A common task is to compute row or column totals. In our example, the row totals give us the total number of medals won by a particular country.

Finding the right index values is a bit tricky, and it is a good idea to make a quick sketch. To compute the total of row i, we need to visit the following elements:

As you can see, we need to compute the sum of counts[i][j], where j ranges from 0 to MEDALS - 1. The following loop computes the total:

```
int total = 0;
for (int j = 0; j < MEDALS; j++)
{
   total = total + counts[i][j];
}
```

Computing column totals is similar. Form the sum of counts[i][j], where i ranges from 0 to COUNTRIES - 1.

```
int total = 0;
for (int i = 0; i < COUNTRIES; i++)
{
    total = total + counts[i][j];
}
```

6.4.4 Two-Dimensional Array Parameters

A two-dimensional array parameter must have a fixed number of columns.

When passing a two-dimensional array to a function, you must specify the number of columns *as a constant* with the parameter type. For example, this function computes the total of a given row.

```
const int COLUMNS = 3;

int row_total(int table[][COLUMNS], int row)
{
    int total = 0;
    for (int j = 0; j < COLUMNS; j++)
    {
        total = total + table[row][j];
    }
    return total;
}
```

This function can compute row totals of a two-dimensional array with an arbitrary number of rows, but the array must have 3 columns. You have to write a different function if you want to compute row totals of a two-dimensional array with 4 columns.

To understand this limitation, you need to know how the array elements are stored in memory. Although the array appears to be two-dimensional, the elements are still stored as a linear sequence. Figure 11 shows how the counts array is stored, row by row.

For example, to reach

counts[3][1]

the program must first skip past rows 0, 1, and 2 and then locate offset 1 in row 3. The offset from the start of the array is

$$3 \times number\ of\ columns + 1$$

Figure 11 A Two-Dimensional Array Is Stored as a Sequence of Rows

Now consider the row_total function. The compiler generates code to find the element

```
table[i][j]
```

by computing the offset

```
i * COLUMNS + j
```

The compiler uses the value that you supplied in the second pair of brackets when declaring the parameter:

```
int row_total(int table[][COLUMNS], int row)
```

Note that the first pair of brackets should be empty, just as with one-dimensional arrays.

The row_total function did not need to know the number of rows of the array. If the number of rows is required, pass it as a variable, as in this example:

```
int column_total(int table[][COLUMNS], int rows, int column)
{
   int total = 0;
   for (int i = 0; i < rows; i++)
   {
      total = total + table[i][column];
   }
   return total;
}
```

Working with two-dimensional arrays is illustrated in the following program. The program prints out the medal counts and the row totals.

ch06/medals.cpp

```
 1  #include <iostream>
 2  #include <iomanip>
 3  #include <string>
 4
 5  using namespace std;
 6
 7  const int COLUMNS = 3;
 8
 9  /**
10     Computes the total of a row in a table.
11     @param table a table with 3 columns
12     @param row the row that needs to be totaled
13     @return the sum of all elements in the given row
14  */
15  double row_total(int table[][COLUMNS], int row)
16  {
17     int total = 0;
18     for (int j = 0; j < COLUMNS; j++)
19     {
20        total = total + table[row][j];
21     }
22     return total;
23  }
24
```

```
25  int main()
26  {
27     const int COUNTRIES = 7;
28     const int MEDALS = 3;
29
30     string countries[] =
31        {
32           "Canada",
33           "China",
34           "Japan",
35           "Russia",
36           "Switzerland",
37           "Ukraine",
38           "United States"
39        };
40
41     int counts[COUNTRIES][MEDALS] =
42        {
43           { 0, 0, 1 },
44           { 0, 1, 1 },
45           { 1, 0, 0 },
46           { 3, 0, 1 },
47           { 0, 1, 0 },
48           { 0, 0, 1 },
49           { 0, 2, 0 }
50        };
51
52     cout << "          Country    Gold  Silver  Bronze    Total" << endl;
53
54     // Print countries, counts, and row totals
55     for (int i = 0; i < COUNTRIES; i++)
56     {
57        cout << setw(15) << countries[i];
58        // Process the ith row
59        for (int j = 0; j < MEDALS; j++)
60        {
61           cout << setw(8) << counts[i][j];
62        }
63        int total = row_total(counts, i);
64        cout << setw(8) << total << endl;
65     }
66
67     return 0;
68  }
```

Program Run

Country	Gold	Silver	Bronze	Total
Canada	0	0	1	1
China	0	1	1	2
Japan	1	0	0	1
Russia	3	0	1	4
Switzerland	0	1	0	1
Ukraine	0	0	1	1
United States	0	2	0	2

SELF CHECK

24. What results do you get if you total the columns in our sample data?

25. Consider an 8 ×8 array for a board game:

```
int board[8][8];
```

Using two nested loops, initialize the board so that zeroes and ones alternate, as on a checkerboard:

```
0 1 0 1 0 1 0 1
1 0 1 0 1 0 1 0
0 1 0 1 0 1 0 1
...
1 0 1 0 1 0 1 0
```

Hint: Check whether i + j is even.

26. Define a two-dimensional array for representing a tic-tac-toe board. The board has three rows and columns and contains strings "x", "o", and " ".

27. Write an assignment statement to place an "x" in the upper right corner of the tic-tac-toe board.

28. Which elements are on the diagonal joining the upper-left and the lower-right corners of the tic-tac-toe board?

COMMON ERROR 6.3

Omitting the Column Size of a Two-Dimensional Array Parameter

When passing a one-dimensional array to a function, you specify the size of the array as a separate parameter:

```
void print(double data[], int size)
```

This function can print arrays of any size. However, for two-dimensional arrays you cannot simply pass the numbers of rows and columns as parameters:

```
void print(double table[][], int rows, int cols) // NO!
```

The function must know *at compile time* how many columns the two-dimensional array has. You must specify the number of columns in the array parameter. This number must be a constant:

```
const int COLUMNS = 3;
void print(const double table[][COLUMNS], int rows) // OK
```

This function can print tables with any number of rows, but the column size is fixed.

WORKED EXAMPLE 6.2

A World Population Table

This Worked Example shows how to print world population data in a table with row and column headers, and totals for each of the data columns.

RANDOM FACT 6.2

International Alphabets

The English alphabet is pretty simple: upper- and lowercase *a* to *z*. Other European languages have accent marks and special characters. For example, German has three so-called *umlaut* characters, ä, ö, ü, and a *double-s* character ß. These are not optional frills; you couldn't write a page of German text without using these characters a few times. German computer keyboards have keys for these characters (see Figure 12).

This poses a problem for computer users and designers. The American standard character encoding (called ASCII, for American Standard Code for Information Interchange) specifies 128 codes: 52 upper- and lowercase characters, 10 digits, 32 typographical symbols, and 34 control characters (such as space, newline, and 32 others for controlling printers and other devices). The umlaut and double-s are not among them. Some German data processing systems replace seldom-used ASCII characters with German letters: [\]{|}~ are replaced with Ä Ö Ü ä ö ü ß. While most people can live without these characters, C++ programmers definitely cannot. Other encoding schemes take advantage of the fact that one byte can encode 256 different characters, of which only 128 are standardized by ASCII. Unfortunately, there are multiple incompatible standards for such encodings, resulting in a certain amount of aggravation among European computer users.

Many countries don't use the Roman script at all. Russian, Greek, Hebrew, Arabic, and Thai letters, to name just a few, have completely different shapes (see Figure 13). To complicate matters, Hebrew and Arabic are typed from right to left. Each of these alphabets has between 30 and 100 letters, and the countries using them have established encoding standards for them.

Figure 12   The German Keyboard

Figure 13   The Thai Script

The situation is much more dramatic in languages that use the Chinese script: the Chinese dialects, Japanese, and Korean. The Chinese script is not alphabetic but *ideographic* (see Figure 14). A character represents an idea or thing. Most words are made up of one, two, or three of these ideographic characters. Over 50,000 ideographs are known, of which about 20,000 are in active use. Therefore, two bytes are needed to encode them. China, Taiwan, Japan, and Korea have incompatible encoding standards for them. (Japanese and Korean writing uses a mixture of native syllabic and Chinese ideographic characters.)

The inconsistencies among character encodings have been a major nuisance for international electronic communication and for software manufacturers vying for a global market. Starting in 1988, a consortium of hardware and software manufacturers developed a uniform 21-bit encoding scheme called *unicode* that is capable of encoding text in essentially all written languages of the world. About 100,000 characters have been given codes, including more than 70,000 Chinese, Japanese, and Korean ideographs. There are even plans to add codes for extinct languages, such as Egyptian hieroglyphs.

						Sm.	Lg.
清 燉 雞	湯	57.	House Chicken Soup (Chicken, Celery, Potato, Onion, Carrot)			1.50	2.75
雞 飯	湯	58.	Chicken Rice Soup			1.85	3.25
雞 麵	湯	59.	Chicken Noodle Soup			1.85	3.25
廣 東 雲 吞		60.	Cantonese Wonton Soup			1.50	2.75
蕃 茄 蛋	湯	61.	Tomato Clear Egg Drop Soup			1.65	2.95
雲 吞	湯	62.	Regular Wonton Soup			1.10	2.10
酸 辣	湯	63. ☙	Hot & Sour Soup			1.10	2.10
蛋 花	湯	64.	Egg Drop Soup			1.10	2.10
雲 蛋	湯	65.	Egg Drop Wonton Mix			1.10	2.10
豆 腐 菜	湯	66.	Tofu Vegetable Soup			NA	3.50
雞 玉 米	湯	67.	Chicken Corn Cream Soup			NA	3.50
蟹 肉 玉 米	湯	68.	Crab Meat Corn Cream Soup			NA	3.50
海 鮮	湯	69.	Seafood Soup			NA	3.50

Figure 14   The Chinese Script

CHAPTER SUMMARY

1. Use an array or vector to collect a sequence of values of the same type.

2. Individual elements in an array data are accessed by an integer index i, using the notation data[i].

3. An array element can be used like any variable.

4. An array index must be at least zero and less than the size of the array.

5. A bounds error, which occurs if you supply an invalid array index, can corrupt data or cause your program to terminate.

6. A vector stores a sequence of values whose size can change.

7. Use the push_back member function to add more elements to a vector. Use pop_back to reduce the size.

8. Use the size function to obtain the current size of a vector.

9. With a partially-filled array, keep a companion variable for the current size.

10. Vectors can occur as function parameters and return values.

11. Array parameters are always passed by reference.

12. A function's return type cannot be an array.

13. Use a two-dimensional array to store tabular data.

14. Individual elements in a two-dimensional array are accessed by using two subscripts, m[i][j].

15. A two-dimensional array parameter must have a fixed number of columns.

REVIEW EXERCISES

Exercise R6.1. Write code that fills a vector data with each set of values below

   a. 1   2   3   4   5   6   7   8   9   10

   b. 0   2   4   6   8 10 12 14 16   18 20

   c. 1   4   9 16 25 36 49 64 81 100

d. 0   0   0   0   0   0   0   0   0   0
e. 1   4   9   16   9   7   4   9   11
f. 0   1   0   1   0   1   0   1   0   1
g. 0   1   2   3   4   0   1   2   3   4

Exercise R6.2. Consider the following array:

```
int a[] = { 1, 2, 3, 4, 5, 4, 3, 2, 1, 0 };
```

What is the value of total after the following loops complete?

a. `int total = 0;`
`for (int i = 0; i < 10; i++) { total = total + a[i]; }`

b. `int total = 0;`
`for (int i = 0; i < 10; i = i + 2) { total = total + a[i]; }`

c. `int total = 0;`
`for (int i = 1; i < 10; i = i + 2) { total = total + a[i]; }`

d. `int total = 0;`
`for (int i = 2; i <= 10; i++) { total = total + a[i]; }`

e. `int total = 0;`
`for (int i = 0; i < 10; i = 2 * i) { total = total + a[i]; }`

f. `int total = 0;`
`for (int i = 9; i >= 0; i--) { total = total + a[i]; }`

g. `int total = 0;`
`for (int i = 9; i >= 0; i = i - 2) { total = total + a[i]; }`

h. `int total = 0;`
`for (int i = 0; i < 10; i++) { total = a[i] - total; }`

Exercise R6.3. Consider the following array:

```
int a[] = { 1, 2, 3, 4, 5, 4, 3, 2, 1, 0 };
```

What are the contents of the array a after the following loops complete?

a. `for (int i = 1; i < 10; i++) { a[i] = a[i - 1]; }`
b. `for (int i = 9; i > 0; i--) { a[i] = a[i - 1]; }`
c. `for (int i = 0; i < 9; i++) { a[i] = a[i + 1]; }`
d. `for (int i = 8; i >= 0; i--) { a[i] = a[i + 1]; }`
e. `for (int i = 1; i < 10; i++) { a[i] = a[i] + a[i - 1]; }`
f. `for (int i = 1; i < 10; i = i + 2) { a[i] = 0; }`
g. `for (int i = 0; i < 5; i++) { a[i + 5] = a[i]; }`
h. `for (int i = 1; i < 5; i++) { a[i] = a[9 - i]; }`

Exercise R6.4. Write a loop that fills a vector data with ten random numbers between 1 and 100. Write code for two nested loops that fill data with ten *different* random numbers between 1 and 100.

Exercise R6.5. Write C++ code for a loop that simultaneously computes both the maximum and minimum of a vector.

Exercise R6.6. What is wrong with the following loop?

```
vector<int> data(10);
for (int i = 1; i <= 10; i++)
{
   data[i] = i * i;
}
```

Explain two ways of fixing the error.

Exercise R6.7. What is an index of a vector or an array? What are the legal index values? What is a bounds error?

Exercise R6.8. Write a program that contains a bounds error. Run the program. What happens on your computer?

Exercise R6.9. Write a loop that reads ten numbers and a second loop that displays them in the opposite order from which they were entered.

Exercise R6.10. Trace the flow of the loop in Section 6.2.4 with the given example. Show two columns, one with the value of i and one with the output.

Exercise R6.11. Trace the flow of the loop in Section 6.2.6, where data contains the values 110 90 100 120 80. Show two columns, for i and matches.

Exercise R6.12. Trace the flow of the loop in Section 6.2.7, where data contains the values 80 90 100 120 110. Show two columns, for pos and found. Repeat the trace when data contains 80 90 100 70.

Exercise R6.13. Trace both mechanisms for removing an element described in Section 6.2.8. Use a vector data with values 110 90 100 120 80, and remove the element at index 2.

Exercise R6.14. From the examples in this chapter, name

a. A function that has a vector as a value parameter.
b. A function that has a vector as a reference parameter.
c. A function that has a vector as a return value.

Exercise R6.15. A function that has a vector as a reference parameter can change the vector in two ways. It can change the contents of individual vector elements, or it can rearrange the elements. From the examples in this chapter, name two functions that change a vector in each of the two ways just described.

Exercise R6.16. Give pseudocode for a function that rotates the elements of a vector by one position, moving the initial element to the end of the vector, like this:

Exercise R6.17. Give pseudocode for a function that removes all negative values from a vector, preserving the order of the remaining elements.

Exercise R6.18. Suppose data is a *sorted* vector of integers. Give pseudocode that describes how a new value can be inserted in its proper position so that the resulting vector stays sorted.

Exercise R6.19. A *run* is a sequence of adjacent repeated values. Give pseudocode for computing the length of the longest run in a vector. For example, the longest run in the vector with elements

    1 2 5 5 3 1 2 4 3 2 2 2 2 3 6 5 5 6 3 1

has length 4.

Exercise R6.20. How do you perform the following tasks with vectors in C++?
   a. Test that two vectors contain the same elements in the same order.
   b. Copy one vector to another.
   c. Fill a vector with zeroes, overwriting all elements in it.
   d. Remove all elements from a vector.

Exercise R6.21. True or false?
   a. All elements of a vector are of the same type.
   b. Vector subscripts must be integers.
   c. Vectors cannot contain strings as elements.
   d. Vectors cannot use strings as subscripts.
   e. Two-dimensional arrays always have the same numbers of rows and columns.
   f. Elements of different columns in a two-dimensional array can have different types.
   g. All vector parameters are reference parameters.
   h. A function cannot return a two-dimensional array.
   i. A function cannot change the dimensions of a two-dimensional array that is passed as a parameter.
   j. A function cannot change the length of a vector that is passed by reference.

PROGRAMMING EXERCISES

Exercise P6.1. Write a program that initializes an array with ten random integers and then prints four lines of output, containing
   • Every element at an even index.
   • Every even element.
   • All elements in reverse order.
   • Only the first and last element.

Exercise P6.2. Modify the `largest.cpp` program to mark both the smallest and the largest element.

Exercise P6.3. Reimplement How To 6.1 on page 262 without removing the minimum from the vector of scores. Instead, compute the final score as the difference of the sum and the minimum of the scores.

Exercise P6.4. Write a function `void remove_min` that removes the minimum value from a vector without calling other methods. *Hint:* You can accomplish this task with two loops if you keep track of the index of the smallest value in the first loop.

Exercise P6.5. Write a function that computes the *alternating sum* of all elements in a vector. For example, if `alternating_sum` is called with a vector containing

$$1 \quad 4 \quad 9 \quad 16 \quad 9 \quad 7 \quad 4 \quad 9 \quad 11$$

then it computes

$$1 - 4 + 9 - 16 + 9 - 7 + 4 - 9 + 11 = -2$$

Exercise P6.6. Write a function `reverse` that reverses the sequence of elements in a vector. For example, if `reverse` is called with a vector containing

$$1 \quad 4 \quad 9 \quad 16 \quad 9 \quad 7 \quad 4 \quad 9 \quad 11$$

then the vector is changed to

$$11 \quad 9 \quad 4 \quad 7 \quad 9 \quad 16 \quad 9 \quad 4 \quad 1$$

Exercise P6.7. Write a function

```
vector<int> append(vector<int> a, vector<int> b)
```

that appends one vector after another. For example, if a is

$$1 \quad 4 \quad 9 \quad 16$$

and b is

$$9 \quad 7 \quad 4 \quad 9 \quad 11$$

then append returns the vector

$$1 \quad 4 \quad 9 \quad 16 \quad 9 \quad 7 \quad 4 \quad 9 \quad 11$$

Exercise P6.8. Write a function

```
vector<int> merge(vector<int> a, vector<int> b)
```

that merges two vectors, alternating elements from both vectors. If one vector is shorter than the other, then alternate as long as you can and then append the remaining elements from the longer vector. For example, if a is

$$1 \quad 4 \quad 9 \quad 16$$

and b is

$$9 \quad 7 \quad 4 \quad 9 \quad 11$$

then `merge` returns the vector

$$1 \quad 9 \quad 4 \quad 7 \quad 9 \quad 4 \quad 16 \quad 9 \quad 11$$

Exercise P6.9. Write a function

```
vector<int> merge_sorted(vector<int> a, vector<int> b)
```

that merges two *sorted* vectors, producing a new sorted vector. Keep an index into each vector, indicating how much of it has been processed already. Each time, append the smallest unprocessed element from either vector, then advance the index. For example, if a is

$$1 \quad 4 \quad 9 \quad 16$$

and b is

$$4 \quad 7 \quad 9 \quad 9 \quad 11$$

then `merge_sorted` returns the vector

$$1 \quad 4 \quad 4 \quad 7 \quad 9 \quad 9 \quad 9 \quad 11 \quad 16$$

Exercise P6.10. Write a function

```
bool equals(vector<int> a, vector<int> b)
```

that checks whether two vectors have the same elements in the same order.

Exercise P6.11. Write a function

```
bool same_set(vector<int> a, vector<int> b)
```

that checks whether two vectors have the same elements in some order, ignoring duplicates. For example, the two vectors

$$1 \quad 4 \quad 9 \quad 16 \quad 9 \quad 7 \quad 4 \quad 9 \quad 11$$

and

$$11 \quad 11 \quad 7 \quad 9 \quad 16 \quad 4 \quad 1$$

would be considered identical. You will probably need one or more helper functions.

Exercise P6.12. Write a predicate function

```
bool same_elements(vector<int> a, vector<int> b)
```

that checks whether two vectors have the same elements in some order, with the same multiplicities. For example,

$$1 \quad 4 \quad 9 \quad 16 \quad 9 \quad 7 \quad 4 \quad 9 \quad 11$$

and

$$11 \quad 1 \quad 4 \quad 9 \quad 16 \quad 9 \quad 7 \quad 4 \quad 9$$

would be considered identical, but

$$1 \quad 4 \quad 9 \quad 16 \quad 9 \quad 7 \quad 4 \quad 9 \quad 11$$

and

$$11 \quad 11 \quad 7 \quad 9 \quad 16 \quad 4 \quad 1$$

would not. You will probably need one or more helper functions.

Exercise P6.13. Write a function that removes duplicates from a vector. For example, if remove_duplicates is called with a vector containing

$$1 \quad 4 \quad 9 \quad 16 \quad 9 \quad 7 \quad 4 \quad 9 \quad 11$$

then the vector is changed to

$$1 \quad 4 \quad 9 \quad 16 \quad 7 \quad 11$$

Exercise P6.14. A *run* is a sequence of adjacent repeated values. Write a program that generates a sequence of 20 random die tosses and that prints the die values, marking the runs by including them in parentheses, like this:

```
1 2 (5 5) 3 1 2 4 3 (2 2 2 2) 3 6 (5 5) 6 3 1
```

Use the following pseudocode:

```
Set a boolean variable in_run to false.
For each valid index i in the vector
{
   If in_run
   {
      If values[i] is different from the preceding value
      {
         Print )
         in_run = false
      }
   }
   Else
   {
      If values[i] is the same as the following value
      {
         Print (
         in_run = true
      }
   }
   Print values[i]
}
If in_run, print )
```

Exercise P6.15. Write a program that generates a sequence of 20 random die tosses and that prints the die values, marking only the longest run, like this:

```
1 2 5 5 3 1 2 4 3 (2 2 2 2) 3 6 5 5 6 3 1
```

If there is more than one run of maximum length, mark the first one.

Exercise P6.16. Write a program that generates a sequence of 20 random values between 0 and 99, prints the sequence, sorts it, and prints the sorted sequence. Use the sort function from the standard C++ library.

Exercise P6.17. Write a program that produces ten random permutations of the numbers 1 to 10. To generate a random permutation, you need to fill a vector with the numbers 1 to 10 so that no two entries of the vector have the same contents. You could do it by brute force, by generating random values until you have a value that is not yet in the vector. But that is inefficient. Instead, follow this algorithm.

```
Make a second vector and fill it with the numbers 1 to 10.
Repeat 10 times
{
    Pick a random element from the second vector.
    Remove it and append it to the permutation vector.
}
```

Exercise P6.18. It is a well-researched fact that men in a restroom generally prefer to maximize their distance from already occupied stalls, by occupying the middle of the longest sequence of unoccupied places.

For example, consider the situation where all ten stalls are empty.

```
_ _ _ _ _ _ _ _ _ _
```

The first visitor will occupy a middle position:

```
_ _ _ _ X _ _ _ _ _
```

The next visitor will be in the middle of the empty area at the right.

```
_ _ _ _ X _ _ X _ _
```

Given an array of `bool` values, where `true` indicates an occupied stall, find the position for the next visitor. Your computation should be placed in a function

```
next_visitor(vector<bool>& occupied)
```

Exercise P6.19. *Magic squares.* An $n \times n$ matrix that is filled with the numbers 1, 2, 3, ..., n^2 is a magic square if the sum of the elements in each row, in each column, and in the two diagonals is the same value.

16	3	2	13
5	10	11	8
9	6	7	12
4	15	14	1

Write a program that reads in 16 values from the keyboard and tests whether they form a magic square when put into a 4 × 4 array. You need to test two features:

1. Does each of the numbers 1, 2, ..., 16 occur in the user input?

2. When the numbers are put into a square, are the sums of the rows, columns, and diagonals equal to each other?

Exercise P6.20. Implement the following algorithm to construct magic $n \times n$ squares; it works only if n is odd.

```
Set row = n - 1, column = n / 2.
For k = 1 ... n
{
    Place k at [row][column].
    Increment row and column.
    If the row or column is n, replace it with 0.
    If the element at [row][column] has already been filled
        or you are in the lower right corner
    {
        Decrement row.
    }
}
```

Here is the 5×5 square that you get if you follow this method:

```
11 18 25  2  9
10 12 19 21  3
 4  6 13 20 22
23  5  7 14 16
17 24  1  8 15
```

Write a program whose input is the number n and whose output is the magic square of order n if n is odd.

Exercise P6.21. Write a function

```
void bar_chart(vector<double> data)
```

that displays a bar chart of the values in data, using asterisks, like this:

```
************************
******************************************
*****************************
***************************
**************
```

You may assume that all values in data are positive. First figure out the maximum value in data. That value's bar should be drawn with 40 asterisks. Shorter bars should use proportionally fewer asterisks.

Exercise P6.22. Improve the bar_chart function of Exercise P6.21 to work correctly when data contains negative values.

Exercise P6.23. Improve the bar_chart function of Exercise P6.21 by adding an array of captions for each bar. The output should look like this:

```
      Egypt ************************
     France ******************************************
      Japan *****************************
    Uruguay ***************************
Switzerland **************
```

Exercise P6.24. A theater seating chart is implemented as a two-dimensional array of ticket prices, like this:

```
10 10 10 10 10 10 10 10 10 10
10 10 10 10 10 10 10 10 10 10
10 10 10 10 10 10 10 10 10 10
10 10 20 20 20 20 20 20 10 10
10 10 20 20 20 20 20 20 10 10
10 10 20 20 20 20 20 20 10 10
20 20 30 30 40 40 30 30 20 20
20 30 30 40 50 50 40 30 30 20
30 40 50 50 50 50 50 50 40 30
```

Write a program that prompts users to pick either a seat or a price. Mark sold seats by changing the price to 0. When a user specifies a seat, make sure it is available. When a user specifies a price, find any seat with that price.

Exercise P6.25. Write a program that plays tic-tac-toe. The tic-tac-toe game is played on a 3 × 3 grid as in

The game is played by two players, who take turns. The first player marks moves with a circle, the second with a cross. The player who has formed a horizontal, vertical, or diagonal sequence of three marks wins. Your program should draw the game board, ask the user for the coordinates of the next mark, change the players after every successful move, and pronounce the winner.

ANSWERS TO SELF-CHECK QUESTIONS

1. `int primes[] = { 2, 3, 5, 7, 11 };`

2. `2, 3, 5, 3, 2`

3. `3, 4, 6, 8, 12`

4. `data[0] = 0;`
   `data[SIZE - 1] = 0;`

5. `for (int i = SIZE - 1; i >= 0; i--)`
   `{`
   `   cout << data[i] << endl;`
   `}`

6. `string words[10];`

7. `string words[] = { "Yes", "No" };`

8.
```
vector<int> primes(5);
primes[0] = 2;
primes[1] = 3;
primes[2] = 5;
primes[3] = 7;
primes[4] = 11;
```
or
```
vector<int> primes;
primes.push_back(2);
primes.push_back(3);
primes.push_back(5);
primes.push_back(7);
primes.push_back(11);
```

9. "Ann", "Cal"

10. Since you know the size of the array at compile time, there is no disadvantage to using an array, and it is easier to initialize:
```
string weekday_names[] = { "Monday", "Tuesday", "Wednesday", "Thursday",
   "Friday", "Saturday", "Sunday" };
```

11.
```
20 <== largest value
10
20 <== largest value
```

12.
```
int count = 0;
for (int i = 0; i < data.size(); i++)
{
   if (data[i] == 0)
   {
      count++;
   }
}
```

13. Simply collect the matches. The count is obtained as `matches.size()`.

14. If all elements of data are negative, then the result is incorrectly computed as 0.

15.
```
for (int i = 0; i < data.size(); i++)
{
   cout << data[i];
   if (i < data.size() - 1)
   {
      cout << " | ";
   }
}
```
Now you know why we set up the loop the other way.

16. If the vector has no elements, then a random value is printed.

17. If there is a match, then `pos` is incremented before the loop exits.

18. This loop sets all elements to `data[pos]`.

19. `target` must be a reference parameter, `source` should be a value parameter.

20. The function will compile and run correctly. However, programmers who look at the definition will scratch their heads.

21. The sum function will add up all the numbers in the data array and the next 900 numbers, yielding a random result. (Actually, there is the chance that the program doesn't have the right to access all those numbers, in which case the operating system will terminate it.)

22. `vector<int> numbers = squares(5);`

23. `int numbers[5];`
`squares(5, numbers);`

24. You get the total number of gold, silver, and bronze medals in the competition. In our example, there are four of each.

25.
```
for (int i = 0; i < 8; i++)
{
   for (j = 0; j < 8; j++)
   {
      board[i][j] = (i + j) % 2;
   }
}
```

26. `string board[3][3];`

27. `board[0][2] = "x";`

28. `board[0][0], board[1][1], board[2][2]`

Pointers

CHAPTER GOALS

- To learn how to declare, initialize, and use pointers

- To become familiar with dynamic memory allocation and deallocation

- To understand the relationship between arrays and pointers

- To be able to convert between string objects and character pointers

A **variable** *contains* a value, but a pointer specifies *where* a value is located. In C++, pointers are important for several reasons. Pointers can refer to values that are allocated on demand. Pointers allow sharing of values. Furthermore, as you will see in Chapter 10, pointers are necessary for implementing *polymorphism*, an important concept in object-oriented programming.

In C++, there is a deep relationship between pointers and arrays. You will see in this chapter how this relationship explains a number of special properties and limitations of arrays.

CHAPTER CONTENTS

7.1   Accessing Variables Through Pointers

Pointers allow you to write code that accesses different variables in a uniform way. Consider a person who wants a program for making bank deposits and withdrawals, but who may not always use the same bank account. By using a pointer, it is possible to switch to a different account without modifying the code for deposits and withdrawals.

Let's start with a variable for storing an account balance:

```
double harrys_account = 0;
```

> A pointer denotes the location of a variable in memory.

If Harry anticipates that he may not always use that account, he can use a pointer to access it or some other account. A pointer tells you *where* a value is located, not what the value is.

Harry declares a pointer variable and initializes it with the address of an account:

```
double* account_pointer = &harrys_account;
```

> The type T* denotes a pointer to a variable of type T.

The type double*, or "pointer to double", denotes the location of a double variable. The & operator yields the location (or *address*) of a variable. Taking the address of a double variable yields a value of type double*.

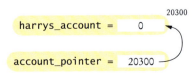

Figure 1
A Pointer Variable

Like a pointer that points to different locations on a blackboard, a C++ pointer can point to different memory locations.

The & operator yields the location of a variable.

Thinking about pointers can be rather abstract, but you can use a simple trick to make it more tangible. Every variable in a computer program is located in a specific memory location. You don't know where each variable is stored, but you can pretend you do. Let's pretend that we know that harrys_account is stored in location 20300. (That is just a made-up value.) As shown in Figure 1, the value of harrys_account is 0, but the value of &harrys_account is 20300. The value of account_pointer is also 20300. In our diagrams, we will draw an arrow from a pointer to the location, but of course the computer doesn't store arrows, just numbers.

By using a pointer, Harry can switch to a different account at any time. To access a different account, simply change the pointer value (see Figure 2):

```
account_pointer = &joint_account;
```

Figure 2 Changing a Pointer

SYNTAX 7.1 Pointer Syntax

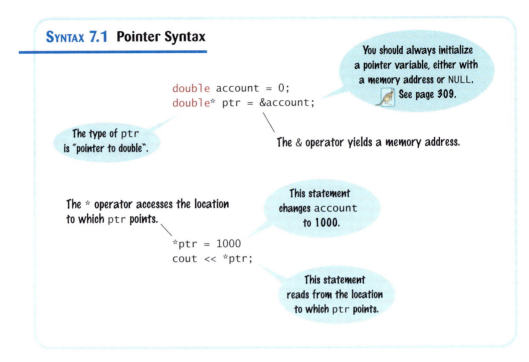

You should always initialize a pointer variable, either with a memory address or NULL.
See page 309.

```
double account = 0;
double* ptr = &account;
```

The type of ptr is "pointer to double".

The & operator yields a memory address.

The * operator accesses the location to which ptr points.

This statement changes account to 1000.

```
*ptr = 1000
cout << *ptr;
```

This statement reads from the location to which ptr points.

> The * operator locates the value to which a pointer points.

When you have a pointer to a variable, you will want to access the value to which it points. In C++ the * operator is used to indicate the location associated with a pointer. (When used with pointers, the * operator has no relationship with multiplication.) For example, this statement makes an initial deposit into the account:

```
*account_pointer = 1000;
```

In other words, you can use *account_pointer in exactly the same way as harrys_account or joint_account. Which account is used depends on the value of the pointer. When the program executes this statement, it fetches the address stored in account_pointer. It then uses the variable at that address, as shown in Figure 3.

An expression such as *account_pointer can be on the left or the right of an assignment. When it occurs on the left, then a value is stored in the location to which the pointer refers. When it occurs on the right, then the value is fetched from the location. For example, this statement prints the account balance.

```
cout << *account_pointer << endl;
```

You can have *account_pointer on both sides of an assignment. The following statement withdraws $100.

```
*account_pointer = *account_pointer - 100;
```

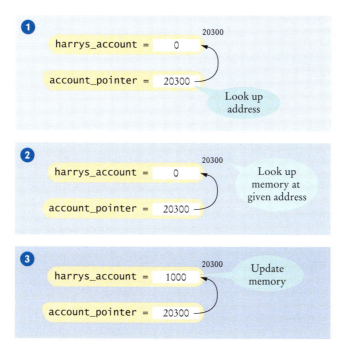

Figure 3   Executing the Assignment *account_pointer = 1000

> It is an error to use an
> uninitialized pointer.

When a pointer variable is first defined, it contains a random address. Using that random address is an error. In practice, your program will likely crash or mysteriously misbehave if you use an uninitialized pointer:

```
double* account_pointer;
    // Forgot to initialize
*account_pointer = 1000;
    // NO! account_pointer contains an unpredictable value
```

> The NULL pointer does not
> point to any object.

There is a special value, NULL, that you can use to indicate a pointer that doesn't point anywhere. If you define a pointer variable and are not ready to initialize it quite yet, it is a good idea to set it to NULL.

```
double* account_pointer = NULL; // Will set later
```

You can later test whether the pointer is still NULL. If it is, don't use it.

```
if (account_pointer != NULL) { cout << *account_pointer; } // OK
```

Trying to access data through a NULL pointer is still illegal, and it will cause your program to terminate.

Table 1 contains additional pointer examples.

Table 1 Pointer Syntax Examples

Assume the following declarations:
```
int m = 10; // Assumed to be at address 20300
int n = 20; // Assumed to be at address 20304
int* p = &m;
```

Expression	Value	Comment
p	20300	The address of m.
*p	10	The value stored at that address.
&n	20304	The address of n.
p = &n;		Set p to the address of n.
*p	20	The value stored at the changed address.
m = *p;		Stores 20 into m.
🚫 m = p;	Error	m is an int value; p is an int* pointer. The types are not compatible.
🚫 &10	Error	You can only take the address of a variable.
&p	The address of p, perhaps 20308	This is the location of a pointer variable, not the location of an integer.

The following program demonstrates the behavior of pointers. We execute the same withdrawal statement twice, but with different values for account_pointer. Each time, a different account is modified.

ch07/accounts.cpp

```
1   #include <iostream>
2
3   using namespace std;
4
5   int main()
6   {
7      double harrys_account = 0;
8      double joint_account = 2000;
9      double* account_pointer = &harrys_account;
10
11     *account_pointer = 1000; // Initial deposit
12
13     *account_pointer = *account_pointer - 100; // Withdraw $100
14     cout << "Balance: " << *account_pointer << endl; // Print balance
15
```

```
16      // Change the pointer value
17      account_pointer = &joint_account;
18
19      // The same statements affect a different account
20      *account_pointer = *account_pointer - 100; // Withdraw $100
21      cout << "Balance: " << *account_pointer << endl; // Print balance
22
23      return 0;
24   }
```

Program Run

```
Balance: 900
Balance: 1900
```

SELF CHECK

1. Consider this set of statements. What is printed?

```
int a = 1;
int b = 2;
int* p = &a;
cout << *p << endl;
p = &b;
cout << *p << endl;
```

2. Consider this set of statements. What is printed?

```
int a = 1;
int b = 2;
int* p = &a;
int* q = &b;
*p = *q;
cout << a << " " << b << endl;
```

3. Consider this set of statements. What is printed?

```
int a = 15;
int* p = &a;
int* q = &a;
cout << *p + *q << endl;
```

4. Consider this set of statements. What is printed?

```
int a = 15;
int* p = &a;
int* q = &a;
*p = *p + 10;
cout << *q << endl;
```

5. Consider this set of statements. What is printed?

```
int a = 15;
int* p = &a;
cout << *p << " " << p << endl;
```

COMMON ERROR 7.1

Confusing Pointers with the Data to Which They Point

A pointer is a memory address—a number that tells where a value is located in memory. It is a common error to confuse the pointer with the variable to which it points:

```
double* account_pointer = &joint_account;
account_pointer = 1000; // ERROR
```

The assignment statement does not set the joint account balance to 1000. Instead, it sets the pointer to point to memory address 1000. The pointer `account_pointer` only describes *where* the joint account variable is, and it almost certainly is not located at address 1000. Most compilers will report an error for this assignment.

To actually access the variable, use `*account_pointer`:

```
*account_pointer = 1000; // OK
```

QUALITY TIP 7.1

Defining Two Pointers on the Same Line

It is legal in C++ to define multiple variables together, like this:

```
int i = 0, j = 1;
```

This style is confusing when used with pointers:

```
double* p, q;
```

The `*` associates only with the first variable. That is, `p` is a `double*` pointer, and `q` is a `double` value. To avoid any confusion, it is best to define each pointer variable separately:

```
double* p;
double* q;
```

7.2 Arrays and Pointers

> The value of an array variable is a pointer to the starting element of the array.

Pointers are particularly useful for understanding the peculiarities of arrays. Consider this declaration of an array:

```
int a[10];
```

As you know, `a[3]` denotes an array element. You can also use the variable name `a` without brackets. The name of the array denotes a pointer to the starting element (see Figure 4). You can capture that pointer in a variable.

```
int* p = a; // Now p points to a[0]
```

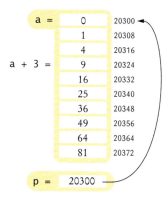

Figure 4   Pointers into an Array

If you prefer, you can use a as a pointer: The statement

```
cout << *a;
```

has the same effect as the statement

```
cout << a[0];
```

> Pointer arithmetic means adding an integer offset to an array pointer, yielding a pointer that skips past the given number of elements.

Moreover, pointers into arrays support *pointer arithmetic.* You can add an integer offset to the pointer to point at another array location. For example,

```
a + 3
```

is a pointer to the array element with index 3. The expression

```
*(a + 3)
```

has exactly the same meaning as a[3]. In fact, for any integer n, it is true that

```
a[n]  is the same as  *(a + n)
```

> The array/pointer duality law states that a[n] is identical to *(a + n), where a is a pointer into an array and n is an integer offset.

This relationship is called the *array/pointer duality law.*
This law explains why all C++ arrays start with an index of zero. The pointer a (or a + 0) points to the starting element of the array. That element must therefore be a[0].

To better understand pointer arithmetic, let's again pretend that we know actual memory addresses. Suppose the array a starts at address 20300. The array contains ten values of type double. A double value occupies 8 bytes of memory. Therefore, the array occupies 80 bytes, from 20300 to 20379. The starting value is located at address 20300, the next one at address 20308, and so on (see Figure 4). Table 2 on page 297 shows pointer arithmetic and the array/pointer duality using this example.

Once you understand the connection between arrays and pointers, it becomes clear why array parameters are different from other parameter types. As an example, consider this function that computes the sum of all values in an array:

```
double sum(double a[], int size)
{
```

```
    double total = 0;
    for (int i = 0; i < size; i++)
    {
        total = total + a[i];
    }
    return total;
}
```

Here is a call to the function (see Figure 5):

```
double data[10];
... // Initialize data
double s = sum(data, 10);
```

> When passing an array to a function, only the starting address is passed.

The value `data` is passed to the `sum` function. It is actually a pointer of type `double*`, pointing to the starting element of the array. One would therefore expect that the function is declared as

```
double sum(double* a, int size)
```

However, if you look closely at the function definition, you will see that the parameter is declared as an array with empty bounds:

```
double sum(double a[], int size)
```

As viewed by the C++ compiler, these parameter declarations are completely equivalent. The `[]` notation is "syntactic sugar" for declaring a pointer. (Computer scientists use the term "syntactic sugar" to describe a notation that is easy to read for humans and that masks a complex implementation detail.) The array notation gives human readers the illusion that an entire array is passed to the function, but in fact the function receives only the starting address for the array.

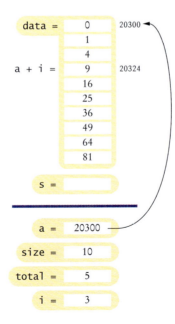

Figure 5   Passing an Array to a Function

Now consider this statement in the body of the function:

```
total = total + a[i];
```

The C++ compiler considers a to be a *pointer*, not an array. The expression a[i] is syntactic sugar for *(a + i). That expression denotes the storage location that is i elements away from the address stored in the variable a, as shown in Figure 5.

You can now understand why it is always necessary to pass the size of the array. The function receives a single memory address, which tells it where the array starts. That memory address enables the function to locate the values in the array. But the function also needs to know where to stop.

Table 2 Arrays and Pointers

Expression	Value	Comment
a	20300	The starting address of the array, here assumed to be 20300.
*a	0	The value stored at that address. (The array contains values 0, 1, 4, 9, ...)
a + 1	20308	The address of the next double value in the array. A double occupies 8 bytes.
a + 3	20324	The address of the element with index 3, obtained by skipping past 3 × 8 bytes.
*(a + 3)	9	The value stored at address 20324.
a[3]	9	The same as *(a + 3) by array/pointer duality.
*a + 3	3	The sum of *a and 3. Since there are no parentheses, the * refers only to a.
&a[3]	20324	The address of the element with index 3, the same as a + 3.

SELF CHECK

For problems 6–9, draw the array and pointer as in Figure 4. Assume a starting address (20300 will work fine), and assume that each int value occupies 4 bytes.

6. What is the contents of the array a after these statements?

```
int a[] = { 2, 3, 5 };
int* p = a;
p++;
*p = 0;
```

7. What is the contents of the array a after these statements?

```
int a[] = { 2, 3, 5 };
int* p = a + 1;
*(p + 1) = 0;
```

8. What is the contents of the array a after these statements?

```
int a[] = { 2, 3, 5 };
int* p = a;
int* q = a + 2;
p++;
q--;
*p = *q;
```

9. What do the following statements print?

```
int a[] = { 2, 3, 5 };
cout << *a + 2 << " ";
cout << *(a + 2) << endl;
```

10. In Chapter 6, we defined a function

```
void squares(int n, int result[])
```

Declare the parameter using pointer notation.

ADVANCED TOPIC 7.1

Using a Pointer to Step Through an Array

Now that you know that the first parameter of the sum function is a pointer, you can implement the function in a slightly different way. Rather than incrementing an integer index, you can increment a pointer variable to visit all array elements in turn:

```
double sum(double* a, int size)
{
    double total = 0;
    double* p = a; // p starts at the beginning of the array
    for (int i = 0; i < size; i++)
    {
        total = total + *p; // Add the value to which p points
        p++; // Advance p to the next array element
    }
    return total;
}
```

Initially, the pointer p points to the element a[0]. The increment

```
p++;
```

moves it to point to the next element (see Figure 6).

It is a tiny bit more efficient to use and increment a pointer than to access an array element as a[i]. For this reason, some programmers routinely use pointers instead of indexes to access array elements.

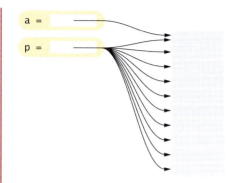

Figure 6 A Pointer Variable Traversing the Elements of an Array

QUALITY TIP 7.2

Program Clearly, Not Cleverly

Some programmers take great pride in minimizing the number of instructions, even if the resulting code is hard to understand. For example, here is a legal implementation of the sum function:

```
double sum(double* a, int size)
{
    double total = 0;
    while (size-- > 0) // Loop size times
    {
        total = total + *a++; // Add the value to which a points; increment a
    }
    return total;
}
```

This implementation uses two tricks. First, the function parameters a and size are variables, and it is legal to modify them. Moreover, the expressions

```
size--
```

and

```
a++
```

mean "decrement or increment the variable and return the old value". Therefore, *a++ increments the pointer to the next element, but it returns the element to which it pointed before the increment.

Please do not use this programming style. Your job as a programmer is not to dazzle other programmers with your cleverness, but to write code that is easy to understand and maintain.

COMMON ERROR 7.2

Returning a Pointer to a Local Variable

Consider this function that tries to return a pointer to an array containing two elements, the first and the last value of an array.

```
double* firstlast(double a[], int size)
{
   double result[2];
   result[0] = a[0];
   result[1] = a[size - 1];
   return result; // ERROR!
}
```

The function returns a pointer to the starting element of the result array. However, that array is a local variable of the firstlast function. The local variable is no longer valid when the function exits, and the values will soon be overwritten by other function calls.

You can solve this problem by returning a vector:

```
vector<double> firstlast(const double a[], int size)
{
   vector<double> result(2);
   result[0] = a[0];
   result[1] = a[size - 1];
   return result; // OK!
}
```

ADVANCED TOPIC 7.2

Constant Pointers

The following definition specifies a constant pointer:

```
const double* p = &balance;
```

You cannot modify the value to which p points. That is, the following statement is illegal:

```
*p = 0; // ERROR
```

Of course, you can read the value:

```
cout << *p; // OK
```

A constant array parameter is syntactic sugar for a constant pointer. For example, consider the function

```
double sum(const double[] a, int size)
```

This definition is equivalent to

```
double sum(const double* a, int size)
```

The function can use the pointer a to read the array elements, but it cannot modify them.

7.3 C and C++ Strings

C++ has two mechanisms for manipulating strings. The string class supports character sequences of arbitrary length and provides convenient operations such as concatenation and string comparison. However, C++ also inherits a more primitive level of string handling from the C language, in which strings are represented as arrays of char values. In the following sections, we will discuss the relationships between these types.

7.3.1 The char Type

A value of type char denotes an individual character. Character literals are enclosed in single quotes.

The char type denotes an individual character. Character literals are delimited by single quotes; for example,

```
char input = 'y';
```

Each character is actually encoded as an integer value. (See Appendix D for the encoding using the ASCII code, which is used on the majority of computers today.)

Note that 'y' is a single character, which is quite different from "y", a string containing the 'y' character.

Table 3 on page 302 shows typical character literals.

7.3.2 C Strings

A literal string (enclosed in double quotes) is an array of char values with a zero terminator.

In the C programming language, strings are always represented as character arrays. C++ programmers often refer to arrays of char values as "C strings".

In particular, a literal string, such as "Harry", is *not* an object of type string. Instead, it is an array of char values. As with all arrays, a string literal can be assigned to a pointer variable that points to the initial character in the array:

```
char* char_pointer = "Harry"; // Points to 'H'
```

A C string is terminated by a special character, called a *null terminator*, denoted '\0'. For example, the C string "Harry" contains *six* characters, namely 'H', 'a', 'r', 'r', 'y' and '\0' (See Figure 7.)

Figure 7
A Character Array

Table 3	Character Literals
`'y'`	The character y
`'0'`	The character for the digit 0. In the ASCII code, `'0'` has the value 48.
`' '`	The space character
`'\n'`	The newline character
`'\t'`	The tab character
`'\0'`	The null terminator of a string
🚫 `"y"`	**Error:** Not a char value

The terminator is a character that is encoded as the number zero—this is different from the character `'0'`, the character denoting the zero digit. (Under the ASCII encoding scheme, the character denoting the zero digit is encoded as the number 48.)

Functions that operate on C strings rely on this terminator. Here is a typical example, the strlen function declared in the <cstring> header that computes the length of a character array. The function counts the number of characters until it reaches the terminator.

```
int strlen(const char s[])
{
   int i = 0;
   while (s[i] != '\0') { i++; } // Count characters before the null terminator
   return i;
}
```

The call strlen("Harry") returns 5.

7.3.3 Character Arrays

A literal string such as "Harry" is a constant. You are not allowed to modify its characters. If you want to modify the characters in a string, define a character array instead. For example:

```
char char_array[] = "Harry"; // An array of 6 characters
```

The char_array variable is an array of 6 characters, containing `'H'`, `'a'`, `'r'`, `'r'`, `'y'`, and a null terminator. The compiler counts the characters in the string that is used for initializing the array, including the null terminator.

You can modify the characters in the array:

```
char_array[0] = 'L';
```

7.3.4 Converting Between C and C++ Strings

Before the C++ string class became widely available, direct manipulation of character arrays was common, but also quite challenging (see Advanced Topic 7.3 on page 304). If you use functions that receive or return C strings, you need to know how to convert between C strings and string objects.

Many library functions use pointers of type char*.

For example, the <cstdlib> header declares a useful function

```
int atoi(const char s[])
```

The atoi function converts a character array containing digits into its integer value:

```
char* year = "2012";
int y = atoi(year); // Now y is the integer 2012
```

The c_str member function yields a char* pointer from a string object.

This functionality is inexplicably missing from the C++ string class. The c_str member function of the string class offers an "escape hatch". If s is a string, then s.c_str() yields a char* pointer to the characters in the string. Here is how you use that member function to call the atoi function:

```
string year = "2012";
int y = atoi(year.c_str());
```

You can initialize C++ string variables with C strings.

Conversely, converting from a C string to a C++ string is very easy. Simply initialize a string variable with the C string. For example, the definition

```
string name = "Harry";
```

initializes the C++ string object name with the C string "Harry".

7.3.5 C++ Strings are Vectors of Characters

Up to this point, we have always used the substr member function to access individual characters in a C++ string. For example, if a string variable is defined as

```
string name = "Harry";
```

the expression

```
name.substr(3, 1)
```

yields a string of length 1 containing the character at index 3.

You can access characters in a C++ string object with the [] operator.

You can access individual characters with the [] operator:

```
name[0] = 'L';
```

Now the string is "Larry". The [] operator is more convenient than the substr function if you want to visit a string one character at a time.

Here is a useful example. The following function makes a copy of a string and changes all characters to uppercase:

```
/**
    Makes an uppercase version of a string.
```

```
        @param str a string
        @return a string with the characters in str converted to uppercase
    */
    string uppercase(string str)
    {
        string result = str; // Make a copy of str
        for (int i = 0; i < result.length(); i++)
        {
            result[i] = toupper(result[i]); // Convert each character to uppercase
        }
        return result;
    }
```

For example, uppercase("Harry") returns a string with the characters "HARRY".

The toupper function is defined in the <cctype> header. It converts lowercase characters to uppercase. (The tolower function does the opposite.)

SELF CHECK

11. How many char values are stored in the character array "Hello, World!\n"?

12. What is strlen("Hello, World!\n")?

13. Allocate a pointer variable that points to the string "Hello".

14. Consider this statement:

```
string title = "Agent" + 007;
```

Does the statement compile? What is its effect?

15. Consider the following statements:

```
cout << "Enter an integer, Q to quit";
string input;
cin >> input;
if (input == "Q") { return; }
```

If the input is not the letter Q, how do you extract the number stored in the string input?

ADVANCED TOPIC 7.3

Working with C Strings

Before the string class became widely available, it was common to work with character arrays directly.

Table 4 shows several commonly used functions for manipulating C strings. All of these functions are declared in the <cstring> header.

Consider the task of concatenating a first name and a last name into a string. The string class makes this very easy:

```
string first = "Harry";
string last = "Smith";
string name = first + " " + last;
```

Let us implement this task with C strings. Allocate an array of characters for the result:

```
const int NAME_SIZE = 40;
char name[NAME_SIZE];
```

This array can hold strings with a length of at most 39, because one character is required for the null terminator.

Now copy the first name, using strncpy:

```
strncpy(name, first, NAME_SIZE - 1);
```

You must be careful not to overrun the target array. It is unlikely that a first name is longer than 39 characters, but a hacker could supply a longer input in order to overwrite memory.

	Table 4 **C String Functions**
	In this table, s and t are character arrays; n is an integer.

Function	Description
strlen(s)	Returns the length of s.
strcpy(t, s)	Copies the characters from s into t.
strncpy(t, s, n)	Copies at most n characters from s into t.
strcat(t, s)	Appends the characters from s after the end of the characters in t.
strncat(t, s, n);	Appends at most n characters from s after the end of the characters in t.
strcmp(s, t)	Returns 0 if s and t have the same contents, a negative integer if s comes before t in lexicographic order, a positive integer otherwise.

Now, if there is still room, add a space and the last name, again being careful not to overrun the array boundaries.

```
int length = strlen(name);
if (length < NAME_SIZE - 1)
{
   strcat(name, " ");
   int n = NAME_SIZE - 2 - length; // Leave room for space, null terminator
   if (n > 0)
   {
      strncat(name, last, n);
   }
}
```

7.4 Dynamic Memory Allocation

Use dynamic memory allocation if you do not know in advance how many values you need.

In many programming situations, you do not know beforehand how many values you need. To solve this problem, you can use *dynamic allocation* and ask the C++ run-time system to create new values whenever you need them. The run-time system keeps a large storage area, called the *heap*, that can allocate values and arrays of any type. When you ask for a

```
new double
```

The new operator allocates memory from the heap.

then a storage location of type `double` is located on the heap, and a pointer to that location is returned. More usefully, the expression

```
new double[n]
```

allocates an array of size n, and yields a pointer to the starting element. (Here n need *not* be a constant.)

You will want to capture that pointer in a variable:

```
double* account_pointer = new double;
double* account_array = new double[n];
```

You now use the pointer as described previously in this chapter. If you allocated an array, the magic of array/pointer duality lets you use the array notation `account_array[i]` to access the ith element.

SYNTAX 7.2 Dynamic Memory Allocation

Capture the pointer in a variable.

The new operator yields a pointer to a memory block of the given type.

```
int* var_ptr = new int;
```

Use the memory.
```
...
*var_ptr = 1000;
...
```

Delete the memory when you are done.
```
delete var_ptr;
```

Use this form to allocate an array of the given size (size need not be a constant).

```
int* array_ptr = new int[size];
...
array_ptr[i] = 1000;
...
delete[] array_ptr;
```

Use the pointer as if it were an array.

Remember to use `delete[]` when deallocating the array.

> You must reclaim dynamically allocated objects with the delete operator.

When your program no longer needs memory that you previously allocated with the new operator, you must return it to the heap, using the delete operator:

```
delete account_pointer;
```

However, if you allocated an array, you must use the delete[] operator.

```
delete[] account_array;
```

This operator reminds the heap that the pointer points to an array, not a single value.

After you delete a memory block, you can no longer use it. The storage space may already be used elsewhere.

```
delete[] account_array;
account_array[0] = 1000; // NO! You no longer own the memory of account_array
```

Heap arrays have one significant advantage over array variables. If you declare an array variable, you must specify a fixed array size when you compile the program. But when you allocate an array on the heap, you can choose the size at run time.

Moreover, if you later need more elements, you are not stuck. You can allocate a bigger heap array, copy the elements from the smaller array into the bigger array, and delete the smaller array (see Figure 8):

```
double* bigger_array = new double[2 * n];
for (int i = 0; i < n; i++)
{
    bigger_array[i] = account_array[i];
}
delete[] account_array;
account_array = bigger_array;
n = 2 * n;
```

This is exactly what a vector does behind the scenes.

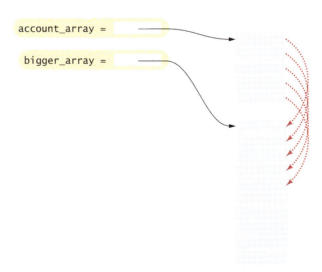

Figure 8
Growing a Dynamic Array

Be sure to recycle any heap memory that your program no longer needs.

Heap allocation is a powerful feature, but you must be very careful to follow all rules precisely:

- Every call to new must be matched by exactly one call to delete.
- Use delete[] to delete arrays.
- Don't access a memory block after it has been deleted.

If you don't follow these rules, your program can crash or run unpredictably. Table 5 shows common errors.

Table 5   Common Memory Allocation Errors

Statements	Error

`int* p;`
`*p = 5;`
`delete p;`
	There is no call to new int.

`int* p = new int;`
`*p = 5;`
`p = new int;`
	The first allocated memory block was never deleted.

`int* p = new int[10];`
`*p = 5;`
`delete p;`
	The delete[] operator should have been used.

`int* p = new int[10];`
`int* q = p;`
`q[0] = 5;`
`delete p;`
`delete q;`
	The same memory block was deleted twice.

`int n = 4;`
`int* p = &n;`
`*p = 5;`
`delete p;`
	You can only delete memory blocks that you obtained from calling new.

16. What does this statement sequence print?

```
int* p = new int;
*p = 3;
cout << *p << endl;
delete p;
```

17. What does this statement sequence print?

```
int* p = new int[10];
for (int i = 0; i < 10; i++) { p[i] = i * i; }
cout << *p << " " << *(p + 1) << " " << p[2] << endl;
delete[] p;
```

18. What is wrong with this sequence of statements?

```
int* p = new int[10];
p[10] = 5;
delete[] p;
```

19. Consider this function

```
int* grow(int a[], int size)
{
    int* result = new int[2 * size];
    for (int i = 0; i < size; i++) { result[i] = a[i]; }
    for (int i = size; i < 2 * size; i++) { result[i] = 0; }
    return result;
}
```

What is the contents of the array to which p points after these statements?

```
int primes[] = { 2, 3, 5, 7, 11 };
int* p = grow(primes, 5);
```

20. Consider the grow function of Self Check 19. What must its caller remember to do?

COMMON ERROR 7.3

Dangling Pointers

A very common pointer error is to use a pointer that has not been initialized, or that has already been deleted. Such a pointer is called a *dangling* pointer, because it does point somewhere. You can create real damage by writing to the location to which it points. Even reading from the location can crash your program.

> Using a dangling pointer (a pointer that has not been initialized or has been deleted) is a serious programming error.

An uninitialized pointer has a good chance of pointing to an address that your program doesn't own. On most operating systems, attempting to access such a location causes a processor error, and the operating system shuts down the program. You may have seen that happen to other programs—a dialog box with a bomb icon or a message such as "general protection fault" or "segmentation fault" comes up, and the program is terminated.

If a dangling pointer points to a valid address inside your program, then writing to it will damage some part of your program. You will change the value of one of your variables, or perhaps damage the control structures of the heap so that it starts returning invalid pointers when you call new.

When your program crashes and you restart it, the problem may not reappear, or it may manifest itself in different ways because the random pointer is now initialized with a different random address.

Programming with pointers requires iron discipline.

- *Always* initialize pointer variables. If you can't initialize them with the return value of new or the & operator, then set them to NULL.

- *Never* use a pointer that has been deleted.

COMMON ERROR 7.4

Memory Leaks

Another very common pointer error is to allocate memory on the heap and never deallocate it. A memory block that is never deallocated is called a *memory leak*.

If you allocate a few small blocks of memory and forget to deallocate them, this is not a huge problem. When the program exits, all allocated memory is returned to the operating system.

But if your program runs for a long time, or if it allocates lots of memory (perhaps in a loop), then it can run out of memory. Memory exhaustion will cause your program to crash. In extreme cases, the computer may freeze up if your program exhausted all available memory. Avoiding memory leaks is particularly important in programs that need to run for months or years, without restarting.

> Every call to new should have a matching call to delete.

Even if you write short-lived programs, you should make it a habit to avoid memory leaks. Make sure that every call to the new operator has a corresponding call to the delete operator.

7.5 Arrays and Vectors of Pointers

When you have a sequence of pointers, you can place them into an array or vector. An array and a vector of ten int* pointers are defined as

```
int* pointer_array[10];
vector<int*> pointer_vector(10);
```

The expression pointer_array[i] or pointer_vector[i] denotes the pointer with index i in the sequence.

One application of such pointer sequences are two-dimensional arrays in which each row has a different length, such as the triangular array shown in Figure 9.

Figure 9 A Triangular Array

In this situation, it would not be very efficient to use a two-dimensional array, because almost half of the elements would be wasted.

We will develop a program that uses such an array for simulating a *Galton board*. A Galton board consists of a pyramidal arrangement of pegs, and a row of bins at the bottom. Balls are dropped onto the top peg and travel toward the bins. At each peg, there is a 50 percent chance of moving left or right. The balls in the bins approximate a bell-curve distribution.

The Galton board can only show the balls in the bins, but we can do better by keeping a counter for each peg, incrementing it as a ball travels past it.

We will simulate a board with ten rows of pegs. Each row requires an array of counters. The following statements initialize the triangular array:

```
int* counts[10];
for (int i = 0; i < 10; i++)
{
    counts[i] = new int[i + 1];
}
```

Note that the first element counts[0] contains a pointer to an array of length 1, and the last element counts[9] contains a pointer to an array of length 10.

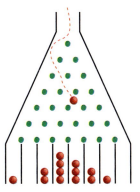

Figure 10
A Galton Board

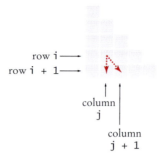

Figure 11

Movement of a Ball in the
Galton Board Array

Before doing the simulation, let us consider how to print out the values. The element counts[i] points to an array. The element of index j of that array is

```
counts[i][j]
```

This loop prints all elements in the ith row:

```
for (int j = 0; j <= i; j++)
{
   cout << setw(4) << counts[i][j];
}
cout << endl;
```

Now let's simulate a falling ball. The movements to the left and right in Figure 10 correspond to movements to the next row, either straight down or to the right, in Figure 11. More precisely, if the ball is currently at row i and column j, then it will go to row i + 1 and, with a 50 percent chance, either stay in column j or go to column j + 1.

The program below has the details. In the sample program run, notice how 1,000 balls have hit the top peg, and how the bottommost row of pegs approximates a bell-curve distribution.

ch07/galton.cpp

```
 1  #include <iostream>
 2  #include <iomanip>
 3  #include <cstdlib>
 4  #include <ctime>
 5
 6  using namespace std;
 7
 8  int main()
 9  {
10     srand(time(0));
11
12     int* counts[10];
13
14     // Allocate the rows
15     for (int i = 0; i < 10; i++)
16     {
17        counts[i] = new int[i + 1];
18        for (int j = 0; j <= i; j++)
19        {
20           counts[i][j] = 0;
```

```
21       }
22     }
23
24     const int RUNS = 1000;
25
26     // Simulate 1,000 balls
27     for (int run = 0; run < RUNS; run++)
28     {
29        // Add a ball to the top
30        counts[0][0]++;
31        // Have the ball run to the bottom
32        int j = 0;
33        for (int i = 1; i < 10; i++)
34        {
35           int r = rand() % 2;
36           // If r is even, move down, otherwise to the right
37           if (r == 1)
38           {
39              j++;
40           }
41           counts[i][j]++;
42        }
43     }
44
45     // Print all counts
46     for (int i = 0; i < 10; i++)
47     {
48        for (int j = 0; j <= i; j++)
49        {
50           cout << setw(4) << counts[i][j];
51        }
52        cout << endl;
53     }
54
55     // Deallocate the rows
56     for (int i = 0; i < 10; i++)
57     {
58        delete[] counts[i];
59     }
60
61     return 0;
62  }
```

Program Run

```
1000
 480 520
 241 500 259
 124 345 411 120
  68 232 365 271   64
  32 164 283 329 161   31
  16  88 229 303 254   88   22
   9  47 147 277 273 190   44   13
   5  24 103 203 288 228 113   33    3
   1  18   64 149 239 265 186   61   15    2
```

SELF CHECK

21. Why didn't we initialize the triangular array with the following loop?

```
for (int i = 0; i < 10; i++)
{
    counts[i] = new int[i];
}
```

22. Suppose a program initializes a triangular array as we did in this section, and then accesses a non-existent element with the statement

```
counts[1][2]++
```

Will the program compile? If so, what happens at run time?

23. Initialize a triangular 10 × 10 array where the first row has length 10 and the last row has length 1.

24. What changes would need to be made to the galton.cpp program so that counts is a vector<int*>?

25. What changes would need to be made to the galton.cpp program so that *each row* is a vector<int>?

How To 7.1

Working with Pointers

You use pointers because you want flexibility in your program: the ability to change the relationships between data. This How To walks you through the decision-making process for using pointers.

We will illustrate the steps with the task of simulating a part of the control logic for a departmental photocopier. A person making a copy enters a user number. There are 100 different users, with numbers 0 to 99. Each user is linked to a copy account, either the master account or one of ten project accounts. That linkage is maintained by the administrator, and it can change as users work on different projects. When copies are made, the appropriate account should be incremented.

Users identify themselves on the copier control panel. Using pointers, the relationships between users and copy accounts can be flexible.

Step 1　Draw a picture.

Start with the data that will be accessed or modified through the pointers. These may be account balances, counters, character strings, or other items. Focus on what is being pointed at.

Then draw the variable or variables that contain the pointers. These will be the front-end to your system. You will start with a pointer, then locate the actual data.

Finally, draw the pointers as arrows. If the pointers will vary as the program executes, draw a typical arrangement.

In our example, we need to track the copy accounts: a master account and ten project accounts. For each user, we need a pointer to the copy account:

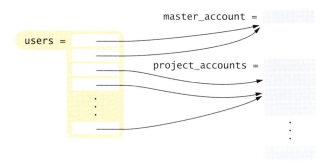

Step 2   Declare pointer variables.

This step is usually easy. With numerical data, you will have pointers of type `int*` or `double*`. If you manipulate character arrays, you use `char*` pointers. In Chapter 10, you will use pointers to objects.

How many pointer variables do you have? If you only have one or two, just declare variables such as

```
double* account_pointer;
```

If you have a sequence of pointers, use a vector or array, such as

```
vector<char*> lines;
```

In our example, the purpose is to manipulate copy counters. Therefore, our data are integers and the pointers have type `int*`. We know that we will have exactly 100 pointers. Therefore, we can choose an array

```
int* users[100];
```

Step 3   Initialize the pointers with variable addresses or heap memory.

Will you allocate variables and then take their addresses with the & operator? That is fine if you have a fixed amount of data that you want to reach through the pointers. Otherwise, use the `new` operator to allocate memory dynamically. Be sure to deallocate the memory when you are done, using the `delete` or `delete[]` operator.

In our example, there is no need for dynamic allocation, so we will just take addresses of variables.

```
int master_account;
int project_accounts[10];
for (int i = 0; i < 100; i++)
{
   users[i] = &master_account;
}
// Link a couple of project accounts to simulate the administrator
users[2] = project_accounts + 1;
users[3] = project_accounts + 2;
users[99] = project_accounts + 2;
```

Step 4   Use the * or [] operator to access your data.

When you access a single variable through a pointer, use the * operator to read or write the variable. For example,

```
*account_pointer = *account_pointer - 100;
```

When you have a pointer to an array, use the [] notation. Simply think of the pointer as the array:

```
account_array[i] = account_array[i] - 100;
```

If you have an array or vector of pointers, then you need brackets to get at an individual pointer. Then supply another * or [] to get at the value. You saw an example in the Galton board simulator where a count was accessed as

```
counts[i][j]
```

Implement your algorithm, keeping these access rules in mind.

In our example, we read the user ID and number of copies. Then we increment the copy account:

```
cin >> id >> copies;
*users[id] = *users[id] + copies;
```

Exercise P7.10 asks you to complete this simulation.

WORKED EXAMPLE 7.1

Producing a Mass Mailing

This Worked Example shows how to use pointers to create a template for a mass mailing.

RANDOM FACT 7.1

Embedded Systems

An *embedded system* is a computer system that controls a device. The device contains a processor and other hardware and is controlled by a computer program. Unlike a personal computer, which has been designed to be flexible and run many different computer programs, the hardware and software of an embedded system are tailored to a specific device. Computer controlled devices are becoming increasingly common, ranging from washing machines to medical equipment, cell phones, automobile engines, and spacecraft.

Several challenges are specific to programming embedded systems. Most importantly, a much higher standard of quality control applies. Vendors are often unconcerned about bugs in personal computer software, because they can always make you install a patch or upgrade to the next version. But in an embedded system, that is not an option. Few consumers would feel comfortable upgrading the software in their washing machines or automobile engines. If you ever handed in a programming assignment that you believed to be correct, only to have the instructor or grader find bugs in it, then you know how hard it is to write software that can reliably do its task for many years without a chance of changing it. Quality standards are especially important in devices whose failure would destroy property or endanger human life. Many personal computer purchasers buy computers that are fast and have a lot of storage, because the investment is paid back over time when many programs are run on the same equipment. But the hardware for an embedded device is not shared—it is dedicated to one device. A separate processor, memory, and so on, are built for every copy of the device (see Figure 12). If it is possible to shave a few pennies off the manufacturing cost of every unit, the savings can add up quickly for devices that are produced in large volumes. Thus, the embedded-system programmer has a much larger economic incentive to conserve resources than the programmer of desktop software. Unfortunately, trying to conserve resources usually makes it harder to write programs that work correctly.

C and C++ are commonly used languages for developing embedded systems.

Figure 12   The Controller of an Embedded System

CHAPTER SUMMARY

1. A pointer denotes the location of a variable in memory.

2. The type T* denotes a pointer to a variable of type T.

3. The & operator yields the location of a variable.

4. The * operator locates the value to which a pointer points.

5. It is an error to use an uninitialized pointer.

6. The NULL pointer does not point to any object.

7. The value of an array variable is a pointer to the starting element of the array.

8. Pointer arithmetic means adding an integer offset to an array pointer, yielding a pointer that skips past the given number of elements.

9. The array/pointer duality law states that a[n] is identical to *(a + n), where a is a pointer into an array and n is an integer offset.

10. When passing an array to a function, only the starting address is passed.

11. A value of type char denotes an individual character. Character literals are enclosed in single quotes.

char_pointer =		
Points to 'H'	'H'	[0]
	'a'	[1]
	'r'	[2]
	'r'	[3]
	'y'	[4]
	'\0'	[5]

12. A literal string (enclosed in double quotes) is an array of char values with a zero terminator.

13. Many library functions use pointers of type char*.

14. The c_str member function yields a char* pointer from a string object.

15. You can initialize C++ string variables with C strings.

16. You can access characters in a C++ string object with the [] operator.

17. Use dynamic memory allocation if you do not know in advance how many values you need.

18. The new operator allocates memory from the heap.

19. You must reclaim dynamically allocated objects with the delete operator.

20. Using a dangling pointer (a pointer that has not been initialized or has been deleted) is a serious programming error.

21. Every call to new should have a matching call to delete.

REVIEW EXERCISES

Exercise R7.1. Trace the following code. Assume that a and b are stored at 20300 and 20308. Your trace table should have entries for a, b, and p.

```
double a = 1000;
double b = 2000;
double* p = &a;
*p = 3000;
p = &b;
a = *p * 2;
```

Exercise R7.2. Trace the following code. Assume that a and b are stored at 20300 and 20308. Your trace table should have entries for a, b, p, and q.

```
double a = 1000;
double b = 2000;
double* p = &a;
double* q = &b;
*p = *q;
p = q;
*p = 3000;
```

Exercise R7.3. What does the following code print?

```
double a = 1000;
double b = 2000;
double* p = &a;
double* q = p;
b = *q;
p = &b;
a = *p + *q;
cout << a << " " << b << endl;
```

Exercise R7.4. Explain the mistakes in the following code. Not all lines contain mistakes. Each line depends on the lines preceding it.

```
1  double a = 1000;
2  double* p = a;
3  int* p = &a;
4  double* q;
5  *q = 2000;
6  int* r = NULL;
7  *r = 3000;
```

Exercise R7.5. Suppose that a system allows the use of any string as a password, even the empty string. However, when a user connects to the system for the first time, no password has been assigned. Describe how you can use a string* variable and the NULL pointer to distinguish unassigned passwords from empty ones.

Exercise R7.6. Given the definitions

```
double primes[] = { 2, 3, 5, 7, 11, 13 };
double* p = primes + 3;
```

draw a diagram that explains the meanings of the following expressions:

a. primes[1]

b. primes + 1

c. *(primes + 1)

d. p[1]

e. p + 1

Exercise R7.7. Suppose the array primes, defined as

```
double primes[] = { 2, 3, 5, 7, 11, 13 };
```

starts at memory location 20300. What are the values of

a. primes

b. *primes

c. primes + 4

d. *(primes + 4)

e. primes[4]

f. &primes[4]

Exercise R7.8. Suppose the array primes is defined as

```
double primes[] = { 2, 3, 5, 7, 11, 13 };
```

Consider the sum function discussed in Section 7.2. What are the values of

a. sum(primes, 6);

b. sum(primes, 4);

c. sum(primes + 2, 4);

d. sum(primes, 0);

e. sum(NULL, 4);

Exercise R7.9. Suppose the array primes, defined as

```
double primes[] = { 2, 3, 5, 7, 11, 13 };
```

starts at memory location 20300. Trace the function call sum(primes, 4), using the definition of sum from Advanced Topic 7.1 on page 298. In your trace table, show the values for a, size, total, p, and i.

Exercise R7.10. Pointers are addresses and have a numerical value. You can print out the value of a pointer as cout << (unsigned)(p). Write a program to compare p, p + 1, q, and q + 1, where p is an int* and q is a double*. Explain the results.

Exercise R7.11. A pointer variable can contain a pointer to a single variable, a pointer to an array, NULL, or a random value. Write code that creates and sets four pointer variables a, b, c, and d to show each of these possibilities.

Exercise R7.12. Implement a function firstlast that obtains the first and last values in an array of integers and stores the result in an array *parameter*.

Exercise R7.13. Explain the meanings of the following expressions:

a. "Harry" + 1

b. *("Harry" + 2)

c. "Harry"[3]

d. [4]"Harry"

Exercise R7.14. What is the difference between the following two variable definitions?

    a. `char a[6] = "Hello";`

    b. `char* b = "Hello";`

Exercise R7.15. What is the difference between the following three variable definitions?

    a. `char* p = NULL;`

    b. `char* q = "";`

    c. `char r[1] = { '\0' };`

Exercise R7.16. Consider this program segment:

```
char a[] = "Mary had a little lamb";
char* p = a;
int count = 0;
while (*p != '\0')
{
   count++;
   while (*p != ' ' && *p != '\0') { p++; }
   while (*p == ' ') { p++; }
}
```

What is the value of `count` at the end of the outer `while` loop?

Exercise R7.17. Consider the following code that repeats a C++ string three times.

```
string a = "Hello";
string b = a + a + a;
```

Suppose s is a C string, and t is declared as

```
char t[100];
```

Write the equivalent code for C strings that stores the threefold repetition of s (or as much of it as will fit) into t.

Exercise R7.18. Which of the following assignments are legal in C++?

```
void f(int p[])
{
   int* q;
   const int* r;
   int s[10];
   p = q;   ❶
   p = r;   ❷
   p = s;   ❸
   q = p;   ❹
   q = r;   ❺
   q = s;   ❻
   r = p;   ❼
   r = q;   ❽
   r = s;   ❾
   s = p;   ❿
   s = q;   ⓫
   s = r;   ⓬
}
```

Exercise R7.19. What happens if you forget to delete an object that you obtained from the heap? What happens if you delete it twice?

Exercise R7.20. Write a program that accesses a deleted pointer, an uninitialized pointer, and a NULL pointer. What happens when you run your program?

Exercise R7.21. Find the mistakes in the following code. Not all lines contain mistakes. Each line depends on the lines preceding it. Watch out for uninitialized pointers, NULL pointers, pointers to deleted objects, and confusing pointers with objects.

```
 1   int* p = new int;
 2   p = 5;
 3   *p = *p + 5;
 4   string s = "Harry";
 5   *s = "Sally";
 6   delete &s;
 7   int* a = new int[10];
 8   *a = 5;
 9   a[10] = 5;
10   delete a;
11   int* q;
12   *q = 5;
13   q = p;
14   delete q;
15   delete p;
```

Exercise R7.22. How do you define a triangular two-dimensional array using just vectors, not arrays or pointers?

PROGRAMMING EXERCISES

Exercise P7.1. Write a function that computes the average value of an array of floating-point data:

```
double average(double* a, int size)
```

In the function, use a pointer variable, not an integer index, to traverse the array elements.

Exercise P7.2. Write a function that returns a pointer to the maximum value of an array of floating-point data:

```
double* maximum(double a[], int size)
```

If size is 0, return NULL.

Exercise P7.3. Write a function that reverses the values of an array of floating-point data:

```
void reverse(double a[], int size)
```

In the function, use two pointer variables, not integer indexes, to traverse the array elements.

Exercise P7.4. Implement the `strncpy` function of the standard library.

Exercise P7.5. Implement the standard library function

```
int strspn(const char s[], const char t[])
```

that returns the length of the initial portion of s consisting of the characters in t (in any order).

Exercise P7.6. Write a function

```
void reverse(char s[])
```

that reverses a character string. For example, "Harry" becomes "yrraH".

Exercise P7.7. Using the `strncpy` and `strncat` functions, implement a function

```
void safe_concat(const char a[], const char b[], char result[],
    int result_maxlength)
```

that concatenates the strings a and b to the buffer result. Be sure not to overrun the buffer. It can hold `result_maxlength` characters, not counting the '\0' terminator. (That is, the buffer has `result_maxlength + 1` bytes available.)

Exercise P7.8. Write a function `int* read_data(int& size)` that reads data from cin until the user terminates input by entering Q. The function should set the size reference parameter to the number of numeric inputs. Return a pointer to an array on the heap. That array should have exactly size elements. Of course, you won't know at the outset how many elements the user will enter. Start with an array of 10 elements, and double the size whenever the array fills up. At the end, allocate an array of the correct size and copy all inputs into it. Be sure to delete any intermediate arrays.

Exercise P7.9. Enhance the Galton board simulation by printing a bar chart of the bottommost counters. Draw the bars vertically, below the last row of numbers.

```
 1  18   64 149 239 265 186  61  15   2
     *    *   *   *   *   *   *   *
          *   *   *   *   *   *
          *   *   *   *   *   *
              *   *   *   *
              *   *   *   *
              *   *   *   *
              *   *   *   *
                  *   *   *
                  *   *   *
                  *   *
                  *   *
                  *   *
                      *
```

Exercise P7.10. Complete the copier simulation of How To 7.1 on page 314. Your program should first show the main menu:

```
U)ser A)dministrator Q)uit
```

For a user, prompt for the ID and the number of copies, increment the appropriate account, and return to the main menu.

For an administrator, show this menu:

```
B)alance M)aster P)roject
```

In the balance option, show the balances of the master account and the ten project accounts. In the master option, prompt for a user ID and link it to the master account. In the project option, prompt for user and project IDs. Afterward, return to the main menu.

Exercise P7.11. Write a program that reads lines of text and appends them to a `char` `buffer[1000]`. Stop after reading 1,000 characters. As you read in the text, replace all newline characters `'\n'` with `'\0'` terminators. Establish an array `char* lines[100]`, so that the pointers in that array point to the beginnings of the lines in the text. Consider only 100 input lines if the input has more lines. Then display the lines in reverse order, starting with the last input line.

Exercise P7.12. The program in Exercise P7.11 is limited by the fact that it can only handle inputs of 1,000 characters or 100 lines. Remove this limitation as follows. Concatenate the input in one long `string` object. Use the `c_str` member function to obtain a `char*` into the string's character buffer. Store the beginnings of the lines as a `vector<char*>`.

Exercise P7.13. Exercise P7.12 demonstrated how to use the `string` and `vector` classes to implement resizable arrays. In this exercise, you should implement that capability manually. Allocate a buffer of 1,000 characters from the heap (`new char[1000]`). Whenever the buffer fills up, allocate a buffer of twice the size, copy the buffer contents, and delete the old buffer. Do the same for the array of `char*` pointers—start with a `new char*[100]` and keep doubling the size.

Exercise P7.14. Modify Exercise P7.11 so that you first print the lines in the order that they were entered, then print them in sorted order. When you sort the lines, only rearrange the pointers in the `lines` array.

Exercise P7.15. When you read a long document, there is a good chance that many words occur multiple times. Instead of storing each word, it may be beneficial to only store unique words, and to represent the document as a vector of pointers to the unique words. Write a program that implements this strategy. Read a word at a time from `cin`. Keep a `vector<char*>` of words. If the new word is not contained in this vector, allocate memory, copy the word into it, and append a pointer to the new memory. If the word is already present, then append a pointer to the existing word.

ANSWERS TO SELF-CHECK QUESTIONS

1. 1
2

2. 2 2

3. 30

4. 25

5. 15 followed by the memory address of the variable a. The address can differ from one program run to the next.

6. 2 0 5

7. 2 3 0

8. 2 3 5

9. 4 5

10. `void squares(int n, int* result)`

11. 15: `'H''e''l''l''o'','' ''W''o''r''l''d''!''\n''\0'`

12. 14. The null terminator is not counted, and `'\n'` counts as a single character.

13. `char* p = "Hello";`

14. The statement compiles, but it has a disastrous effect. The type of `"Agent"` is a `char*`. It is legal to add an integer to a `char*`. The result is a pointer that is seven characters away from the start of the array. The array only contains 6 characters, so the result points to some other part of memory. The `title` string will be constructed with whatever characters are found there, until a zero is encountered. The result is unpredictable.

15. `int number = atoi(input.c_str());`

16. 3

17. 0 1 4

18. The access p[10] is illegal; the returned array has elements with index 0 ... 9.

19. p points to an array of size 10 with elements 2, 3, 5, 7, 11, 0, 0, 0, 0, 0.

20. Call `delete[]` on the returned pointer after it is no longer needed.

21. Then the first row would have had 0 elements and the last row would have had 9 elements.

22. The program will compile. `counts[1]` is an `int*` pointer, and it is legal to apply `[2]`. `counts[1][2]` will access the memory address `counts[1] + 2`, which unfortunately points to some other memory. That memory will be overwritten, and it is not possible to predict the effect.

23.
```
int* triangular_array[10];
for (int i = 0; i < 10; i++)
{
    triangular_array[i] = new int[10 - i];
}
```

24. Include the `<vector>` header and replace the declaration of counts with vec-tor`<int*>` counts(10). The remainder of the program need not change.

25. Change the declaration of counts to vector`<int>` counts[10]. Change the row allocation loop body to

```
counts[i] = vector<int>(i + 1);
```

Drop the deallocation loop.

Streams

CHAPTER GOALS

- To be able to read and write files
- To convert between strings and numbers using string streams
- To learn how to process the command line
- To understand the concepts of sequential and random access
- To learn about encryption

All of the programs that you have written until now have read their input from the keyboard and displayed their output on the screen. However, many programs need to be able to use disk files for reading input and writing output. In this chapter, you will learn how to use the C++ stream library for file processing.

8.1 Reading and Writing Files

The C++ input/output library is based on the concept of *streams*. An *input stream* is a source of data, and an *output stream* is a destination for data. The most common sources and destinations for data are the files on your hard disk.

Data arrive in an input stream just like items on a conveyor belt, one at a time.

> To read or write disk files, you use variables of type fstream, ifstream, or ofstream.

To access a disk file, you use a file stream. There are three types of file streams: ifstream (for input), ofstream (for output), and fstream (for both input and output). Include the <fstream> header when you use any of these file streams.

In the following sections, you will learn how to process data from files.

8.1.1 Opening a Stream

To read anything from a file stream, you need to *open* it. When you open a stream, you give the name of the disk file. Suppose you want to read data from a file named input.dat, located in the same directory as the program. Then you use the following command to open the file:

```
in_file.open("input.dat");
```

When opening a file
stream, you supply the
name of the disk file.

This command call associates the variable `in_file` with the disk file named `input.dat`.

Note that all streams are objects, and you use the dot notation for calling functions that manipulate them.

To open a file for writing, you use an `ostream` variable. To open the same file for both reading and writing, you use an `fstream` variable.

File names can contain directory path information, such as

```
~/homework/input.dat (UNIX)
c:\homework\input.dat (Windows)
```

When you specify the file name as a string literal, and the name contains backslash characters (as in a Windows filename), you must supply each backslash *twice*:

```
in_file.open("c:\\homework\\input.dat");
```

Recall that a single backslash inside a string literal is an *escape character* that is combined with another character to form a special meaning, such as \n for a newline character. The \\ combination denotes a single backslash.

If you want to pass a name that is stored in a `string` variable, use the `c_str` function to convert the C++ `string` to a C string.

```
cout << "Please enter the file name:";
string filename;
cin >> filename;
ifstream in_file;
in_file.open(filename.c_str());
```

When the program ends, all streams that you have opened will be automatically closed. You can also manually close a stream with the `close` member function:

```
in_file.close();
```

Manual closing is only necessary if you want to open the file again in the same program run.

8.1.2 Reading from a File

Read from a file stream
with the same operations
that you use with `cin`.

Reading data from a file stream is completely straightforward: You simply use the same functions that you have always used for reading from `cin`.

```
string name;
double value;
in_file >> name >> value;
```

The `fail` function tells you whether input has failed. You have already used this function with `cin`, to check for errors in numeric input. File streams behave in the same way. When you try to read a number from a file, and the next data item is not a properly formatted number, then the stream fails. After reading data, you should test for success before processing:

```
if (!in_file.fail())
{
```

```
        Process input
    }
```

Alternatively, you can use the fact that the >> operator returns a "not failed" condition, allowing you to combine an input statement and a test:

```
    if (in_file >> name >> value)
    {
        Process input
    }
```

When you read input from a file, number format errors are not the only reason for failure. Suppose you have consumed all of the data contained in a file and try to read more items. A file stream enters the failed state, whereas cin would just wait for more user input. Moreover, if you open a file and the name is invalid, or if there is no file of that name, then the file stream is also in a failed state. It is a good idea to test for failure immediately after calling open.

8.1.3 Writing to a File

> Write to a file stream with the same operations that you use with cout.

In order to write to a file, you define an ostream or fstream variable and open it. Then you send information to the output file, using the same operations that you used with cout.

```
    ofstream out_file;
    out_file.open("output.txt");
    out_file << name << " " << value << endl;
```

SYNTAX 8.1 **Working with File Streams**

Include this header when you use file streams. — `#include <fstream>`

Call c_str if the file name is a C++ string.

Use ifstream for input, ofstream for output, fstream for both input and output.

```
ifstream in_file;
in_file.open(filename.c_str());
in_file >> name >> value;
```

Use \\ for each backslash in a string literal.

Use the same operations as with cin.

```
ofstream out_file;
out_file.open("c:\\output.txt");
out_file << name << " " << value << endl;
```

Use the same operations as with cout.

8.1.4 A File Processing Example

Here is a typical example of processing data in a file. The Social Security Administration publishes lists of the most popular baby names on their web site http://www.ssa.gov/OACT/babynames/. When querying the 1,000 most popular names for a given decade, the browser displays the result on the screen (see Figure 1).

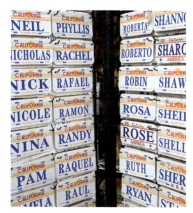

To save the data as text, one simply selects it and pastes the result into a file. The book code contains a file babynames.txt with the data for the 1990s.

Each line in the file contains seven entries:

- The rank (from 1 to 1,000)
- The name, frequency, and percentage of the male name of that rank
- The name, frequency, and percentage of the female name of that rank

Sellers of personalized items can find trends in popular names by processing data files from the Social Security Administration.

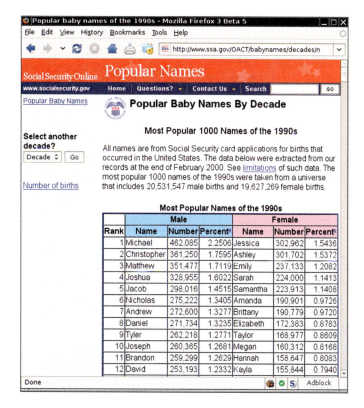

Figure 1
Querying Baby Names

For example, the line

```
10  Joseph  260365  1.2681  Megan  160312  0.8168
```

shows that the 10th most common boy's name was Joseph, with 260,365 births, or 1.2681 percent of all births during that period. The 10th most common girl's name was Megan. Why are there many more Josephs than Megans? Parents seem to use a wider set of girl's names, making each one of them less frequent.

Let us test that conjecture, by determining the names given to the top 50 percent of boys and girls in the list.

To process each line, we first read the rank:

```
int rank;
in_file >> rank;
```

We then read a set of three values for the boy's name:

```
string name;
int count;
double percent;
in_file >> name >> count >> percent;
```

Then we repeat that step for girls. Because the actions are identical, we supply a helper function process_name for that purpose. To stop processing after reaching 50 percent, we can add up the frequencies and stop when they reach 50 percent. However, it turns out to be a bit simpler to initialize a total with 50 and subtract the frequencies. We need separate totals for boys and girls. When a total falls below 0, we stop printing. When both totals fall below 0, we stop reading.

> **Always use a reference parameter for a stream.**

Note that the ifstream parameter of the process_name function is passed by *reference*. Reading or writing modifies a stream variable. The file variable monitors how many characters have been read or written so far. Any read or write operation changes that data. For that reason, you must always pass stream variables by reference.

The complete program is shown below. As you can see, reading from a file is just as easy as reading keyboard input.

Have a look at the program output. Remarkably, only 69 boy names and 153 girl names account for half of all births. That's good news for those who are in the business of producing personalized doodads. Exercise P8.10 asks you to study how this distribution changed over the years.

ch08/babynames.cpp

```
 1  #include <iostream>
 2  #include <fstream>
 3  #include <string>
 4
 5  using namespace std;
 6
 7  /**
 8     Reads name information, prints the name if total >= 0, and adjusts the total.
 9     @param in_file the input stream
10     @param total the total percentage that should still be processed
11  */
```

```
12  void process_name(ifstream& in_file, double& total)
13  {
14      string name;
15      int count;
16      double percent;
17      in_file >> name >> count >> percent;
18
19      if (in_file.fail()) { return; } // Check for failure after each input
20      if (total > 0) { cout << name << " "; }
21      total = total - percent;
22  }
23
24  int main()
25  {
26      ifstream in_file;
27      in_file.open("babynames.txt");
28      if (in_file.fail()) { return 0; } // Check for failure after opening
29
30      double boy_total = 50;
31      double girl_total = 50;
32
33      while (boy_total > 0 || girl_total > 0)
34      {
35          int rank;
36          in_file >> rank;
37          if (in_file.fail()) { return 0; }
38
39          cout << rank << " ";
40
41          process_name(in_file, boy_total);
42          process_name(in_file, girl_total);
43
44          cout << endl;
45      }
46
47      return 0;
48  }
```

Program Run

```
1 Michael Jessica
2 Christopher Ashley
3 Matthew Emily
4 Joshua Sarah
5 Jacob Samantha
6 Nicholas Amanda
7 Andrew Brittany
8 Daniel Elizabeth
9 Tyler Taylor
10 Joseph Megan
...
68 Dustin Gabrielle
69 Noah Katie
```

```
70 Caitlin
71 Lindsey
...
150 Hayley
151 Rebekah
152 Jocelyn
153 Cassidy
```

SELF CHECK

1. What happens if you call `in_file.open("")`?

2. What is wrong with the following code?

```
ifstream out_file;
out_file.open("output.txt");
out_file << "Hello, World!" << endl;
```

3. What is wrong with the following function?

```
double sum(ifstream in)
{
   double total = 0;
   double input;
   while (in >> input) { total = total + input; }
   return total;
}
```

4. How do you modify the `babynames.cpp` program so that you get the most common names that make up 10 percent of the population?

5. How do you modify the `babynames.cpp` program so that the program output is saved to a file `output.txt`?

8.2 Reading Text Input

In the following sections, you will learn how to process text with complex contents that often occurs in real life situations.

8.2.1 Reading Words

You already know how to read the next word from a stream, using the >> operator.

```
string word;
in_file >> word;
```

Here is precisely what happens when that operation is executed. Input characters that are *white space* are consumed first. White space includes spaces, tab characters, and the newline characters that separate lines. The first character that is not white space is added to word. More characters are added until either another white space character occurs, or the end of the file has been reached.

8.2.2 Reading Characters

You can get individual characters from a stream and unget the last one.

Instead of reading an entire word, you can read one character at a time by calling the get method:

```
char ch;
in_file.get(ch);
```

The get function returns the "not failed" condition. The following loop processes all characters in a file:

```
while (in_file.get(ch))
{
   Process the character ch
}
```

The get method reads white space characters. If you want to skip past white space, use the >> operator instead:

```
in_file >> ch; // ch is set to the next non-white space character
```

If you read a character and you regretted it, you can *unget* it, so that the next input operation can read it again. However, you can unget only the last character. This is called *one-character lookahead.* You get a chance to look at the next character in the input stream, and you can make a decision whether you want to consume it or put it back.

A typical situation for lookahead is to look for numbers:

```
char ch;
in_file.get(ch);
if (isdigit(ch))
{
   in_file.unget(); // Put the digit back so that it is part of the number
   int n;
   data >> n; // Read integer starting with ch
}
```

The isdigit function is one of several useful functions that categorize characters—see Table 1 on page 337. You must include the <cctype> header to use these functions.

If you read a character from a stream and you don't like what you get, you can unget it.

8.2.3 Reading Lines

When each line of a file is a data record, it is often best to read entire lines with the `getline` function:

```
string line;
getline(in_file, line);
```

The next input line (without the newline character) is placed into the string `line`.

The `getline` function returns the "not failed" condition. You can use the following loop to process each line in a file:

```
while (getline(in_file, line))
{
    Process line
}
```

Note that `getline` is not a member function, but an ordinary function that is not called with the dot notation.

Here is a typical example of processing lines in a file. A file with population data from the CIA Fact Book site (http://www.cia.gov/library/publications/the-world-factbook/) contains lines such as the following:

```
China   1330044605
India   1147995898
United States 303824646
...
```

Because each line is a data record, it is natural to use the `getline` function for reading lines into a string variable. To extract the data from that string, you need to find out where the name ends and the number starts.

Locate the first digit:

```
int i = 0;
while (!isdigit(line[i])) { i++; }
```

Then go backward and skip white space:

```
int j = i - 1;
while (isspace(line[j])) { j--; }
```

Finally, extract the country name and population:

```
string country_name = line.substr(0, j + 1);
string population = line.substr(i);
```

There is just one problem. The population is stored in a string, not a number. You will see in Section 8.4 how to extract the population number.

Table 1	Character Predicate Functions in <cctype>
Function	**Accepted Characters**
isdigit	0 ... 9
isalpha	a ... z, A ... Z
islower	a ... z
isupper	A ... Z
isalnum	a ... z, A ... Z, 0 ... 0
isspace	White space (space, tab, newline, and the rarely used carriage return, form feed, and vertical tab)

SELF CHECK

6. Suppose the input stream contains the characters 6,995.0. What is the value of number and ch after these statements?

```
int number;
char ch;
in_file >> number;
in_file.get(ch);
```

7. Suppose the input stream contains the characters Hello, World!. What is the value of word and ch after these statements?

```
string word;
char ch;
in_file >> word >> ch;
if (isupper(ch)) { in_file.unget(); in_file >> word; }
```

8. Your input file contains a sequence of numbers, but sometimes a value is not available and marked as N/A. How can you read the numbers and skip over the markers?

9. What is the effect of the following loop?

```
char ch;
while (in_file.get(ch) && isspace(ch)) { }
in_file.unget();
```

10. Why can't you simply read the population data file with the following loop?

```
while (in_file >> country_name >> population)
{
    Process country name and population
}
```

8.3 Writing Text Output

You use the >> operator to send strings and numbers to a stream. To write a single character, use

```
strm.put(ch);
```

To control how the output is formatted, you use stream *manipulators*. A manipulator is an object that is sent to a stream using the << operator, and that affects the behavior of the stream. The setw manipulator, which you have already used, is a typical example. The statement

```
strm << setw(10);
```

does not cause any immediate output, but when the next item is written, it is padded with sufficient spaces so that the output spans ten characters. (If a value does not fit into the given width, it is not truncated.)

Occasionally, you need to pad numbers with leading zeroes, for example to print hours and minutes as 09:01. This is achieved with the setfill manipulator:

```
strm << setfill('0') << setw(2) << hours
     << ":" << setw(2) << minutes << setfill(' ');
```

Now, a zero is used to pad the field. Afterward, the space is restored as the fill character.

By default, the fill characters appear before the item:

```
strm << setw(10) << 123 << endl << setw(10) << 4567;
```

produces

```
       123
      4567
```

The numbers line up to the right. That alignment works well for numbers, but not for strings. Usually, you want strings to line up at the left. You use the left and right manipulators to set the alignment. The following example uses left alignment for a string and then switches back to right alignment for a number:

```
strm << left << setw(10) << word << right << setw(10) << number;
```

A manipulator is like a control button on a sound mixer. It doesn't produce an output, but it affects how the output looks.

The default format for floating-point numbers is called *general* format. That format displays as many digits as are specified by the *precision* (6 by default), switching to scientific notation for large and small numbers. For example,

```
strm << 12.3456789 << " " << 123456789.0;
```

yields

```
12.3457 1.23457e+08
```

The *fixed* format prints all values with the same number of digits after the decimal point. In the fixed format, the same numbers are displayed as

```
12.345679 123456789.000000
```

Use the `fixed` manipulator to select that format, and the `setprecision` manipulator to change the precision.

For example,

```
strm << fixed << setprecision(2) << 1.2 << " " << 1.235
```

yields

```
1.20 1.24
```

Table 2 summarizes the stream manipulators. Note that all manipulators set the state of the stream object for all subsequent operations, with the exception of `setw`. After each output operation, the field width is reset to 0.

Table 2   Stream Manipulators

Manipulator	Purpose	Example	Output

setw	Sets the field width of the next item only.	`strm << setw(6) << 123 << endl`
		`<< 123 << endl`
		`<< setw(6) << 12345678;`
			123
			123
			12345678

setfill	Sets the fill character for padding a field. (The default character is a space.)	`strm << setfill('0') << setw(6)` `<< 123;`	000123
left	Selects left alignment.	`strm << left << setw(6) << 123;`	123
right	Selects right alignment (default).	`strm << right << setw(6) << 123;`	123
fixed	Selects fixed format for floating-point numbers.	`double x = 123.4567;` `strm << x << endl << fixed << x;`	123.457 123.456700

setprecision	Sets the number of significant digits for general format, the number of digits after the decimal point for fixed format.	`double x = 123.4567;`
		`strm << fixed << x << endl`
		`<< setprecision(2) << x;`
			123.456700
			123.46

11. What is the output of the following statement?

```
cout << fixed << 123456.0;
```

12. How do you change the statement so that the result is 123456.00?

13. What is the output of the following statement?

```
cout << setw(8) << setfill('0') << 123456;
```

14. What is the output of the following statement?

```
cout << setw(2) << setfill('0') << 123456;
```

15. Why doesn't the following statement sequence line up the numbers?

```
cout << setw(10) << setprecision(2) << fixed << 1.234 << endl << 56.7;
```

8.4 String Streams

> Use string streams to read numbers that are contained in strings, or to convert between numbers and strings.

In the preceding section, you saw how file streams read characters from a file and write characters to a file. The `istringstream` class reads characters from a string, and the `ostringstream` class writes characters to a string. That doesn't sound so exciting—we already know how to access and change the characters of a string. However, the string stream classes have the same *interface* as the other stream classes. In particular, you can use the familiar `>>` and `<<` operators to read and write numbers that are contained in strings. For that reasons, the `istringstream` and `ostringstream` classes are called *adapters*—they adapt strings to the stream interface. Include the `<sstream>` header when you use string streams.

Like an adapter that converts international power plugs to your outlets, the string stream adapters allow you to access strings as streams.

Here is a typical example. Suppose the string date contains a date such as "January 24, 1973", and we want to separate it into month, day, and year. First, construct an `istringstream` object. Then use the `str` function to set the string that you want to read:

```
istringstream strm;
strm.str("January 24, 1973");
```

Next, simply use the `>>` operator to read off the month name, the day, the comma separator, and the year:

```
string month;
int day;
```

```
string comma;
int year;
strm >> month >> day >> comma >> year;
```

Now month is "January", day is 24, and year is 1973. Note that this input statement yields day and year as *integers*. Had we taken the string apart with substr, we would have obtained only strings, not numbers.

In fact, converting strings that contain digits to their integer values is such a common operation that it is useful to write a helper function for this purpose:

```
int string_to_int(string s)
{
   istringstream strm;
   strm.str(s);
   int n = 0;
   strm >> n;
   return n;
}
```

For example, string_to_int("1973") is the *integer* 1973.

By writing to a string stream, you can convert numbers to strings. First construct an ostringstream object:

```
ostringstream strm;
```

Next, use the << operator to add a number to the stream. The number is converted into a sequence of characters:

```
strm << fixed << setprecision(5) << 10.0 / 3;
```

Now the stream contains the string "3.33333". To obtain that string from the stream, call the str member function:

```
string output = strm.str();
```

You can build up more complex strings in the same way. Here we build a data string of the month, day, and year:

```
string month = "January";
int day = 24;
int year = 1973;
ostringstream strm;
strm << month << " " << day << "," << year;
string output = strm.str();
```

Now output is the string "January 24, 1973". Note that we converted the *integers* day and year into a string. Again, converting an integer into a string is such a common operation that is useful to have a helper function for it:

```
string int_to_string(int n)
{
   ostringstream strm;
   strm << n;
   return strm.str();
}
```

For example, int_to_string(1973) is the string "1973".

16. What is the value of n after these statements?

```
istrstream strm;
strm.str("123,456");
int n;
int m;
char ch;
strm >> n >> ch >> m;
n = 1000 * n + m;
```

17. What does string_to_int("123,456") return?

18. What does string_to_int("$123") return?

19. What is the value of strm.str() after these statements?

```
ostringstream strm;
strm << setprecision(5) << 10.0 / 3;
```

20. Write a function that converts a floating-point number into a string. Provide a parameter for the number of digits after the decimal point.

8.5 Command Line Arguments

Depending on the operating system and C++ development system used, there are different methods of starting a program—for example, by selecting "Run" in the compilation environment, by clicking on an icon, or by typing the name of the program at a prompt in a command shell window. The latter method is called "invoking the program from the command line". When you use this method, you must of course type the name of the program, but you can also type in additional information that the program can use. These additional strings are called *command line arguments*. For example, if you start a program with the command line

```
prog -v input.dat
```

then the program receives two command line arguments: the strings "-v" and "input.dat". It is entirely up to the program what to do with these strings. It is customary to interpret strings starting with a - as options and other strings as file names.

> Programs that start from the command line can receive the name of the program and the command line arguments in the main function.

To receive command line arguments, you need to define the main function in a different way. You define two parameters: an integer and an array of pointers to C character arrays.

```
int main(int argc, char* argv[])
{
   ...
}
```

Here argc is the count of arguments, and argv contains the values of the arguments. In our example, argc is 3, and argv contains the three strings

```
argv[0]:  "prog"
argv[1]:  "-v"
argv[2]:  "input.dat"
```

Note that argv[0] is always the name of the program and that argc is always at least 1.

Let us write a program that *encrypts* a file—that is, scrambles it so that it is unreadable except to those who know the decryption method. Ignoring 2000 years of progress in the field of encryption, we will use a method familiar to Julius Caesar, replacing A with a D, B with an E, and so on (see Figure 2).

The program takes the following command line arguments:

- An optional -d flag to indicate decryption instead of encryption
- The input file name
- The output file name

For example,

```
caesar input.txt encrypt.txt
```

encrypts the file input.txt and places the result into encrypt.txt.

```
caesar -d encrypt.txt output.txt
```

decrypts the file encrypt.txt and places the result into output.txt.

The emperor Julius Caesar used a simple scheme to encrypt messages.

Figure 2 Caesar Cipher

ch08/caesar.cpp

```cpp
1   #include <iostream>
2   #include <fstream>
3   #include <string>
4   #include <sstream>
5
6   using namespace std;
7
8   /**
9       Encrypts a stream using the Caesar cipher.
10      @param in the stream to read from
11      @param out the stream to write to
12      @param k the encryption key
13  */
14  void encrypt_file(istream& in, ostream& out, int k)
15  {
```

```
16      char ch;
17      while (in.get(ch))
18      {
19          out.put(ch + k);
20      }
21  }
22
23  int main(int argc, char* argv[])
24  {
25      int key = 3;
26      int file_count = 0;  // The number of files specified
27      ifstream in_file;
28      ofstream out_file;
29
30      for (int i = 1; i < argc; i++) // Process all command-line arguments
31      {
32          string arg = argv[i]; // The currently processed argument
33          if (arg == "-d") // The decryption option
34          {
35              key = -3;
36          }
37          else // It is a file name
38          {
39              file_count++;
40              if (file_count == 1) // The first file name
41              {
42                  in_file.open(arg.c_str());
43                  if (in_file.fail()) // Exit the program if opening failed
44                  {
45                      cout << "Error opening input file " << arg << endl;
46                      return 1;
47                  }
48              }
49              else if (file_count == 2) // The second file name
50              {
51                  out_file.open(arg.c_str());
52                  if (out_file.fail())
53                  {
54                      cout << "Error opening output file " << arg << endl;
55                      return 1;
56                  }
57              }
58          }
59      }
60
61      if (file_count != 2) // Exit if the user didn't specify two files
62      {
63          cout << "Usage: " << argv[0] << " [-d] infile outfile" << endl;
64          return 1;
65      }
66
67      encrypt_file(in_file, out_file, key);
68      return 0;
69  }
```

21. If the program is invoked with caesar -d encrypt.txt, what is argc, and what are the elements of argv?

22. Trace the program when it is invoked as described in Self Check 21.

23. Encrypt CAESAR using the Caesar cipher.

24. What does the program do with spaces?

RANDOM FACT 8.1

Encryption Algorithms

The exercises at the end of this chapter give a few algorithms to encrypt text. Don't actually use any of those methods to send secret messages to your lover. Any skilled cryptographer can *break* these schemes in a very short time—that is, reconstruct the original text without knowing the secret keyword.

In 1978 Ron Rivest, Adi Shamir, and Leonard Adleman introduced an encryption method that is much more powerful. The method is called *RSA encryption*, after the last names of its inventors. The exact scheme is too complicated to present here, but it is not actually difficult to follow. You can find the details in http://theory.lcs.mit.edu/~rivest/rsapaper.pdf.

RSA is a remarkable encryption method. There are two keys: a public key and a private key. (See Figure 3.) You can print the public key on your business card (or in your e-mail signature block) and give it to anyone. Then anyone can send you messages that only you can decrypt. Even though everyone else knows the public key, and even if they intercept all the messages coming to you, they cannot break the scheme and actually read the messages. In 1994, hundreds of researchers, collaborating over the Internet, cracked an RSA message encrypted with a 129-digit key. Messages encrypted with a key of 230 digits or more are expected to be secure.

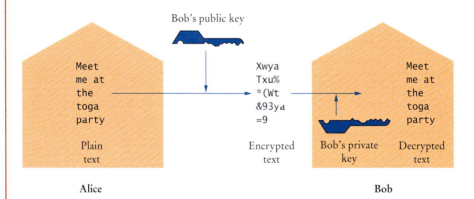

Figure 3　Public-Key Encryption

The inventors of the algorithm obtained a *patent* for it. A patent is a deal that society makes with an inventor. For a period of 20 years, the inventor has an exclusive right for its commercialization, may collect royalties from others wishing to manufacture the invention, and may even stop competitors from using it altogether. In return, the inventor must publish the invention, so that others may learn from it, and must relinquish all claim to it after the monopoly period ends. The presumption is that in the absence of patent law, inventors would be reluctant to go through the trouble of inventing, or they would try to cloak their techniques to prevent others from copying their devices.

There has been some controversy about the RSA patent. Had there not been patent protection, would the inventors have published the method anyway, thereby giving the benefit to society without the cost of the 20-year monopoly? In this case, the answer is probably yes. The inventors were academic researchers, who live on salaries rather than sales receipts and are usually rewarded for their discoveries by a boost in their reputation and careers. Would their followers have been as active in discovering (and patenting) improvements? There is no way of knowing, of course. Is an algorithm even patentable, or is it a mathematical fact that belongs to nobody? The patent office did take the latter attitude for a long time. The RSA inventors and many others described their inventions in terms of imaginary electronic devices, rather than algorithms, to circumvent that restriction. Nowadays, the patent office will award software patents.

There is another interesting aspect to the RSA story. A programmer, Phil Zimmermann, developed a program called PGP (for *Pretty Good Privacy*) that is based on RSA. Anyone can use the program to encrypt messages, and decryption is not feasible even with the most powerful computers. You can get a copy of a free PGP implementation from the GNU project (`http://www.gnupg.org`). The existence of strong encryption methods bothers the United States government to no end. Criminals and foreign agents can send communications that the police and intelligence agencies cannot decipher. The government considered charging Zimmermann with breaching a law that forbids the unauthorized export of munitions, arguing that he should have known that his program would appear on the Internet. There have been serious proposals to make it illegal for private citizens to use these encryption methods, or to keep the keys secret from law enforcement.

HOW TO 8.1

Processing Text Files

Processing text files that contain real data can be surprisingly challenging. This How To gives you step-by-step guidance.

As an example, we will consider this task: Read two country data files, `worldpop.txt` and `worldarea.txt` (supplied with the book code). Both files contain the same countries in the same order. Write a file `world_pop_density.txt` that contains country names and population densities (people per square km), with the country names aligned left and the numbers aligned right:

```
Afghanistan                                  50.56
Akrotiri                                    127.64
Albania                                     125.91
Algeria                                      14.18
American Samoa                              288.92
...
```

Step 1 Understand the processing task.

As always, you need to have a clear understanding of the task before designing a solution. Can you carry out the task by hand (perhaps with smaller input files)? If not, get more information about the problem.

The following pseudocode describes our processing task.

```
While there are more lines to be read
{
    Read a line from each file.
    Extract the country name.
    population = number following the country name in the first line
    area = number following the country name in the second line
    If area != 0
    {
        density = population / area
    }
    Print country name and density.
}
```

Step 2 Determine which files you need to read and write.

This should be clear from the problem. In our example, there are two input files, the population data and the area data, and one output file.

Step 3 Choose a method for obtaining the file names.

There are three options:

- Hard-coding the file names (such as "worldpop.txt")
- Asking the user:

  ```
  cout << "Enter filename: ";
  cin >> filename;
  in_file.open(filename.c_str());
  ```

- Using command-line parameters

In our example, we use hard-coded file names for simplicity.

Step 4 Choose between line, word, and character-based input.

As a rule of thumb, read lines if the input data is grouped by lines. That is the case with tabular data, such as in our example, or when you need to report line numbers.

When gathering data that can be distributed over several lines, then it makes more sense to read words or characters.

Step 5 With line-oriented input, extract the required data.

It is simple to read a line of input with the getline command. Then you need to get the data out of that line. You can extract substrings, as described in Section 8.2. Alternatively, you can turn the line into an istringstream and extract its components with the >> operator. The latter approach is easier when the number of items on each line is constant. In our example, that is not the case—country names can consist of more than one string. Therefore, we choose to extract substrings from each input line.

If you need any of the substrings as numbers, you must convert them, as discussed in Section 8.4.

Step 6   Use functions to factor out common tasks.

Processing input files usually has repetitive tasks, such as skipping over white space or extracting numbers from strings. It really pays off to develop a set of functions to handle these tedious operations.

In our example, we have a common task that calls for a helper function: extracting the country name and the value that follows. This task can be implemented in a helper function

```
void read_line(string line, string& country, double& value)
```

We also need a helper function `string_to_double` to convert the population and area values to floating-point numbers. This function is similar to `string_to_int` that was developed in Section 8.4.

Step 7   If required, use manipulators to format the output.

If you are asked to format your output, use manipulators, as described in Section 8.3. Usually, you want to switch to fixed format for the output and set the precision. Then use setw before every value, and use `left` for aligning strings and `right` for aligning numbers:

```
out << setw(40) << left << country << setw(15) << right << density << endl;
```

Here is the complete program:

ch08/popdensity.cpp

```
1  #include <cctype>
2  #include <fstream>
3  #include <iostream>
4  #include <iomanip>
5  #include <sstream>
6  #include <string>
7
8  using namespace std;
9
10 /**
11     Converts a string to a floating-point number, e.g. "3.14" -> 3.14.
12     @param s a string representing a floating-point number
13     @return the equivalent floating-point number
14 */
15 double string_to_double(string s)
16 {
17     istringstream stream;
18     stream.str(s);
19     double x = 0;
20     stream >> x;
21     return x;
22 }
23
24 /**
25     Extracts the country and associated value from an input line.
26     @param line a line containing a country name, followed by a number
27     @param country the string for holding the country name
```

```
28       @param value  the variable for holding the associated value
29       @return  true if a line has been read, false at the end of the stream
30  */
31  void read_line(string line, string& country, double& value)
32  {
33      int i = 0; // Locate the start of the first digit
34      while (!isdigit(line[i])) { i++; }
35      int j = i - 1; // Locate the end of the preceding word
36      while (isspace(line[j])) { j--; }
37
38      country = line.substr(0, j + 1); // Extract the country name
39      value = string_to_double(line.substr(i)); // Extract the number value
40  }
41
42  int main()
43  {
44      ifstream in1;
45      ifstream in2;
46      in1.open("worldpop.txt"); // Open input files
47      in2.open("worldarea.txt");
48
49      ofstream out;
50      out.open("world_pop_density.txt"); // Open output file
51      out << fixed << setprecision(2);
52
53      string line1;
54      string line2;
55
56      // Read lines from each file
57      while (getline(in1, line1) && getline(in2, line2))
58      {
59          string country;
60          double population;
61          double area;
62
63          // Split the lines into country and associated value
64          read_line(line1, country, population);
65          read_line(line2, country, area);
66
67          // Compute and print the population density
68          double density = 0;
69          if (area != 0) // Protect against division by zero
70          {
71              density = population * 1.0 / area;
72          }
73          out << setw(40) << left << country
74              << setw(15) << right << density << endl;
75      }
76
77      return 0;
78  }
```

Looking for for Duplicates

This Worked Example processes a file to locate lines that contain repeated words.

8.6 Random Access and Binary Files

In the following sections, you will learn how to read and write data at arbitrary positions in a file, and how to edit image files.

8.6.1 Random Access

> You can access any position in a random access file by moving the *file pointer* prior to a read or write operation.

So far, you've read from a file an item at a time and written to a file an item at a time, without skipping forward or backward. That access pattern is called *sequential access*. In many applications, we would like to access specific items in a file without first having to read all preceding items. This access pattern is called *random access* (see Figure 4). There is nothing "random" about random access—the term means that you can read and modify any item stored at any location in the file.

Only file streams support random access; the cin and cout streams, which are attached to the keyboard and the terminal, do not. Each file stream has two special positions: the *get* position and the *put* position (see Figure 5). These positions determine where the next character is read or written.

The following function calls move the get and put positions to a given value, counted from the beginning of the stream.

```
strm.seekg(position);
strm.seekp(position);
```

To determine the current values of the get and put positions (counted from the beginning of the file), use

```
position = strm.tellg();
position = strm.tellp();
```

Figure 4 Sequential and Random Access   **Figure 5** Get and Put Positions

At a sit-down dinner, food is served sequentially. At a buffet, you have "random access" to all food items.

8.6.2 Binary Files

Many files, in particular those containing images and sounds, do not store information as text but as binary numbers. The numbers are represented as sequences of *bytes*, just as they are in the memory of the computer. (Each byte is a value between 0 and 255.) In binary format, a floating-point number always occupies 8 bytes. We will study random access with a binary file format for images.

We have to cover a few technical issues about binary files. To open a binary file for reading and writing, use the following command:

```
fstream strm;
strm.open(filename, ios::in | ios::out | ios::binary);
```

You read a byte with the call

```
int input = strm.get();
```

This call returns a value between 0 and 255. To read an integer, read four bytes b_0, b_1, b_2, b_3 and combine them to $b_0 + b_1 \cdot 256 + b_2 \cdot 256^2 + b_3 \cdot 256^3$. We will supply a helper function for this task.

The >> operator cannot be used to read numbers from a binary file.

8.6.3 Processing Image Files

In this section, you will learn how to write a program for editing image files in the BMP format. Unlike the more common GIF, PNG, and JPEG formats, the BMP format is quite simple because it does not use data compression. As a consequence, BMP files are huge and you will rarely find them in the wild. However, image editors can convert any image into BMP format.

There are different versions of the BMP format; we will only cover the simplest and most common one, sometimes called the 24-bit true color format. In this format, each pixel is represented as a sequence of three bytes, one each for the blue, green, and red value. For example, the color cyan (a mixture of blue and green) is 255 255 0, red is 0 0 255, and medium gray is 128 128 128.

A BMP file starts with a header that contains various pieces of information. We only need the following items:

Position	Item
2	The size of this file in bytes
10	The start of the image data
18	The width of the image in pixels
22	The height of the image in pixels

The image is stored as a sequence of pixel rows, starting with the pixels of the bottommost row of the image. Each pixel row contains a sequence of blue/green/red triplets. The end of the row is padded with additional bytes so that the number of bytes in the row is divisible by 4. (See Figure 6.) For example, if a row consisted of merely three pixels, one cyan, one red, and one medium gray one, the row would be encoded as

```
255 255 0 0 0 255 128 128 128 x y z
```

where $x \, y \, z$ are padding bytes to bring the row length up to 12, a multiple of 4. It is these little twists that make working with real-life file formats such a joyful experience.

The sample program at the end of this section reads every pixel of a BMP file and replaces it with its negative, turning white to black, cyan to red, and so on. The result is a negative image of the kind that old-fashioned film cameras used to produce (see Figure 7). To try out this program, take one of your favorite images, use an image editor to convert to BMP format (or use queen-mary.bmp from the sample files for this book), then run the program and view the transformed file in an image editor. Exercises P8.21 and P8.22 ask you to produce more interesting effects.

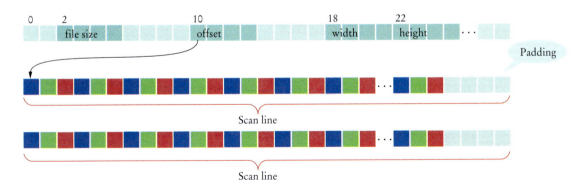

Figure 6   The BMP File Format for 24-bit True Color Images

Figure 7 An Image and Its Negative

ch08/imagemod.cpp

```cpp
1   #include <iostream>
2   #include <fstream>
3   #include <cstdlib>
4
5   using namespace std;
6
7   /**
8      Processes a pixel by forming the negative.
9      @param blue the blue value of the pixel
10     @param green the green value of the pixel
11     @param red the red value of the pixel
12  */
13  void process(int& blue, int& green, int& red)
14  {
15     blue = 255 - blue;
16     green = 255 - green;
17     red = 255 - red;
18  }
19
20  /**
21     Gets an integer from a binary stream.
22     @param stream the stream
23     @param offset the offset at which to read the integer
24     @return the integer starting at the given offset
25  */
```

```
26  int get_int(fstream& stream, int offset)
27  {
28     stream.seekg(offset);
29     int result = 0;
30     int base = 1;
31     for (int i = 0; i < 4; i++)
32     {
33        result = result + stream.get() * base;
34        base = base * 256;
35     }
36     return result;
37  }
38
39  int main()
40  {
41     cout << "Please enter the file name: ";
42     string filename;
43     cin >> filename;
44
45     fstream stream;
46     // Open as a binary file
47     stream.open(filename.c_str(), ios::in | ios::out | ios::binary);
48
49     int file_size = get_int(stream, 2); // Get the image dimensions
50     int start = get_int(stream, 10);
51     int width = get_int(stream, 18);
52     int height = get_int(stream, 22);
53
54     // Scan lines must occupy multiples of four bytes
55     int scanline_size = width * 3;
56     int padding = 0;
57     if (scanline_size % 4 != 0)
58     {
59        padding = 4 - scanline_size % 4;
60     }
61
62     if (file_size != start + (scanline_size + padding) * height)
63     {
64        cout << "Not a 24-bit true color image file." << endl;
65        return 1;
66     }
67
68     stream.seekg(start); // Go to the start of the pixels
69
70     for (int i = 0; i < height; i++) // For each scan line
71     {
72        for (int j = 0; j < width; j++) // For each pixel
73        {
74           int pos = stream.tellg(); // Go to the start of the pixel
75
76           int blue = stream.get(); // Read the pixel
77           int green = stream.get();
78           int red = stream.get();
79
```

```
80              process(blue, green, red); // Process the pixel
81
82              stream.seekp(pos); // Go back to the start of the pixel
83
84              stream.put(blue); // Write the pixel
85              stream.put(green);
86              stream.put(red);
87          }
88
89          stream.seekg(padding, ios::cur); // Skip the padding
90      }
91
92      return 0;
93  }
```

SELF CHECK

25. In plain English, what does the following code segment do?

```
strm.seekp(0);
strm.put(0);
```

26. How would you modify the imagemod.cpp program to flip the green and blue values of each pixel for a psychedelic effect?

27. What happens if you run the imagemod.cpp program twice on the same image file?

28. Could we have implemented the image modification program with sequential access only? If not, why not?

29. Suppose a BMP file stores a 100 × 100 pixel image in BMP format, with the image data starting at offset 64. What is the total file size?

RANDOM FACT 8.2

Databases and Privacy

Most companies use computers to keep huge data files of customer records and other business information. Databases not only lower the cost of doing business; they improve the quality of service that companies can offer. Nowadays it is almost unimaginable how time-consuming it used to be to withdraw money from a bank branch or to make travel reservations.

Today most databases are organized according to the *relational model*. Suppose a company stores your orders and payments. They will probably not repeat your name and address on every order; that would take unnecessary space. Instead, they will keep one file of all their customer names and identify each customer by a unique customer number. Only that customer number, not the entire customer information, is kept with an order record. (See Figure 8.)

To print an invoice, the database program must issue a *query* against both the customer and order files and pull the necessary information (name, address, articles ordered) from both. Frequently, queries involve more than two files. For example, the company may have a file of addresses of car owners and a file of people with good payment history and may want

Customers   Orders

Cust. #:	Name	
11439	Doe, John	

Order #:	Cust. #:	Item	
59673	11439	DOS for Historians	
59897	11439	C++ for Everyone	
61013	11439	Big C++	

Figure 8   Relational Database Files

to find all of its customers who placed an order in the last month, drive an expensive car, and pay their bills, so they can send them another catalog. This kind of query is, of course, much faster if all customer files use the *same* key, which is why so many organizations in the United States try to collect the Social Security numbers of their customers.

The Social Security Act of 1935 provided that each contributor be assigned a Social Security number to track contributions into the Social Security Fund. These numbers have a distinctive format, such as 078-05-1120. (This particular number was printed on sample cards that were inserted in wallets. It actually was the Social Security number of the secretary of a vice president at the wallet manufacturer. When thousands of people used it as their own, the number was voided, and the secretary received a new number.) Figure 9 shows a Social Security card. Although they had not originally been intended for use as a universal identification number, Social Security numbers have become just that.

Figure 9   Social Security Card

Some people are very concerned about the fact that just about every organization wants to store their Social Security number and other personal information. There is the possibility that companies and the government can merge multiple databases and derive information about us that we may wish they did not have or that simply may be untrue. An insurance company may deny coverage, or charge a higher premium, if it finds that you have too many relatives with a certain disease. You may be denied a job because of an inaccurate credit or medical report, and you may not even know the reason. These are very disturbing developments that have had a very negative impact for a small but growing number of people.

In many industrialized countries (but not currently in the United States), citizens have a right to control what information about themselves should be communicated to others and under what circumstances.

CHAPTER SUMMARY

1. To read or write disk files, you use variables of type `fstream`, `ifstream`, or `ofstream`.

2. When opening a file stream, you supply the name of the disk file.

3. Read from a file stream with the same operations that you use with `cin`.

4. Write to a file stream with the same operations that you use with `cout`.

5. Always use a reference parameter for a stream.

6. You can get individual characters from a stream and unget the last one.

7. Control stream formatting with manipulators.

8. Use string streams to read numbers that are contained in strings, or to convert between numbers and strings.

9. Programs that start from the command line can receive the name of the program and the command line arguments in the `main` function.

10. You can access any position in a random access file by moving the file pointer prior to a read or write operation.

REVIEW EXERCISES

Exercise R8.1. When do you open a file as an `ifstream`, as an `ofstream`, or as an `fstream`? Could you simply open all files as an `fstream`?

Exercise R8.2. What happens if you write to a file that you only opened for reading? Try it out if you don't know.

Exercise R8.3. What happens if you try to open a file for reading that doesn't exist? What happens if you try to open a file for writing that doesn't exist?

Exercise R8.4. What happens if you try to open a file for writing, but the file or device is write-protected (sometimes called read-only)? Try it out with a short test program.

Exercise R8.5. How do you open a file whose name contains a backslash, such as `temp\output.dat` or `c:\temp\output.dat`?

Exercise R8.6. Why is the `ifstream` parameter of the `process_name` function in Section 8.1.4 a reference parameter and not a value parameter?

Exercise R8.7. How can you convert the string `"3.14"` into the floating-point number 3.14? How can you convert the floating-point number 3.14 into the string `"3.14"`?

Exercise R8.8. What is a command line? How can a program read its command line?

Exercise R8.9. If a program `woozle` is started with the command

```
woozle -DNAME=Piglet -I\eeyore -v heff.cpp a.cpp lump.cpp
```

what is the value of `argc`, and what are the values of `argv[0]`, `argv[1]`, and so on?

Exercise R8.10. What is the difference between sequential access and random access?

Exercise R8.11. What is the difference between a text file and a binary file?

Exercise R8.12. What are the get and put positions in a file? How do you move them? How do you tell their current positions?

Exercise R8.13. What happens if you try to move the get or put position past the end of a file? What happens if you try to move the get or put position of `cin` or `cout`? Try it out and report your results.

PROGRAMMING EXERCISES

Exercise P8.1. Write a program that carries out the following tasks:

```
Open a file with the name hello.txt.
Store the message "Hello, World!" in the file.
Close the file.
Open the same file again.
Read the message into a string variable and print it.
```

Exercise P8.2. Write a program that reads a file containing floating-point numbers. Print the average of the numbers in the file. Prompt the user for the file name.

Exercise P8.3. Repeat Exercise P8.2, but allow the user to specify the file name on the command-line. If the user doesn't specify any file name, then prompt the user for the name.

Exercise P8.4. Write a program that reads a file containing two columns of floating-point numbers. Prompt the user for the file name. Print the average of each column.

Exercise P8.5. Write a program find that searches all files specified on the command line and prints out all lines containing a keyword. For example, if you call

```
find Tim report.txt address.txt homework.cpp
```

then the program might print

```
report.txt: discussed the results of my meeting with Tim T
address.txt: Torrey, Tim|11801 Trenton Court|Dallas|TX
address.txt: Walters, Winnie|59 Timothy Circle|Detroit|MI
homework.cpp: Time now;
```

The keyword is always the first command-line argument.

Exercise P8.6. Write a program that checks the spelling of all words in a file. It should read each word of a file and check whether it is contained in a word list. A word list is available on most UNIX systems (including Linux and Mac OS X) in the file /usr/share/dict/words. (If you don't have access to a UNIX system, you can find a copy of the file on the Internet by searching for /usr/share/dict/words.) The program should print out all words that it cannot find in the word list. Follow this pseudocode:

```
Open the dictionary file.
Define a vector of strings called words.
For each word in the dictionary file
{
    Append the word to the words vector.
}
Open the file to be checked.
For each word in that file
{
    If the word is not contained in the words vector
    {
        Print the word.
    }
}
```

Exercise P8.7. Write a program that reads each line in a file, reverses its characters, and writes the resulting line to another file. For example, if the file input.txt contains the lines

```
Mary had a little lamb
Its fleece was white as snow
And everywhere that Mary went
the lamb was sure to go.
```

and you run

```
reverse input.txt output.txt
```

then output.txt contains

```
bmal elttil a dah yraM
wons sa etihw saw eceelf stI
tnew yraM taht erehwyreve dnA
.og ot erus saw bmal ehT
```

Exercise P8.8. Write a program that reads each line in a file, reverses its characters, and writes the resulting line to the same file. Use the following pseudocode:

```
While the end of the file has not been reached
{
    pos1 = current get position
    Read a line.
    If the line was successfully read
    {
        pos2 = current get position
        Set put position to pos1.
        Write the reversed line.
        Set get position to pos2.
    }
}
```

Exercise P8.9. Write a program that reads each line in a file, reverses its lines, and writes them to another file. For example, if the file input.txt contains the lines

```
Mary had a little lamb
Its fleece was white as snow
And everywhere that Mary went
The lamb was sure to go.
```

and you run

```
reverse input.txt output.txt
```

then output.txt contains

```
The lamb was sure to go.
And everywhere that Mary went
Its fleece was white as snow
Mary had a little lamb
```

Exercise P8.10. Get the data for names in prior decades from the Social Security Administration. Paste the table data in files named babynames80s.txt, etc. Modify the babynames.cpp program so that it prompts the user for a file name. The numbers in the files have comma separators, so modify the program to handle them. Can you spot a trend in the frequencies?

Exercise P8.11. Write a program that reads in babynames.txt and produces two files boynames.txt and girlnames.txt, separating the data for the boys and girls.

Exercise P8.12. Write a program that reads a file in the same format as babynames.txt and prints all names that are both boy and girl names (such as Alexis or Morgan).

Exercise P8.13. Write a program that reads the country data in the file `worldpop.txt` (included with the book code). Do not edit the file. Use the following algorithm for processing each line. Add non-white space characters to the country name. When you encounter a white space, locate the next non-white space character. If it is not a digit, add a space and that character to the country name. Otherwise unget it and read the number. Print the total of all country populations (excepting the entries for "World" and "European Union") and compare it with the entry for "World."

Exercise P8.14. Write a program that asks the user for a file name and displays the number of characters, words, and lines in that file. Then have the program ask for the name of the next file. When the user enters a file that doesn't exist (such as the empty string), the program should exit.

Exercise P8.15. Write a program `copyfile` that copies one file to another. The file names are specified on the command line. For example,

```
copyfile report.txt report.sav
```

Exercise P8.16. Write a program that *concatenates* the contents of several files into one file. For example,

```
catfiles chapter1.txt chapter2.txt chapter3.txt book.txt
```

makes a long file `book.txt` that contains the contents of the files `chapter1.txt`, `chapter2.txt`, and `chapter3.txt`. The target file is always the last file specified on the command line.

Exercise P8.17. *Random monoalphabet cipher.* The Caesar cipher, which shifts all letters by a fixed amount, is far too easy to crack. Here is a better idea. As the key, don't use numbers but words. Suppose the key word is FEATHER. Then first remove duplicate letters, yielding FEATHR, and append the other letters of the alphabet in reverse order:

F E A T H R Z Y X W V U S Q P O N M L K J I G D C B

Now encrypt the letters as follows:

Write a program that encrypts or decrypts a file using this cipher. For example,

```
crypt -d -kFEATHER encrypt.txt output.txt
```

decrypts a file using the keyword FEATHER. It is an error not to supply a keyword.

Exercise P8.18. *Letter frequencies.* If you encrypt a file using the cipher of Exercise P8.17, it will have all of its letters jumbled up, and will look as if there is no hope of decrypting it without knowing the keyword. Guessing the keyword seems hopeless too. There are just too many possible keywords. However, someone who is trained in decryption will be able to break this cipher in no time at all. The average letter frequencies of English letters are well known. The most common letter is E, which occurs about 13 percent of the time. Here are the average frequencies of the letters.

A	8%	H	4%	O	7%	U	3%
B	<1%	I	7%	P	3%	V	<1%
C	3%	J	<1%	Q	<1%	W	2%
D	4%	K	<1%	R	8%	X	<1%
E	13%	L	4%	S	6%	Y	2%
F	3%	M	3%	T	9%	Z	<1%
G	2%	N	8%				

Write a program that reads an input file and displays the letter frequencies in that file. Such a tool will help a code breaker. If the most frequent letters in an encrypted file are H and K, then there is an excellent chance that they are the encryptions of E and T.

Exercise P8.19. *Vigenère cipher.* In order to defeat a simple letter frequency analysis, the Vigenère cipher encodes a letter into one of several cipher letters, depending on its position in the input document. Choose a keyword, for example TIGER. Then encode the first letter of the input text like this:

The encoded alphabet is just the regular alphabet shifted to start at T, the first letter of the keyword TIGER. The second letter is encrypted according to the following map.

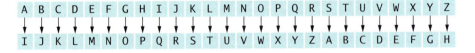

The third, fourth, and fifth letters in the input text are encrypted using the alphabet sequences beginning with characters G, E, and R, and so on. Because the key is only five letters long, the sixth letter of the input text is encrypted in the same way as the first.

Write a program that encrypts or decrypts an input text according to this cipher.

Exercise P8.20. *Playfair cipher.* Another way of thwarting a simple letter frequency analysis of an encrypted text is to encrypt *pairs* of letters together. A simple scheme to do this is the Playfair cipher. You pick a keyword and remove duplicate letters

from it. Then you fill the keyword, and the remaining letters of the alphabet, into a
5 × 5 square. (Since there are only 25 squares, I and J are considered the same letter.)
Here is such an arrangement with the keyword PLAYFAIR.

```
P L A Y F
I R B C D
E G H K M
N O Q S T
U V W X Z
```

To encrypt a letter pair, say AM, look at the rectangle with corners A and M:

```
P L A Y F
I R B C D
E G H K M
N O Q S T
U V W X Z
```

The encoding of this pair is formed by looking at the other two corners of the rectangle, in this case, FH. If both letters happen to be in the same row or column, such
as GO, simply swap the two letters. Decryption is done in the same way.

Write a program that encrypts or decrypts an input text according to this cipher.

Exercise P8.21. Write a program that edits an image file and reduces the blue and
green values by 30 percent, giving it a "sunset" effect.

Exercise P8.22. Write a program that edits an image file, turning it into grayscale.

Replace each pixel with a pixel that has the same grayness level for the blue, green,
and red component. The grayness level is computed by adding 30 percent of the red
level, 59 percent of the green level and 11 percent of the blue level. (The color-
sensing cone cells in the human eye differ in their sensitivity for red, green, and
blue light.)

Exercise P8.23. *Junk mail.* Write a program that reads in two files: a *template* and a *database.* The template file contains text and tags. The tags have the form |1| |2| |3|… and need to be replaced with the first, second, third, … field in the current database record.

A typical database looks like this:

```
Mr.|Harry|Morgan|1105 Torre Ave.|Cupertino|CA|95014
Dr.|John|Lee|702 Ninth Street Apt. 4|San Jose|CA|95109
Miss|Evelyn|Garcia|1101 S. University Place|Ann Arbor|MI|48105
```

And here is a typical form letter:

```
To:
|1| |2| |3|
|4|
|5|, |6| |7|

Dear |1| |3|:

You and the |3| family may be the lucky winners of $10,000,000 in the C++
compiler clearinghouse sweepstakes! ...
```

Exercise P8.24. Write a program that manipulates three database files. The first file contains the names and telephone numbers of a group of people. The second file contains the names and Social Security numbers of a group of people. The third file contains the Social Security numbers and annual salaries of a group of people. The groups of people should overlap but need not be completely identical. Your program should ask the user for a telephone number and then print the name, Social Security number, and annual income, if it can determine that information.

Exercise P8.25. Write a program that prints out a student grade report. There is a file, classes.txt, that contains the names of all classes taught at a college, such as

classes.txt
```
1   CSC1
2   CSC2
3   CSC46
4   CSC151
5   MTH121
6   ...
```

For each class, there is a file with student ID numbers and grades:

csc2.txt
```
1   11234 A-
2   12547 B
3   16753 B+
4   21886 C
5   ...
```

Write a program that asks for a student ID and prints out a grade report for that student, by searching all class files. Here is a sample report

```
Student ID 16753
CSC2 B+
MTH121 C+
CHN1 A
PHY50 A-
```

ANSWERS TO SELF-CHECK QUESTIONS

1. The stream will be in a failed state since there is no file with an empty name.
2. The stream variable is declared as an input stream. It should have been an ofstream.
3. The stream is not passed by reference.
4. Initialize boy_total and girl_total with 10.
5. Add the following code to the beginning of main:

   ```
   ofstream out_file;
   out_file.open("output.txt");
   ```

   Change every cout to out_file.

   Add an out_file parameter of type ofstream& to process_name.
6. number is 6 because the comma is not recognized as a part of the number. ch is ','.
7. word is "World!" (including the !) and ch is 'W'.
8. ```
   char ch;
   double number;
   string marker;
   in_file >> ch;
   in_file.unget();
   if (isdigit(ch) || ch == '-') { cin >> number; } else { cin >> marker; }
   ```
9. The loop skips a sequence of white space.
10. Some country names (such as United States) consist of multiple words.
11. 123456.000000, because the default precision is 6.
12. cout << fixed << setprecision(2) << 123456.0;
13. 00123456
14. 123456
15. Because the setw command only affects the first output.
16. 123456
17. 123
18. 0
   ```

19. 3.3333. Note that in general format, the precision denotes the total number of digits, not the number of digits after the decimal point.

20.
```
string double_to_string(double x, int digits)
{
   ostringstream strm;
   strm << fixed << setprecision(digits) << x;
   return strm.str();
}
```

21. `argc` is 3, and `argv` contains the strings `"caesar"`, `"-d"`, and `"encrypt.txt"`.

22.

key	file_count	i	arg
3	0	1	-d
-3	1	2	encrypt.txt
		3	

Then the program prints a message

`Usage: caesar [-d] infile outfile`

and exits.

23. FDHVDU

24. It turns them into # characters. The ASCII code for a space is 32, and the # character has code 35.

25. It replaces the initial byte of a file with 0.

26. Change the `process` function to swap the values of the `green` and `blue` parameters. The remainder of the program stays unchanged.

27. You get the original image back.

28. We could have read the header values and pixel data sequentially, but to update the pixels, we had to move backwards.

29. We need 3×100 bytes for each scan line. There is no padding since this number is divisible by 4. The total size $= 3 \times 100 \times 100 + 64 = 30{,}064$ bytes.

Classes

CHAPTER GOALS

- To be able to implement your own classes
- To master the separation of interface and implementation
- To understand the concept of encapsulation
- To design and implement accessor and mutator member functions
- To understand object construction
- To learn how to distribute a program over multiple source files

At this point, you are familiar with using objects from the string class and the stream classes. You have learned how to work with these objects by using member functions—functions that are called with the dot notation.

In this chapter you will learn how to implement your own classes. You will see how to design classes that help you solve programming problems, and you will study the mechanics of defining classes, constructors, and member functions.

CHAPTER CONTENTS

9.1 Object-Oriented Programming

You have learned how to structure your programs by decomposing tasks into functions. This is an excellent practice, but experience shows that it does not go far enough. As programs get larger, it becomes increasingly difficult to maintain a large collection of functions. It is common for larger programs to use a set of global variables that are manipulated by many functions. Because every function is able to change any of the global variables, diagnosing errors and managing changes becomes a challenge. Whenever some part of the global data is to be changed to improve performance or to add new capabilities, a large number of functions may be affected, making program modifications expensive or impractical (see Figure 1).

> An object holds data members that are accessed by member functions.

To overcome this problem, computer scientists invented *object-oriented programming*, a programming style in which tasks are solved by collaborating objects. An object has a set of variables (which are called data members) and functions that can act upon them (which are called member functions). The data members are *encapsulated*—hidden from other parts of the program and accessible only through their own member functions (see Figure 2). When we want to change the way that an object is implemented, only a small number of functions need to be updated. Program evolution becomes much more manageable. Because most real-world programs need to be updated often during their lifetime, this is an important advantage of object-oriented programming.

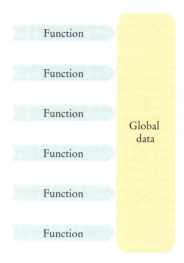

Figure 1
A Program Using Functions

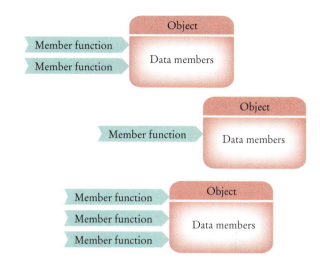

Figure 2
An Object-Oriented Program

> Encapsulation is the act of hiding implementation details.

Consider your own experience with using string or stream objects. When you access an object, you do not know its data members. Encapsulation means that they are hidden from you. You can only access the object through its member functions. You need not know how a string organizes a character sequence, or how a stream communicates with a file. You simply call member functions such as substr, or an operator such as [] or >>. (These operators are also implemented as functions—see Advanced Topic 9.2 on page 386).

You can drive a car by operating the steering wheel and pedals, without knowing how the engine works. Similarly, you use an object through its member functions. The implementation is hidden.

Encapsulation benefits the programmer who uses an object. That programmer only needs to know about the set of functions that can be invoked on the objects. It is also a benefit for the programmer who implements objects. That programmer is able to choose a more efficient implementation without impacting the object user.

> A class describes a set of objects with the same behavior.

In C++, a programmer doesn't implement a single object. Instead, the programmer implements a *class*. A class describes a set of objects with the same behavior. To define a class, you must specify the behavior by providing implementations for the member functions, and by defining the data members for the objects. We will discuss this process in the following sections.

When classifying real-life objects, you can group together objects with the same behavior. For example, a Car class describes all passenger vehicles that have a certain capacity and shape.

SELF CHECK

1. Suppose a program consists of 1,000 functions, and one of the global data items has been set to the wrong value. How many functions could have caused the error? Suppose the program is instead implemented using 100 objects, each having 10 member functions. If a data member has been set to the wrong value, how many functions could have caused the error?

2. In C++, is cin an object or a class? Is string an object or a class?

3. When using a string object, you do not know how it stores its characters. How can you access them?

4. Describe two possible ways in which a string object might store its characters.

5. Suppose the providers of your C++ compiler decide to change the way that a string object stores its characters, and they update the string member functions accordingly. Which parts of your code do you need to change when you get the new compiler?

9.2 Interfaces

> Every class has a public interface: a collection of member functions through which the objects of the class can be manipulated.

To define a class, we first need to specify its public *interface*. The interface of a class consists of all functions that we want to apply to its objects.

Let's consider a simple example. We want to use objects that simulate cash registers. A cashier who rings up a sale presses a key to start the sale, then rings up each item. A display shows the amount owed as well as the total number of items purchased.

In our simulation, we want to call the following member functions on a cash register object:

- Clear the cash register to start a new sale.
- Add the price of an item.
- Get the total amount owed, and the count of items purchased.

Our first example of a class simulates a cash register.

The interface is specified in the *class definition*, summarized in Syntax 9.1 on page 372. We will call our class CashRegister. (We follow the convention that the name of a programmer-defined class starts with an uppercase letter, as does each word within the name. This naming convention is called *camel case* because the uppercase letters in the middle of the name look like the humps of a camel.)

Here is the C++ syntax for the CashRegister class definition:

```
class CashRegister
{
public:
    void clear();
    void add_item(double price);

    double get_total() const;
    int get_count() const;

private:
    data members—see Section 9.3
};
```

The member functions are declared in the *public section* of the class. Any part of the program can call the member functions. The data members are defined in the *private section* of the class. Only the member functions of the class can access those data members; they are hidden from the remainder of the program.

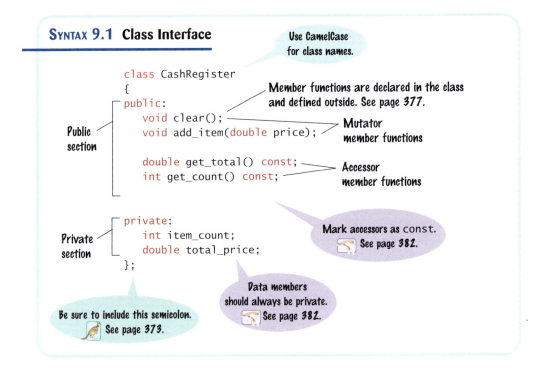

SYNTAX 9.1 Class Interface

Use CamelCase for class names.

```
class CashRegister
{
public:
    void clear();
    void add_item(double price);

    double get_total() const;
    int get_count() const;

private:
    int item_count;
    double total_price;
};
```

Public section

Private section

Member functions are declared in the class and defined outside. See page **377**.

Mutator member functions

Accessor member functions

Mark accessors as const. See page **382**.

Data members should always be private. See page **382**.

Be sure to include this semicolon. See page **373**.

The member function declarations look similar to the declarations of regular functions. These declarations do not provide any implementation. You will see in Section 9.4 how to implement the member functions.

Member functions are invoked using the dot notation that you have already seen with string and stream functions:

```
CashRegister register1; // Defines a CashRegister object
register1.clear(); // Invokes a member function
```

A mutator member function changes the object on which it operates.

There are two kind of member functions, called *mutators* and *accessors*. A mutator is a function that modifies the data members of the object. The CashRegister class has two mutators: clear and add_item. After you call either of these functions, the amount due and item count are changed.

An accessor member function does not change the object on which it operates. Use const with accessors.

Accessors just query the object for some information without changing it. The CashRegister class has two accessors: get_total and get_count. Applying either of these functions to a CashRegister object simply returns a value and does not modify the object. In C++, you should use the const reserved word to mark accessor functions (see Quality Tip 9.2 on page 382), like this:

```
double get_total() const;
```

Now we know *what* a CashRegister object can do, but not *how* it does it. Of course, to use CashRegister objects in our programs, we don't need to know. We

Figure 3 The Interface of the CashRegister Class

simply use the public interface. Figure 3 shows the interface of the CashRegister class. The mutator functions are shown with arrows pointing inside the private data to indicate that they modify the data. The accessor functions are shown with arrows pointing the other way to indicate that they just read the data.

SELF CHECK

6. What does the following code segment print?

```
CashRegister reg;
reg.clear();
reg.add_item(0.95);
reg.add_item(0.95);
cout << reg.get_count() << " " << reg.get_total() << endl;
```

7. What is wrong with the following code segment?

```
CashRegister reg;
reg.clear();
reg.add_item(0.95);
cout << reg.get_amount_due() << endl;
```

8. Declare a member function get_dollars of the CashRegister class that yields the dollar value of the total amount of the sale.

9. Name two accessor member functions of the string class.

10. Is the get member function of the ifstream class an accessor or a mutator?

COMMON ERROR 9.1

Forgetting a Semicolon

Braces { } are common in C++ code, and usually you do not place a semicolon after the closing brace. However, class definitions always end in };. A common error is to forget that semicolon:

```
class CashRegister
{
```

```
public:
   ...
private:
   ...
} // Forgot semicolon

int main()
{ // Many compilers report the error in this line
   ...
}
```

This error can be extremely confusing to many compilers. There is syntax, now obsolete but supported for compatibility with old code, to define class types and variables of that type simultaneously. Because the compiler doesn't know that you don't use that obsolete construction, it tries to analyze the code wrongly and ultimately reports an error. Unfortunately, it may report the error *several lines away* from the line in which you forgot the semicolon.

If the compiler reports bizarre errors in lines that you are sure are correct, check that each of the preceding class definitions is terminated by a semicolon.

9.3 Encapsulation

Each `CashRegister` object must store the total price and item count of the sale that is currently rung up. We have to choose an appropriate *data representation*. In our example, we simply store the total price and the item count. (Different data representations are explored in Exercises P9.1 and P9.2.)

The data members are defined in the private section of the class definition.

```
class CashRegister
{
public:
   // See Section 9.2
private:
   int item_count;
   double total_price;
};
```

A driver of an electric car doesn't have to learn new controls even though the car engine is very different. Neither does the programmer who uses an object with an improved implementation—as long as the same member functions are used.

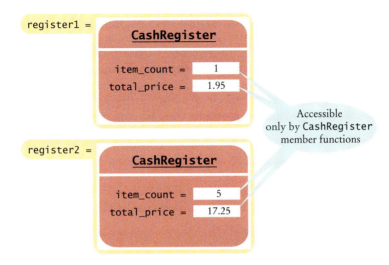

Figure 4 Data Members of CashRegister Objects

Every `CashRegister` object has a separate copy of these data members (see Figure 4).

> Every object has its own set of data members.

Because the data members are defined to be private, only the member functions of the class can access them. Programmers using the `CashRegister` class cannot access the data members directly:

```
int main()
{
   ...
   cout << register1.item_count; // Error—use get_count() instead
   ...
}
```

> Private data members can only be accessed by member functions of the same class.

All data access must occur through the public interface. Thus, the data members of an object are effectively hidden from the programmer using the class. While it is theoretically possible in C++ to leave data members unencapsulated (by placing them into the public section), this is very uncommon in practice. We will always make all data members private in this book.

The `CashRegister` class is so simple that it is not obvious what benefit we gain from the encapsulation.

> By keeping the implementation private, we protect it from being accidentally corrupted.

One benefit of the encapsulation mechanism is the guarantee that the object data cannot accidentally be put in an incorrect state. For example, we can be assured that `item_count` cannot be set to a negative value. There are only two functions that can change the value, the `add_item` and `clear` mutators. As you will see in the next section, these functions will never let `item_count` be negative. Since no other function can touch the private data members, we can *guarantee* that their values are always valid, thanks to the encapsulation mechanism.

> Encapsulation enables changes in the implementation without affecting users of a class.

There is a second benefit of encapsulation that is particularly important in larger programs. Typically, implementation details need to change over time. You want to be able to make your classes more efficient or more capable, without affecting the programmers that use your classes. As long as those programmers do not depend on the implementation details, you are free to change them at any time.

SELF CHECK

11. What is the value of register1.item_count, register1.total_price, register2.item_count, and register2.total_price after these statements?

```
CashRegister register1;
register1.clear();
register1.add_item(0.90);
register1.add_item(0.95);
CashRegister register2;
register2.clear();
register2.add_item(1.90);
```

12. What is wrong with this code segment?

```
CashRegister register2;
register2.clear();
register2.add_item(0.95);
cout << register2.total_price << endl;
```

13. Consider a class Time that represents a point in time, such as 9 A.M. or 3:30 P.M. Give two different sets of data members that can be used for implementing the Time class.

14. Suppose the implementor of the Time class changes from one implementation strategy to another, keeping the public interface unchanged. What do the programmers who use the Time class need to do?

15. Consider a class Grade that represents a letter grade, such as A+ or B. Give two different sets of data members that can be used for implementing the Grade class.

9.4 Member Functions

The definition of a class declares its member functions. Each member function is defined separately, after the class definition. The following sections show how to define member functions.

9.4.1 Implementing Member Functions

Here is the implementation of the add_item function of the CashRegister class.

```
void CashRegister::add_item(double price)
{
   item_count++;
   total_price = total_price + price;
}
```

> Use the *ClassName*:: prefix when defining member functions.

The CashRegister:: prefix makes it clear that we are defining the add_item function of the CashRegister class. In C++ it is perfectly legal to have add_item functions in other classes as well, and it is important to specify exactly which add_item function we are defining. (See Syntax 9.2 on page 379.) You use the *ClassName*::add_item syntax only when *defining* the function, not when calling it. When you call the add_item member function, the call has the form *object*.add_item(...).

When defining an accessor member function, supply the reserved word const following the closing parenthesis of the parameter list. Here is the get_count member function:

```
int CashRegister::get_count() const
{
   return item_count;
}
```

You will find the other member functions with the sample program at the end of this section.

9.4.2 Implicit and Explicit Parameters

Whenever you refer to a data member, such as item_count or total_price, in a member function, it denotes that data member *of the object on which the member function was invoked*. For example, consider the call

```
register1.add_item(1.95);
```

The first statement in the CashRegister::add_item function is

```
item_count++;
```

Which item_count is incremented? In this call, it is the item_count of the register1 object. (See Figure 5.)

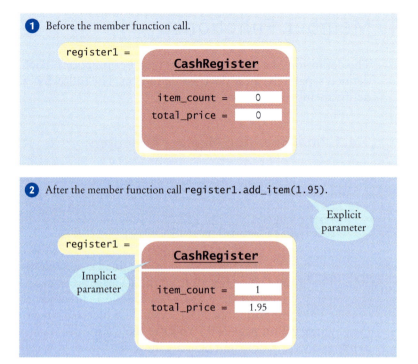

❶ Before the member function call.

register1 =

CashRegister

item_count = 0
total_price = 0

❷ After the member function call register1.add_item(1.95).

Explicit parameter

register1 =

CashRegister

Implicit parameter

item_count = 1
total_price = 1.95

Figure 5 Implicit and Explicit Parameters

> The object on which a member function is applied is the implicit parameter.

The object on which a member function is invoked is called the *implicit parameter* of the member function.

You can think of the code of the add_item function like this:

```
void CashRegister::add_item(double price)
{
    implicit parameter.item_count++;
    implicit parameter.total_price = implicit parameter.total_price + price;
}
```

In C++, you do not actually write the implicit parameter in the function definition. For that reason, the parameter is called "implicit".

> Explicit parameters of a member function are listed in the function definition.

In contrast, parameters that are explicitly mentioned in the function definition, such as the price parameter, are called *explicit parameters*. Every member function has exactly one implicit parameter and zero or more explicit parameters.

9.4.3 Calling a Member Function from a Member Function

When calling another member function on the same object, do not use the dot notation.

When one member function calls another member function *on the same object*, you do not use the dot notation. Instead, you simply use the name of the other function. Here is an example. Suppose we want to implement a member function to add multiple instances of the same item. An easy way to implement this function is to repeatedly call the add_item function:

```
void CashRegister::add_items(int quantity, double price)
{
   for (int i = 1; i <= quantity; i++)
   {
      add_item(price);
   }
}
```

Here, the add_item member function is invoked on the implicit parameter.

```
for (int i = 1; i <= quantity; i++)
{
   implicit parameter.add_item(price);
}
```

That parameter is the object on which the add_items function is invoked. For example, in the call

```
register1.add_items(6, 0.95);
```

the add_item method is invoked six times on register1.

SYNTAX 9.2 Member Function Definition

Use *ClassName*:: before the name of the member function.

Explicit parameter

```
void CashRegister::add_item(double price)
{
   item_count++;
   total_price = total_price + price;
}
```

Data members of the implicit parameter

```
int CashRegister::get_count() const
{
   return item_count;
}
```

Data member of the implicit parameter

Use const for accessor functions.
See page 382.

ch09/registertest1.cpp

```cpp
1   #include <iostream>
2   #include <iomanip>
3
4   using namespace std;
5
6   /**
7       A simulated cash register that tracks the item count and
8       the total amount due.
9   */
10  class CashRegister
11  {
12  public:
13     /**
14         Clears the item count and the total.
15     */
16     void clear();
17
18     /**
19         Adds an item to this cash register.
20         @param price  the price of this item
21     */
22     void add_item(double price);
23
24     /**
25         @return  the total amount of the current sale
26     */
27     double get_total() const;
28
29     /**
30         @return  the item count of the current sale
31     */
32     int get_count() const;
33
34  private:
35     int item_count;
36     double total_price;
37  };
38
39  void CashRegister::clear()
40  {
41     item_count = 0;
42     total_price = 0;
43  }
44
45  void CashRegister::add_item(double price)
46  {
47     item_count++;
48     total_price = total_price + price;
49  }
50
51  double CashRegister::get_total() const
52  {
53     return total_price;
```

```
54  }
55
56  int CashRegister::get_count() const
57  {
58     return item_count;
59  }
60
61  /**
62     Displays the item count and total price of a cash register.
63     @param reg the cash register to display
64  */
65  void display(CashRegister reg)
66  {
67     cout << reg.get_count() << " $" << fixed << setprecision(2)
68        << reg.get_total() << endl;
69  }
70
71  int main()
72  {
73     CashRegister register1;
74     register1.clear();
75     register1.add_item(1.95);
76     display(register1);
77     register1.add_item(0.95);
78     display(register1);
79     register1.add_item(2.50);
80     display(register1);
81     return 0;
82  }
```

Program Run

```
1 $1.95
2 $2.90
3 $5.40
```

SELF CHECK

16. What is wrong with this implementation of the get_total member function?

```
int get_total()
{
   return total_price;
}
```

17. Implement the add_items member function described in Section 9.4.3 without calling add_item.

18. Implement a member function get_dollars of the CashRegister class that yields the amount of the total sale as a dollar value without the cents.

19. Consider the substr member function of the string class. How many parameters does it have, and what are their types?

20. Consider the length member function of the string class. How many parameters does it have, and what are their types?

QUALITY TIP 9.1

All Data Members Should Be Private; Most Member Functions Should Be Public

It is possible to define data members in the public section of a class, but you should not do that in your own code. Always use encapsulation, with private data members that are manipulated with member functions.

Generally, member functions should be public. However, sometimes you have a member function that is only used as a helper function by other member functions. In that case, you can make the helper function private. Simply declare it in the private section of the class.

QUALITY TIP 9.2

const Correctness

You should declare all accessor functions in C++ with the const reserved word. (Recall that an accessor function is a member function that does not modify its implicit parameter.)

For example, suppose you design the following class:

```
class CashRegister
{
    void display(); // Bad style—no const
    ...
};
```

When you compile your code, no error is reported. But now suppose that another programmer uses your CashRegister class in a function

```
void display_all(const CashRegister registers[])
{
    for (int i = 0; i < NREGISTERS; i++) { registers[i].display(); }
}
```

That programmer is conscientious and declares the registers parameter as const. But then the call registers[i].display() will not compile. Because CashRegister::display is not tagged as const, the compiler suspects that the call registers[i].display() may modify registers[i]. But the function promised not to modify the registers array.

If you write a program with other team members who are conscientious about const, it is very important that you do your part as well. You should therefore get into the habit of using const with all accessor member functions.

9.5 Constructors

A constructor is a member function that initializes the data members of an object. The constructor is automatically called whenever an object is created. By supplying a constructor, you can ensure that all data members are properly set before any member functions act on an object.

> A constructor is called automatically whenever an object is created.

To understand the importance of constructors, consider the following statements:

```
CashRegister register1;
register1.add_item(1.95);
int count = register1.get_count(); // May not be 1
```

Here, the programmer forgot to call `clear` before adding items. Therefore, the data members of the `register1` object were initialized with random values. Constructors guarantee that an object is always fully initialized when it is defined.

> The name of a constructor is the same as the class name.

The name of a constructor is identical to the name of its class. You declare constructors in the class definition, for example:

```
class CashRegister
{
public:
    CashRegister(); // A constructor
    ...
};
```

Constructors never return values, but you do not use the `void` reserved word when declaring them.

Here is the definition of that constructor:

```
CashRegister::CashRegister()
{
    item_count = 0;
    total_price = 0;
}
```

A constructor is like a set of assembly instructions for an object.

In the constructor definition, the first `CashRegister` (before the `::`) indicates that we are about to define a member function of the `CashRegister` class. The second `CashRegister` is the name of that member function.

> A default constructor has no parameters.

The constructor that you just saw has no parameters. Such a constructor is called a *default constructor*. It is used whenever you define an object and do not specify any parameters for the construction. For example, if you define

```
CashRegister register1;
```

then the default constructor is called. It sets `register1.item_count` and `register1.total_price` to zero.

> A class can have multiple constructors.

Many classes have more than one constructor. This allows you to define objects in different ways. Consider for example a `BankAccount` class that has two constructors:

```
class BankAccount
{
public:
    BankAccount(); // Sets balance to 0
    BankAccount(double initial_balance); // Sets balance to initial_balance
    // Member functions omitted
private:
    double balance;
};
```

Both constructors have the same name as the class, `BankAccount`. But the default constructor has no parameters, whereas the second constructor has a `double` parameter.

> The compiler picks the constructor that matches the construction parameters.

When you construct an object, the compiler chooses the constructor that matches the parameters that you supply. For example,

```
BankAccount joes_account;
    // Uses default constructor
BankAccount lisas_account(499.95);
    // Uses BankAccount(double) constructor
```

> Be sure to initialize all number and pointer data members in a constructor.

When implementing a constructor, you need to pay particular attention to all data members that are numbers or pointers. These types are not classes and therefore have no constructors. If you have a data member that is an object of a class (such as a `string` object), then that class has a constructor, and the object will be initialized. For example, all string objects are automatically initialized to the empty string. Consider this class:

```
class Item
{
public:
    Item();
    // Additional member functions omitted
private:
    string description;
    double price;
};
```

In the `Item` constructor, you need to set `price` to 0, but you need not initialize the `description` data member. It is automatically initialized to the empty string.

If you do not supply any constructor for a class, the compiler automatically generates a default constructor that initializes all data members of class type with their default constructors.

SELF CHECK

21. Provide an implementation for the default constructor of the BankAccount class.

22. Provide an implementation for the BankAccount(double) constructor.

23. Provide an implementation for the default constructor of the Item class.

24. Provide an implementation for the default constructor of the CashRegister class that calls the clear member function.

25. Which constructor is called in each of the following definitions?

    a. Item item1;

    b. Item item2("Corn flakes");

    c. Item item3(3.95);

    d. Item item4("Corn flakes", 3.95);

    e. Item item5();

COMMON ERROR 9.2

Trying to Call a Constructor

The constructor is invoked only when an object is first created. You cannot invoke it again. For example, you cannot call the constructor to clear an object:

```
CashRegister register1;
...
register1.CashRegister(); // Error
```

It is true that the default constructor sets a *new* CashRegister object to the cleared state, but you cannot invoke a constructor on an *existing* object.

ADVANCED TOPIC 9.1

Initializer Lists

When you construct an object whose data members are themselves objects, those objects are constructed by their class's default constructor. However, if a data member belongs to a class without a default constructor, you need to invoke the member's constructor explicitly. Here is an example.

This Item class has no default constructor.

```
class Item
{
```

```
   public:
       Item(string item_description, double item_price);
       // No other constructors
       ...
   };
```

This Order class has a data member of type Item.

```
   class Order
   {
   public:
       Order(string customer_name, string item_description, double item_price);
       ...
   private:
       Item article;
       string customer;
   };
```

The Order constructor must call the Item constructor. That is achieved with an *initializer list*. The initializer list is placed before the opening brace of the constructor. The list starts with a colon and contains names of data members with their construction parameters.

```
   Order(string customer_name, string item_description, double item_price)
       : article(item_description, item_price)
   {
       customer = customer_name;
   }
```

Initializers are separated by commas. The Order constructor can also be written like this:

```
   Order(string customer_name, string item_description, double item_price)
       : article(item_description, item_price), customer(customer_name)
   {
   }
```

ADVANCED TOPIC 9.2

Overloading

When the same function name is used for more than one function, then the name is *overloaded*. In C++ you can overload function names provided the parameter types are different. For example, you can define two functions, both called print:

```
   void print(CashRegister r)
   void print(Item i)
```

When the print function is called,

```
   print(x);
```

the compiler looks at the type of x. If x is a CashRegister object, the first function is called. If x is an Item object, the second function is called. If x is neither, the compiler generates an error.

We have not used the overloading feature in this book. Instead, we gave each function a unique name, such as print_register or print_item. However, we have no choice with constructors. C++ demands that the name of a constructor equal the name of the class. If a class has more than one constructor, then that name must be overloaded.

In addition to name overloading, C++ also supports *operator overloading*. It is possible to give new meanings to the familiar C++ operators such as +, ==, and <<. This is an advanced technique that we do not discuss in this book.

HOW TO 9.1

Implementing a Class

A very common task is to implement a class whose objects can carry out a set of specified actions. This How To walks you through the necessary steps.

As an example, consider a class Menu. An object of this class can display a menu such as

```
1) Open new account
2) Log into existing account
3) Help
4) Quit
```

Then the menu waits for the user to supply a value. If the user does not supply a valid value, the menu is redisplayed, and the user can try again.

Step 1 Get an informal list of the responsibilities of your objects.

Be careful that you restrict yourself to features that are actually required in the problem. With real-world items, such as cash registers or bank accounts, there are potentially dozens of features that might be worth implementing. But your job is not to faithfully model the real world. You need to determine only those responsibilities that you need for solving your specific problem.

In the case of the menu, you need to

> Display the menu.
> Get user input.

Now look for hidden responsibilities that aren't part of the problem description. How do objects get created? Which mundane activities need to happen, such as clearing the cash register at the beginning of each sale?

In the menu example, consider how a menu is produced. The programmer creates an empty menu object and then adds options "Open new account", "Help", and so on. There is a hidden responsibility:

> Add an option.

Step 2 Specify the public interface.

Turn the list in Step 1 into a set of member functions, with specific types for the parameters and the return values. Be sure to mark accessors as const. Many programmers find this step simpler if they write out member function calls that are applied to a sample object, like this:

```
Menu main_menu;
main_menu.add_option("Open new account");
// Add more options
int input = main_menu.get_input();
```

Now we have a specific list of member functions.

- `void add_option(string option)`
- `int get_input() const`

What about displaying the menu? There is no sense in displaying the menu without also asking the user for input. However, `get_input` may need to display the menu more than once if the user provides a bad input. Thus, `display` is a good candidate for a private member function.

To complete the public interface, you need to specify the constructors. Ask yourself what information you need in order to construct an object of your class. Sometimes you will want two constructors: one that sets all fields to a default and one that sets them to user-supplied values.

In the case of the menu example, we can get by with a single constructor that creates an empty menu.

Here is the public interface:

```
class Menu
{
public:
   Menu();
   void add_option(string option);
   int get_input() const
private:
   ...
};
```

Step 3 Document the public interface.

Supply a documentation comment for the class, then comment each member function.

```
/**
   A menu that is displayed on a console.
*/
class Menu
{
public:
   /**
      Constructs a menu with no options.
   */
   Menu();

   /**
      Adds an option to the end of this menu.
      @param option  the option to add
   */
   void add_option(string option);

   /**
      Displays the menu, with options numbered starting with 1,
      and prompts the user for input. Repeats until a valid input
      is supplied.
      @return the number that the user supplied
   */
   int get_input() const;
```

```
private:
    ...
};
```

Step 4   Determine data members.

Ask yourself what information an object needs to store to do its job. Remember, the member functions can be called in any order! The object needs to have enough internal memory to be able to process every member function using just its data members and the member function parameters. Go through each member function, perhaps starting with a simple one or an interesting one, and ask yourself what you need to carry out the member function's task. Make data members to store the information that the member function needs.

In the menu example, we clearly need to store the menu options so that the menu can be displayed. How should we store them? As a vector of strings? As one long string? Both approaches can be made to work. We will use a vector here. Exercise P9.5 asks you to implement the other approach.

```
class Menu
{
    ...
private:
    ...
    vector<string> options;
};
```

When checking for user input, we need to know the number of menu items. Because we store them in a vector, the number of menu items is simply obtained as the size of the vector. If you stored the menu items in one long string, you might want to keep another data member that stores the item count.

Step 5   Implement constructors and member functions.

Implement the constructors and member functions in your class, one at a time, starting with the easiest ones. For example, here is the implementation of the add_option member function:

```
void Menu::add_option(string option)
{
    options.push_back(option);
}
```

Here is the get_input member function. This member function is a bit more sophisticated. It loops until a valid input has been obtained, and it calls the private display member function to display the menu.

```
int Menu::get_input() const
{
    int input;
    do
    {
        display();
        cin >> input;
    }
    while (input < 1 || input > options.size());
    return input;
}
```

Finally, here is the `display` member function:

```
void Menu::display() const
{
   for (int i = 0; i < options.size(); i++)
   {
      cout << i + 1 << ") " << options[i] << endl;
   }
}
```

The `Menu` constructor is a bit odd. We need to construct a menu with no options. A vector is a class, and it has a default constructor. That constructor does exactly what we want, namely to construct an empty vector. Nothing else needs to be done:

```
Menu::Menu()
{
}
```

If you find that you have trouble with the implementation of some of your member functions, you may need to rethink your choice of data members. It is common for a beginner to start out with a set of data members that cannot accurately describe the state of an object. Don't hesitate to go back and rethink your implementation strategy.

Once you have completed the implementation, compile your class and fix any compiler errors. (See ch09/menu.cpp in your book code for the completed class.)

Step 6 Test your class.

Write a short tester program and execute it. The tester program should carry out the member function calls that you found in Step 2.

```
int main()
{
   Menu main_menu;
   main_menu.add_option("Open new account");
   main_menu.add_option("Log into existing account");
   main_menu.add_option("Help");
   main_menu.add_option("Quit");
   int input = main_menu.get_input();
   cout << "Input: " << input << endl;
   return 0;
}
```

Program Run

```
1) Open new account
2) Log into existing account
3) Help
4) Quit
5
1) Open new account
2) Log into existing account
3) Help
4) Quit
3
Input: 3
```

WORKED EXAMPLE 9.1

Implementing a Bank Account Class

This Worked Example shows how to develop a class that simulates a bank account.

RANDOM FACT 9.1

Electronic Voting Machines

In the 2000 presidential elections in the United States, votes were tallied by a variety of machines. Some machines processed cardboard ballots into which voters punched holes to indicate their choices (see Figure 6). When voters were not careful, remains of paper—the now infamous "chads"—were partially stuck in the punch cards, causing votes to be miscounted. A manual recount was necessary, but it was not carried out everywhere due to time constraints and procedural wrangling. The election was very close, and there remain doubts in the minds of many people whether the election outcome would have been different if the voting machines had accurately counted the intent of the voters.

Subsequently, voting machine manufacturers have argued that electronic voting machines would avoid the problems caused by punch cards or optically scanned forms. In an electronic voting machine, voters indicate their preferences by pressing buttons or touching icons on a computer screen. Typically, each voter is presented with a summary screen for review before casting the ballot. The process is very similar to using an automatic bank teller machine (see Figure 7).

It seems plausible that these machines make it more likely that a vote is counted in the same way that the voter intends. However, there has been significant controversy surrounding some types of electronic voting machines. If a machine simply records the votes and prints out the totals after the election has been completed, then how do you know that

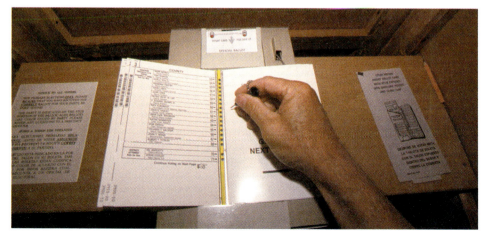

Figure 6 Punch Card Ballot

Figure 7
Touch Screen Voting Machine

the machine worked correctly? Inside the machine is a computer that executes a program, and, as you may know from your own experience, programs can have bugs.

In fact, some electronic voting machines do have bugs. There have been isolated cases where machines reported tallies that were impossible. When a machine reports far more or far fewer votes than voters, then it is clear that it malfunctioned. Unfortunately, it is then impossible to find out the actual votes. Over time, one would expect these bugs to be fixed in the software. More insidiously, if the results are plausible, nobody may ever investigate.

Many computer scientists have spoken out on this issue and confirmed that it is impossible, with today's technology, to tell that software is error free and has not been tampered with. Many of them recommend that electronic voting machines should employ a *voter verifiable audit trail*. (A good source of information is http://verifiedvoting.org.) Typically, a voter-verifiable machine prints out a ballot. Each voter has a chance to review the printout, and then deposits it in an old-fashioned ballot box. If there is a problem with the electronic equipment, the printouts can be scanned or counted by hand.

As this book is written, this concept is strongly resisted both by manufacturers of electronic voting machines and by their customers, the cities and counties that run elections. Manufacturers are reluctant to increase the cost of the machines because they may not be able to pass the cost increase on to their customers, who tend to have tight budgets. Election officials fear problems with malfunctioning printers, and some of them have publicly stated that they actually prefer equipment that eliminates bothersome recounts.

What do you think? You probably use an automatic bank teller machine to get cash from your bank account. Do you review the paper record that the machine issues? Do you check your bank statement? Even if you don't, do you put your faith in other people who double-check their balances, so that the bank won't get away with widespread cheating?

At any rate, is the integrity of banking equipment more important or less important than that of voting machines? Won't every voting process have some room for error and fraud anyway? Is the added cost for equipment, paper, and staff time reasonable to combat a potentially slight risk of malfunction and fraud? Computer scientists cannot answer these questions—an informed society must make these tradeoffs. But, like all professionals, they have an obligation to speak out and give accurate testimony about the capabilities and limitations of computing equipment.

9.6 Discovering Classes

> To discover classes, look for nouns in the problem description.

When you are given a problem description and aim to provide a solution using objects and classes, you need to determine the classes required for the implementation. You may be able to reuse existing classes, or you may need to implement new ones. One simple approach for discovering classes and member functions is to look for the nouns and verbs in the problem description. Often times, nouns correspond to classes, and verbs correspond to member functions.

Many classes are abstractions of real-life entities.

- BankAccount
- CashRegister

> Concepts from the problem domain are good candidates for classes.

Generally, concepts from the problem domain, be it science, business, or a game, make good classes. The name for such a class should be a noun that describes the concept. Other frequently used classes represent system services such as files or menus.

What might not be a good class? If you can't tell from the class name what an object of the class is supposed to do, then you are probably not on the right track. For example, your homework assignment might ask you to write a program that prints paychecks. Suppose you start by trying to design a class PaycheckProgram. What would an object of this class do? An object of this class would have to do everything that the homework needs to do. That doesn't simplify anything. A better class would be Paycheck. Then your program can manipulate one or more Paycheck objects.

Another common mistake, particularly by students who are used to writing programs that consist of functions, is to turn an action into a class. For example, if your homework assignment is to compute a paycheck, you may consider writing a class ComputePaycheck. But can you visualize a "ComputePaycheck" object? The fact that "ComputePaycheck" isn't a noun tips you off that you are on the wrong track. On the other hand, a Paycheck class makes intuitive sense. The word "paycheck" is a noun. You can visualize a paycheck object. You can then think about useful member functions of the Paycheck class, such as compute_taxes, that help you solve the assignment.

When you analyze a problem description, you often find that you need multiple classes. It is then helpful to consider how these classes are related. One of the fundamental relationships between classes is the "aggregation" relationship (which is informally known as the "has-a" relationship).

> A class aggregates another if its objects contain objects of the other class.

The aggregation relationship states that objects of one class contain objects of another class. Consider a quiz that is made up of questions. Since each quiz has one or more questions, we say that the class Quiz aggregates the class Question. There is a standard notation, called a UML (Unified Modeling Language) class diagram, to describe class relationships. In the UML notation, aggregation is denoted by a line with a diamond-shaped symbol (see Figure 8).

Figure 8 Class Diagram

Finding out about aggregation is very helpful for deciding how to implement classes. For example, when you implement the Quiz class, you will want to store the questions of a quiz as a data member. Since a quiz can have any number of questions, you will choose a vector:

```
class Quiz
{
    ...
private:
    vector<Question> questions;
};
```

In summary, when you analyze a problem description, you will want to carry out these tasks:

- Find the concepts that you need to implement as classes. Often, these will be nouns in the problem description.
- Find the responsibilities of the classes. Often, these will be verbs in the problem description.
- Find relationships between the classes that you have discovered. In this section, we described the aggregation relationship. In the next chapter, you will learn about another important relationship between classes, called inheritance.

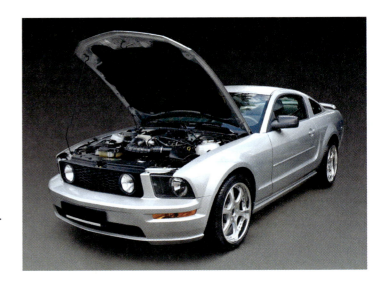

A car has a motor and tires. In object-oriented design, this "has-a" relationship is called aggregation.

SELF CHECK

26. What is the rule of thumb for finding classes?

27. Your job is to write a program that plays chess. Might ChessBoard be an appropriate class? How about MovePiece?

28. In an e-mail system, messages are stored in a mailbox. Draw a UML diagram that shows the appropriate aggregation relationship.

29. You are implementing a system to manage a library, keeping track of which books are checked out by whom. Should the Book class aggregate Patron or the other way around?

30. In a library management system, what would be the relationship between classes Patron and Author?

QUALITY TIP 9.3

Make Parallel Vectors into Vectors of Objects

Sometimes, you find yourself using vectors of the same length, each of which stores a part of what conceptually should be an object. In that situation, it is a good idea to reorganize your program and use a single vector whose elements are objects.

For example, suppose an invoice contains a series of item descriptions and prices. One solution is to keep two vectors:

```
vector<string> descriptions;
vector<double> prices;
```

Each of the vectors will have the same length, and the ith *slice*, consisting of descriptions[i] and prices[i], contains data that needs to be processed together. These vectors are called *parallel vectors* (see Figure 9).

Parallel vectors become a headache in larger programs. The programmer must ensure that the vectors always have the same length and that each slice is filled with values that actually belong together. Moreover, any function that operates on a slice must get all vectors as parameters, which is tedious to program.

descriptions =   prices =

                    [i]   [i]   A slice

Figure 9   Parallel Vectors

The remedy is simple. Look at the slice and find the *concept* that it represents. Then make the concept into a class. In this example, each slice contains the description and price of an *item;* turn this into a class.

```
class Item
{
public:
    ...
private:
    string description;
    double price;
};
```

> Avoid parallel vectors by changing them into vectors of objects.

You can now eliminate the parallel vectors and replace them with a single vector:

```
vector<Item> items;
```

Each slot in the resulting vector corresponds to a slice in the set of parallel vectors (see Figure 10).

Parallel vectors

A vector of objects

Figure 10 Eliminating Parallel Vectors

9.7 Separate Compilation

> The code of complex programs is distributed over multiple files.

When you write and compile small programs, you can place all your code into a single source file. When your programs get larger or you work in a team, that situation changes. You will want to split your code into separate source files. There are two reasons why this split becomes necessary. First, it takes time to compile a file, and it seems silly to wait for the compiler to keep translating code that doesn't change. If your code is distributed over several source files, then only those files that you changed need to be recompiled. The second reason becomes apparent when you work with other programmers in a team. It would be very difficult for multiple programmers to edit a single source file simultaneously. Therefore, the program code is broken up so that each programmer is solely responsible for a separate set of files.

If your program is composed of multiple files, some of these files will define data types or functions that are needed in other files. There must be a path of communication between the files. In C++, that communication happens through the inclusion of header files.

A header file contains

> Header files contain the definitions of classes and declarations of nonmember functions.

- Definitions of classes.
- Definitions of constants.
- Declarations of nonmember functions.

The source file contains

> Source files contain function implementations.

- Definitions of member functions.
- Definitions of nonmember functions.

For the `CashRegister` class, you create a pair of files, `cashregister.h` and `cashregister.cpp`, that contain the interface and the implementation, respectively.

The header file contains the class definition.

ch09/cashregister.h

```
 1  #ifndef CASHREGISTER_H
 2  #define CASHREGISTER_H
 3
 4  /**
 5      A simulated cash register that tracks the item count and
 6      the total amount due.
 7  */
 8  class CashRegister
 9  {
10  public:
11     /**
12         Constructs a cash register with cleared item count and total.
13     */
14     CashRegister();
15
16     /**
17         Clears the item count and the total.
18     */
19     void clear();
20
21     /**
22         Adds an item to this cash register.
23         @param price the price of this item
24     */
25     void add_item(double price);
```

```
26
27    /**
28       @return the total amount of the current sale
29    */
30    double get_total() const;
31
32    /**
33       @return the item count of the current sale
34    */
35    int get_count() const;
36
37 private:
38    int item_count;
39    double total_price;
40 };
41
42 #endif
```

You include this header file whenever the definition of the CashRegister class is required. Since this file is not a standard header file, you must enclose its name in quotes, not <...>, when you include it, like this:

```
#include "cashregister.h"
```

Note the set of directives that bracket the header file.

```
#ifndef CASHREGISTER_H
#define CASHREGISTER_H
...
#endif
```

Suppose a file includes two header files: cashregister.h, and another header file that itself includes cashregister.h. The effect of the directives is to skip the file when it is encountered the second time. If we did not have that check, the compiler would complain when it saw the definition for the CashRegister class twice. (Sadly, it doesn't check whether the definitions are identical.)

The source file simply contains the definitions of the member functions (including constructors).

Note that the source file cashregister.cpp includes its own header file cashregister.h. The compiler needs to know how the CashRegister class is defined in order to compile the member functions.

ch09/cashregister.cpp

```
1  #include "cashregister.h"
2
3  CashRegister::CashRegister()
4  {
5     clear();
6  }
7
8  void CashRegister::clear()
9  {
10    item_count = 0;
```

```
11      total_price = 0;
12   }
13
14   void CashRegister::add_item(double price)
15   {
16      item_count++;
17      total_price = total_price + price;
18   }
19
20   double CashRegister::get_total() const
21   {
22      return total_price;
23   }
24
25   int CashRegister::get_count() const
26   {
27      return item_count;
28   }
```

Note that the function comments are in the header file, since they are a part of the interface, not the implementation.

The `cashregister.cpp` file does *not* contain a main function. There are many potential programs that might make use of the `CashRegister` class. Each of these programs will need to supply its own main function, as well as other functions and classes.

Here is a simple test program that puts the `CashRegister` class to use. Its source file includes the `cashregister.h` header file.

ch09/registertest2.cpp

```
1   #include <iostream>
2   #include <iomanip>
3   #include "cashregister.h"
4
5   using namespace std;
6
7   /**
8      Displays the item count and total price of a cash register.
9      @param reg the cash register to display
10  */
11  void display(CashRegister reg)
12  {
13     cout << reg.get_count() << " $" << fixed << setprecision(2)
14        << reg.get_total() << endl;
15  }
16
17  int main()
18  {
19     CashRegister register1;
20     register1.clear();
21     register1.add_item(1.95);
22     display(register1);
23     register1.add_item(0.95);
```

```
24    display(register1);
25    register1.add_item(2.50);
26    display(register1);
27    return 0;
28 }
```

To build the complete program, you need to compile both the `registertest2.cpp` and `cashregister.cpp` source files (see Figure 11). The details depend on your compiler. For example, with the Gnu compiler, you issue the command

```
g++ -o registertest registertest2.cpp cashregister.cpp
```

You have just seen the simplest and most common case for designing header and source files. There are a few additional technical details that you should know.

- A header file should include all headers that are necessary for defining the class. For example, if a class uses the `string` class, include the `<string>` header as well. Anytime you include a header from the standard library, also include the directive

  ```
  using namespace std;
  ```

  item.h

  ```
  1  #include <string>
  2  using namespace std;
  3
  4  class Item
  5  {
  6     ...
  7  private:
  8     string description
  9  };
  ```

- Place shared constants into a header file. For example,

  volume.h

  ```
  11  const double CAN_VOLUME = 0.355;
  ```

- To share a nonmember function, place the function declaration into a header file and the definition of the function into the corresponding source file.

  cube.h

  ```
  15  double cube_volume(double side_length);
  ```

  cube.cpp

  ```
  1  #include "cube.h"
  2
  3  double cube_volume(double side_length)
  4  {
  5     double volume = side_length * side_length * side_length;
  6     return volume;
  7  }
  ```

Figure 11   Compiling a Program from Multiple Source Files

SELF CHECK

31. Suppose the cash register is enhanced to carry out direct debits from bank accounts, and a member function debit(BankAccount&) is added to the Cash-Register class. Which header file do you need to include in cashregister.h?

32. In the enhancement described in Self Check 31, what additional file do you need to include in cashregister.cpp?

33. In the enhancement described in Self Check 31, what additional file do you need to include in the bankaccount.h file?

34. Suppose we want to move the display function from registertest2.cpp to the cashregister.h and cashregister.cpp files. Explain how those files need to change.

35. Where is the header file located that you include with the #include <iostream> directive?

9.8 Pointers to Objects

The following sections discuss how to work with pointers to objects. As you will see in the next chapter, pointers to objects are important when you work with multiple objects from related classes.

9.8.1 Dynamically Allocating Objects

It is common to allocate objects on the heap. As discussed in Section 7.4, you use the new operator to obtain memory from the heap. For example, the call

```
new CashRegister
```

returns a pointer to a CashRegister object. You can also supply construction parameters:

```
new BankAccount(1000)
```

You usually want to store the pointer that the new operator returns:

```
CashRegister* register_pointer = new CashRegister;
BankAccount* account_pointer = new BankAccount(1000);
```

Note that each of these definitions allocates two entities: a pointer variable and an object on the heap—see Figure 12.

When you no longer need a heap object, be sure to delete it:

```
delete account_pointer;
```

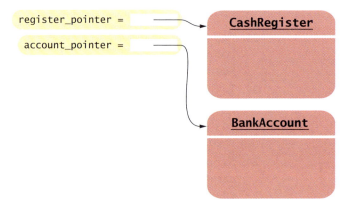

Figure 12
Pointers and the Objects
to Which They Point

9.8.2 The -> Operator

Because register_pointer is a pointer to a CashRegister object, the value *register_pointer denotes the CashRegister object itself. To invoke a member function on that object, you might call

```
(*register_pointer).add_item(1.95);
```

The parentheses are necessary because in C++ the dot operator takes precedence over the * operator. The expression without the parentheses would be a syntax error:

```
*register_pointer.add_item(1.95); // Error—you can't apply . to a pointer
```

Because the dot operator has higher precedence than *, the dot would be applied to a pointer, not an object.

Use the -> operator to invoke a member function through a pointer.

Because calling a member function through a pointer is very common, the designers of C++ supply an operator to abbreviate the "follow pointer and access member" operation. That operator is written -> and usually pronounced as "arrow". Here is how you use the "arrow" operator:

```
register_pointer->add_item(1.95);
```

This call means: Invoke the `add_item` member function with implicit parameter `*register_pointer` and explicit parameter 1.95.

9.8.3 The this Pointer

Each member function has a special parameter variable, called `this`, which is a pointer to the implicit parameter. For example, consider the `CashRegister::add_item` function. If you call

```
register1.add_item(1.95)
```

then the `this` pointer has type `CashRegister*` and points to the `register1` object.

You can use the `this` pointer inside the definition of a member function. For example, you can implement the `add_item` function as

```
void CashRegister::add_item(double price)
{
    this->item_count++;
    this->total_price = this->total_price + price;
}
```

In a member function, the this pointer points to the implicit parameter.

Here, the expression `this->item_count` refers to the `item_count` data member of the object to which `this` points, that is, the `item_count` member of the implicit parameter (which is `register1.item_count` in our example). The `this` pointer is not necessary, since by convention the expression `item_count` also refers to the field of the implicit parameter. Nevertheless, some programmers like to use the `this` pointer to make it clear that `item_count` is a data member and not a variable.

SELF CHECK

36. Write a statement that dynamically allocates a `string` object and saves the address in a pointer variable `str_pointer`.

37. Write a statement that deallocates the object that was allocated in Self Check 36.

38. Write a statement that dynamically allocates a `string` object with contents `"Hello"` and saves the address in a pointer variable `str_pointer`.

39. Write a statement that invokes the `length` member function on the object that was allocated in Self Check 38 and prints the result.

40. What is the type of `this` when the `string::length` member function is called?

ADVANCED TOPIC 9.3

Destructors and Resource Management

A destructor is a special member function that is automatically executed under two circumstances:

- At the end of the block in which an object variable is defined
- When a heap object is deleted

To understand the need for destructors, consider an implementation of a string class, similar to that of the C++ library. The characters of a string are stored on the heap, and each `String` object contains a pointer to the array holding its characters.

```cpp
class String
{
   ...
private:
   char* char_array;
}
```

The constructor allocates and initializes the character array.

```cpp
String::String(const char initial_chars[])
{
   char_array = new char[strlen(initial_chars) + 1];
   strcpy(char_array, initial_chars);
}
```

It is the job of the destructor to deallocate this memory. The name of the destructor is the ~ character followed by the class name, that is, ~String in our case. A class can have only one destructor, and it has no parameters.

```cpp
String::~String()
{
   delete[] char_array;
}
```

When a `String` object is no longer needed, the destructor is automatically invoked, and the memory for the characters is properly recycled (see Figure 13):

```cpp
void fun()
{
   String name("Harry"); // ① Heap memory is allocated by the constructor
   ...
} // ② The destructor is invoked on name, and its heap memory is deallocated
```

As a rule of thumb, if a constructor calls `new`, you should supply a destructor that calls `delete`.

Unfortunately, just supplying a destructor is not enough. Consider this scenario:

```cpp
String name1("Harry");
String name2("Sally");
name1 = name2;
```

The assignment has a very unfortunate effect: The memory for the first `String` has not been deallocated. (The destructor is only called at the end of the block in which name1 is defined.)

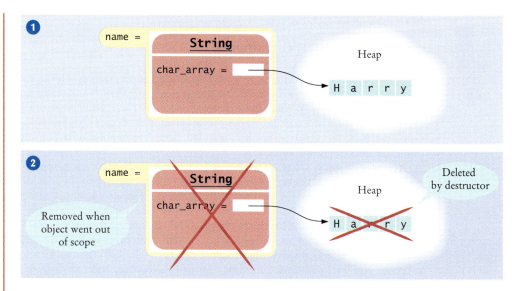

Figure 13 The Destructor Deallocates Heap Memory

And the two String objects now share a pointer to the same area of heap memory. Eventually, that memory location will be deleted twice (see Figure 14).

To overcome this problem, you must define an operator= function so that the assignment of one string to another manages heap memory correctly. However, doing so is beyond the scope of this book. (See Horstmann & Budd, *Big C++, 2nd Edition*, Ch. 15, for details.)

Figure 14 A Bad Assignment

RANDOM FACT 9.2

Open Source and Free Software

Most companies that produce software regard the source code as a trade secret. After all, if customers or competitors had access to the source code, they could study it and create similar programs without paying the original vendor. For the same reason, customers dislike secret source code. If a company goes out of business or decides to discontinue support for a computer program, its users are left stranded. They are unable to fix bugs or adapt the program to a new operating system.

Nowadays, some software packages are distributed with "open source" or "free software" licenses. Here, the term "free" doesn't refer to price, but to the freedom to inspect and modify the source code. Richard Stallman, a famous computer scientist and winner of a MacArthur "genius" grant, pioneered the concept of free software. He is the inventor of the Emacs text editor and the originator of the GNU project that aims to create an entirely free version of a Unix compatible operating system. All programs of the GNU project are licensed under the General Public License or GPL. The GPL allows you to make as many copies as you wish, make any modifications to the source, and redistribute the original and modified programs, charging nothing at all or whatever the market will bear. In return, you must agree that your modifications also fall under the GPL. You must give out the source code to any changes that you distribute, and anyone else can distribute them under the same conditions. The GPL, and similar open source licenses, form a social contract. Users of the software enjoy the freedom to use and modify the software, and in return they are obligated to share any improvements that they make. Many programs, such as the Linux operating system and the GNU C++ compiler, are distributed under the GPL.

Some commercial software vendors have attacked the GPL as "viral" and "undermining the commercial software sector". Other companies have a more nuanced strategy, producing proprietary software while also contributing to open source projects.

Frankly, open source is not a panacea and there is plenty of room for the commercial software sector. Open source software often lacks the polish of commercial software because many of the programmers are volunteers who are interested in solving their own problems, not in making a product that is easy to use by others. Some product categories are not available at all as open source software because the development work is unattractive when there is little promise of commercial gain. Open source software has been most successful in areas that are of interest to programmers, such as the Linux operating system, Web servers, and programming tools.

On the positive side, the open software community can be very competitive and creative. It is quite common to see several competing projects that take ideas from each other, all rapidly becoming more capable. Having many programmers involved, all reading the source code, often means that bugs tend to get squashed quickly. Eric Raymond describes open source development in his famous article "The Cathedral and the Bazaar" (`http://catb.org/~esr/writings/cathedral-bazaar/cathedral-bazaar/index.html`). He writes "Given enough eyeballs, all bugs are shallow".

CHAPTER SUMMARY

1. An object holds data members that are accessed by member functions.

2. Encapsulation is the act of hiding implementation details.

3. A class describes a set of objects with the same behavior.

4. Every class has a public interface: a collection of member functions through which the objects of the class can be manipulated.

5. A mutator member function changes the object on which it operates.

6. An accessor member function does not change the object on which it operates. Use const with accessors.

7. Every object has its own set of data members.

8. Private data members can only be accessed by member functions of the same class.

9. By keeping the implementation private, we protect it from being accidentally corrupted.

10. Encapsulation enables changes in the implementation without affecting users of a class.

11. Use the *ClassName*:: prefix when defining member functions.

12. The object on which a member function is applied is the implicit parameter.

13. Explicit parameters of a member function are listed in the function definition.

14. When calling another member function on the same object, do not use the dot notation.

15. A constructor is called automatically whenever an object is created.

16. The name of a constructor is the same as the class name.

17. A default constructor has no parameters.

18. A class can have multiple constructors.

19. The compiler picks the constructor that matches the construction parameters.

20. Be sure to initialize all number and pointer data members in a constructor.

21. To discover classes, look for nouns in the problem description.

22. Concepts from the problem domain are good candidates for classes.

23. A class aggregates another if its objects contain objects of the other class.

24. Avoid parallel vectors by changing them into vectors of objects.

25. The code of complex programs is distributed over multiple files.

26. Header files contain the definitions of classes and declarations of nonmember functions.

27. Source files contain function implementations.

28. Use the -> operator to invoke a member function through a pointer.

29. In a member function, the this pointer points to the implicit parameter.

REVIEW EXERCISES

Exercise R9.1. What value is returned by the calls reg1.get_count(), reg1.get_total(), reg2.get_count(), and reg2.get_total() after these statements?

```
CashRegister reg1;
reg1.clear();
reg1.add_item(0.90);
reg1.add_item(1.95);
CashRegister reg2;
reg2.clear();
reg2.add_item(1.90);
```

Exercise R9.2. Consider the Menu class in How To 9.1 on page 387. What is displayed when the following calls are executed?

```
Menu simple_menu;
simple_menu.add_option("Ok");
simple_menu.add_option("Cancel");
int response = simple_menu.get_input();
```

Exercise R9.3. What is the *interface* of a class? How does it differ from the *implementation* of a class?

Exercise R9.4. What is a member function, and how does it differ from a nonmember function?

Exercise R9.5. What is a mutator function? What is an accessor function?

Exercise R9.6. What happens if you forget the const in an accessor function? What happens if you accidentally supply a const in a mutator function?

Exercise R9.7. What is an implicit parameter? How does it differ from an explicit parameter?

Exercise R9.8. How many implicit parameters can a member function have? How many implicit parameters can a nonmember function have? How many explicit parameters can a function have?

Exercise R9.9. What is a constructor?

Exercise R9.10. What is a default constructor? What is the consequence if a class does not have a default constructor?

Exercise R9.11. How many constructors can a class have? Can you have a class with no constructors? If a class has more than one constructor, which of them gets called?

Exercise R9.12. What is encapsulation? Why is it useful?

Exercise R9.13. Data members are hidden in the private section of a class, but they aren't hidden very well at all. Anyone can read the private section. Explain to what extent the private reserved word hides the private members of a class.

Exercise R9.14. You can read the item_count data member of the CashRegister class with the get_count accessor function. Should there be a set_count mutator function to change it? Explain why or why not.

Exercise R9.15. In a nonmember function, it is easy to differentiate between calls to member functions and calls to nonmember functions. How do you tell them apart? Why is it not as easy for functions that are called from a member function?

Exercise R9.16. Consider the following problem description:

> Users place coins in a vending machine and select a product by pushing a button. If the inserted coins are sufficient to cover the purchase price of the product, the product is dispensed and change is given. Otherwise, the inserted coins are returned to the user.

What classes should you use to implement it?

Exercise R9.17. Consider the following problem description:

> Employees receive their biweekly paychecks. They are paid their hourly rates for each hour worked; however, if they worked more than 40 hours per week, they are paid overtime at 150 percent of their regular wage.

What classes should you use to implement it?

Exercise R9.18. Consider the following problem description:

> Customers order products from a store. Invoices are generated to list the items and quantities ordered, payments received, and amounts still due. Products are shipped to the shipping address of the customer, and invoices are sent to the billing address.

What classes should you use to implement it?

Exercise R9.19. Suppose a vending machine contains products, and users insert coins into the vending machine to purchase products. Draw a UML diagram showing the aggregation relationships between the classes VendingMachine, Coin, and Product.

Exercise R9.20. Suppose an Invoice object contains descriptions of the products ordered, and the billing and shipping address of the customer. Draw a UML diagram showing the aggregation relationships between the classes Invoice, Address, Customer, and Product.

PROGRAMMING EXERCISES

Exercise P9.1. Reimplement the CashRegister class so that it keeps track of the price of each added item in a vector<double>. Remove the item_count and total_price data members. Reimplement the clear, add_item, get_total, and get_count member functions. Add a member function display_all that displays the prices of all items in the current sale.

Exercise P9.2. Reimplement the CashRegister class so that it keeps track of the total price as an integer: the total cents of the price. For example, instead of storing 17.29, store the integer 1729. Such an implementation is commonly used because it avoids the accumulation of roundoff errors. Do not change the public interface of the class.

Exercise P9.3. Add a feature to the CashRegister class for computing sales tax. The tax rate should be supplied when constructing a CashRegister object. Add add_taxable_item and get_total_tax member functions. (Items added with add_item are not taxable.)

Exercise P9.4. After closing time, the store manager would like to know how much business was transacted during the day. Modify the CashRegister class to enable this functionality. Supply member functions get_sales_total and get_sales_count to get the total amount of all sales and the number of sales. Supply a member function reset_sales that resets any counters and totals so that the next day's sales start from zero.

Exercise P9.5. Reimplement the Menu class so that it stores all menu items in one long string. *Hint:* Keep a separate counter for the number of options. When a new option is added, append the option count, the option, and a newline character.

Exercise P9.6. Implement a class Address. An address has a house number, a street, an optional apartment number, a city, a state, and a postal code. Supply two constructors: one with an apartment number and one without. Supply a print member function that prints the address with the street on one line and the city, state, and postal code on the next line. Supply a member function comes_before that tests whether one address comes before another when the addresses are compared by postal code.

Exercise P9.7. Implement a class Portfolio. This class has two objects, checking and savings, of the type BankAccount that was developed in Worked Example 9.1 (ch09/account.cpp in your code files). Implement four member functions:

```
deposit(double amount, string account)
withdraw(double amount, string account)
```

```
transfer(double amount, string account)
print_balances()
```

Here the account string is "S" or "C". For the deposit or withdrawal, it indicates which account is affected. For a transfer, it indicates the account from which the money is taken; the money is automatically transferred to the other account.

Exercise P9.8. Implement a class SodaCan with member functions get_surface_area() and get_volume(). In the constructor, supply the height and radius of the can.

Exercise P9.9. Implement a class Car with the following properties. A car has a certain fuel efficiency (measured in miles/gallon) and a certain amount of fuel in the gas tank. The efficiency is specified in the constructor, and the initial fuel level is 0. Supply a member function drive that simulates driving the car for a certain distance, reducing the fuel level in the gas tank, and member functions get_gas_level, to return the current fuel level, and add_gas, to tank up. Sample usage:

```
Car my_hybrid(50); // 50 miles per gallon
my_hybrid.add_gas(20); // Tank 20 gallons
my_hybrid.drive(100); // Drive 100 miles
cout << my_hybrid.get_gas_level() << endl; // Print fuel remaining
```

Exercise P9.10. Implement a class Student. For the purpose of this exercise, a student has a name and a total quiz score. Supply an appropriate constructor and functions get_name(), add_quiz(int score), get_total_score(), and get_average_score(). To compute the latter, you also need to store the *number of quizzes* that the student took.

Exercise P9.11. Modify the Student class of Exercise P9.10 to compute grade point averages. Member functions are needed to add a grade, and get the current GPA. Specify grades as elements of a class Grade. Supply a constructor that constructs a grade from a string, such as "B+". You will also need a function that translates grades into their numeric values (for example, "B+" becomes 3.3).

Exercise P9.12. Define a class ComboLock that works like the combination lock in a gym locker, as shown here. The lock is constructed with a combination—three numbers between 0 and 39. The reset function resets the dial so that it points to 0. The turn_left and turn_right functions turn the dial by a given number of ticks to the left or right. The open function attempts to open the lock. The lock opens if the user first turned it right to the first number in the combination, then left to the second, and then right to the third.

```
class ComboLock
{
public:
    ComboLock(int secret1, int secret2, int secret3);
    void reset();
    void turn_left(int ticks);
    void turn_right(int ticks);
    bool open() const;
private:
    ...
}
```

Exercise P9.13. Define a class `Country` that stores the name of the country, its population, and its area. Using that class, write a program that reads in a set of countries and prints

- The country with the largest area.
- The country with the largest population.
- The country with the largest population density (people per square kilometer).

Exercise P9.14. Design a class `Message` that models an e-mail message. A message has a recipient, a sender, and a message text. Support the following member functions:

- A constructor that takes the sender and recipient and sets the time stamp to the current time
- A member function `append` that appends a line of text to the message body
- A member function `to_string` that makes the message into one long string like this: `"From: Harry Hacker\nTo: Rudolf Reindeer\n ..."`
- A member function `print` that prints the message text. *Hint:* Use `to_string`.

Write a program that uses this class to make a message and print it.

Exercise P9.15. Design a class `Mailbox` that stores e-mail messages, using the `Message` class of Exercise P9.14.

Implement the following member functions:

```
void Mailbox::add_message(Message m);
Message Mailbox::get_message(int i) const;
void remove_message(int i);
```

Exercise P9.16. Implement a `VotingMachine` class that can be used for a simple election. Have member functions to clear the machine state, to vote for a Democrat, to vote for a Republican, and to get the tallies for both parties. Extra credit if your program gives the nod to your favored party if the votes are tallied after 8 P.M. on the first Tuesday in November, but acts normally on all other dates. (*Hint:* Use a function in the `<cctime>` header to get the current date.)

Exercise P9.17. Provide a class for authoring a simple letter. In the constructor, supply the names of the sender and the recipient:

```
Letter(string from, string to)
```

Supply a member function

```
void add_line(string line)
```

to add a line of text to the body of the letter. Supply a member function

```
string get_text()
```

that returns the entire text of the letter. The text has the form:

```
Dear recipient name:
blank line
first line of the body
```

second line of the body
. . .
last line of the body
blank line
Sincerely,
blank line
sender name

Also supply a `main` function that prints this letter.

```
Dear John:

I am sorry we must part.
I wish you all the best.

Sincerely,

Mary
```

Construct an object of the `Letter` class and call `add_line` twice.

Exercise P9.18. Write a class `Bug` that models a bug moving along a horizontal line. The bug moves either to the right or left. Initially, the bug moves to the right, but it can turn to change its direction. In each move, its position changes by one unit in the current direction. Provide a constructor

```
Bug(int initial_position)
```

and member functions

```
void turn()
void move()
int get_position()
```

Sample usage:

```
Bug bugsy(10);
bugsy.move(); // Now the position is 11
bugsy.turn();
bugsy.move(); // Now the position is 10
```

Your `main` function should construct a bug, make it move and turn a few times, and print the actual and expected positions.

Exercise P9.19. Implement a class `Moth` that models a moth flying in a straight line. The moth has a position, the distance from a fixed origin. When the moth moves toward a point of light, its new position is halfway between its old position and the position of the light source. Supply a constructor

```
Moth(double initial_position)
```

and member functions

```
void move_to_light(double light_position)
void get_position()
```

Your `main` function should construct a moth, move it toward a couple of light sources, and check that the moth's position is as expected.

Exercise P9.20. Design a class `Cannonball` to model a cannonball that is fired into the air. A ball has

- An *x*- and a *y*-position.
- An *x*- and a *y*-velocity.

Supply the following member functions:

- A constructor with a weight and an *x*-position (the *y*-position is initially 0)
- A member function `move(double sec)` that moves the ball to the next position (First compute the distance traveled in `sec` seconds, using the current velocities, then update the *x*- and *y*-positions; then update the *y*-velocity by taking into account the gravitational acceleration of -9.81 m/sec²; the *x*-velocity is unchanged.) (See Exercise P4.22 for additional details.)
- Member functions `get_x` and `get_y` that get the current location of the cannonball
- A member function `shoot` whose parameters are the angle α and initial velocity *v* (Compute the *x*-velocity as $v \cos \alpha$ and the *y*-velocity as $v \sin \alpha$; then keep calling `move` with a time interval of 0.1 seconds until the *x*-position is 0; call `get_x` and `get_y` after every move and display the position.)

Use this class in a program that prompts the user for the starting angle and the initial velocity. Then call `shoot`.

ANSWERS TO SELF-CHECK QUESTIONS

1. 1,000. 10.
2. `cin` is an object, `string` is a class.
3. Through the `substr` member function and the `[]` operator.
4. As a `vector<char>`. As a char array.
5. None. The member functions will have the same effect, and your code could not have manipulated `string` objects in any other way.
6. 2 1.90
7. There is no member function named `get_amount_due`.
8. `int get_dollars() const;`
9. `length`, `substr`
10. A mutator. Getting a character removes it from the stream, thereby modifying it. Not convinced? Consider what happens if you call the `get` function twice. You will usually get two different characters. But if you call an accessor twice on an object (without a mutation between the two calls), you are sure to get the same result.
11. 2 1.85 1 1.90
12. The code tries to access a private data member.

13. (1)

```
int hours; // Between 1 and 12
int minutes; // Between 0 and 59
bool pm; // True for P.M., false for A.M.
```

(2)

```
int hours; // Military time, between 0 and 23
int minutes; // Between 0 and 59
```

(3)

```
int total_minutes // Between 0 and 60 * 24 - 1
```

14. They need not change their programs at all since the public interface has not changed. They need to recompile with the new version of the Time class.

15. (1)

```
string letter_grade; // "A+", "B"
```

(2)

```
double number_grade; // 4.3, 3.0
```

16. (1) The CashRegister:: is missing. (2) The const is missing.

17.
```
void CashRegister::add_items(int quantity, double price)
{
    item_count = item_count + quantity;
    total_price = total_price + quantity * price;
}
```

18.
```
int CashRegister::get_dollars() const
{
    int dollars = total_price; // Truncates cents
    return dollars;
}
```

19. Three parameters: two explicit parameters of type int, and one implicit parameter of type string.

20. One parameter: the implicit parameter of type string. The function has no explicit parameters.

21. `BankAccount::BankAccount() { balance = 0; }`

22.
```
BankAccount::BankAccount(double initial_balance)
{
    balance = initial_balance;
}
```

23.
```
Item::Item()
{
    price = 0;
}
```

Note that the description data member need not be initialized.

24.
```
CashRegister::CashRegister()
{
    clear();
}
```

25. (a) Default constructor. (b) `Item(string)` or `Item(const char[])` (c) `Item(double)` (d) `Item(string, double)` (e) Does not define an object.

26. Look for nouns in the problem description.

27. Yes (`ChessBoard`) and no (`MovePiece`).

28.

29. Typically, a library system wants to track which books a patron has checked out, so it makes more sense to have `Patron` aggregate `Book`. However, there is not always one true answer in design. If you feel strongly that it is important to identify the patron who had checked out a particular book (perhaps to notify the patron to return it because it was requested by someone else), then you can argue that the aggregation should go the other way around.

30. There would be no relationship.

31. The header file that defines the `BankAccount` class, probably named `bankaccount.h`.

32. None. The `cashregister.cpp` file includes `cashregister.h`, which includes `bankaccount.h`.

33. None. The bank account need not know anything about cash registers.

34. Add the following line to `cashregister.h`:

```
void display(CashRegister reg);
```

Add the implementation of the `display` function to `cashregister.cpp`.

35. The answer depends on your system. On my system, the file is located at /usr/include/c++/4.2/iostream.

36. `string* str_pointer = new string;`

37. `delete str_pointer;`

38. `string* str_pointer = new string("Hello");`

or

```
string* str_pointer = new string;
*str_pointer = "Hello";
```

39. `cout << str_pointer->length();`

40. `string*`, or more accurately, `const string*` because `length` is an accessor function.

Inheritance

- To understand the concepts of inheritance and polymorphism
- To learn how to inherit and override member functions
- To be able to implement constructors for derived classes
- To be able to design and use virtual functions

In this chapter you will learn two of the most important concepts in object-oriented programming: inheritance and polymorphism. Through inheritance, you will be able to define new classes that are extensions of existing classes.

Polymorphism allows you to take advantage of the commonality between related classes, while still giving each class the flexibility to implement specific behavior. Using polymorphism, it is possible to build very flexible and extensible systems.

CHAPTER CONTENTS

10.1 Inheritance Hierarchies

A derived class inherits data and behavior from a base class.

In object-oriented design, *inheritance* is a relationship between a more general class (called the *base class*) and a more specialized class (called the *derived class*). The derived class inherits data and behavior from the base class. For example, consider the relationships between different kinds of vehicles depicted in Figure 1. Every car *is a* vehicle. Cars share the common traits of all vehicles, such as the ability to transport people from one place to another. We say that the class Car inherits from the class Vehicle. In this relationship, the Vehicle class is the base class and the Car class is the derived class.

You can always use a derived class object in place of a base class object.

Suppose we have an algorithm that manipulates a Vehicle object. Since a car is a special kind of vehicle, we can supply a Car object to such an algorithm, and it will work correctly. This is an example of the *substitution principle* that states that you can always use a derived-class object when a base-class object is expected.

The inheritance relationship can give rise to hierarchies where classes get ever more specialized, as shown in Figure 1. The C++ stream classes, shown in Figure 2, are another example of such a hierarchy. Figure 2 uses the UML notation for inheritance where the base and derived class are joined with an arrow that points to the base class.

As you can see, an ifstream (an input stream that reads from a file) is a special case of an istream (an input stream that reads data from any source). If you have an ifstream, you can pass it to a function that expects an istream.

```
void process_input(istream& in) // Can call with an ifstream object
```

Figure 1 An Inheritance Hierarchy of Vehicle Classes

Why provide a function that processes istream objects instead of ifstream objects? That function is more useful because it can handle *any* kind of input stream (such as an istringstream, which is convenient for unit testing). This again is the substitution principle at work.

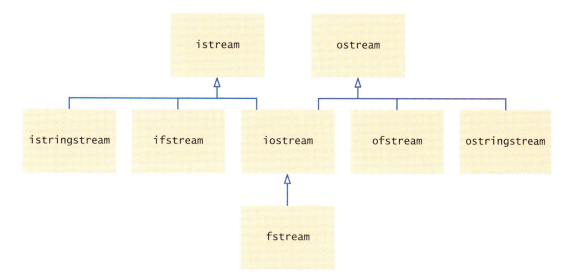

Figure 2 The Inheritance Hierarchy of Stream Classes

In this chapter, we will consider a simpler hierarchy of classes. Most likely, you have taken computer-graded quizzes. A quiz consists of questions, and there are different kinds of questions:

- Fill-in-the-blank
- Choice (single or multiple)
- Numeric (where an approximate answer is ok; e.g., 1.33 when the actual answer is 4/3)
- Free response

We will develop a simple but flexible quiz-taking program to illustrate inheritance.

Figure 3 shows an inheritance hierarchy for these question types.

At the root of this hierarchy is the Question type. A question can display its text, and it can check whether a given response is a correct answer:

```cpp
class Question
{
public:
   Question();
   void set_text(string question_text);
   void set_answer(string correct_response);
   bool check_answer(string response) const;
   void display() const;
private:
   string text;
   string answer;
};
```

How the text is displayed depends on the question type. Later in this chapter, you will see some variations, but the base class simply sends the question text to cout.

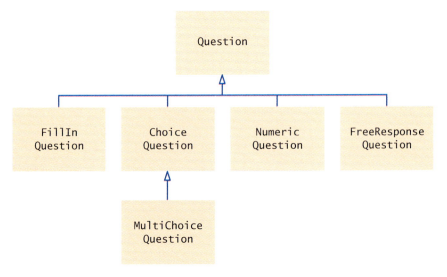

Figure 3 Inheritance Hierarchy of Question Types

How the response is checked also depends on the question type. As already mentioned, a numeric question might accept approximate answers (see Exercise P10.1). In Exercise P10.3, you will see another way of checking the response. But in the base class, we will simply require that the response match the correct answer exactly.

In the following sections, you will see how to form derived classes that inherit the member functions and data members of this base class.

Here is the implementation of the Question class and a simple test program. Note the the Question class constructor needs to do no work because the text and answer fields are automatically set to the empty string. The boolalpha stream manipulator in the main function causes Boolean values to be displayed as true and false instead of the default 1 and 0.

ch10/quiz1/test.cpp

```cpp
1  #include <iostream>
2  #include <sstream>
3  #include <string>
4
5  using namespace std;
6
7  class Question
8  {
9  public:
10     /**
11        Constructs a question with empty text and answer.
12     */
13     Question();
14
15     /**
16        @param question_text the text of this question
17     */
18     void set_text(string question_text);
19
20     /**
21        @param correct_response the answer for this question
22     */
23     void set_answer(string correct_response);
24
25     /**
26        @param response the response to check
27        @return true if the response was correct, false otherwise
28     */
29     bool check_answer(string response) const;
30
31     /**
32        Displays this question.
33     */
34     void display() const;
35
36  private:
37     string text;
38     string answer;
39  };
```

```
40
41  Question::Question()
42  {
43  }
44
45  void Question::set_text(string question_text)
46  {
47     text = question_text;
48  }
49
50  void Question::set_answer(string correct_response)
51  {
52     answer = correct_response;
53  }
54
55  bool Question::check_answer(string response) const
56  {
57     return response == answer;
58  }
59
60  void Question::display() const
61  {
62     cout << text << endl;
63  }
64
65  int main()
66  {
67     string response;
68     cout << boolalpha; // Show Boolean values as true, false
69
70     Question q1;
71     q1.set_text("Who was the inventor of C++?");
72     q1.set_answer("Bjarne Stroustrup");
73
74     q1.display();
75     cout << "Your answer: ";
76     getline(cin, response);
77     cout << q1.check_answer(response) << endl;
78
79     return 0;
80  }
```

Program Run

```
Who was the inventor of C++?
Your answer: Bjarne Stroustrup
true
```

SELF CHECK

1. Consider classes `Manager` and `Employee`. Which should be the base class and which should be the derived class?

2. What are the inheritance relationships between classes `BankAccount`, `CheckingAccount`, and `SavingsAccount`?

3. Consider the function do_something(istream& stream). List all stream classes from Figure 2 whose objects can be passed to this function.

4. Consider the function do_something(Car& c). List all vehicle classes from Figure 1 whose objects *cannot* be passed to this function.

5. Should a class Quiz inherit from the class Question? Why or why not?

QUALITY TIP 10.1

Use a Single Class for Variation in Values, Inheritance for Variation in Behavior

The purpose of inheritance is to model objects with different *behavior*. When students first learn about inheritance, they have a tendency to overuse it, by creating multiple classes even though the variation could be expressed with a simple data member.

Consider a program that tracks the fuel efficiency of a fleet of cars by logging the distance traveled and the refueling amounts. Some cars in the fleet are hybrids. Should you create a derived class HybridCar? Not in this application. Hybrids don't behave any differently than other cars when it comes to driving and refueling. They just have a better fuel efficiency. A single Car class with a data member

```
double miles_per_gallon;
```

is entirely sufficient.

However, if you write a program that shows how to repair different kinds of vehicles, then it makes sense to have a separate class HybridCar. When it comes to repairs, hybrid cars behave differently from other cars.

10.2 Implementing Derived Classes

In C++, you form a derived class from a base class by specifying what makes the derived class different. You define the member functions that are new to the derived class. The derived class inherits all member functions from the base class, but you can change the implementation if the inherited behavior is not appropriate.

The derived class automatically inherits all data members from the base class. You only define the added data members.

Here is the syntax for the definition of a derived class:

```
class ChoiceQuestion : public Question
{
public:
    New and changed member functions
private:
    Additional data members
};
```

The : symbol denotes inheritance. The reserved word public is required for a technical reason (see Common Error 10.1 on page 426).

Like the manufacturer of a stretch limo, who starts with a regular car and modifies it, a programmer makes a derived class by modifying another class.

A ChoiceQuestion object differs from a Question object in three ways:

- Its objects store the various choices for the answer.
- There is a member function for adding another choice.
- The display function of the ChoiceQuestion class shows these choices so that the respondent can choose one of them.

When the ChoiceQuestion class inherits from the Question class, it needs only to spell out these three differences:

```
class ChoiceQuestion : public Question
{
public:
   ChoiceQuestion();
   void add_choice(string choice, bool correct);
   void display() const;
private:
   vector<string> choices;
};
```

Figure 4 shows the layout of a ChoiceQuestion object. It inherits the text and answer data members from the Question base object, and it adds an additional data member: the choices vector.

> A derived class can override a base class function by providing a new implementation.

The add_choice function is specific to the ChoiceQuestion class. You can only apply it to ChoiceQuestion objects, not general Question objects. However, the display function is a redefinition of a function that exists in the base class, to take into account the special needs of the derived class. We say that the derived class *overrides* this function.

> The derived class inherits all data members and all functions that it does not override.

In the ChoiceQuestion class definition you specify only new member functions and data members. All other member functions and data members of the Question class are automatically inherited by the Question class. For example, each ChoiceQuestion object still has text and answer data members, and set_text, set_answer, and check_answer member functions.

Figure 4
Data Layout of Derived Object

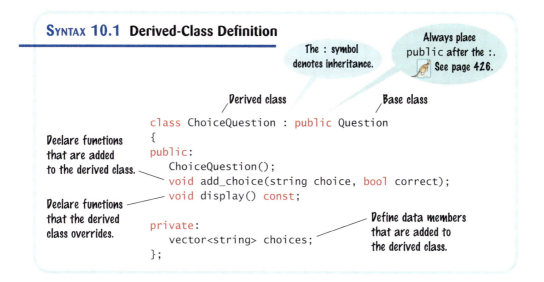

SYNTAX 10.1 Derived-Class Definition

The : symbol denotes inheritance.

Always place public after the :. See page 426.

Derived class

Base class

Declare functions that are added to the derived class.

Declare functions that the derived class overrides.

Define data members that are added to the derived class.

```
class ChoiceQuestion : public Question
{
public:
    ChoiceQuestion();
    void add_choice(string choice, bool correct);
    void display() const;

private:
    vector<string> choices;
};
```

You can call the inherited member functions on a derived-class object:

```
choice_question.set_answer("2");
```

However, the inherited data members are inaccessible. Since these members are private data of the base class, only the base class has access to them. The derived class has no more access rights than any other class.

In particular, the `ChoiceQuestion` member functions cannot directly access the `answer` member. These member functions must use the public interface of the `Question` class to access its private data, just like every other function.

To illustrate this point, let us implement the `add_choice` member function. The function has two parameters: the choice to be added (which is appended to the vector of choices), and a Boolean value to indicate whether this choice is correct. If it is true, set the answer to the current choice number. (We use an `ostringstream` to convert the number to a string—see Section 8.4 for details.)

```
void ChoiceQuestion::add_choice(string choice, bool correct)
{
    choices.push_back(choice);
    if (correct)
    {
        // Convert choices.size() to string
        ostringstream stream;
        stream << choices.size();
        string num_str = stream.str();
        // Set num_str as the answer
        ...
    }
}
```

You can't just access the `answer` member in the base class. Fortunately, the `Question` class has a `set_answer` member function. You can call that member function. On which object? The question that you are currently modifying—that is, the implicit parameter of the `ChoiceQuestion::add_choice` function. As you saw in Chapter 9, if you invoke a member function on the implicit parameter, you don't specify the parameter but just write the member function name:

```
set_answer(num_str);
```

The compiler interprets this call as

implicit parameter`.set_answer(num_str);`

SELF CHECK

6. Suppose q is an object of the class `Question` and cq an object of the class `Choice-Question`. Which of the following calls are legal?

   a. `q.set_answer(response)`

   b. `cq.set_answer(response)`

   c. `q.add_option(option, true)`

   d. `cq.add_option(option, true)`

7. Define a class `Manager` that inherits from the class `Employee` and adds a data member bonus for storing a salary bonus. Omit the constructor declaration.

8. Suppose the class `Employee` is defined as follows:

```
class Employee
{
public:
   Employee();
   void set_name(string new_name);
   void set_base_salary(double new_salary);
   string get_name();
   double get_salary() const;
private:
   string name;
   double base_salary;
}
```

   Which data members does the `Manager` class from Self Check 7 have?

9. Define a class `Manager` that inherits from the class `Employee` and overrides the `get_salary` function.

10. Which member functions does the `Manager` class from Self Check 9 inherit?

COMMON ERROR 10.1

Private Inheritance

It is a common error to forget the reserved word `public` that must follow the colon after the derived-class name.

```
class ChoiceQuestion : Question // Error
{
   ...
};
```

The class definition will compile. The ChoiceQuestion still inherits from Question, but it inherits *privately*. That is, only the member functions of ChoiceQuestion get to call member functions of Question. Whenever another function invokes a Question member function on a ChoiceQuestion object, the compiler will flag this as an error:

```
int main()
{
   ChoiceQuestion q;
   ...
   cout << q.check_answer(response); // Error
}
```

This private inheritance is rarely useful. In fact, it violates the spirit of using inheritance in the first place—namely, to create objects that are usable just like the base-class objects. You should always use public inheritance and remember to supply the public reserved word in the definition of the derived class.

ADVANCED TOPIC 10.1

Calling the Base-Class Constructor

> Unless specified otherwise, the base-class data members are initialized with the default constructor.

Consider the process of constructing a derived-class object. A derived-class constructor can only initialize the data members of the derived class. But the base-class data members also need to be initialized. Unless you specify otherwise, the base-class data members are initialized with the default constructor of the base class.

In order to specify another constructor, you use an initializer list, as described in Advanced Topic 9.1. Specify the name of the base class and the construction parameters in the initializer list. For example, suppose the Question base class had a constructor for setting the question text. Here is how a derived-class constructor could call that base-class constructor:

```
ChoiceQuestion::ChoiceQuestion(string question_text)
   : Question(question_text)
{
}
```

SYNTAX 10.2 Constructor with Base-Class Initializer

The base-class constructor is called first.

```
ChoiceQuestion::ChoiceQuestion(string question_text)
   : Question(question_text)
{

}
```

This block can contain additional statements.

If you omit the base-class constructor call, the default constructor is invoked.

> The constructor of a derived class can pass parameters to a base-class constructor.

The derived-class constructor calls the base-class constructor before executing the code inside the { }.

In our example program, we used the default constructor of the base class. However, if a base class has no default constructor, you must use the initializer list syntax.

COMMON ERROR 10.2

Replicating Base-Class Members

A derived class has no access to the data members of the base class.

```
ChoiceQuestion::ChoiceQuestion(string question_text)
{
    text = question_text; // Error—tries to access private base-class member
}
```

When faced with a compiler error, beginners commonly "solve" this issue by adding *another* data member with the same name to the derived class:

```
class ChoiceQuestion : public Question
{
    ...
private:
    vector<string> choices;
    string text; // Don't!
}
```

Sure, now the constructor compiles, but it doesn't set the correct text! Such a `ChoiceQuestion` object has two data members, both named `text`. The constructor sets one of them, and the `display` member function displays the other.

10.3 Overriding Member Functions

The derived class inherits the member functions from the base class. If you are not satisfied with the behavior of the inherited member function, you can *override* it by specifying a new implementation in the derived class.

Consider the `display` function of the `ChoiceQuestion` class. It needs to override the base-class `display` function in order to show the choices for the answer. Specifically, the derived-class function needs to

- **Display the question text.**
- **Display the answer choices.**

The second part is easy since the answer choices are a data member of the derived class.

```
int ChoiceQuestion::display() const
{
    // Display the question text
    ...
    // Display the answer choices
    for (int i = 0; i < choices.size(); i++)
    {
        cout << i + 1 << ": " << choices[i] << endl;
    }
}
```

But how do you get the question text? You can't access the `text` member of the base class directly since it is private.

Instead, you can call the `display` function of the base class.

```
int ChoiceQuestion::display() const
{
    // Display the question text
    display(); // Invokes implicit parameter.display()
    // Display the answer choices
    ...
}
```

However, this won't quite work. Because the implicit parameter of `ChoiceQuestion::display` is of type `ChoiceQuestion`, and there is a function named `display` in the `ChoiceQuestion` class, that function will be called—but that is just the function you are currently writing! The function would call itself over and over.

To display the question text, you must be more specific about which function named `display` you want to call. You want `Question::display`:

```
int ChoiceQuestion::display() const
{
    // Display the question text
    Question::display(); // OK
    // Display the answer choices
    ...
}
```

Use *BaseClass*::*function* notation to explicitly call a base-class function.

When you override a function, you usually want to *extend* the functionality of the base-class version. Therefore, you often need to invoke the base-class version before extending it. To invoke it, you need to use the *BaseClass*::*function* notation. However, you have no obligation to call the base-class function. Occasionally, a derived class overrides a base-class function and specifies an entirely different functionality.

Here is the complete program that displays a plain `Question` object and a `Choice-Question` object. (The definition of the `Question` class, which you have already seen, is placed into `question.h`, and the implementation is in `question.cpp`.) This example shows how you can use inheritance to form a more specialized class from a base class.

ch10/quiz2/test.cpp

```
1  #include <iostream>
2  #include <sstream>
3  #include <vector>
4  #include "question.h"
5
6  class ChoiceQuestion : public Question
7  {
8  public:
9     /**
10       Constructs a choice question with no choices.
11    */
12    ChoiceQuestion();
13
14    /**
15       Adds an answer choice to this question.
16       @param choice the choice to add
17       @param correct true if this is the correct choice, false otherwise
18    */
19    void add_choice(string choice, bool correct);
20
21    void display() const;
22  private:
23    vector<string> choices;
24  };
25
26  ChoiceQuestion::ChoiceQuestion()
27  {
28  }
29
30  void ChoiceQuestion::add_choice(string choice, bool correct)
31  {
32    choices.push_back(choice);
33    if (correct)
34    {
35       // Convert choices.size() to string
36       ostringstream stream;
37       stream << choices.size();
38       string num_str = stream.str();
39       set_answer(num_str);
40    }
41  }
42
43  void ChoiceQuestion::display() const
44  {
45    // Display the question text
46    Question::display();
```

```
47     // Display the answer choices
48     for (int i = 0; i < choices.size(); i++)
49     {
50         cout << i + 1 << ": " << choices[i] << endl;
51     }
52 }
53
54 int main()
55
56     string response;
57     cout << boolalpha;
58
59     // Ask a basic question
60
61     Question q1;
62     q1.set_text("Who was the inventor of C++?");
63     q1.set_answer("Bjarne Stroustrup");
64
65     q1.display();
66     cout << "Your answer: ";
67     getline(cin, response);
68     cout << q1.check_answer(response) << endl;
69
70     // Ask a choice question
71
72     ChoiceQuestion q2;
73     q2.set_text("In which country was the inventor of C++ born?");
74     q2.add_choice("Australia", false);
75     q2.add_choice("Denmark", true);
76     q2.add_choice("Korea", false);
77     q2.add_choice("United States", false);
78
79     q2.display();
80     cout << "Your answer: ";
81     getline(cin, response);
82     cout << q2.check_answer(response) << endl;
83
84     return 0;
85 }
```

Program Run

```
Who was the inventor of C++?
Your answer: Bjarne Stroustrup
true
In which country was the inventor of C++ born?
1: Australia
2: Denmark
3: Korea
4: United States
Your answer: 2
true
```

SELF CHECK

11. What is wrong with the following implementation of the `display` function?

```
void ChoiceQuestion::display() const
{
   cout << text << endl;
   for (int i = 0; i < choices.size(); i++)
   {
      cout << i + 1 << ": " << choices[i] << endl;
   }
}
```

12. What is wrong with the following implementation of the `display` function?

```
void ChoiceQuestion::display() const
{
   this->display();
   for (int i = 0; i < choices.size(); i++)
   {
      cout << i + 1 << ": " << choices[i] << endl;
   }
}
```

13. Look again at the implementation of the `add_choice` function that calls the `set_answer` function of the base class. Why don't you need to call `Question::set_answer`?

14. In the `Manager` class of Self Check 9, override the `get_name` function so that managers have a * before their name (such as *Lin, Sally).

15. In the `Manager` class of Self Check 7, override the `get_salary` function so that it returns the sum of the salary and the bonus.

COMMON ERROR 10.3

Forgetting the Base-Class Name

A common error in extending the functionality of a base-class function is to forget the base-class name. For example, to compute the salary of a manager, get the salary of the underlying `Employee` object and add a bonus:

```
double Manager::get_salary() const
{
   double base_salary = get_salary();
      // Error—should be Employee::get_salary()
   return base_salary + bonus;
}
```

Here `get_salary()` refers to the `get_salary` function applied to the implicit parameter of the member function. The implicit parameter is of type `Manager`, and there is a `Manager::get_salary` function, so that function is called. Of course, that is a recursive call to the function that we are writing. Instead, you must be precise which `get_salary` function you want to call. In this case, you need to call `Employee::get_salary` explicitly.

Whenever you call a base-class function from a derived-class function with the same name, be sure to give the full name of the function, including the base-class name.

10.4 Virtual Functions and Polymorphism

In the preceding sections you saw one important use of inheritance: to form a more specialized class from a base class. In the following sections you will see an even more powerful application of inheritance: to work with a collection of objects whose type can vary at run time and that carry out common tasks in different ways.

10.4.1 The Slicing Problem

In this section, we will discuss a problem that commonly arises when you work with a collection of objects that belong to different classes in a class hierarchy.

If you look into the main function of quiz2/test.cpp, you will find that there was some repetitive code to display each question and check the responses. It would be nicer if all questions were collected in a vector and one could use a loop to present them to the user:

```
vector<Question> quiz(2);
quiz[0].set_text("Who was the inventor of C++?");
quiz[0].set_answer("Bjarne Stroustrup");
ChoiceQuestion cq;
cq.set_text("In which country was the inventor of C++ born?");
cq.add_choice("Australia", false);
...
quiz[1] = cq;

for (int i = 0; i < quiz.size(); i++)
{
   quiz[i].display();
   cout << "Your answer: ";
   getline(cin, response);
   cout << quiz[i].check_answer(response) << endl;
}
```

The vector quiz holds objects of type Question. The compiler realizes that a Choice-Question is a special case of a Question. Thus it permits the assignment from a choice question to a question:

```
quiz[1] = cq;
```

However, a ChoiceQuestion object has three data members, whereas a Question object has just two. There is no room to store the derived-class data. That data simply gets *sliced away* when you assign a derived-class object to a base-class variable (see Figure 5).

Figure 5 Slicing Away Derived-Class Data

If you run the resulting program, the options are not displayed:

```
Who was the inventor of C++?
Your answer: Bjarne Stroustrup
true
In which country was the inventor of C++ born?
Your answer:
```

> When converting a derived class object to a base class, the derived class data is sliced away.

This problem is very typical of code that needs to manipulate objects from a mixture of classes in an inheritance hierarchy. Derived-class objects are usually bigger than base-class objects, and objects of different derived classes have different sizes. A vector of objects cannot deal with this variation in sizes.

Instead, you need to store the actual objects elsewhere and collect their locations in a vector by storing pointers. We will discuss the use of pointers in the next section.

10.4.2 Pointers to Base and Derived Classes

To access objects from different classes in a class hierarchy, use pointers. Pointers to the various objects all have the same size—namely, the size of a memory address—even though the objects themselves may have different sizes.

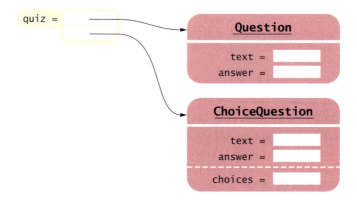

Figure 6 A Polymorphic Vector

Here is the code to set up the vector of pointers:

```
vector<Question*> quiz(2);
quiz[0] = new Question;
quiz[0]->set_text("Who was the inventor of C++?");
quiz[0]->set_answer("Bjarne Stroustrup");
ChoiceQuestion* cq_pointer = new ChoiceQuestion;
cq_pointer->set_text("In which country was the inventor of C++ born?");
cq_pointer->add_choice("Australia", false);
...
quiz[1] = cq_pointer;
```

As the highlighted code shows, you simply define the vector to hold pointers, allocate all objects by calling new, and use the -> operator instead of the dot operator.

> A derived-class pointer can be converted to a base-class pointer.

Note that the last assignment assigns a derived-class pointer of
type ChoiceQuestion* to a base-class pointer of type Question*. This
is perfectly legal. A pointer is the starting address of an object.
Because every ChoiceQuestion is a special case of a Question, the
starting address of a ChoiceQuestion object is, in particular, the starting
address of a Question object. The reverse assignment—from a base-class pointer to a
derived-class pointer—is an error.

The code to present all questions is

```
for (int i = 0; i < quiz.size(); i++)
{
   quiz[i]->display();
   cout << "Your answer: ";
   getline(cin, response);
   cout << quiz[i]->check_answer(response) << endl;
}
```

Again, note the use of the -> operators because quiz[i] is a pointer.

10.4.3 Virtual Functions

When you collect objects of different classes in a class hierarchy, and then invoke a
member function, you want the appropriate member function to be applied. For
example, when you call the display member function on a Question* pointer that
happens to point to a ChoiceQuestion, you want the choices to be displayed.

For reasons of efficiency, this is not the default in C++. By default, a call

```
quiz[i]->display();
```

always calls Question::display because the type of quiz[i] is Question*.

However, in this case you really want to determine the actual type of the object
to which quiz[i] points, which can be either a Question or a ChoiceQuestion object,
and then call the appropriate function. In C++, you must alert the compiler that the
function call needs to be preceded by the appropriate function selection, which can
be a different one for every iteration in the loop. You use the virtual reserved word
for this purpose:

```
class Question
{
```

```
public:
   Question();
   void set_text(string question_text);
   void set_answer(string correct_response);
   virtual bool check_answer(string response) const;
   virtual void display() const;
private:
   ...
};
```

The virtual reserved word must be used in the *base class*. All functions with the same name and parameter types in derived classes are then automatically virtual. However, it is considered good taste to supply the virtual reserved word for the derived-class functions as well.

```
class ChoiceQuestion : public Question
{
public:
   ChoiceQuestion();
   void add_choice(string choice, bool correct);
   virtual void display() const;
private:
   ...
};
```

You do not supply the reserved word virtual in the function definition:

```
void Question::display() const // No virtual reserved word
{
   cout << text << endl;
}
```

> When a virtual function is called, the version belonging to the actual type of the implicit parameter is invoked.

Whenever a virtual function is called, the compiler determines the type of the implicit parameter in the particular call at run time. The appropriate function for that object is then called. For example, when the display function is declared virtual, the call

```
quiz[i]->display();
```

always calls the function belonging to the actual type of the object to which display[i] points—either Question::display or ChoiceQuestion::display.

In the same way that vehicles can differ in their method of locomotion, polymorphic objects carry out tasks in different ways.

10.4.4 Polymorphism

Polymorphism (literally, "having multiple shapes") describes objects that share a set of tasks and execute them in different ways.

The quiz vector collects a mixture of both kinds of questions. Such a collection is called *polymorphic* (literally, "of multiple shapes"). Objects in a polymorphic collection have some commonality but are not necessarily of the same type. Inheritance is used to express this commonality, and virtual functions enable variations in behavior.

Virtual functions give programs a great deal of flexibility. The question presentation loop describes only the general mechanism: "Display the question, get a response, and check it". Each object knows on its own how to carry out the specific tasks: "Display the question" and "Check a response".

Using virtual functions makes programs *easily extensible*. Suppose we want to have a new kind of question for calculations, where we are willing to accept an approximate answer. All we need to do is to define a new class NumericQuestion, with its own check_answer function. Then we can populate the quiz vector with a mixture of plain questions, choice questions, and numeric questions. The code that presents the questions need not be changed at all! The calls to the virtual functions automatically select the correct member functions of the newly defined classes.

Here is the final version of the quiz program, using pointers and virtual functions. When you run the program, you will find that the appropriate versions of the virtual functions are called.

ch10/quiz3/question.h

```
 1  #ifndef QUESTION_H
 2  #define QUESTION_H
 3
 4  #include <string>
 5
 6  using namespace std;
 7
 8  class Question
 9  {
10  public:
11     /**
12        Constructs a question with empty question and answer.
13     */
14     Question();
15
16     /**
17        @param question_text the text of this question
18     */
19     void set_text(string question_text);
20
21     /**
22        @param correct_response the answer for this question
23     */
24     void set_answer(string correct_response);
25
```

```
26    /**
27        @param response  the response to check
28        @return  true if the response was correct, false otherwise
29    */
30    virtual bool check_answer(string response) const;
31
32    /**
33        Displays this question.
34    */
35    virtual void display() const;
36 private:
37    string text;
38    string answer;
39 };
40
41 #endif
```

ch10/quiz3/choicequestion.h

```
1  #ifndef CHOICEQUESTION_H
2  #define CHOICEQUESTION_H
3
4  #include <vector>
5  #include "question.h"
6
7  class ChoiceQuestion : public Question
8  {
9  public:
10    /**
11        Constructs a choice question with no choices.
12    */
13    ChoiceQuestion();
14
15    /**
16        Adds an answer choice to this question.
17        @param choice  the choice to add
18        @param correct  true if this is the correct choice, false otherwise
19    */
20    void add_choice(string choice, bool correct);
21
22    virtual void display() const;
23 private:
24    vector<string> choices;
25 };
26
27 #endif
```

ch10/quiz3/test.cpp

```
1  #include <iostream>
2  #include "question.h"
3  #include "choicequestion.h"
4
5  int main()
6  {
```

```
 7     string response;
 8     cout << boolalpha;
 9
10     // Make a quiz with two questions
11     vector<Question*> quiz(2);
12     quiz[0] = new Question;
13     quiz[0]->set_text("Who was the inventor of C++?");
14     quiz[0]->set_answer("Bjarne Stroustrup");
15
16     ChoiceQuestion* cq_pointer = new ChoiceQuestion;
17     cq_pointer->set_text(
18        "In which country was the inventor of C++ born?");
19     cq_pointer->add_choice("Australia", false);
20     cq_pointer->add_choice("Denmark", true);
21     cq_pointer->add_choice("Korea", false);
22     cq_pointer->add_choice("United States", false);
23     quiz[1] = cq_pointer;
24
25     // Check answers for all questions
26     for (int i = 0; i < quiz.size(); i++)
27     {
28        quiz[i]->display();
29        cout << "Your answer: ";
30        getline(cin, response);
31        cout << quiz[i]->check_answer(response) << endl;
32     }
33
34     return 0;
35  }
```

SELF CHECK

16. Why did the test program introduce the variable `cq_pointer` instead of directly calling `quiz[1]->add_choice("Australia", false)`?

17. Which of the following statements are legal?

    a. `ChoiceQuestion q;`
       `Question a = q;`

    b. `ChoiceQuestion b = a;`

    c. `a.add_choice("Yes", true);`

    d. `b.add_choice("No", false);`

18. Which of the following statements are legal?

    a. `Question* p = new ChoiceQuestion;`

    b. `ChoiceQuestion* q = p;`

    c. `p->add_choice("Yes", true);`

    d. `q->add_choice("No", false);`

19. What is displayed as the result of the following statements?

```
ChoiceQuestion* p = new ChoiceQuestion;
p->set_text("What is the answer?");
p->add_choice("42", true);
p->add_choice("Something else", false);
Question q = *p;
q.display();
```

20. Suppose check_answer was not declared virtual in question.h. How would the behavior of test.cpp change?

QUALITY TIP 10.2

Don't Use Type Tags

Some programmers build inheritance hierarchies in which each object has a tag that indicates its type, commonly a string. They then query that string:

```
if (q->get_type() == "Question")
{
   // Do something
}
else if (q->get_type() == "ChoiceQuestion")
{
   // Do something else
}
```

This is a poor strategy. If a new class is added, then all these queries need to be revised. In contrast, consider the addition of a class NumericQuestion to our quiz program. *Nothing* needs to change in that program because it uses virtual functions, not type tags.

Whenever you find yourself adding a type tag to a hierarchy of classes, reconsider and use virtual functions instead.

COMMON ERROR 10.4

Slicing an Object

In C++ it is legal to copy a derived-class object into a base-class variable. However, any derived-class information is lost in the process. For example, when a Manager object is assigned to a variable of type Employee, the result is only the employee portion of the manager data:

```
Manager m;
...
Employee e = m; // Holds only the Employee base data of m
```

Any information that is particular to managers is sliced off, because it would not fit into a variable of type Employee. To avoid slicing, you can use pointers.

The slicing problem commonly occurs when a function has a polymorphic parameter (that is, a parameter that can belong to a base class or a derived class). In that case, the parameter must be a pointer or a reference. Consider this example:

```
void ask(Question q) // Error
{
```

```
        q.display();
        cout << "Your answer: ";
        getline(cin, response);
        cout << q.check_answer(response) << endl;
    }
```

If you call this function with a ChoiceQuestion object, then the parameter variable q is initialized with a copy of that object. But q is a Question object; the derived-class information is sliced away. The simplest remedy is to use a reference:

```
    void ask(const Question& q)
```

Now only the *address* is passed to the function. A reference is really a pointer in disguise. No slicing occurs, and virtual functions work correctly.

ADVANCED TOPIC 10.2

Virtual Self-Calls

Suppose we add the following function to the Question class:

```
    void Question::ask() const
    {
        display();
        cout << "Your answer: ";
        getline(cin, response);
        cout << check_answer(response) << endl;
    }
```

Now consider the call

```
    ChoiceQuestion cq;
    cq.set_text("In which country was the inventor of C++ born?");
    ...
    cq.ask();
```

Which display and check_answer function will the ask function call? If you look inside the code of the Question::ask function, you can see that these functions are executed on the implicit parameter.

```
    void Question::ask() const
    {
        implicit parameter.display();
        cout << "Your answer: ";
        getline(cin, response);
        cout << implicit parameter.check_answer(response) << endl;
    }
```

The implicit parameter in our call is cq, an object of type ChoiceQuestion. Because the display and check_answer functions are virtual, the ChoiceQuestion versions of the functions are called automatically. This happens even though the ask function is defined in the Question class, which has *no knowledge* of the ChoiceQuestion class.

As you can see, virtual functions are a very powerful mechanism. The Question class supplies an ask function that specifies the common nature of asking a question, namely to display it and check the response. How the displaying and checking are carried out is left to the derived classes.

HOW TO 10.1

Developing an Inheritance Hierarchy

When you work with a set of classes, some of which are more general and others more specialized, you want to organize them into an inheritance hierarchy. This enables you to process objects of different classes in a uniform way.

As an example, we will consider a bank that offers its customers the following account types:

- A savings account that earns interest. The interest compounds monthly and is computed on the minimum monthly balance.

- A checking account that has no interest, gives you three free withdrawals per month, and charges a $1 transaction fee for each additional withdrawal.

The program will manage a set of accounts of both types, and it should be structured so that other account types can be added without affecting the main processing loop. Supply a menu

```
D)eposit  W)ithdraw  M)onth end  Q)uit
```

For deposits and withdrawals, query the account number and amount. Print the balance of the account after each transaction.

In the "Month end" command, accumulate interest or clear the transaction counter, depending on the type of the bank account. Then print the balance of all accounts.

Step 1   List the classes that are part of the hierarchy.

In our case, the problem description yields two classes: SavingsAccount and CheckingAccount. To express the commonality between them, we will introduce a class BankAccount.

Step 2   Organize the classes into an inheritance hierarchy.

Draw a UML diagram that shows base and derived classes. Here is the diagram for our example.

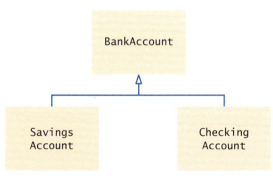

Step 3   Determine the common responsibilities.

In Step 2, you will have identified a class at the base of the hierarchy. That class needs to have sufficient responsibilities to carry out the tasks at hand.

To find out what those tasks are, write pseudocode for processing the objects.

```
For each user command
{
    If it is a deposit or withdrawal
    {
        Deposit or withdraw the amount from the specified account.
        Print the balance.
    }
    If it is month end processing
    {
        For each account
        {
            Call month end processing.
            Print the balance.
        }
    }
}
```

From the pseudocode, we obtain the following list of common responsibilities that every bank account must carry out:

```
Deposit money.
Withdraw money.
Get the balance.
Carry out month end processing.
```

Step 4 Decide which functions are overridden in derived classes.

For each derived class and each of the common responsibilities, decide whether the behavior can be inherited or whether it needs to be overridden. Declare any functions that are overridden as virtual in the root of the hierarchy.

Getting the balance is common to all account types. Withdrawing and end of month processing are different for the derived classes, so they need to be declared virtual. Because it is entirely possible that some future account type will levy a fee for deposits, it seems prudent to declare the deposit member function virtual as well.

```
class BankAccount
{
public:
    virtual void deposit(double amount);
    virtual void withdraw(double amount);
    virtual void month_end();
    double get_balance() const;
private:
    ...
};
```

Step 5 Define the public interface of each derived class.

Typically, derived classes have responsibilities other than those of the base class. List those, as well as the member functions that need to be overridden. You also need to specify how the objects of the derived classes should be constructed.

In this example, we need a way of setting the interest rate for the savings account. In addition, we need to specify constructors and overridden functions.

```
class SavingsAccount : public BankAccount
{
public:
   /**
       Constructs a savings account with a zero balance.
   */
   SavingsAccount();

   /**
      Sets the interest rate for this account.
      @param rate  the monthly interest rate in percent
   */
   void set_interest_rate(double rate);

   virtual void withdraw(double amount);
   virtual void month_end();
private:
   . . .
};

class CheckingAccount : public BankAccount
{
public:
   /**
       Constructs a checking account with a zero balance.
   */
   CheckingAccount();

   virtual void withdraw(double amount);
   virtual void month_end();
private:
   . . .
};
```

Step 6 Identify data members.

List the data members for each class. If you find a data member that is common to all classes, be sure to place it in the base of the hierarchy.

All accounts have a balance. We store that value in the BankAccount base class.

```
class BankAccount
{
   . . .
private:
   double balance;
};
```

The SavingsAccount class needs to store the interest rate. It also needs to store the minimum monthly balance, which must be updated by all withdrawals.

```
class SavingsAccount : public BankAccount
{
   . . .
```

```
private:
    double interest_rate;
    double min_balance;
};
```

The CheckingAccount class needs to count the withdrawals, so that the charge can be applied after the free withdrawal limit is reached.

```
class CheckingAccount : public BankAccount
{
    ...
private:
    int withdrawals;
};
```

Step 7 Implement constructors and member functions.

The member functions of the BankAccount class update or return the balance.

```
BankAccount::BankAccount()
{
    balance = 0;
}

void BankAccount::deposit(double amount)
{
    balance = balance + amount;
}

void BankAccount::withdraw(double amount)
{
    balance = balance - amount;
}

double BankAccount::get_balance() const
{
    return balance;
}
```

At the level of the BankAccount base class, we can say nothing about end of month processing. We choose to make that function do nothing.

```
void BankAccount::month_end()
{
}
```

In the withdraw member function of the SavingsAccount class, the minimum balance is updated. Note the call to the base-class member function.

```
void SavingsAccount::withdraw(double amount)
{
    BankAccount::withdraw(amount);
    double balance = get_balance();
    if (balance < min_balance)
    {
        min_balance = balance;
    }
}
```

In the `month_end` member function of the `SavingsAccount` class, the interest is deposited into the account. We must call the `deposit` member function since we have no direct access to the `balance` data member. The minimum balance is reset for the next month.

```cpp
void SavingsAccount::month_end()
{
   double interest = min_balance * interest_rate / 100;
   deposit(interest);
   min_balance = get_balance();
}
```

The `withdraw` function of the `CheckingAccount` class needs to check the withdrawal count. If there have been too many withdrawals, a charge is applied. Again, note how the function invokes the base-class function, using the `BankAccount::` syntax.

```cpp
void CheckingAccount::withdraw(double amount)
{
   const int FREE_WITHDRAWALS = 3;
   const int WITHDRAWAL_FEE = 1;

   BankAccount::withdraw(amount);
   withdrawals++;
   if (withdrawals > FREE_WITHDRAWALS)
   {
      BankAccount::withdraw(WITHDRAWAL_FEE);
   }
}
```

End of month processing for a checking account simply resets the withdrawal count.

```cpp
void CheckingAccount::month_end()
{
   withdrawals = 0;
}
```

Step 8 Allocate objects on the heap and process them.

For polymorphism (that is, variation of behavior) to work in C++, you need to call virtual functions through pointers. The easiest strategy is to allocate all polymorphic objects on the heap, using the `new` operator.

In our sample program, we allocate 5 checking accounts and 5 savings accounts and store their addresses in an array of bank accounts. Then we accept user commands and execute deposits, withdrawals, and monthly processing.

```cpp
int main()
{
   cout << fixed << setprecision(2);

   // Create accounts
   const int ACCOUNTS_SIZE = 10;
   BankAccount* accounts[ACCOUNTS_SIZE];
   for (int i = 0; i < ACCOUNTS_SIZE / 2; i++)
   {
      accounts[i] = new CheckingAccount;
   }
   for (int i = ACCOUNTS_SIZE / 2; i < ACCOUNTS_SIZE; i++)
   {
```

```
        SavingsAccount* account = new SavingsAccount;
        account->set_interest_rate(0.75);
        accounts[i] = account;
    }

    // Execute commands
    bool more = true;
    while (more)
    {
        cout << "D)eposit  W)ithdraw  M)onth end  Q)uit: ";
        string input;
        cin >> input;
        if (input == "D" || input == "W")   // Deposit or withdrawal
        {
            cout << "Enter account number and amount: ";
            int num;
            double amount;
            cin >> num >> amount;

            if (input == "D") { accounts[num]->deposit(amount); }
            else { accounts[num]->withdraw(amount); }

            cout << "Balance: " << accounts[num]->get_balance() << endl;
        }
        else if (input == "M")   // Month end processing
        {
            for (int n = 0; n < ACCOUNTS_SIZE(); n++)
            {
                accounts[n]->month_end();
                cout << n << " " << accounts[n]->get_balance() << endl;
            }
        }
        else if (input == "Q")
        {
            more = false;
        }
    }

    return 0;
}
```

See ch10/accounts.cpp for the complete program.

WORKED EXAMPLE 10.1

Implementing an Employee Hierarchy for Payroll Processing

This Worked Example shows how to implement payroll processing that works for different kinds of employees.

The Limits of Computation

Have you ever wondered how your instructor or grader makes sure your programming homework is correct? In all likelihood, they look at your solution and perhaps run it with some test inputs. But usually they have a correct solution available. That suggests that there might be an easier way. Perhaps they could feed your program and their correct program into a "program comparator", a computer program that analyzes both programs and determines whether they both compute the same results. Of course, your solution and the program that is known to be correct need not be identical—what matters is that they produce the same output when given the same input.

How could such a program comparator work? Well, the C++ compiler knows how to read a program and make sense of the classes, functions, and statements. So it seems plausible that someone could, with some effort, write a program that reads two C++ programs, analyzes what they do, and determines whether they solve the same task. Of course, such a program would be very attractive to instructors, because it could automate the grading process. Thus, even though no such program exists today, it might be tempting to try to develop one and sell it to universities around the world.

However, before you start raising venture capital for such an effort, you should know that theoretical computer scientists have proven that it is impossible to develop such a program, *no matter how hard you try*.

There are quite a few of these unsolvable problems. The first one, called the *halting problem*, was discovered by the British researcher Alan Turing in 1936 (see Figure 7). Because his research occurred before the first actual computer was constructed, Turing had to devise a theoretical device, the *Turing machine*, to explain how computers could work. The Turing machine consists of a long magnetic tape, a read/write head, and a program that has numbered instructions of the form: "If the current symbol under the head is x, then replace it with y, move the head one unit left or right, and continue with instruction n" (see Figure 8). Interestingly enough, with just these instructions, you can program just as much as with C++, even though it is incredibly tedious to do so. Theoretical computer scientists like Turing machines because they can be described using nothing more than the laws of mathematics.

Figure 7 Alan Turing

Program

Instruction number	If tape symbol is	Replace with	Then move head	Then go to instruction
1	0	2	right	2
1	1	1	left	4
2	0	0	right	2
2	1	1	right	2
2	2	0	left	3
3	0	0	left	3
3	1	1	left	3
3	2	2	right	1
4	1	1	right	5
4	2	0	left	4

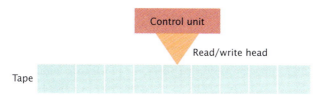

Control unit

Read/write head

Tape

Figure 8   A Turing Machine

Expressed in terms of C++, the halting problem states: "It is impossible to write a program with two inputs, namely the source code of an arbitrary C++ program P and a string I, that decides whether the program P, when executed with the input I, will halt without getting into an infinite loop". Of course, for some kinds of programs and inputs, it is possible to decide whether the programs halt with the given input. The halting problem asserts that it is impossible to come up with a single decision-making algorithm that works with all programs and inputs. Note that you can't simply run the program P on the input I to settle this question. If the program runs for 1,000 days, you don't know that the program is in an infinite loop. Maybe you just have to wait another day for it to stop.

Such a "halt checker", if it could be written, might also be useful for grading homework. An instructor could use it to screen student submissions to see if they get into an infinite loop with a particular input, and then not check them any further. However, as Turing demonstrated, such a program cannot be written. His argument is ingenious and quite simple.

Suppose a "halt checker" program existed. Let's call it H. From H, we will develop another program, the "killer" program K. K does the following computation. Its input is a string containing the source code for a program R. It then applies the halting checker on the input program R and the input string R. That is, it checks whether the program R halts if its input is its own source code. It sounds bizarre to feed a program to itself, but it isn't impossible. For example, the C++ compiler is written in C++, and you can use it to compile itself. Or, as a simpler example, you can use a word count program to count the words in its own source code.

When K gets the answer from H that R halts when applied to itself, it is programmed to enter an infinite loop. Otherwise K exits. In C++, the program might look like this:

```
int main()
{
```

```
    string r = read program input;
    HaltChecker checker;
    if (checker.check(r, r))
    {
        while (true) { } // Infinite loop
    }
    else
    {
        return 0;
    }
}
```

Now ask yourself: What does the halt checker answer when asked if *K* halts when given *K* as the input? Maybe it finds out that *K* gets into an infinite loop with such an input. But wait, that can't be right. That would mean that checker.check(r, r) returns false when r is the program code of *K*. As you can plainly see, in that case, the main function returns, so *K* didn't get into an infinite loop. That shows that *K* must halt when analyzing itself, so checker.check(r, r) should return true. But then the main function doesn't terminate—it goes into an infinite loop. That shows that it is logically impossible to implement a program that can check whether *every* program halts on a particular input.

It is sobering to know that there are *limits* to computing. There are problems that no computer program, no matter how ingenious, can answer.

Theoretical computer scientists are working on other research involving the nature of computation. One important question that remains unsettled to this day deals with problems that in practice are very time-consuming to solve. It may be that these problems are intrinsically hard, in which case it would be pointless to try to look for better algorithms. Such theoretical research can have important practical applications. For example, right now, nobody knows whether the most common encryption schemes used today could be broken by discovering a new algorithm (see Random Fact 8.1 for more information on encryption algorithms). Knowing that no fast algorithms exist for breaking a particular code could make us feel more comfortable about the security of encryption.

CHAPTER SUMMARY

1. A derived class inherits data and behavior from a base class.

2. You can always use a derived class object in place of a base class object.

3. A derived class can override a base class function by providing a new implementation.

4. The derived class inherits all data members and all functions that it does not override.

5. Unless specified otherwise, the base-class data members are initialized with the default constructor.

6. The constructor of a derived class can pass parameters to a base-class constructor.

7. Use *BaseClass*::*function* notation to explicitly call a base-class function.

8. When converting a derived class object to a base class, the derived class data is sliced away.

9. A derived-class pointer can be converted to a base-class pointer.

10. When a virtual function is called, the version belonging to the actual type of the implicit parameter is invoked.

11. Polymorphism (literally, "having multiple shapes") describes objects that share a set of tasks and execute them in different ways.

REVIEW EXERCISES

Exercise R10.1. Identify the base class and the derived class in each of the following pairs of classes.

a. `Employee, Manager`

b. `Polygon, Triangle`

c. `GraduateStudent, Student`

d. `Person, Student`

e. `Employee, Professor`

f. `BankAccount, CheckingAccount`

g. `Vehicle, Car`

h. `Vehicle, Minivan`

i. `Car, Minivan`

j. `Truck, Vehicle`

Exercise R10.2. What inheritance relationships would you establish among the following classes?

```
Student              Professor
TeachingAssistant    Employee
Secretary            DepartmentChair
Janitor              Person
Course               Seminar
Lecture              LabCourse
```

Exercise R10.3. An object-oriented traffic simulation system has the following classes:

```
Vehicle              PickupTruck
Car                  SportUtilityVehicle
Truck                Minivan
Sedan                Bicycle
Coupe                Motorcycle
```

Draw a UML diagram that shows the inheritance relationships between these classes.

Exercise R10.4. What inheritance relationships would you establish among the following classes?

```
Student              Professor
Employee             Secretary
DepartmentChair      Janitor
Person
```

Exercise R10.5. Draw a UML diagram that shows the inheritance and aggregation relationships between the classes:

```
Person               Employee
Student              Instructor
Course
```

Exercise R10.6. Consider a program for managing inventory in a small appliance store. Why isn't it useful to have a base class SmallAppliance and derived classes Toaster, CarVacuum, TravelIron, and so on?

Exercise R10.7. Which functions does the SavingsAccount class in How To 10.1 on page 442 inherit from its base class? Which functions does it override? Which functions does it add?

Exercise R10.8. Which data members does the CheckingAccount class in How To 10.1 on page 442 inherit from its base class? Which data members does it add?

Exercise R10.9. Design an inheritance hierarchy for geometric shapes: rectangles, squares, and circles. Draw a UML diagram. Provide a virtual function to compute the area of a shape. Provide appropriate constructors for each class. Write the class definitions but do not provide implementations of the member functions.

Exercise R10.10. Continue Exercise R10.9 by writing a main function that executes the following steps:

> Fill a vector of shape pointers with a rectangle, a square, and a circle.
> Print the area of each shape.
> Deallocate all heap objects.

Exercise R10.11. Can you convert a base-class object into a derived-class object? A derived-class object into a base-class object? A base-class pointer into a derived-class pointer? A derived-class pointer into a base-class pointer? If so, give examples. If not, explain why not.

Exercise R10.12. Consider a function process_file(ostream& str). Objects from which of the classes in Figure 2 can be passed as parameters to this function?

Exercise R10.13. What does the following program print?

```
class B
{
public:
   void print(int n) const;
};

void B::print(int n) const
{
   cout << n << endl;
}

class D : public B
{
public:
   void print(int n) const;
};

void D::print(int n) const
{
   if (n <= 1) B::print(n);
   else if (n % 2 == 0) print(n / 2);
   else print(3 * n + 1);
}

int main()
{
   D d;
   d.print(3);
   return 0;
}
```

Determine the answer by hand, not by compiling and running the program.

Exercise R10.14. Suppose the class D inherits from B. Which of the following assignments are legal?

```
B b;
D d;
B* pb;
D* pd;
```

a. b = d;

b. d = b;

c. pd = pb;

d. pb = pd;

e. d = pd;

f. b = *pd;

g. *pd = *pb;

Exercise R10.15. Suppose the class Sub is derived from the class Sandwich. Which of the following assignments are legal?

a. Sandwich* x = new Sandwich();

b. Sub* y = new Sub();

c. x = y;

d. y = x;

e. y = new Sandwich();

f. x = new Sub();

g. *x = *y;

h. *y = *x;

Exercise R10.16. What does the program print? Explain your answers by tracing the flow of each call.

```
class B
{
public:
   B();
   virtual void p() const;
   void q() const;
};

B::B() {}
void B::p() const { cout << "B::p\n"; }
void B::q() const { cout << "B::q\n"; }

class D : public B
{
public:
   D();
   virtual void p() const;
   void q() const;
};
```

```
D::D() {}
void D::p() const { cout << "D::p\n"; }
void D::q() const { cout << "D::q\n"; }

int main()
{
   B b;
   D d;
   B* pb = new B;
   B* pd = new D;
   D* pd2 = new D;

   b.p(); b.q();
   d.p(); d.q();
   pb->p(); pb->q();
   pd->p(); pd->q();
   pd2->p(); pd2->q();
   return 0;
}
```

Exercise R10.17. Using the Employee class from Worked Example 10.1 (ch10/sala-ries.cpp in your code files), form a subclass Volunteer of Employee and provide a constructor Volunteer(string name) that sets the salary to 0.

Exercise R10.18. In the accounts.cpp program of How To 10.1, would it be reasonable to make the get_balance function virtual? Explain your reasoning.

Exercise R10.19. What is the effect of declaring the display member function virtual only in the ChoiceQuestion class?

PROGRAMMING EXERCISES

Exercise P10.1. Add a class NumericQuestion to the question hierarchy of Section 10.1. If the response and the expected answer differ by no more than 0.01, then accept it as correct.

Exercise P10.2. Add a class FillInQuestion to the question hierarchy of Section 10.1. Such a question is constructed with a string that contains the answer, surrounded by _ _, for example, "The inventor of C++ was _Bjarne Stroustrup_". The question should be displayed as

```
The inventor of C++ was _____
```

Exercise P10.3. Modify the check_answer member function of the Question class so that it does not take into account different spaces or upper/lowercase characters. For example, the response " bjarne stroustrup" should match an answer of "Bjarne Stroustrup".

Exercise P10.4. Add a class MultiChoiceQuestion to the question hierarchy of Section 10.1 that allows multiple correct choices. The respondent should provide any one of the correct choices. The answer string should contain all of the correct choices, separated by spaces.

Exercise P10.5. Add a class ChooseAllCorrect to the question hierarchy of Section 10.1 that allows multiple correct choices. The respondent should provide all correct choices, separated by spaces.

Exercise P10.6. Add a member function add_text to the Question base class and provide a different implementation of ChoiceQuestion that calls add_text rather than storing a vector of choices.

Exercise P10.7. Change the CheckingAccount class in How To 10.1 so that a $1 fee is levied for deposits or withdrawals in excess of three free monthly transactions. Place the code for computing the fee into a private member function that you call from the deposit and withdraw member functions.

Exercise P10.8. Derive a class Programmer from Employee. Supply a constructor Programmer(string name, double salary) that calls the base-class constructor. Supply a function get_name that returns the name in the format "Hacker, Harry (Programmer)".

Exercise P10.9. Implement a base class Person. Derive classes Student and Instructor from Person. A person has a name and a birthday. A student has a major, and an instructor has a salary. Write the class definitions, the constructors, and the member functions display for all classes.

Exercise P10.10. Derive a class Manager from Employee. Add a data member named department of type string. Supply a function display that displays the manager's name, department, and salary. Derive a class Executive from Manager. Supply a function display that displays the string Executive, followed by the information stored in the Manager base object.

Exercise P10.11. Implement a base class Account and derived classes Savings and Checking. In the base class, supply member functions deposit and withdraw. Provide a function daily_interest that computes and adds the daily interest. For calculations, assume that every month has 30 days. Checking accounts yield interest of 3 percent annually on balances over $1,000. Savings accounts yield interest of 6 percent annually on the entire balance. Write a driver program that makes a month's worth of deposits and withdrawals and calculates the interest every day.

Exercise P10.12. Implement a base class Appointment and derived classes Onetime, Daily, Weekly, and Monthly. An appointment has a description (for example, "see the dentist") and a date and time. Write a virtual function occurs_on(int year, int month, int day) that checks whether the appointment occurs on that date. For example, for a monthly appointment, you must check whether the day of the month matches. Then fill a vector of Appointment* with a mixture of appointments. Have the user enter a date and print out all appointments that happen on that date.

Exercise P10.13. Improve the appointment book program of Exercise P10.12. Give the user the option to add new appointments. The user must specify the type of the appointment, the description, and the date and time.

Exercise P10.14. Improve the appointment book program of Exercises P10.12 and P10.13 by letting the user save the appointment data to a file and reload the data from a file. The saving part is straightforward: Make a virtual function save. Save out the type, description, date, and time. The loading part is not so easy. You must first determine the type of the appointment to be loaded, create an object of that type with its default constructor, and then call a virtual load function to load the remainder.

Exercise P10.15. Use polymorphism to carry out image manipulations such as those described in Exercise P8.10 and P8.11. Design a base class Effect and derived classes Sunset and Grayscale. Use a virtual function process. The file processing part of your program should repeatedly call process on an Effect* pointer, without having to know which effect is applied.

ANSWERS TO SELF-CHECK QUESTIONS

1. Because every manager is an employee but not the other way around, the Manager class is more specialized. It is the derived class, and Employee is the base class.

2. CheckingAccount and SavingsAccount both inherit from the more general class BankAccount.

3. istream, istringstream, ifstream, iostream, fstream

4. Vehicle, truck, motorcycle

5. It shouldn't. A quiz isn't a question; it *has* questions.

6. a, b, d

7.
```
class Manager : public Employee
{
private:
   double bonus;
}
```

8. name, base_salary, and bonus

9.
```
class Manager : public Employee
{
public:
   double get_salary() const;
}
```

10. get_name, set_name, set_base_salary

11. The function is not allowed to access the text member from the base class.

12. The type of the this pointer is ChoiceQuestion*. Therefore, the display function of ChoiceQuestion is selected, and the function calls itself.

13. Because there is no ambiguity. The derived class doesn't have a `set_answer` function.

14.
```
string Manager::get_name() const
{
    return "*" + Employee::get_name();
}
```

15.
```
double Manager::get_salary() const
{
    return Employee::get_salary() + bonus;
}
```

16. The type of `quiz[1]` is `Question*`, and the `Question` class has no member function called `add_choice`.

17. a and d are legal.

18. a and d are legal.

19. Only the question text, not the choices. The choices are sliced away when `*p` is assigned to the object q.

20. It wouldn't change. The function is never overridden in the classes used in our test program.

C++ Language Coding Guidelines

Introduction

This coding style guide is a simplified version of one that has been used with good success both in industrial practice and for college courses. It lays down rules that you must follow for your programming assignments.

A style guide is a set of mandatory requirements for layout and formatting. Uniform style makes it easier for you to read code from your instructor and classmates. You will really appreciate the consistency if you do a team project. It is also easier for your instructor and your grader to grasp the essence of your programs quickly.

A style guide makes you a more productive programmer because it *reduces gratuitous choice*. If you don't have to make choices about trivial matters, you can spend your energy on the solution of real problems.

In these guidelines a number of constructs are plainly outlawed. That doesn't mean that programmers using them are evil or incompetent. It does mean that the constructs are of marginal utility and can be expressed just as well or even better with other language constructs.

If you have already programmed in C or C++, you may be initially uncomfortable about giving up some fond habits. However, it is a sign of professionalism to set aside personal preferences in minor matters and to compromise for the benefit of your group.

These guidelines are necessarily somewhat long and dull. They also mention features that you may not yet have seen in class. Here are the most important highlights:

- Tabs are set every three spaces.
- Variable and function names are lowercase.
- Constant names are uppercase. Class names start with an uppercase letter.
- There are spaces after reserved words and between binary operators.
- Braces must line up.
- No magic numbers may be used.
- Every function must have a comment.
- At most 30 lines of code may be used per function.
- No goto, continue, or break is allowed.
- At most two global variables may be used per file.

A note to the instructor: Of course, many programmers and organizations have strong feelings about coding style. If this style guide is incompatible with your own preferences or with local custom, please feel free to modify it. For that purpose, this coding style guide is available in electronic form in the WileyPLUS course and the web site for this book.

Source Files

Each program is a collection of one or more files or modules. The executable program is obtained by compiling and linking these files. Organize the material in each file as follows:

- Header comments
- #include statements
- Constants
- Classes
- Functions

It is common to start each file with a comment block. Here is a typical format:

```
/**
   @file invoice.cpp
   @author Jenny Koo
   @date 2009-01-24
   @version 3.14
*/
```

You may also want to include a copyright notice, such as

```
/* Copyright 2009 Jenny Koo */
```

A valid copyright notice consists of

- the copyright symbol © or the word "Copyright" or the abbreviation "Copr."
- the year of first publication of the work
- the name of the owner of the copyright

(Note: To save space, this header comment has been omitted from the programs in this book as well as the programs on disk so that the actual line numbers match those that are printed in the book.)

Next, list all included header files.

```
#include <iostream>
#include "question.h"
```

Do not embed absolute path names, such as

```
#include "c:\me\my_homework\widgets.h"   // Don't !!!
```

After the header files, list constants that are needed throughout the program file.

```
const int GRID_SIZE = 20;
const double CLOCK_RADIUS = 5;
```

Then supply the definitions of all classes.

```
class Product
{
   ...
};
```

Order the class definitions so that a class is defined before it is used in another class.

Finally, list all functions, including member functions of classes and nonmember functions. Order the nonmember functions so that a function is defined before it is called. As a consequence, the main function will be the last function in your file.

Functions

Supply a comment of the following form for every function.

```
/**
    Explanation.
    @param argument₁   explanation
    @param argument₂   explanation
    ...
    @return explanation
*/
```

The introductory explanation is required for all functions except main. It should start with an uppercase letter and end with a period. Some documentation tools extract the first sentence of the explanation into a summary table. Thus, if you provide an explanation that consists of multiple sentences, formulate the explanation such that the first sentence is a concise explanation of the function's purpose.

Omit the @param comment if the function takes no parameters. Omit the @return comment for void functions. Here is a typical example.

```
/**
    Converts calendar date into Julian day. This algorithm is from Press
    et al., Numerical Recipes in C, 2nd ed., Cambridge University Press, 1992.
    @param year  the year of the date to be converted
    @param month  the month of the date to be converted
    @param day  the day of the date to be converted
    @return  the Julian day number that begins at noon of the given
    calendar date
*/
long dat2jul(int year, int month, int day)
{
    ...
}
```

Parameter names must be explicit, especially if they are integers or Boolean.

```
Employee remove(int d, double s); // Huh?
Employee remove(int department, double severance_pay); // OK
```

Of course, for very generic functions, short names may be very appropriate.

Do not write void functions that return exactly one answer through a reference. Instead, make the result into a return value.

```
void find(vector<Employee> c, bool& found); // Don't!
bool find(vector<Employee> c); // OK
```

Of course, if the function computes more than one value, some or all results can be returned through reference parameters.

Functions must have at most 30 lines of code. (Comments, blank lines, and lines containing only braces are not included in this count.) Functions that consist of one long if/else/else statement sequence may be longer, provided each branch is 10 lines or less. This rule forces you to break up complex computations into separate functions.

Local Variables

Do not define all local variables at the beginning of a block. Define each variable just before it is used for the first time.

Every variable must be either explicitly initialized when defined or set in the immediately following statement (for example, through a >> instruction).

```
int pennies = 0;
```

or

```
int pennies;
cin >> pennies;
```

Move variables to the innermost block in which they are needed.

```
while (...)
{
   double xnew = (xold + a / xold) / 2;
   ...
}
```

Do not define two variables in one statement:

```
int dimes = 0, nickels = 0; // Don't
```

When defining a pointer variable, place the * with the type, not the variable:

```
Link* p; // OK
```

not

```
Link *p; // Don't
```

Constants

In C++, do not use #define to define constants:

```
#define CLOCK_RADIUS 5 // Don't
```

Use const instead:

```
const double CLOCK_RADIUS = 5; // The radius of the clock face
```

You may not use magic numbers in your code. (A magic number is an integer constant embedded in code without a constant definition.) Any number except 0, 1, or 2 is considered magic:

```
if (p.get_x() < 10) // Don't
```

Use a const variable instead:

```
const double WINDOW_XMAX = 10;
if (p.get_x() < WINDOW_XMAX) // OK
```

Even the most reasonable cosmic constant is going to change one day. You think there are 365 days per year? Your customers on Mars are going to be pretty unhappy about your silly prejudice.

Make a constant

```
const int DAYS_PER_YEAR = 365;
```

so that you can easily produce a Martian version without trying to find all the 365's, 364's, 366's, 367's, and so on in your code.

Classes

Lay out the items of a class as follows:

```
class ClassName
{
public:
    constructors
    mutators
    accessors
private:
    data
};
```

All data fields of classes must be private.

Control Flow

The for Statement

Use for loops only when a variable runs from somewhere to somewhere else with some constant increment/decrement.

```
for (i = 0; i < a.size(); i++) { cout << a[i] << endl; }
```

Do not use the for loop for weird constructs such as

```
for (xnew = a / 2; count < ITERATIONS; cout << xnew) // Don't
{
    xold = xnew;
    xnew = xold + a / xold;
    count++;
}
```

Make such a loop into a while loop, so the sequence of instructions is much clearer.

```
xnew = a / 2;
while (count < ITERATIONS) // OK
{
    xold = xnew;
    xnew = xold + a / xold;
    count++;
    cout << xnew;
}
```

Nonlinear Control Flow

Don't use the switch statement. Use if/else instead.

Do not use the break, continue, or goto statement. Use a bool variable to control the execution flow.

Lexical Issues

Naming Conventions

The following rules specify when to use upper- and lowercase letters in identifier names.

1. All variable and function names and all data fields of classes are in lowercase, sometimes with an underscore in the middle. For example, `first_player`.
2. All constants are in uppercase, with an occasional underscore. For example, `CLOCK_RADIUS`.
3. All class names start with uppercase and are followed by lowercase letters, with an occasional uppercase letter in the middle. For example, `BankTeller`.

Names must be reasonably long and descriptive. Use `first_player` instead of `fp`. No drppng f vwls. Local variables that are fairly routine can be short (`ch`, `i`) as long as they are really just boring holders for an input character, a loop counter, and so on. Also, do not use `ctr`, `c`, `cntr`, `cnt`, `c2` for five counter variables in your function. Surely each of these variables has a specific purpose and can be named to remind the reader of it (for example, `ccurrent`, `cnext`, `cprevious`, `cnew`, `cresult`).

Indentation and White Space

Use tab stops every three columns. Save your file so that it contains no tabs at all. That means you will need to change the tab stop setting in your editor! In the editor, make sure to select "3 spaces per tab stop" and "save all tabs as spaces". Every programming editor has these settings. If yours doesn't, don't use tabs at all but type the correct number of spaces to achieve indentation.

Use blank lines freely to separate logically distinct parts of a function.

Use a blank space around every binary operator:

```
x1 = (-b - sqrt(b * b - 4 * a * c)) / (2 * a); // Good
x1=(-b-sqrt(b*b-4*a*c))/(2*a); // Bad
```

Leave a blank space after (and not before) each comma, semicolon, and reserved word, but not after a function name.

```
if (x == 0) ...
f(a, b[i]);
```

Every line must fit in 80 columns. If you must break a statement, add an indentation level for the continuation:

```
a[n] = .................................................
   + .................;
```

Braces

Opening and closing braces must line up, either horizontally or vertically.

```
while (i < n) { cout << a[i] << endl; i++; }  // OK
```

```
while (i < n)
{
   cout << a[i] << endl;
   i++;
}  // OK
```

Some programmers don't line up vertical braces but place the { *behind* the while:

```
while (i < n) {   // Don't
   cout << a[i] << endl;
   i++;
}
```

This style saves a line, but it is difficult to match the braces.

Always use braces with if, while, do, and for statements, even if the body is only a single statement.

```
if (floor > 13)
{              // OK
   floor--;
}
if (floor > 13)
   floor--;   // Don't
```

Unstable Layout

Some programmers take great pride in lining up certain columns in their code:

```
class Employee
{
   ...
private:
   string  name;
      int  age;
   double  hourly_wage;
     Time  start_time;
};
```

This is undeniably neat, and we recommend it if your editor does it for you, but *don't* do it manually. The layout is not *stable* under change. A data type that is longer than the preallotted number of columns requires that you move *all* entries around.

Some programmers like to format multiline comments so that every line starts with **:

```
/* This is a comment
** that extends over
** three source lines
*/
```

Again, this is neat if your editor has a command to add and remove the asterisks, and if you know that all programmers who will maintain your code also have such an editor. Otherwise, it can be a powerful method of *discouraging* programmers from editing the comment. If you have to choose between pretty comments and comments that reflect the current facts of the program, facts win over beauty.

Reserved Word Summary

Reserved Word	Description	Reference Location
bool	The Boolean type	Section 3.5
break	Break out of a loop or switch	Advanced Topic 3.3, 4.1
case	A label in a switch statement	Advanced Topic 3.3
char	The character type	Section 7.3
class	Definition of a class	Section 9.2
const	Definition of a constant value, reference, member function, or pointer	Section 2.2.4, Advanced Topic 5.2, Advanced Topic 6.3, Section 9.2
default	The default case of a switch statement	Advanced Topic 3.3
delete	Return a memory block to the heap	Section 7.4
do	A loop that is executed at least once	Section 4.3
double	The double-precision, floating-point type	Section 2.1.2
else	The alternative clause in an if statement	Section 3.1
false	The false Boolean value	Section 3.5
float	The single-precision, floating-point type	Advanced Topic 2.1
for	A loop that is intended to initialize, test, and update a variable	Section 4.2

Reserved Word	Description	Reference Location
if	The conditional branch statement	Section 3.1
int	The integer type	Section 2.1
long	A modifier for the int and double types that indicates that the type may have more bytes	Advanced Topic 2.1
namespace	A name space for disambiguating names	Section 1.6
new	Allocate a memory block from the heap	Section 7.4
private	Features of a class that can only be accessed by this class and its friends	Section 9.2
public	Features of a class that can be accessed by all functions	Section 9.2
return	Returns a value from a function	Section 5.4
short	A modifier for the int type that indicates that the type may have fewer bytes	Advanced Topic 2.1
static_cast	Convert from one type to another	Advanced Topic 2.4
switch	A statement that selects among multiple branches, depending upon the value of an expression	Advanced Topic 3.3
this	The pointer to the implicit parameter of a member function	Section 9.8.3
true	The true value of the Boolean type	Section 3.5
unsigned	A modifier for the int and char types that indicates that values of the type cannot be negative	Advanced Topic 2.1
using	Importing a name space	Section 1.6
virtual	A member function with dynamic dispatch	Section 10.4
void	The empty type of a function or pointer	Section 5.5
while	A loop statement that is controlled by a condition	Section 4.1

The following reserved words are not covered in this book:

asm	explicit	operator	static	type_info
auto	export	protected	struct	typename
catch	extern	register	template	union
const_cast	friend	reinterpret_c	throw	volatile
continue	goto	ast	try	wchar_t
dynamic_cast	inline	signed	typedef	
enum	mutable	sizeof	typeid	

Operator Summary

The operators are listed in groups of decreasing precedence in the table on the next two pages. The horizontal lines in the table indicate a change in operator precedence. For example,

```
z = x - y;
```

means

```
z = (x - y);
```

because = has a lower precedence than - .

The prefix unary operators and the assignment operators associate right-to-left. All other operators associate left-to-right. For example,

```
x - y - z
```

means

```
(x - y) - z
```

because - associates left-to-right, but

```
x = y = z
```

means

```
x = (y = z)
```

because = associates right-to-left.

Operator	Description	Reference Location
::	Scope resolution	Section 9.4.1
.	Access member	Section 2.5
->	Dereference and access member	Section 9.8
[]	Vector or array subscript	Section 6.1
()	Function call	Section 5.1
++	Increment	Section 2.2.2
--	Decrement	Section 2.2.2
!	Boolean NOT	Section 3.6
~	Bitwise NOT	Appendix G
+ (unary)	Positive	Section 2.3.1
- (unary)	Negative	Section 2.3.1
* (unary)	Pointer dereferencing	Section 7.1
& (unary)	Address of variable	Section 7.1
new	Heap allocation	Section 7.4
delete	Heap recycling	Section 7.4
sizeof	Size of variable or type	Appendix F
(*type*)	Cast	not covered
.*	Access pointer to member	not covered
->*	Dereference and access pointer to member	not covered
*	Multiplication	Section 2.3.1
/	Division or integer division	Section 2.3.1
%	Integer remainder	Section 2.3.2
+	Addition	Section 2.3.1
-	Subtraction	Section 2.3.1
<<	Output	Section 1.6, Appendix G
>>	Input	Section 2.2.3, Appendix G

Operator	Description	Reference Location
<	Less than	Section 4.3
<=	Less than or equal	Section 4.3
>	Greater than	Section 4.3
>=	Greater than or equal	Section 4.3
==	Equal	Section 4.3
!=	Not equal	Section 4.3
&	Bitwise AND	Appendix G
^	Bitwise XOR	Appendix G
|	Bitwise OR	Appendix G
&&	Boolean AND	Section 3.6
||	Boolean OR	Section 3.6
? :	Selection	Advanced Topic 3.4
=	Assignment	Section 2.2.1
+= -= *= /= %= &= |= ^= >>= <<=	Combined operator and assignment	Advanced Topic 2.3
,	Sequencing of expressions	not covered

Character Codes

These escape sequences can occur in strings (for example, "\n") and characters for example, '\'').

Escape Sequence	Description
\n	Newline
\r	Carriage return
\t	Tab
\v	Vertical tab
\b	Backspace
\f	Form feed
\a	Alert
\\	Backslash
\"	Double quote
\'	Single quote
\?	Question mark
\x$h_1h_2$	Code specified in hexadecimal
\o$_1$o$_2$o$_3$	Code specified in octal

ASCII Code Table

Dec. Code	Hex Code	Char-acter	Dec. Code	Hex Code	Char-acter	Dec. Code	Hex Code	Char-acter	Dec. Code	Hex Code	Char-acter
0	00		32	20	Space	64	40	@	96	60	`
1	01		33	21	!	65	41	A	97	61	a
2	02		34	22	"	66	42	B	98	62	b
3	03		35	23	#	67	43	C	99	63	c
4	04		36	24	$	68	44	D	100	64	d
5	05		37	25	%	69	45	E	101	65	e
6	06		38	26	&	70	46	F	102	66	f
7	07	\a	39	27	'	71	47	G	103	67	g
8	08	\b	40	28	(	72	48	H	104	68	h
9	09	\t	41	29	)	73	49	I	105	69	i
10	0A	\n	42	2A	*	74	4A	J	106	6A	j
11	0B	\v	43	2B	+	75	4B	K	107	6B	k
12	0C	\f	44	2C	,	76	4C	L	108	6C	l
13	0D	\r	45	2D	-	77	4D	M	109	6D	m
14	0E		46	2E	.	78	4E	N	110	6E	n
15	0F		47	2F	/	79	4F	O	111	6F	o
16	10		48	30	0	80	50	P	112	70	p
17	11		49	31	1	81	51	Q	113	71	q
18	12		50	32	2	82	52	R	114	72	r
19	13		51	33	3	83	53	S	115	73	s
20	14		52	34	4	84	54	T	116	74	t
21	15		53	35	5	85	55	U	117	75	u
22	16		54	36	6	86	56	V	118	76	v
23	17		55	37	7	87	57	W	119	77	w
24	18		56	38	8	88	58	X	120	78	x
25	19		57	39	9	89	59	Y	121	79	y
26	1A		58	3A	:	90	5A	Z	122	7A	z
27	1B		59	3B	;	91	5B	[	123	7B	{
28	1C		60	3C	<	92	5C	\	124	7C		
29	1D		61	3D	=	93	5D	]	125	7D	}
30	1E		62	3E	>	94	5E	^	126	7E	~
31	1F		63	3F	?	95	5F	_	127	7F	

C++ Library Summary

Standard Code Libraries

<cmath>

- double **sqrt**(double x)
  Function: Square root, $\sqrt{x}$

- double **pow**(double x, double y)
  Function: Power, x^y. If $x > 0$, y can be any value. If x is 0, y must be > 0.
  If $x < 0$, y must be an integer.

- double **sin**(double x)
  Function: Sine, sin x (x in radians)

- double **cos**(double x)
  Function: Cosine, cos x (x in radians)

- double **tan**(double x)
  Function: Tangent, tan x (x in radians)

- double **log10**(double x)
  Function: Decimal log, $\log_{10}(x)$, $x > 0$

- double **fabs**(double x)
  Function: Absolute value, $|x|$

<cstdlib>

- int **abs**(int x)
  Function: Absolute value, $|x|$
- void **exit**(int n)
  Function: Exits the program with status code n.
- int **rand**()
  Function: Random integer
- void **srand**(int n)
  Function: Sets the seed of the random number generator to n.

<cctype>

- bool **isalpha**(char c)
  Function: Tests whether c is a letter.
- char **isalnum**(char c)
  Function: Test whether c is a letter or a number.
- bool **isdigit**(char c)
  Function: Tests whether c is a digit.
- bool **isspace**(char c)
  Function: Tests whether c is white space.
- bool **islower**(char c)
  Function: Tests whether c is lowercase.
- bool **isupper**(char c)
  Function: Tests whether c is uppercase.
- char **tolower**(char c)
  Function: Returns the lowercase of c.
- char **toupper**(char c)
  Function: Returns the uppercase of c.

<ctime>

- time_t **time**(time_t* p)
  Function: Returns the number of seconds since January 1, 1970, 00:00:00 GMT. If p is not NULL, the return value is also stored in the location to which p points.

<string>

- istream& **getline**(istream& in, string s)
  Function: Gets the next input line from the input stream in and stores it in the string s.

Class string

- int string::**length**() const
  Member function: Returns the length of the string.
- string string::**substr**(int i) const
  Member function: Returns the substring from index i to the end of the string.

- `string string::`**`substr`**`(int i, int n) const`
  Member function: Returns the substring of length n starting at index i.
- `const char* string::`**`c_str`**`() const`
  Member function: Returns a char array with the characters in this string.

`<iostream>`

Class `istream`

- `bool istream::`**`fail`**`() const`
  Function: True if input has failed.
- `istream& istream::`**`get`**`(char& c)`
  Function: Gets the next character and places it into c.
- `istream& istream::`**`unget`**`()`
  Function: Puts the last character read back into the stream, to be read again in the next input operation; only one character can be put back at a time.
- `istream& istream::`**`seekg`**`(long p)`
  Function: Moves the get position to position p.
- `long istream::`**`tellg`**`()`
  Function: Returns the get position.

Class `ostream`

- `ostream& ostream::`**`seekp`**`(long p)`
  Function: Moves the put position to position p.
- `long ostream::`**`tellp`**`()`
  Function: Returns the put position.

`<iomanip>`

- **`setw`**`(int n)`
  Manipulator: Sets the width of the next field.
- **`setprecision`**`(int n)`
  Manipulator: Sets the precision of floating-point values to n digits after the decimal point.
- **`fixed`**
  Manipulator: Selects fixed floating-point format, with trailing zeroes.
- **`setfill`**`(char c)`
  Manipulator: Sets the fill character to the character c.

`<fstream>`

Class `ifstream`

- `void ifstream::`**`open`**`(const char n[])`
  Function: Opens a file with name n for reading.

Class `ofstream`

- `void ofstream::`**`open`**`(const char n[])`
  Function: Opens a file with name n for writing.

Class fstream

- void fstream::**open**(const char n[])
  Function: Opens a file with name n for reading and writing.

Class fstreambase

- void fstreambase::**close**()
  Function: Closes the file stream.

Notes:
- fstreambase is the common base class of ifstream, ofstream, and fstream.
- To open a binary file both for input and output, use f.open(n, ios::in | ios::out | ios::binary)

\<strstream>

Class istringstream

- istringstream::**istringstream**(string s)
  Constructs a string stream that reads from the string s.

Class ostringstream

- string ostringstream::**str**() const
  Function: Returns the string that was collected by the string stream.

Notes:
- Call istrstream(s.c_str()) to construct an istrstream.
- Call s = string(out.str()) to get a string object that contains the characters collected by the ostrstream out.

\<vector>

Class vector\<T>

- int vector\<T>::**size**() const
  Function: Returns the number of elements in the container.
- vector\<T>::**vector**(int n)
  Function: Constructs a vector with n elements.
- void vector\<T>::**push_back**(const T& x)
  Function: Inserts x after the last element.
- void vector\<T>::**pop_back**()
  Function: Removes (but does not return) the last element.
- T& vector\<T>::**operator**[](int n)
  Function: Accesses the element at index n.
- T& vector\<T>::**at**(int n)
  Function: Accesses the element at index n, checking that the index is in range.

Glossary

Accessor function A function that accesses an object but does not change it.

Actual parameter The expression supplied by the caller for a formal parameter of a function.

Address A value that specifies the location of a variable in memory.

Aggregation relationship The "has-a" relationship between classes.

Algorithm An unambiguous, executable, and terminating specification to solve a problem.

ANSI/ISO C++ Standard The standard for the C++ language that was developed by the American National Standards Institute and the International Standards Organization.

Argument A parameter value in a function call, or one of the values combined by an operator.

Array A collection of values of the same type, each of which can be accessed by an integer index.

Arrow operator The -> operator. p->m is the same as (*p).m.

ASCII code The American Standard Code for Information Interchange, which associates code values between 0 and 127 to letters, digits, punctuation marks, and control characters.

Assignment Placing a new value into a variable.

Base class A class from which another class is derived.

Binary file A file in which values are stored in their binary representation and cannot be read as text.

Binary operator An operator that takes two arguments, for example, + in x + y.

Bit Binary digit; the smallest unit of information, having two possible values, 0 and 1. A data element consisting of n bits has 2^n possible values.

Black-box testing Testing functions without knowing their implementation.

Block A group of statements bracketed by {}.

Boolean operator See **Logical operator**.

Boolean type A type with two values, true and false.

Boundary test case A test case involving values that are at the outer boundary of the set of legal values. For example, if a function is expected to work for all nonnegative integers, then 0 is a boundary test case.

Bounds error Trying to access an array element that is outside the legal range.

break statement A statement that terminates a loop or switch statement.

Byte A number between 0 and 255 (eight bits). Essentially all currently manufactured computers use a byte as the smallest unit of storage in memory.

Capacity The number of values that a data structure such as a vector or deque can potentially hold, in contrast to the size (the number of elements it currently holds).

Case-sensitive Distinguishing upper- and lowercase characters.

Cast Converting a value from one type to a different type. For example, the cast from a floating-point number x to an integer is expressed in C++ by the static cast notation, static_cast<int>(x).

Class A programmer-defined data type.

Command line The line you type when you start a program in a command window. It consists of the program name and the command line arguments.

Comment An explanation to make the human reader understand a section of a program; ignored by the compiler.

Compiler A program that translates code in a high-level language such as C++ to machine instructions.

Compile-time error See **Syntax error**.

Concatenation Placing one string after another.

Constant A value that cannot be changed by the program. In C++, constants are marked with the reserved word const.

Constructor A function that initializes a newly allocated object.

CPU (Central Processing Unit) The part of a computer that executes the machine instructions.

Dangling pointer A pointer that does not point to a valid location.

Data field A variable that is present in every object of a class.

Declaration A statement that announces the existence of a variable, function, or class but does not define it.

Default constructor A constructor that can be invoked with no parameters.

Definition A statement or series of statements that fully describes a variable, a function and its implementation, a type, or a class and its properties.

delete operator The operator that recycles memory to the heap.

Derived class A class that modifies a base class by adding data fields or member functions or by redefining member functions.

Directory A structure on a disk that can hold files or other directories; also called a folder.

Dot notation The notation *object.function(parameters)* used to invoke a member function on an object.

Encapsulation The hiding of implementation details.

Escape character A character in text that is not taken literally but has a special meaning when combined with the character or characters that follow it. The \ character is an escape character in C++ strings.

Executable file The file that contains a program's machine instructions.

Explicit parameter A parameter of a member function other than the object on which the function is invoked.

Expression A syntactical construct that is made up of constants, variables, and/or function calls, and the operators combining them.

Extension The last part of a file name, which specifies the file type. For example, the extension .cpp denotes a C++ file.

Failed stream state The state of a stream after an invalid operation has been attempted, such as reading a number when the next stream position yielded a nondigit, or reading after the end of file was reached.

File A sequence of bytes that is stored on disk.

File pointer The position within a file of the next byte to be read or written. It can be moved so as to access any byte in the file.

Floating-point number A number with a fractional part.

Folder Directory.

Formal parameter A variable in a function definition; it is initialized with an actual parameter value when the function is called.

Function A sequence of statements that can be invoked multiple times, with different values for its parameters.

Global variable A variable whose scope is not restricted to a single function.

Header file A file that informs the compiler of features that are available in another module or library.

Heap A reservoir of storage from which memory can be allocated when a program runs.

IDE (Integrated Development Environment) A programming environment that includes an editor, compiler, and debugger.

#if directive A directive to the preprocessor to include the code contained between the #if and the matching #endif if a condition is true.

Implicit parameter The object on which a member function is called. For example, in the call x.f(y), the object x is the implicit parameter of f.

#include directive An instruction to the preprocessor to include a header file.

Inheritance The "is-a" relationship between a general base class and a specialized derived class.

Initialization Setting a variable to a well-defined value when it is created.

Integer A number without a fractional part.

Integer division Taking the quotient of two integers and discarding the remainder. In C++, the / symbol denotes integer division if both arguments are integers. For example, 11 / 4 is 2, not 2.75.

Interface The set of functions that can be applied to objects of a given type.

Lexicographic ordering Ordering strings in the same order as in a dictionary, by skipping all matching characters and comparing the first nonmatching characters of both strings. For example, "orbit" comes before "orchid" in the lexicographic ordering. Note that in C++, unlike a dictionary, the ordering is case-sensitive: Z comes before a.

Library A set of precompiled functions that can be included in programs.

Linker The program that combines object and library files into an executable file.

Local variable A variable whose scope is a single block.

Logic error An error in a syntactically correct program that causes it to act differently from its specification.

Logical operator An operator that can be applied to Boolean values. C++ has three logical operators: &&, ||, and !.

Loop A sequence of instructions that is executed repeatedly.

Loop and a half A loop whose termination decision is neither at the beginning nor at the end.

Machine code Instructions that can be executed directly by the CPU.

Magic number A number that appears in a program without explanation.

main function The function that is called first when a program executes.

Member function A function that is defined by a class and operates on objects of that class.

Memory leak Memory that is dynamically allocated but never returned to the heap manager. A succession of memory leaks can cause the heap manager to run out of memory.

Modulus operator The % operator that yields the remainder of an integer division.

Mutator function A member function that changes the state of an object.

Nested block A block that is contained inside another block.

new operator The operator that allocates new memory from the heap.

Newline The '\n' character, which indicates the end of a line.

Object-oriented programming A programming style in which tasks are solved by collaborating objects.

Off-by-one error A common programming error in which a value is one larger or smaller than it should be.

Opening a file Preparing a file for reading or writing.

Operator A symbol denoting a mathematical or logical operation, such as + or &&.

Operator associativity The rule that governs in which order operators of the same precedence are executed. For example, in C++ the - operator is left-associative, since a - b - c is interpreted as (a - b) - c, and = is right-associative, since a = b = c is interpreted as a = (b = c).

Operator precedence The rule that governs which operator is evaluated first. For example, in C++ the && operator has a higher precedence than the || operator. Hence a || b && c is interpreted as a || (b && c).

Overriding Redefining a function from a base class in a derived class.

Parameter value The expression supplied for a parameter by the caller of a function.

Parameter variable A variable in a function that is initialized with the parameter value when the function is called.

Pointer A value that denotes the memory location of an object.

Polymorphism Selecting a function among several functions with the same name, by comparing the actual types of the parameters.

Private feature A feature that is accessible only by functions of the same class, its friends, and its nested classes.

Prompt A string that prompts the program user to provide input.

Pseudocode A mixture of English and C++ used when developing the code for a program.

RAM (random-access memory) The computer memory that stores code and data of running programs.

Random access The ability to access any value directly without having to read the values preceding it.

Recursive function A function that can call itself with simpler values. It must handle the simplest values without calling itself.

Reference parameter A parameter that is bound to a variable supplied in the call. Changes made to the parameter within the function affect the variable outside the function.

Regression testing Keeping old test cases and testing every revision of a program against them.

Reserved word A word that has a special meaning in a programming language and therefore cannot be used as a name by the programmer.

Return value The value returned by a function through a return statement.

Roundoff error An error introduced by the fact that the computer can store only a finite number of digits of a floating-point number.

Run-time error See **Logic error**.

Scope The part of a program in which a variable is defined.

Sentinel A value in input that is not to be used as an actual input value but to signal the end of input.

Sequential access Accessing values one after another without skipping over any of them.

Slicing an object Copying an object of a derived class into a variable of the base class, thereby losing the derived-class data.

Source file A file containing instructions in a programming language.

Stepwise refinement Solving a problem by breaking it into smaller problems and then further decomposing those smaller problems.

Stream An abstraction for a sequence of bytes from which data can be read or to which data can be written.

String A sequence of characters.

Stub A function with no or minimal functionality.

Substitution principle The rule that states that you can use a derived-class object whenever a base-class object is expected.

Syntax Rules that define how to form instructions in a particular programming language.

Syntax error An instruction that does not follow the programming language rules and is rejected by the compiler.

Tab character The '\t' character, which advances the next character on the line to the next one of a set of fixed screen positions known as tab stops.

Test coverage The instructions of a program that are executed when a set of test cases are run.

Test suite A set of test cases for a program.

Text file A file in which values are stored in their text representation.

Trace message A message that is printed during a program run for debugging purposes.

Unary operator An operator with one argument.

Unicode A standard code that assigns values consisting of two bytes to characters used in scripts around the world.

Uninitialized variable A variable that has not been set to a particular value. It is filled with whatever "random" bytes happen to be present in the memory location that the variable occupies.

Unit test A test of a function by itself, isolated from the remainder of the program.

Value parameter A function parameter whose value is copied into a parameter variable of a function. If a variable is passed as a value parameter, changes made to the parameter inside the function do not affect the original variable outside the program.

Variable A storage location that can hold different values.

Vector The standard C++ template for a dynamically-growing array.

Virtual function A function that can be redefined in a derived class. The actual function called depends on the type of the object on which it is invoked at run time.

void A reserved word indicating no type or an unknown type.

Walkthrough Simulating a program or a part of a program by hand to test for correct behavior.

White-box testing Testing that takes a function's implementation into account; for example, by selecting boundary test cases and ensuring that all branches of the code are covered by some test case.

White space A sequence consisting of space, tab, and/or newline characters.

Index

Page numbers followed by *t* indicate material in tables. Functions and classes from the C++ libraries are included by name. For functions and classes created for application examples, refer to the program listed under the main heading "applications."

Illustration Credits

Page 102: iStockphoto.
Page 108: Bananastock/Media Bakery.
Page 109, 122: © 2008 Sidney Harris.
Page 110: Alamy.
Page 116: Vaughn Youtz/Zuma Press.
Page 117: Tetra Images/Media Bakery.
Page 119: Bruce M. BEEHLER/AFP/Getty Images.

Chapter 4

Page 136: iStockphoto.
Page 137, 170: Fermi National Accelerator Laboratory/Photo Researchers, Inc.
Page 143: M.C. Escher's "Ascending and Descending" © 2008 The M.C. Escher Company-Holland. All rights reserved. www.mcescher.com.
Page 144: Karen Town/iStockphoto.
Page 145: Naval Surface Weapons Center, Dahlgren, VA.
Page 146, 170: Enrico Fianchini/iStockphoto.
Page 152, 170: iStockphoto.
Page 154: Steve Geer/iStockphoto.
Page 157, 170: david kahn/iStockphoto.
Page 160, 170: Altrendo Travel/Getty Images.
Page 166, 170: Kiyoshi Takahase/iStockphoto.
Page 167: Tim Starkey/iStockphoto.
Page 169: Don Bayley/iStockphoto.

Chapter 5

Page 188 (top), 226: Yenwen Lu/iStockphoto.
Page 188 (bottom): dieter Spears/iStockphoto.
Page 194 (collage), 226: Klaudia Steiner/iStockphoto (cherries); christine balderas/iStockphoto (cherry pie); iStockphoto (apples); dieter Spears/iStockphoto (apple pie).
Page 196, 226: Natalia Bratslavsky/iStockphoto.
Page 198: Holger Mette/iStockphoto.
Page 211 (collage), 226: Joan Champ/iStockphoto (Railway and Main); Steven Johnson/iStockphoto (Main and N. Putnam); Jeffrey Smith/iStockphoto (Main and South).
Page 216: Winston Davidian/iStockphoto.
Page 219: Janice Richard/iStockphoto.
Page 221, 226: Nicolae Popovici/iStockphoto.
Page 224: Reprint Courtesy of International Business Machines Corporation, copyright © International Business Machines Corporation.
Page 228: Stacey Newman/iStockphoto.

Chapter 6

Page 242, 275: Max Dimyadi/iStockphoto.
Page 251, 275: matt matthews/iStockphoto.
Page 266 (top), 275: Chris Burt/iStockphoto.
Page 266 (bottom): Gian Mattia D'Alberto/LaPresse/Zuma Press.
✚ Worked Example 6.1: Ryan Ruffatti/iStockphoto.

Chapter 7

Page 289, 317: Alexey Chuvarkov/iStockphoto.
Page 308, 318: Carrie Bottomley/iStockphoto.
Page 314: Bartosz Liszkowski/iStockphoto.
Page 317: Courtesy of Professor Naehyuck Chang, Computer Systems Lab, Department of Computer Engineering, Seoul National University.

Chapter 8

Page 328: iStockphoto.
Page 331, 357: age fotostock/SUPERSTOCK.
Page 335, 357: altrendo images/Getty Images.
Page 338, 357: iStockphoto.
Page 340, 357: iStockphoto.
Page 343: iStockphoto.
Page 351, 357: iStockphoto.
Page 353, 363: Cay Horstmann.

Chapter 9

Page 369, 407: Damir Cudic/iStockphoto.
Page 370, 407: Michael Shake/iStockphoto.
Page 371 (top): James Richey/iStockphoto.
Page 371 (bottom): Eric Isselée/iStockphoto.
Page 374, 407: Photo by Gary Lee/UPPA/Zuma Press. © Copyright 2006 by UPPA.
Page 383, 407: Ann Marie Kurtz/iStockphoto.
Page 391: David Young-Wolff/PhotoEdit.
Page 392: Lisa F. Young/iStockphoto.
Page 394, 408: Anastaslya Maksymenko/iStockphoto.
Page 411: Steve Dibblee/iStockphoto.

Chapter 10

Page 419, 450: Tony Tremblay/iStockphoto (vehicle); Peter Dean/iStockphoto (motorcycle); nicholas belton/iStockphoto (car); Robert Pernell/iStockphoto (truck); Clay Blackburn/iStockphoto (sedan); iStockphoto (SUV).
Page 420: paul kline/iStockphoto.
Page 424, 451: Ivan Cholavov/iStockphoto.
Page 436, 451: Aleksandr Popov/iStockphoto.
Page 448: Science Photo Library/Photo Researchers, Inc.